·DIOCLETIAN·
AND THE ROMAN
RECOVERY

To the Memory of
Arthur Peachey and Jim Miller

·DIOCLETIAN·
AND THE ROMAN
RECOVERY

STEPHEN WILLIAMS

Methuen, Inc., New York

First Published 1985 in the United States of America
by Methuen, Inc., 733 Third Avenue, New York, N.Y. 10017

Library of Congress Cataloging in Publication Data

Williams, Stephen, 1942–
  Diocletian and the Roman Recovery
  Bibliography: P.
  Includes index.
    1. Diocletian, Emperor of Rome, 245–313.   2. Rome——
History——Diocletian, 284–305.   3. Rome——History——
Constantines, 306–363.   I. Title.
DG313.W54   1985   937′.06′0924   85-3013
ISBN 0-416-01151-9

Printed in
Great Britain

·CONTENTS·

·ILLUSTRATIONS·

·ACKNOWLEDGEMENTS·

I am especially grateful to Professor Robert Browning for his kind help and encouragement, and to Professor Fergus Millar for his generous and indispensable guidance at several stages of this book, on what must often have seemed quite naïve questions. Whatever errors and faults remain despite his advice, are entirely my own.

I am indebted too to Professor Tony Honoré for his ready help in the area of Roman Law and Diocletian's contribution to its codification. Thanks are also due to Professor John Wilkes, and particularly to Professor Tomislav Marasović of Split Urban Planning Institute, and Dr Branko Kirigin of Split Archaeological Museum, who were both very welcoming on our visit to the city and palace. The presence of Diocletian hovers over Split; and I would be most happy to think that this book might make him a little better known to some of the many visitors there.

My deep thanks to Patricia Morgan, who read and commented on several drafts of the chapters and gave unstinting support in every other way. For their moral encouragement and other help, Herbert Jarmany and Charles Langley have my warm appreciation.

I also thank Professor Ramsay MacMullen for permission to quote from his excellent study of this period, and for facilitating my use of the Worcester bust photo. I do indeed agree with him that Diocletian was one of that rare species in imperial history, an Emperor with ideas, and I hope I have sustained that claim.

Stephen Williams

·PROLOGUE·

When the young Marcus Aurelius became Emperor of the Roman world in the spring of 161, he had never even seen a real army, far less commanded one in the field.[1] The long reign of his predecessor and adoptive father Antoninus ('the Pious') had been one of almost unbroken peace and internal tranquillity: on the far-flung frontiers the static garrisons had continued their careful and orderly routine, legionary commanders had been appointed, served their time and been replaced without once leading their forces into battle. It was well over a generation since an Emperor had conducted a serious war in person. The Empire of the second century was a supreme achievement of statecraft, never since repeated, in which all the diverse nationalities of the Mediterranean world from the Atlantic coast to the Euphrates were ruled by a single state which ensured that peace and security were the normal conditions of existence.[2]

Antoninus Pius had been a patient, urbane Emperor without military experience, and while he had taken great care over the education of Marcus as his chosen successor, he had not felt the need to give him a military apprenticeship. Rather, the young prince was steeped in philosophy and rhetoric and introduced to public responsibility through holding the various civil magistracies at Rome, including a consulship at the very early age of 19. Marcus was naturally aware of the honourable position of the soldier in Rome's history and greatness, but his awareness was of an academic, historical kind, half infused with the traditional view of the Roman soldier as a citizen in arms. His only concrete acquaintance with professional military force was in the shape of the plumed and privileged Praetorian Guard who attended the imperial family everywhere, decorated the palace and public places of Rome, and upheld imperial authority there by their mere presence.

Marcus and his adoptive brother Lucius Verus were duly invested by the Senate with all the traditional powers of Emperors – powers that were still republican in style and carefully avoided any mention of kingship. Then they went in solemn procession through the *Porta Viminalis* to the Guards camp to the north of the City, where the National Library now stands. They addressed the assembled troops with the conventional formulae and received in reply the oath of loyalty, after which every man received a donative of 5,000 denarii, equal to several years' pay. The transfer of power went off smoothly and legally, as it had done for the last four reigns. Marcus and Lucius had been nominated joint successors by the long-dead Hadrian, and although it was clear to everyone that in practice Marcus would be the senior partner, he scrupulously carried out the bequest to the letter. The successful Antonine dynasty, which had presided over nearly a century of political stability and toleration, was not a hereditary one at all, but a mixture of accident and wise expedient which, if anything, concealed the lack of a settled method of imperial succession. Lacking male blood relations to follow them, each ruler had chosen a successor early on, adopted him into the imperial family and carefully devolved powers on him in preparation for eventual supremacy. The arrangement had worked well, but it was not an established system: it was a substitute for hereditary succession rather than an alternative to it. Marcus was to be the last in this adoptive line, and to later generations he would represent in so many ways the end of an epoch which would never return. So severe and prolonged were the convulsions that followed, so sharp the contrast in the manner of government, that the historian Dio Cassius understandably describes the change as a degeneration from an age of gold to an age of iron and rust.[5]

Like the vanished world before 1914, perhaps, it is easy to invest this golden age with a mythical quality, or to ask: golden for whom? To the senatorial aristocracy, Marcus, due to his Stoic upbringing, would always be a model Emperor. This was not just because of his self-conscious devotion to duty, nor even his outstanding justice and humanity, but above all because of his *civilitas,* because he behaved publicly as their fellow-citizen and not as a monarch at all. In the imperial council he once agreed to be outvoted because, he said, it was right that one man should bow to the opinion of so many friends.[4] In allocating money from the treasury he asked the Senate to grant it him, maintaining the pious fiction that all public money and property still belonged to the Senate and People.[5] In his meditations he told himself, 'Take care you do not become dyed in purple',[6] and followed this precept most conscientiously in his public style. To outward appearances it might almost have seemed that the Empire was still ruled by the cultured élite of senators and upper equestrians at Rome, and that Marcus was merely the first among them, acting with their consent: so, at least, a visitor from China might have concluded. As one admirer sums it up, the virtue of his reign was that he ruled *as if it were a free state.*[7]

Now the reality was very different, and when the realities of power become too removed from the formal procedures, a state becomes very brittle in coping with new kinds of challenge. Whether he liked it or not, Marcus Aurelius was virtually an absolute monarch. He was the sole source of laws, and the supreme judge and interpreter of them; he controlled all armed force, all important public appointments, all public finance and taxation, and decided on peace and war and relations with foreign peoples. He was irremovable except by death, and limited by no constitutional checks beyond his respect for the law and his own self-restraint. The real basis of his power was not the Senate, but the legions strung out along the endless frontiers and nearer at home, the Guards cohorts in the City. The legionaries were professionals, recruited mainly from provincial peasant classes who knew and cared little about the republican traditions of Rome, and whose career prospects were unrelated to its civil institutions. Their notions of government were honestly monarchical, far removed from the polite illusion of republican magistracies to which Marcus and the senatorial class were so attached.

Within a short time the Empire was plunged into war, first against Parthia and then on the Danube. After a generation of peace, military deficiencies showed up quickly. In the East an unskilful commander lost a whole legion.[8] The effort to restore Roman supremacy required transferring such large forces eastwards that for the first time Rome was rudely awakened to the true scale of the threat on its northern frontiers. The Quadi and Marcomanni were powerful Germanic peoples who now invaded the Roman provinces with a force never before experienced, penetrating deep into the peaceful undefended heartland of the Empire. They actually threatened Athens, and besieged Aquileia, the gateway to Italy. They were expelled again, but Marcus had to fight a long series of campaigns to restore the position, which proved more difficult than anyone had anticipated. The invasions set off a temporary panic in many cities, who clamoured for permission to build defensive walls. Marcus did his duty and commanded the Danube wars in person – militarily inexperienced, in failing health and inwardly longing for the calm of retirement. After years of dogged warfare in these frozen, mountainous regions he died at his headquarters at Vindobona (Vienna), the enemy subdued but the wars still unfinished. What Rome was experiencing was only the first of an enormous turmoil of new migrations by distant peoples in the Central European land mass, which before long would bring new enemies pressing in on every sector of the Rhine and Danube frontiers.

Marcus was succeeded by his natural son Commodus, who had none of his father's qualities. He did not consolidate the hard-won military gains, and his rule at Rome was weak, capricious and despotic: he made many enemies, executed many innocent senators but followed no policies consistently and built up no base of support. He was eventually strangled in his palace. After such a reign, all the latent tensions around the throne between the Senate and the Praetorian Guard erupted into the open. The precarious threads of respected tradition, so essential to the orderly transfer of power, were so violently broken that at one stage the Guards, flaunting their power, cynically put the throne up for public auction.[9] A rich, vain senator Julianus won the bidding at a price of 25,000 sesterces per man, but this did not prevent him being murdered by the same Guards a few months later.

In these circumstances it was almost inevitable that the main fighting armies, especially the Upper Danube legions within shortest march of Italy, should take a hand and decide to restore the disgraced state, with their own commander as the new imperial candidate. But if they could set up their own Emperor just because they were geographically close to Rome, why should not other equally valiant legions do the same at a distance? In the long civil war of 193 to 197 three contenders were involved, with the legions in Pannonia, Syria and Britain. The short-lived dynasty of the Severi which followed strengthened the trends of absolutism and militarism, the power of Emperor against Senate, soldiers against civilians, provincials against Italians. Septimius Severus on his deathbed was alleged to have advised his two sons: 'Stick together, pay the soldiers, and forget all the rest'.[10] They failed to do so, both were murdered, and the dynasty proved no more than a breathing space before an escalation of military rebellions and barbarian invasions, both of which became endemic in the next 30 years.

It would be half a century of unheard-of calamities before the Empire was again restored, after indefatigable efforts, and the most painful sacrifices and adaptations. It was restored, not as a dignified civic forum but rather as a great fortress, its life organised around the need to survive indefinite siege. Its restorer was a soldier-Emperor of the humblest social origins, Diocletian, who was compelled to dye himself and his successors so deeply in purple that henceforth the Roman Emperor resembled a godlike Pharoah more than a first magistrate – a figure the Chinese visitor would instantly have recognised.

part one

CRISIS

chapter one

·THE THIRD-CENTURY·
·COLLAPSE·

SUCH WERE THE BARBARIANS, AND SUCH THE TYRANTS, WHO, UNDER THE
REIGNS OF VALERIAN AND GALLIENUS, DISMEMBERED THE PROVINCES, AND
REDUCED THE EMPIRE TO THE LOWEST PITCH OF DISGRACE AND RUIN, FROM
WHENCE IT SEEMED IMPOSSIBLE THAT IT SHOULD EVER EMERGE.
·GIBBON, CHAPTER X·

Rome had long been familiar with its immediate Germanic neighbours, as Tacitus'
unrivalled study of them illustrates. But in the recent century, slow but inexorable
changes had been at work which made them a very different political entity to that
which Tacitus had described. Great population expansions, migrations, displace-
ments and social changes had taken place, originating in remote lands of which the
Romans knew nothing. The main migration currents across Eurasia were westward
and southward. From Scandinavia the Gothic peoples in their great tribal groupings
(Ostrogoths, Visigoths, Heruli) had shifted slowly south down the Vistula and the
Russian rivers, pushing into the Ukraine, the lower Danube and the shores of the
Black Sea. In South-East Europe they struggled for territory with the Sarmatians, an
Iranian plains people who were expanding from the Caucasus westward as far as the
Hungarian plain. Two other continuous tides, also from the Silesia–Vistula region,
were the Vandals, south-westward to the Carpathians; and the Burgundians,
westward to the Elbe and thence to the Main, putting increasing pressure on the
indigenous tribes of West and Central Germany.[1]

Partly as a result of these pressures the more familiar, sedentary, West German
tribes underwent a gradual process of closer federation into much larger units,
accompanied by the emergence of a distinct warrior aristocracy. The earlier Germans
had been a great collection of relatively small clans, practising a primitive slash-burn
agriculture and regular communal allotment of land. The basic political unit was the
tribe, based solely on kin ties, in which every free adult male bore arms and
participated in the tribal assembly which decided important issues such as peace and
war. Apart from priests and certain hereditary offices the leaders were mainly elective
and charismatic: they held authority merely through their continuous prowess in
war, and had no organised coercive power over the whole people. If the society was
'democratic' it was also semi-anarchic, and unsuited to large planned undertakings
demanding authority and direction. Seasonal inter-tribal warfare was a normal,

honoured activity, and Roman diplomacy did everything to encourage these rivalries. As Tacitus put it: 'I pray that what continues among the German nations is, if not affection for us, then at least hostility to one another ... Neither the Samnite, nor Carthagian, nor Spaniard, nor Gaul, nor even the Parthian, have taught us more lessons. The German fighting for his freedom has been a deadlier enemy than the despotism of Arsaces'.[2]

But the contacts with Rome had also led to expanding trade in the ostentatious luxuries beloved of warrior societies—gold, ornaments, robes, weapons, wine, slaves, silverware—which enhanced the standing of successful war-chiefs and promoted the rise of a nobility. Even more potent in this process was the growth of the war-chief's retinue—a personal following of warriors recruited from the bravest young men of several different tribes, bound by oath to fight and die with him in return for his gifts and the hospitality of his hall. This became a standing force, no longer confined to seasonal fighting or to a particular tribal territory, bound to one leader, and dedicated to glory and plunder. In it can be discerned the germ of the much later feudal concept of personal loyalty to a lord.

This institution was the main catalyst in the fusion into great tribal confederations in the second century, in response both to the aggression of newer peoples to the east, and to the opportunities of what seemed limitless reserves of booty in the Roman provinces. By the early third century three groupings had emerged. The central German Suevic tribes, with whom Caesar had first made contact and been unnerved by their ferocity,[3] had formed into the Alemanni (*Aller Manner*); the lower Rhineland group into the Franks; and the sea-peoples at the mouth of the Elbe and Weser into the Saxons. Though still of loose internal unity, the scale of military expedition these groupings could now mount was of an entirely new order, beyond what the carefully planned Roman frontier defences had been designed to deal with. These functioned on the assumption that tribal aggression in any particular sector could be anticipated and neutralised outside Roman territory. But when for the first time very large penetrations did occur, then, as Marcus Aurelius had found, the provincial road system gave the barbarians a rapid route into the heart of the Empire. After 30 more years of mounting danger, Rome was forced to recognise that it was confronted by a continuous belt of tribal enemies from the North Sea to the Black Sea: Saxons, Franks, Alemanni, Marcomanni, Quadi, Sarmatians, Jazyges, Goths, Carpi. The old diplomacy, with the threat of force more or less in the background, was now proving ineffective. That force had to be immediately and palpably available in overwhelming concentration. This placed a mounting burden on military resources, since it meant that hardly any stretch of frontier could safely have its garrisons diminished for long.

It has to be stressed that Roman military superiority, such as it was, did not rest on a more advanced technology. Although the Romans were more skilled in building and siege tactics and had better supplies of weapons and armour, both they and the Germans were still essentially Iron Age peoples. Any tempting parallel with modern colonial riflemen facing African nations is quite misleading. Where the Romans scored was not weaponry, but the organisation and method made possible by a more advanced political culture.[4] Yet this too made their territories vulnerable. The simpler Germans might lack organisation and planning but their whole society was based around war, and every man a warrior: a far higher ratio than Rome with its complex division of labour and large populations of slaves, *coloni* (tenants), and urban proletariat. For these reasons, in the longer term the Germans could inflict disproportionate damage on the elaborately interdependent urban society and economy of the Empire. With the primitive, wandering farmer-warrior ethos in which each tribe was ready to expand into the space of its nearest neighbour, the Germans could recover quickly from all but the most punitive defeats. Man for man they were physically stronger than the Romans and certainly as brave: their fierce fighting qualities had long compelled admiration: Tacitus, prophetically, saw in their warlike freedom a new reservoir of enormous energies which could have profound consequences for the Roman future.[5]

Independently but simultaneously, a major revolution had come about in Rome's great eastern neighbour, which was to present a far greater military challenge than before. The old Parthian kingdom of the Arsacids had been a quasi-feudal structure of powerful family domains and perpetual internal tensions, whose western regions were considerably influenced by Hellenic culture. Early in the third century the Arsacids were overthrown by a powerful nationalist movement based on the Iranian plateau, led by the house of Sassan and claiming spiritual descent from the ancient Achaemenid Empire of Darius and Xerxes. Having defeated his political enemies in battle, the first Sassanid king, Ardashir, was crowned King of Kings in the old capital of Ctesiphon, near modern Baghdad, in 226. The Sassanids worked to build a strong, centralised Iranian state, purged of all foreign influences and pursuing an expansionist, imperialist policy. The ancient Zoroastrian religion was revived and made state orthodoxy, the Magi organised into a church, fire temples established everywhere and other cults – Jews, Buddhists, Hindus, Christians – suppressed. Militarily, the Sassanids proved more capable and more aggressive than their predecessors. Ardashir launched successful wars of conquest as far east as the Punjab, and soon afterwards attacked the Roman provinces. These new military skills were evident in the Sassanids' corps of heavy mailed shock cavalry, and their greater capacity for siege warfare. In besieging the Roman fortress city of Dura Europos on the Euphrates they used mining for the first time, and the dramatic subsidence of one of the great defensive towers is evident in the ruins today. In 241 Ardashir was succeeded by his equally energetic son Shapur I, who conquered the Kushans, Armenia and Georgia, and made no secret of his ambition to restore the empire of his Achaemenid ancestors, which meant nothing less than conquest of the whole Roman East as far as the Bosporus. His first offensive took several Roman stronghold cities and finally captured Antioch, the great commerical capital of Hellenic Syria, only a short distance inland from the Mediterranean coast. Roman Antioch had never before fallen to an enemy. It was retaken with some difficulty, but henceforth Antioch was to be a piece in the strategic Rome–Persia chessboard that had now shifted alarmingly about 500 miles westward.[6]

By the mid-century, war had become almost continuous along the Rhine, Danube and Euphrates frontiers, at the same time that imperial authority was at its most precarious, being openly fought over by rival generals. The two were of course partly connected. The external threat had brought the real importance of the professional army strikingly to the fore, breaking the restraints of aristocratic civil administration: the soldiers could claim what price they liked, and they knew it. But the generals and Emperors who were caught in the perpetual private wars were obviously thereby hampered in the task of territorial defence, having to guard in at least two directions. In extreme cases a contender for power stripped the frontier of troops for a dash against Rome, letting the barbarians ravage the exposed territories and hoping to expel them once again when his power was secure.

Thus, in 244 the Praetorian Prefect Philip the Arab concluded an unfavourable peace with Persia in order to get back to Rome and seize the purple. Then Decius, commander of the army in Pannonia (Western Hungary) marched into Italy against Philip at a time when the Gothic danger was at its height. He defeated Philip's army at Verona, but behind him the Danube defences broke completely and the invaders poured across the Balkans. Decius spent the next three years trying to expel them, but was himself defeated and killed in battle at the river Dobrudja,[7] while Trebonianus Gallus, governor of Moesia (Bulgaria) was declared Emperor by the troops. The Goths were eventually expelled, but the victor Aemilianus turned and marched into Italy against Gallus, just as Decius had done. He ruled four months before being assassinated by the army. The near-suicidal pattern had become permanent. It was no longer a case of brief civil war followed by consolidation under a new dynasty, as had happened after Nero, for example. Imperial authority and effective central power were now so weak, so overwhelmed by multiple crises and utterly dependent on the volatile moods of the armies, that this had become impossible. Some imperial candidates were indeed reluctant: but, rather than murder by their unruly troops or execution by a suspicious Emperor they had no choice but to take the hazard of civil war. If they won, they somehow had to raise higher sums of money to buy the loyalty of the troops, throw back the barbarians and put down every new usurper, until at the first setback they were cut down and the cycle began again. In the 50 years from the assassination of Severus Alexander to the coup of Diocletian there were 15 'legitimate' Emperors and many more pretenders, and almost all died violently: an average reign of about three years (see Appendix III). During this time the frontiers were repeatedly overrun and the great Empire split into several pieces.[8]

An unchanging element in the disintegration was of course the distances themselves. To move an army from the Rhine frontier to Rome took eight or nine weeks: to the Euphrates frontier, six months. Dispatches and orders still had to travel at the speed of a horseman. With interrupted communications and the continually changing military situations on distant fronts, no Emperor could gain a very reliable overall picture of events, let alone impose his direct control on them. Of necessity, military power was localised on the frontiers and the main decisions were made by the commander in that region: in beleaguered conditions of poor infor-mation and disputed authority, they were the effective power centres whether they wished it or not. Once again, the system of communications and military administration had worked adequately only so long as serious external threats did not occur simultaneously; when they did, it seized, then broke down.

One great barbarian war, however costly, need not have had irreversible effects on society and economy. The Empire had recovered from this scale of war many times before. But the repeated shocks of invasions, year after year for generations, and getting tangibly worse, were ruinous to civil life. Agriculture, population, cities, and trade all suffered progressively in the chronic insecurity. Lands in the exposed frontier provinces were abandoned, cities sacked and pillaged, at the same time that Emperors had to raise ever new armies, equip them, pay them and transport them thousands of miles. If, owing to military diversions, they could not immediately resist the invaders, they tried to bribe them into keeping quiet—an expedient that soon proved mountingly expensive and, like all appeasement, merely advertised Roman weakness and raised German appetites.

From this shrinking, dislocated economic base the State had to wring unheard-of levels of taxes: and in concrete terms 'the State' increasingly meant the armed soldiery. Emperors debased the coinage again and again, resulting in uncontrolled inflation which naturally drove up army pay demands. To supply and placate the troops, compulsory purchase at the outdated prices soon became outright requisition, then arbitrary military plundering. As the currency became so worthless that the soldiers would not accept it as pay, and the State in turn would not accept it as taxes, requisition of supplies became a barely disguised taxation in kind, the *annona militaris*. The propertied classes who had once eagerly sought the honours and financial responsibilities of city magistracies to which their wealth entitled them, now did everything to avoid such expenses, which had grown into unsupportable burdens. There are records of men offering two-thirds of their estates to escape the obligations of a magistracy.[9] The rapid rise in status of the military man thus occurred in the most brutal ways. When soldier could plunder civilian, when property rights counted for little compared with the one great difference between the armed and the unarmed, when the Emperors could not be relied on to protect one's villa or estates, or did so only at the price of bankruptcy, what help was one's social position? One could and did petition governors and Emperors, but beyond empty promises they did little. Where adminstration was functioning again, the governorship itself would often be filled by a half-educated military man who doubtless did his best, but was desperately preoccupied with other matters.[10]

Increasingly, those who could had to fend for themselves, and the immediate result, like that of the haphazardly oppressive taxation and seizures, was to compound the crisis. Add to these miseries the fact that throughout the 250s a great epidemic of plague moved across North Africa and the Balkans, assisted by the famines following the invasions, and it is little wonder men believed apocalyptic visions of the End of the World. ('Nation shall rise against nation, and kingdom against kingdom, and there will be plagues, earthquakes and famines . . .')[11] Christian sources painted the most lurid pictures of the coming end of Rome: Nero raised from Hell coming out of the East, Satan at the head of a Gothic horde, and so on. It is impossible to quantify the sufferings of the Empire's populations with any accuracy, and ancient sources are notoriously unreliable with statistics. The plague was sufficently widespread for at least two rulers, Timethesius and Claudius, to succumb to it.[12] Famine must have accounted for many more. The physical area of towns shrank dramatically (Paris, for example, was reduced simply to the Ile de la Cité),[13] and the endlessly reiterated concern with deserted agricultural land leaves no doubt that the total population of the Empire fell measurably, as did the living standards of every class.

The most common response of the civil populations to these calamities could almost be summed up in one word: flight. Flight from the barbarians, from the plague, from the clash of armies, from tax extortion, from plundering soldiers and officials, from forced labour duties – the list reads like a monotonous prayer for deliverance. Archaeological evidence tells a grim and uniform tale: charred foundations of houses and villas, and hoard after hoard of buried coins which the owners never returned to unearth. The standard questions addressed to an oracle illustrate people's most common anxieties: 'Will I become a beggar? Will I take to flight? Will my flight be stopped?'[14] A desperate petition to the Emperor Philip the Arab in about 245 is typical:

> We are suffering extortion and illegal exactions beyond all reason at the hands of those who ought to be preserving the public welfare . . . Soldiers, powerful men from the cities, and your own officials leave the highways, descend on us, take us from our work, seize our plough and oxen and illegally extort what is not due to them . . . We wrote about this to your majesty, Augustus, when you were Prefect of the Guard . . . but . . . we are still suffering extortion at the hands of officials, our resources are exhausted and the estates deserted . . .'[15]

Many towns were abandoned as indefensible, their inhabitants moving to safer sites, sometimes reoccupying far older hilltop settlements. Other cities were successfully fortified, usually with drastically shorter wall circuits and often by pulling down the public buildings of a more prosperous age for building stone. In Athens we can still see remains of a wall enclosing a small area around the Agora, hastily thrown up by the citizens against the sea raids of the Goths, its stones punctuated with anomalous fragments of decorative frieze and cornice.[16] The rich could sometimes bribe their way out of tax obligations, or convert their wealth into moveables that could be hidden, or emigrate to a remote country villa. The poor who fled their land might seek some land-owner in a safer area for whom they might work as *coloni*, or else might join the growing bands of brigands roaming over the devastated and unruly provinces, robbing and scavenging in the wake of the barbarians. A different type of self-help, which promoted territorial fragmentation, was seen when cities repudiated their allegiance to a remote government in Rome which had failed them, and set up their own national rulers, or lent support to any local military usurper who promised protection. The stripping of the Rhine defences had opened the way for a great invasion of Franks, occupying Eastern Gaul and North-Eastern Spain; Gaul was also cut off from Italy by a separate invasion of the Alemanni which threatened Milan. With the support of the civil population the Rhine army commander Postumus murdered the imperial heir, occupied Cologne and had himself proclaimed Emperor, not of the Roman world but of an independent Gaul only, *Imperium Galliarum*. He might be a harsh ruler, but at least he remained in Gaul trying to protect its people, and at least his tax burdens might eventually bring results for

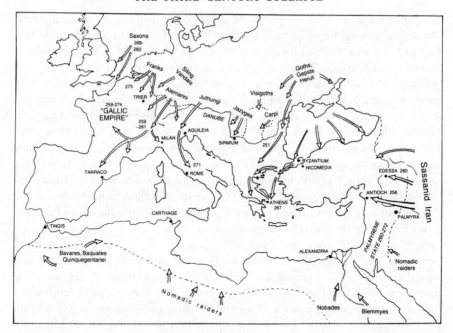

1 The crisis of the third century. The main invasion routes during the years *c.* 250–285, greatly simplified. The frequent interruption of land communications by the invaders, and the tying down of regionally based armies, facilitated breakaway states in Gaul and the East.

them.[17] Needing the military support of Gaul, the governors of Britain and Spain declared allegiance to this new state. A similar, but less successful attempt was made in Egypt.[18]

By the time Valerian had been installed as Emperor in 253, the Rhine and Danube frontiers were both in ruins. The Alemanni had overrun Raetia (Switzerland) and penetrated into Italy, the Marcomanni laid waste Pannonia (Western Hungary), and in the same year Persia took the opportunity to invade in strength, overrunning Syria and again taking Antioch and many other cities. Valerian took his army east to meet the Persians, and installed his son Gallienus as Caesar in Rome, to deal with the western crisis as best he could. In the Black Sea, large fleets of Goths and Borani sacked in succession the undefended coastal Greek cities: Byzantium, Chalcedon, Nicomedia, Nicea, Prusa, Pityus, Trebizond.

Then in 259 came disaster in Mesopotamia. Having relieved Antioch and made some headway against the main Persian forces, Valerian's army was encircled at Edessa. After unsuccessful attempts to break out it was reduced to a capitulation, in which tens of thousands of Romans, including the Emperor himself, were led into captivity. The Persian figure of 60,000 is certainly an exaggeration, but it was nonetheless the greatest single Roman defeat in memory, and one of the worst in her history. There was nothing Gallienus in the West could do as Shapur retook Antioch with great slaughter, and seemed on the point of fulfilling his dynastic ambitions. The unprecedented humiliation of a captive Roman Emperor forced to kneel to a Persian King was recorded for all time by Shapur in the great rock monuments at Bishapur and Naqshe-e-Rustan, which are still tourist attractions today.[19]

Gallienus now assumed full power, made important reforms in the armies he controlled, and fought back with some success against the Alemanni in Raetia and Italy, although his area of effective control was now confined to Italy, Dalmatia, Greece, the Western Danube and the North African coast. Beyond the Alps Postumus ruled his separatist Gaul, but was still unable to prevent a new Alemannic invasion from occupying the Rhône valley and the Auvergne, or Saxon raiders from ravaging the coastal towns of Britain and Gaul. In the Eastern Balkans, Thrace and Asia Minor the Goths roamed without hindrance and their fleets penetrated the Aegean and attacked the ancient cities of Ephesus, Chrysopolis, Sparta and Athens. Usurpers were springing up everywhere.

Of course, not all regions or classes suffered equally, and of course there were still great resources – human, moral and material – left to meet the crises and at least save something, if only they could be effectively organised. If one looks simply at territory overrun, inflation levels, military defeats, rebellions and palace revolutions, then the nadir of disintegration appears roughly in the years 250 to 270. But beneath the surface events, drastic and harsh improvisations were going on, which would later enable the State to surmount the calamities.

This, then, was the political world into which Diocletian was born, and the military ethos through which he, and many like him, were able to rise from utter social obscurity to the highest positions in the State. Most of what we have of Diocletian's background is a tradition, perhaps a fusion of two traditions, of modest reliability. He came from Dalmatia, and was probably born in 243, probably at Salona, where he grew up with the name of Diocles. According to the sources he was either a freedman himself, or the son of a freedman, in the household of the senator Anullinus; a contemporary senatorial family of that name is certainly recorded. It is also claimed that his father was a scribe. If Diocles was himself a freedman, then he would actually have been born a slave; if he was the son of a freedman he would have been of free birth but of the lowest social strata, the *humiliores*. Either way he would have received nothing of what Romans counted as education. At most, he would have acquired the practical skills of a servant and perhaps, if his father was indeed a scribe, an elementary literacy of the type appropriate to his station.[20]

The province of Dalmatia had originally been conquered during the reign of Augustus. It was later colonised by wealthy Italians, and flourishing cities grew up at Pola, Emona, Salona, Doclea and elsewhere. Protected by the Dinaric Alps, these regions were spared the great barbarian onslaughts that devastated the Northern Danube provinces in the third century, although they naturally felt the secondary effects of spiralling taxes and inflation.[21]

Today Salona (Solin) is a suburb a mile or so outside Split, containing a housing estate and industrial complex. But the copious ruins there and in the archaeological museum testify to the splendour of the old Roman city. Large stretches of the great aqueduct are still standing, and there are variously preserved ruins of the city gates, baths, temples, basilicae, Christian churches, theatre and the great amphitheatre, built to hold 15,000. In a nearby cemetery and in the museum, among many more elaborate memorials, are the funerary inscriptions to the gladiators who fought and died there, usually in their early twenties.[22] In the village of Solin almost every one of the old houses has Roman grave monuments, often of fine quality, built into its walls. The tables of the cafés are slabs of massive cornice, and projecting from the low roof of one house are the unmistakable four identical heads of Diocletian and his brother Emperors.

Apart from natural curiosity it is not important that we know next to nothing about his early years. The influences which mattered were undoubtedly in the army, which he joined some time before 270 and whose composition was undergoing great changes. The social status of the ordinary legionary soldier in the Roman Empire was always high (in contrast with most of European history), but it was never so high as in the mid-third century when the different military power centres were fighting for their existence. In contrast with the common citizenry, soldiers were *honestiores,* men of rank;[23] 'Our most noble soldiers' became a common official style of reference. For several generations it had been the recruits from the Danube provinces, including Dalmatia, who had filled the ranks, and then the lower officer posts, of Rome's finest legions. The general region of the Balkans, loosely termed 'Illyricum', had become as synonymous with soldiery traditions as Prussia in our own era (it was indeed German scholars who were first struck by the parallel). By sheer results, these Danubian professional soldiers worked their way up through the crisis years to the highest commands, and behind them trailed ready ladders of opportunity which could not fail to favour their own countrymen.

chapter two

·VIRTUS ILLYRICI·

IF YOU WANT TO BE A TRIBUNE, OR EVEN IF YOU JUST WANT TO STAY ALIVE,
THEN RESTRAIN THE PLUNDERING HANDS OF YOUR SOLDIERS. LET NONE OF
THEM STEAL PEOPLES' FOWL OR SHEEP, OR TAKE OFF GRAPES, OR THRESH OUT
GRAIN, OR EXTORT OIL OR SALT OR FUEL. LET THEM BE CONTENT WITH
THEIR ALLOWANCE. IF THEY WANT BOOTY, LET THEM TAKE IT FROM THE
CONQUERED ENEMY, NOT FROM THE TEARS OF THE PROVINCES.
·ALLEGED LETTER OF AURELIAN, IN *Historia Augusta* ·

The critical years of Diocles' army career were times of great wars, revolts and far-reaching changes in which ambitious commanders at the top fought for supreme power, ruled briefly and then perished, while lower down fast promotion was to be had by the brave and resourceful who distinguished themselves in the perpetual fighting. Gallienus, struggling to save the central heartland of the Empire from the greatest threat since Hannibal, made sweeping innovations in strategy, command structure and appointments, not from any comprehensive plan but in a bold response to the immediate and desperate crisis.

The traditional self-contained legion with its backbone of heavy infantry and full supporting services was a very formidable weapon in a positional war of marches and set battles, but it suffered from poor mobility. Legions had become more or less settled on the frontiers themselves, where many soldiers had put down family roots. The torrential barbarian invasions had been very different from the kind of war they had been designed for: simultaneous puncturing of the frontier lines at many points of the enemy's choosing allowed them to reach deep into the provinces before a strong Roman force could get to grips with them. Gallienus' reaction to this was to develop the cavalry arm beyond anything that had gone before, into a fast, independent striking force which could take advantage of the road system (now that fighting inevitably took place inside Roman territory) to intercept and destroy the enemy.[1]

This force was assembled from the legionary cavalry, and particularly the specialised contingents of mounted auxiliaries such as the Moorish, Dalmatian and Osrhoene horse, whose battle reputations had grown dramatically in the third century. It could fight in co-operation with infantry or on its own, its tactics relying on speed, surprise, skilful manoeuvre and a great use of missile weapons. (It was said that the Moorish horsemen could transfix a man accurately with a javelin through body or head, from the gallop.) Gallienus stationed this powerful force at Milan, in a pivotal position to meet attacks from any direction into the North Italian plain. He frequently commanded it in person, and gained important victories over the Alemanni and the Heruli.

The central cavalry force had another function: as a decisive concentration of force around the Emperor, in instant readiness to pounce on any rebel who might arise. The strategic base at Milan served not just against the Alemanni and Danube invaders but, after about 265, against an anticipated invasion by Postumus across the Alps from Gaul. But the new strategy created political risks of its own. If command of the cavalry force was delegated, as it sometimes had to be, its commander automatically became the most powerful, hence most dangerous, subject in the Empire, a new counterpart of the Praetorian Guards commander. The very first commander of cavalry, Aureolus, himself revolted against Gallienus.[2]

These changes were accompanied by a significant shift in the social composition of the higher command, the culmination of a process that had been working through the army for a long time. Traditionally a legionary commander and his immediate deputy (the *Tribunus Laticlavius*) were nobles at different stages in their Senatorial careers, which might lead to a proconsular governorship or some similar prestigious position. They were not full-time soldiers: higher military commands were reserved for them, just like other top posts. This meant that experience of generalship, and the possibility of gaining that experience, was monopolised by a very small class of independent aristocrats. On the other hand the rest of the regular army – the Primipilarii, Centurions and below – contained a far larger reservoir of experienced, professional soldiers who were prevented from being tested in command solely by their birth. The older class system of appointments had been adequate in more normal times, but in the present emergencies when it was imperative to find the best military leaders quickly, it had to give way.[3]

Already the intermediate officer posts, traditionally open to the Equestrian classes, were in practice being filled by regular soldiers of lower social levels. The small, mobile detachments (*vexillationes*) were commanded by regular officers, usually promoted from centurions, and larger forces made up of these units came under *Duces,* representing a further rung up the ladder for regular officers. Finally Gallienus took the logical step which ended the day of the gentlemen: after 260, senators lost the exclusive right to command legions, and their sons to the deputy rank of military tribunes. The posts were filled by career soldiers, many of whom had worked their way up from the bottom. Some, indeed, had been the sons of soldiers, brought up in a camp environment since childhood.[4]

By furthering military excellence, Gallienus encouraged the growth of an élite corps of higher officers, the *Protectores*. The title was designed to give a sense of professional solidarity to these 'new men' in place of that of birth and education. This *ésprit de corps* was further underlined by the common origin of so many of them in the Balkan provinces, the military cities along the vital Danube highways: Mursa, Sirmium, Singidunum, Naissus, Serdica, where they had acquired a certain social standing. The Emperor acknowledged as much in his coin slogans *Genius Illyrici, Genius Pannoniae* and so on. The *Protectores* seem to have functioned as a general staff whose officers were trained from early on to take up the most important assignments. What is clear is that they formed a pool of proven ability, and that a Protector was in a fast stream of promotion to the highest positions. This included civil offices too, since in these turbulent times provincial governorships and their staffs were increasingly being filled by trusted, former military men.[5]

After the 250s there appears a striking number of Protectors who rose from the ranks to brilliant careers in the army and administration. Traianus Mucianus began as a soldier, became centurion and Protector, then legionary commander, *Dux,* and eventually governor (*Praefectus*) of Mesopotamia.[6] Volusianus rose from centurion to the heights of Praetorian Prefect, then Prefect of the City of Rome, one of the most coveted public offices in the Empire.[7] A century earlier no mere legionary soldier could have dreamed of rising to these positions. Nor were these careers the rare, glittering exceptions: the barriers really were down, and able military men of lowly origins were permeating the system in greater numbers at every level. The displaced senatorial class hated and despised these 'barbarian' Illyrici, an attitude which was to colour the writing of history for centuries afterwards.[8]

It is in the decade following Gallienus that we first hear the briefest mention of Diocles. He was, it seems, *Dux Moesiae,* that is, commander of sizeable forces on the lower Danube front of Moesia (roughly modern Bulgaria).[9] The literary sources are scattered: the two Victors, Eutropius, Lactantius, and later writers such as Zosimus and Zonaras, who drew on material now lost. The notoriously unreliable *Historia Augusta* describes him serving in Gaul (where he received omens of future rule), but this is not corroborated. But we can, with caution, put together a certain portrait of the man from these sources. Masterful, able, ambitious, of course. But a naturally shrewd, calculating nature, keeping his own counsel, trying to see more moves ahead than others. A man who would accomplish the most difficult tasks through tireless attention to planning, seeking always to compute all the contingencies and build up sufficient resources before launching into action: the kind of commander who would not forgive sloppy staff work, even if an operation was successful.

His detractor Lactantius flatly labels this prudence, cowardice (as usual wrecking his own case by exaggeration).[10] Still, the fact emerges that Diocles was not the natural warrior, not easily carried away by the reckless impulse and bravado frequently found in professional officers. Nor was he the convivial popular soldier drinking and joking with his men, though he might adopt this pose when it served his purpose. One cannot help thinking he applied himself to master the profession of war in just the same methodical way he would have mastered any other, had it been available. While his military talents were entirely respectable (he would never have risen far were they not) they were the outcome of careful intelligence and will, not the heroic dash of some other commanders, true worshippers of Mars, for whom glory was the main purpose of battles. But in this respect he was in excellent company, according to one recent writer:

> The ideal Roman general was not a figure in the heroic style, leading his troops in a reckless charge to victory or death. He would rather advance in a slow and carefully prepared march, building supply roads behind him and fortified camps each night to avoid the unpredictable risks of rapid manoeuvre. He preferred to let the enemy

retreat into fortified positions rather than accept the inevitable losses of open warfare, and would wait to starve out an enemy in a prolonged siege rather than suffer great casualties taking the fortification by storm. Overcoming the spirit of a culture still infused with Greek martial ideas ... the great generals of Rome were noted for their extreme caution.[11]

Translated into third-century tactical terms, this describes him admirably. War was a means to an end, not an arena of personal prowess in which to tempt the gods with daring. And, as Diocles observed one Illyrian soldier-Emperor after another fall like ninepins, everything confirmed him in this attitude. A determined man, immensely hard working, clear-headed and controlled. Also, genuinely pious in the traditional religion of the Romans: one who would meet the approval of the great Puritans.

But he was also, most importantly, a thinking man, ceaselessly observing and questioning the appearance of things. Though his education was confined to the practical requirements of military organisation, he had a real intellectual need to understand the dangerous, confused world he was grappling with, sparing no pains to analyse the problems in front of him and organise it all into a coherent picture to his own satisfaction. And his standard of satisfaction was so high that it gradually set him apart from others. The mature result of this untiring quality of mind, was that supremely useful combination in a ruler: a thoroughgoing mastery of detail *and* a large, original view of the whole. If he was cautious, meticulous and devious, it was all in the service of truly bold designs:

> ... a man outstanding, wise, devoted to the State and to his kindred, always
> prepared for whatever the occasion demanded, ceaselessly evolving plans that were
> always deep and subtle, although sometimes too bold. A man whose prudence and
> great firmness held in check the impulses of his restless spirit.[12]

Here Gibbon is worth quoting also:

> His abilities were useful rather than splendid – a vigorous mind improved by the
> experience and study of mankind, dexterity and application in business; a judicious
> mixture of liberality and economy, or mildness and rigour; profound dissimulation
> under the guise of military frankness; steadiness to pursue his ends; flexibility to
> vary his means; and above all the great art of submitting his own passions, as well
> as those of others, to the interest of his ambition, and of colouring his ambition
> with the most specious pretences of public utility.[13]

The best idea of his appearance is probably the imperial bust found at Nicomedia, now in the Istanbul Museum. (Coin portraits, except on the finest medallions, pay very little attention to naturalistic likeness; indeed, so rapidly did Emperors succeed one another up to 284 that the die-cutters sometimes just superimposed the new name over the old profile.) The Istanbul head shows a vigorous, wide face of a man perhaps in his forties, with a broad cranium, eyes distinctly far apart and a watchful expression. He wears the civic crown and has a close beard, in the Illyrian officer fashion of the day.[14]

He clearly shared the general outlook of these *Viri Militares,* as they gathered all the threads of power one by one into their hands. As with all new ruling groups, it was an outlook that became more complex and less consistent as they acquired responsibility. They were conscious of lacking the humane education and social background of those they supplanted; but they did not resent this culture or try to assert some rival to it. Their dominant attitude was that of the iron soldier clearing out the dead wood and putting the State on a proper basis; not the envious political upstart violently rejecting an aristocratic culture which has excluded him. They saw themselves emphatically as Romans and as guardians of Roman traditions. But this was tradition as *they* had imbibed it, the patriotic loyalty and devotion of the soldier making his oath to the gods, Emperor and eagles; or the proud Roman-ness of the successful provincial notables. It was not at all the sentimental republican tradition which lived on among the literati. Apart from their strong dedication to 'order', these officers were as innocent of those political values, as they were of classical inspiration generally.[15]

Yet, in other respects, the Illyrian officers tended to be even more 'Roman' than the contemporary senatorial class – a feature not unfamiliar among provincial arrivistes. Many of them (and Diocles was an example) cultivated what they took to be the strict old Roman manners, especially in family life and traditional religious piety: a style which grew easily out of their military *disciplina,* giving it an extra dimension of social respectability and solidity. In this way they were at pains to distance themselves from the pampered, licentious Praetorian Guards in Rome who had indulged in all the vices and crime of the City instead of facing the enemies on the frontiers. The Illyrians by contrast thought of themselves as politically responsible. What better qualifications for a consulship, than having risen by one's own virtues to command in arduous and successful wars? These men alone could save the Empire from being carved into pieces, and they were determined to do it. Thereby they became the rightful custodians of its destinies.

As younger men and officers who had participated in the frequent revolutions to topple Emperors and been well rewarded for it, they would not have regarded their actions as mutinous. Even in narrow legalistic terms, the choice of a legitimate Emperor had always required the 'consent' of the armies, as well as the 'authority' of the Senate. While modern military juntas typically try to cloak their ambitions in appeals to civic values (presenting themselves as the true saviours of the Constitution, or the Revolution, or as a Government of National Unity pending elections, etc.), the third-century armies advanced the claim to choose Emperors in their own right. *Fides Militum, Concordia Militum* became quite literal assertions of legitimacy on an Emperor's coinage.[16]

But, as they themselves entered the topmost circles of power, the army leaders of course experienced the great disadvantages of this very pliable doctrine. As he saw the possibility of the purple coming within his grasp, each one also realised how dangerous was the endless cycle of assassinations and civil wars, how necessary it was to find firm foundations again. It was not just that each successive coup weakened the imperial authority: they had produced great uncertainty about where the basis of that authority really lay, and laid bare the deep ambiguities at the very heart of the Roman monarchy. From the beginning it had uneasily tried to combine a dynastic principle of succession with that of 'election' by Senate and army. The latter was at bottom quite artificial, and easily turned into the right of the strongest and fittest to make himself Emperor. If the Emperor's natural or adoptive son was a capable leader, the army could usually be counted on to recognise his right to rule, and all would be well. But if there were no son, or if he was incompetent or tyrannical or even just too young, then it could be a positive duty to support an able, patriotic general in supplanting him. Who could really say when election became mutiny, except the gods who would decide the issue in battle? Thus the Illyrian generals, men who managed all their affairs by the strictest discipline and demanded unswerving obedience from their troops, were genuinely confused about the ultimate object to which all this loyalty should be directed. Their own actions had stirred up old, unresolved constitutional conflicts in a very acute form.

There was no simple turning point in the long military struggle against multiple invasions, since the same enemies had to be fought time and again. But as successive Emperors mobilised all their resources and put to use the harsh lessons they had learned, the exhausted and fragmented Empire was brought painfully back from the abyss. The Germanic nations had not (yet) clear and concerted plans of conquest; some of their most dangerous invasions were in fact mere plundering expeditions on a huge scale. Even when the object was land, they rarely attempted to stake out and defend a coherent area for settlement, nor would they stay and occupy the cities they took. Often there was no definite overall goal: the tribes would be constantly moving, herd-like, as opportunity or resistance dictated. Although they now acted in very large conglomerations, this was about the limit of their strategic co-operation. With a few notable exceptions their 'kings' lacked the political apparatus to impose a rational long-term policy, even if they realised the need for it.

In the East, the Empire of Persia threatened to eclipse Roman power after the disaster at Edessa. Help came, however, from an unexpected quarter. The North Arabian trading city of Palmyra (modern Tadmor) had risen to considerable military power and commercial prosperity as a nominal ally of Rome, and saw itself likewise threatened with extinction by expansionist Persia. Its king, Odenath, launched a counter-offensive which succeeded in driving Shapur back across the Euphrates. In the next few years Palmyrene power itself expanded phenomenally into the vacuum in the Orient, effectively ruling Syria, Palestine, Arabia and Mesopotamia, still in alliance with Rome. Gallienus belatedly appointed King Odenath supreme 'Roman' commander of the Orient: he could do little else in any case.[17]

In 268 Gallienus was murdered by his cavalry commanders. The Illyrian generals had at last broken through to the topmost pinnacle of power, and henceforth the purple remained almost exclusively in the hands of their caste.[18] A succession of soldier-Emperors – Claudius, Aurelian, Probus, Carus – spent almost the whole of their short reigns in continuous and victorious wars. On the Danube, Claudius met a great invasion of Goths, this time a true migration of people aimed at occupying the Balkans. Using the new mobile tactics with devastating effect, he was able to destroy them completely in battles at Naissus and in the Haemus mountains. The survivors who capitulated were settled as *coloni* in the depopulated areas.[19]

His successor, the heroic Aurelian, was faced with simultaneous invasions of Vandals on the Danube and Alemanni into the North Italian plain. The Italian defences collapsed, and Aurelian was beaten at Placentia. The German tide advanced, apparently irresistibly, down the Via Aemilia into Central Italy, threatening Rome itself. As the terrified, undefended cities hurriedly made what preparations they could, Aurelian regrouped his army and was able to turn back the invasion at Fano, then destroy it completely at Ticinum in the North. But during these struggles the new Oriental Empire of Palmyra, now ruled by the ambitious Queen Zenobia, seized the opportunity to break completely with Rome. Aurelian's eastern war against Zenobia has been tinged with romantic legend: the marches across hundreds of miles of desert, the near impregnable fortress of Palmyra, the negotiations with the beautiful and formidable queen, her capture and display in Aurelian's triumph through the streets of Rome. But what comes over clearly, once again, is the new and unexpected speed with which Aurelian was able to move his armies. In two great battles the Palmyrenes were defeated and their citadel besieged until it capitulated on honourable terms. But shortly afterwards, we are told, it revolted and this time was stormed and sacked in ferocious manner.[20]

Having brought the East again firmly under his grip, Aurelian turned to the separatist Empire of Gaul, Britain and Spain, which had been pursuing its independent course with some success for over a decade. Postumus had been murdered and the present ruler, Tetricus, was in a weak position, and had no wish to fight a new civil war against Aurelian. In the unavoidable battle at Chalons he courted defeat and capture: the experiment of *Imperium Galliarum* was snuffed out.[21] Thus, by stupendous military exertions, Aurelian had physically reunited the Empire under his iron rule. But it was a weakened, traumatised Empire, fearful of the future. This is graphically illustrated by Aurelian's greatest surviving monument, the 12-mile fortified wall he built around Rome, following its narrow escape from the Alemannic invasion.[22]

Aurelian was assassinated by his own bodyguard in a personal plot, allegedly engineered by one of his secretaries. Whatever the truth of the matter, the received account indicates the growing embarrassment by the military grandees at these casual Emperor-murders. The conspirators were ostentatiously punished, and after a confused interval the throne passed to Aurelian's lieutenant, Probus, who extolled his memory and continued his policies.[23] Gaul, recently pacified but inadequately defended, was deluged by new invasions on a more terrible scale than those it had already suffered. Franks, Alemanni, Vandals and Burgundians crossed the Rhine on a very wide front: over 60 towns, including Paris, were sacked.[24] Probus rushed his mobile armies to Gaul and, unlike previously protracted campaigns, was able to turn the tide quickly. In a double offensive he defeated and expelled all the invaders, and then carried the war across the Rhine in a punitive expedition deep into German territory. The resulting peace treaty established forts across the Rhine and attempted to disarm the tribes in the immediate frontier zone, as well as securing large numbers of hostages and German recruits.[25]

These great victories, in which Diocles played a part, were only achieved at enormous cost to economy and civil society. A higher officer like Diocles would have seen plenty of the signs as he travelled about his business. Especially in the frontier regions he would be quite familiar with mile after mile of abandoned farmland reverting to forest, swamp and wilderness, with the delapidated and abject towns. Only in the larger military cities along important highways was there visible growth and activity, all of which was centred on the armies. Granaries, warehouses, stables and billets had to be established, fortifications built, roads maintained, transport procured, troops armed, fed and clothed, and mints created to pay them. All this generated a ceaseless demand for labour and services as well as offering security, and city suburbs grew accordingly.

But it was a military order, not a civil one. The local propertied classes, the *curiales,* who should have provided normal municipal administration, were few and far between, and in many towns soldiers themselves had to take over these functions in addition to their proper business. Willy-nilly, they would police the roads, supervise markets, conscript plebeians into corvées for building and other heavy labour, and the higher officers would sometimes even sit as judges in the lawcourts. Above all, they were heavily involved in taxation and requisition – the two had virtually merged into one, in the ubiquitous system of the *annona.* Towns and armies depended crucially on the countryside, and this was where the effects of the crisis would be most visible. Through a wide swathe along the armies' line of march supplies had to be raised in enormous quantities, and in the concrete forms they were needed: food, clothing, fodder, horses, wagons and pack animals, billets, fuel, recruits, workers and slaves. The villas and farms close to the route would simply have to bear the brunt of these demands. The centurions had their assigned quotas to obtain from somewhere, and if these goods could not be had from a particular taxpayer, then they would take a rough equivalent in some other form, hoping to balance it all up later. The near-worthless 'silver' currency was not acceptable, except perhaps in huge multiples of its nominal value: but better silver, such as older denarii, or plate and ornament, was. Faced with armed soldiers who descended like locusts on their property, people had no option but to pay up with whatever wealth was visible.[26]

Of course, civilians had always wailed about their taxes, always lied in their declarations, blamed the weather, their tenants, or somebody else for the short deliveries. But when all this special pleading was ignored, a reflective officer could nonethless see from other evidence how makeshift and unsatisfactory it all was. His understanding of economics might be hazy, yet he could hardly avoid the sense of things hugely distorted in so many directions. His own pay would be mainly in multiples of rations and other goods, which he had to exchange for whatever he wanted: even so, it was many times less than it should have been in relation to an ordinary soldier.[27] Even after victorious wars, in areas well away from danger of invasion, there were the telltale signs of deserted land and depopulation. Of course, the armies had to be supplied and paid, and civilians should expect to make sacrifices for the noble soldiers who defended them. But, inevitably, those whose landed property was within easy reach had to pay far more than others whose farms were less accessible. Was it really surprising if they took up roots and migrated? Added to all the other abnormal duties they now had to take on, soldiers were needed in various places to quell the growing menace of brigands who were terrorising country districts. They had deserted the plough for crime and predation, and the enfeebled civil authorities were powerless to deal with them.

The downward spiral was visible to many of those wrestling with the administration. War placed extraordinary, quite unavoidable tax burdens on the countryside, at the very time that invasions reduced the amount of land under cultivation. Emergency taxation caused even more people to desert their land. The demands on the remaining rural population therefore had to be even higher, which accelerated flight from the land and reduced the cultivated areas still further. Men sensed that it could not go on like this, but their efforts to stem the process were piecemeal and only partially successful. Aurelian, a stern disciplinarian, managed to curb the very worst excesses of military seizures; but his more orderly taxation was every bit as heavy and inequitable. Municipal councils were made liable for the full tax on vacant land, but the incentive of a three-year tax exemption was offered to anyone undertaking recultivation.[28] Probus embarked on extensive schemes of drainage and land reclamation, using army labour.[29] A more direct means of recultivation was to settle land-hungry barbarians on reserved territories, to provide a source of both taxes and military manpower.

The imperative was to get land back under the plough and producing a yield, and it mattered less whose hand held the plough: deserters were deemed to have forfeited their ownership. But the device of granting vacant land to a newcomer made sense only if, eventually, his tenure was more tolerable. Somehow, conditions had to be created that made it worthwhile for him to till the land and pay tax on it: or at least, worthwhile for his landlord or his community to hold him on it.

In 282 the upper Danube legions of Raetia and Noricum proclaimed the Praetorian Prefect Carus Emperor, and before the issue could come to battle the tide had deserted Probus, who was slain by his army. (One reason might have been widespread resentment by soldiers at being used as manual labour on the land.)[30] Diocles may possibly have had some involvement in the coup, since under Carus he rose to the topmost circle of military leaders around the Emperor.

Carus, now nearly 60, had two adult sons and was determined to found a dynasty. Both were immediately invested with the title of Caesar, and the elder, Carinus, was given responsibility for the defence of Italy and the Western Provinces, while Carus himself led his army against the Sarmatians on the Danube. Carinus has been depicted as the stock Roman figure of the dissolute tyrant, executing men at whim and far more fond of circuses, gluttony and fornication than serious affairs of state. He is supposed to have turned over the palace to actors and whores, and debauched virtuous Roman ladies and young boys in about equal numbers. Some of this may be true – such as his alleged cruelty – but it has large elements of slanderous propaganda. When the need arose, Carinus was no Caligula or Nero, but an able and vigorous commander.[31]

The younger son and Caesar, Numerian, accompanied his father on his campaigns. He is portrayed in contrast to his brother as a gentle youth of literary talent, composing verses – very out of place in the tough world of soldiers and politics. There was, however, a rising influence close to both of them in the person of Carus'

Praetorian Prefect, Lucius Aper, who had persuaded the Emperor into a marriage alliance between his own daughter and the young Numerian. Such a powerful connection with the dynasty had obvious implications, and one who saw them readily enough was Diocles, who now also stood high in Carus' favour. Within a short time of the elevation of the new ruler he had become commander of the *Protectores Domestici,* the élite 'household' cavalry force which surrounded the Emperor and accompanied him on every campaign. He was thus one of Carus' intimate military advisers, and the immediate commander of a strong, perhaps decisive body of armed force in any crisis. In 283 his eminent position was acknowledged in the honour of a consulship.[32]

Having campaigned successfully on the Danube, Carus assembled his forces for the ambitious gamble of a great war against Persia. There were strong temptations beckoning him, for the balance of power in the Orient was now – temporarily – very different from that 20 years earlier when Valerian's army had been destroyed and Antioch taken. The formidable Shapur was dead, and his successor, Vahram II, distracted by internal disunity. Tactically too, the Roman army was now more adept at fast cavalry and missile warfare, and could meet the heavy Persian mailed horse on much more favourable terms. Only on larger strategic grounds was the invasion questionable. It meant Emperor and armies displacing themselves very great distances from their home territories, while other fronts were still fragile; and it meant an enormous investment in men, wealth and effort which might be better used elsewhere.

The vast army crossed the Euphrates and moved south-east down the corridor of Mesopotamia. This region had long been an area of contention between the two empires, which adapted itself to either power as best it could. Somewhere in Mesopotamia a Persian army gave battle, and was thoroughly defeated. The Romans encountered no further resistance as they rolled victoriously down into the lush heartland between the two rivers, chequered with irrigation canals and abundantly fertile. Here stood the two mighty fortified cities of Seleucia and Ctesiphon, the latter the new capital of the Sassanid kings: to capture them would take an elaborate siege and considerable time. But Vahram, preoccupied in the East, appears to have abandoned them, for both fell without a long struggle. These were great prizes: in a single summer, it seemed, Carus had lopped off half the Persian Empire.[33]

The next stage is disputed. Did Carus intend to press on and conquer the whole Empire of the Sassanids – as some sources claim, adding that he was warned by an oracle that Rome should not cross the allotted boundary of the Tigris? In many ways, the expedition typified Roman confusion in its war aims towards Persia. In these pendulum-like swings between the two powers, Rome had often defeated the Persian army, but had then been faced just as often with the simple problem: what next? The siren spell of Alexander lured them on to annex huge, perfectly useless salients of territory, sometimes as far as the Persian Gulf. They were inordinately expensive, not seriously defensible, and were sooner or later lost again in the next great wave of Persian ascendancy.

What Carus intended will never be known, because very suddenly he died. The circumstances were mysterious. In one version he was laid low by illness, in another, he was supposed to have been struck by lightning in his tent. (As one writer comments, the bolt of lightning might have been forged in a legionary armoury.) But whatever the truth, the blow caused confusion and uncertainty throughout the army. It is of course quite possible the Emperor's death was a genuine accident, such as a heart attack; but in an age full of omens, miracles and political intrigue there was not much room for the notion of a 'genuine accident' in the conceptual scheme of the soldiers. The atmosphere was one of suspicion, rumour, and the portentous shifting of allegiances among the courtiers of the dead Emperor.[34]

Carus had, however, made careful provision for the succession in such an event as this, and all felt bound by it. The young Numerian was therefore acknowledged as Augustus, and the army swore allegiance. It soon became clear that his father-in-law, the Praetorian Prefect Aper, was the dominant influence over the young Emperor. His first decision was to abandon all idea of further conquests. No formal treaty was made with the defeated Persia: perhaps, like Napoleon at Moscow, there was no one to make it with. Shortly after Numerian's accession, as soon as the season and supplies allowed, the main army began retracing its long journey back up the Euphrates. Throughout 284 it wound its way along the 1,200 miles through the semi-arid regions of Mesopotamia, the bleak mineral wilderness of Cappadocia, thence to Bithynia, and eventually the Bosporus. Below the bare surface events, the thick sense of treachery during this great march is almost palpable.

Should an unfortunate accident befall Numerian, Diocles had no intention of letting Aper take power, and he made his dispositions accordingly. As Prefect, Aper was attempting to gather as much military authority as possible into his own hands, but this was still a delegated authority from the acknowledged Emperor. Were Numerian removed for any reason, then in a naked count of armed strength Aper could probably rely on his Praetorian troops, but most of the army, especially the higher officers and the Illyrian elements, would have very different ideas.

Whether Diocles actively plotted Numerian's death we cannot know. But he knew he stood to gain from it, provided it occurred in a way that distanced him from suspicion. Did he then intrigue with Aper to engineer the young ruler's end, and then betray Aper immediately afterwards? The problem with this theory is that it allows Aper hardly any astuteness at all. If Diocles already had the support of the army, or a sizeable part of it, then he would have no need of Aper once Numerian was dead. When two rivals want only one and the same prize, there is little scope for rational bargaining between them. Perhaps Diocles merely 'wished' the Emperor's death; perhaps he simply read the signs and let it happen. But at all events, the odds were against the weak, inexperienced youth ruling a long time, and one cannot avoid the conclusion that by the summer of 284 his fate was more or less sealed. Numerian is a pathetic figure: friendless, helpless and doomed, his only crime that he was gentle and unmilitary. As Gibbon says, he deserved to reign in a happier time.[35]

The question why someone wants to be ruler of the world does not always allow a sensible answer. There were some eligible men, it is true, who saw all the perils, difficulties, crimes and betrayals they would be entangled in, and genuinely wanted none of it: but they were not many. Others had neither the ability nor the solid support, but were carried on a temporary wave of enthusiasm to glory, and then

destruction. Diocles was far too hard-headed to be hypnotised by the external pomp
and magnificence of imperial power. On the contrary, he later used these things to
hypnotise others. It would be fair to say that he knew, soberly, that he was better
able to rule than anyone else, and his pride could not tolerate the idea of anyone but
himself in supreme control. There was too, of course, an immense undertaking to be
faced, even a sacred duty, that was implicit in all the values of the Illyrian Emperors:
to Restore the Empire. This meant many things, and in his case it was later to mean
the most sweeping reforms. But as an ideal it was inherently conservative. The best
that could be aspired to had already existed. This civilisation, this Eternal State,
represented all there was: and it was in danger of crumbling. The Great Task, the
one goal of the truly virtuous, dedicated Emperor, was to stem this process. What
greater ideal could there be?

Diocles had adopted very completely the older religious beliefs of the State he
served and hoped to rebuild. Jupiter, ruler of the universe, had guided and helped
and shielded Rome in its fabulous history from a village on the Tiber to mistress of
the world. Only a fool could regard these fortunes, and the present misfortunes, as
mere blind accident. An upright, simple people who revered the gods, kept their
oaths, and took up their duties bravely in the face of all adversities, had been helped
to success in a way that had happened to no other nation. If they acted again in the
right manner, with piety and courage, they would again enjoy divine help.

Diocles was prepared to intrigue, to kill if he had to, and risk being killed. In the
dangerous game he had been observing for so long, his turn was at last approaching.
This was not entirely inconsistent with a sincerely religious attitude. The traditional
Roman religion, at least as he had received it, was of an active, political kind, with no
room for withdrawal from public duty and little concern for salvation in an afterlife.
Its stress was on courage, responsibility, fidelity (the latter concept was somewhat
elastic in these confused times). If the gods were offended by one's actions, one could
expect failure and ruin; conversely, if one's enterprise prospered it was not just
random luck, but deserved fortune. However careful his preparations, the prize
would fall to Diocles' grasp only if the gods wished it.

As the army moved slowly through Asia and Bithynia towards the city of
Nicomedia, the story goes that the Emperor Numerian had been suffering for some
time from an eye complaint (possibly conjunctivitis caused by desert conditions). He
had been forced to remain inside a covered litter, unseen except by a few attendants,
who were Aper's men. The Prefect alone had charge of the invalid, and issued all
orders and instructions on his behalf. Suspicions grew among the soldiers, and the
rumour passed around that Numerian was dead, that he had been dead some time
and was actually stinking inside the litter. Aper had repeatedly reassured them that
he was merely indisposed, but finally they determined to see for themselves, and
forced their way past his guards. Numerian was indeed dead. Without hesitation the
soldiers on the spot arrested Aper.[36]

There was no armed clash. Whatever Aper's intentions, they had misfired badly.
The whole army halted in the vicinity of Nicomedia, where the senior officers
convened a grand army council. Its purpose could be none other than to choose a
successor. Although Numerian's brother Carinus was legitimate Emperor in the

West and had a natural claim to succeed, he was on the other side of the world: such a powerful assemblage of military force as this could not remain leaderless. This is the first time we hear of such a formal body as an army council, and it probably indicated the shrewdness of the leader it was about to choose. Its public role was to present the elevation of Diocles *not* as the unruly whim of the soldiers, but as the result of careful, orderly deliberation. The conscious and unanimous will of the army was to be expressed with the utmost consitutional propriety. It was therefore essential that the various military units drawn up on the famous hill outside Nicomedia, should represent all sections of the army.[37]

We can reconstruct the scene on 20 November 284. A raised and decorated tribunal, and facing it, rank after rank of legionary infantry, with walls of shields in red, green, yellow, white and black. The glittering scale armour and conical helmets of the heavy cavalry; the Moorish javelin men with their small round shields; the German units with their trousers and sleeveless tunics. Above them a forest of lances and javelins, punctuated by the legionary eagles and the long, silk dragon pennants fluttering in the wind.

The men all knew what was to come, the part they had to play, and the cash donatives they would receive. Some would have observed the officers hastily gathering in all their good silver helmets, bracelets and plate for melting, and heard the minters' anvils busily striking fresh bright coins for the great occasion. It was part of a ritual for Emperor-making which most of them knew by heart, and thoroughly enjoyed. Not only did it mean money in their belts, but it was the one supreme occasion when they were made to feel their worth and importance, when they would be flattered and courted, when an Emperor of their own kind would reaffirm with solemn pageantry and pomp that they, the invincible soldiers, were the true heart and backbone of eternal Rome.

Trumpets sounded, and the leading commanders stepped up to the tribunal in their gleaming breastplates and plumed parade helmets, surrounded by their bodyguard and the purple banners. All eyes were on the commander of the *Domestici*. One of the generals addressed them, in carefully rehearsed phrases. All had been shocked by the treacherous murder of their Emperor. Now they had searched earnestly for the best and fittest man to succeed, imploring the guidance of heaven, carefully consulting every opinion; and the unanimous choice had been Diocles, commander of the household troops. Did the army give its approval? All the troops clashed their weapons and set up the deafening shout of '*Augustus*!' which rolled irrevocably from one end of the great assembly to the other. The purple cloak was placed on his shoulders.[38]

Level-headed though he was, even he could not fail to have been affected by this heady display, the ecstatic illusion of being invincible and godlike, if only for a brief moment. Thousands on thousands of warriors in numberless myriads as far as the eye could see, the mightiest force on earth, were roaring in perfect unison that they would obey him, die for him, follow him to the end of the world: Command us! We will do anything! It was the supreme intoxication, the appallingly corrupting experience of sheer power, the union of countless individuals in a single irresistible will, which represented the climax of all ambition for so many men.

Their new Emperor stepped forward to address them. On to the tribunal was brought the luckless Lucius Aper, under guard. Diocles first held up his sword to the visible god of the sun, and swore the most terrible oath that he was completely unconnected with the death of Numerian, that he had not plotted to gain the purple, and had been reluctant to accept it. He then brought the captive Aper forward for all to see. This man, he shouted, was the murderer of Numerian, his own son-in-law, whose safety had been entrusted to him. As the orchestrated clamour for vengeance rose against Aper, Diocles promptly stabbed the helpless Prefect to death on the spot. Whether Aper had any incriminating revelations to make in his defence we shall never know: perhaps Diocles did not intend us to know. Any misgiving was decisively smothered in the communion of this bloody sacrifice.

With the question of Numerian's death sealed and avenged, Diocles, spattered with blood like a priest, could now speak as Emperor in his own right. He would have reminded them of the conquest of Persia they had achieved together, promised them that if each kept the solemn oaths they had sworn this day, they would triumph over every enemy. The gods approved their compact, and would uphold it. Then would come the long-awaited donatives; to each man, so many gold pieces and so much weight of silver. He was in his fortieth year. Shortly afterwards he was to modify his name to the full, dignified version: Gaius Aurelius Valerius Diocletianus.

But in November 284 his actual realm was more or less confined to the provinces the army had occupied or passed through: Syria, Cilicia, Cappadocia, Asia, Bithynia, possibly Egypt. The Western Provinces were controlled by Carinus in Rome, and there could be no question of a settlement between them. The following spring they would have to fight for mastery. The winter was therefore taken up in feverish preparations for the inevitable clash. Distant governors and provinces had to be secured, gaps filled in the army, supply dumps established, key towns occupied. The vital region was the Balkans, which contained not only the best recruiting grounds, but also the essential communication routes between East and West: whoever controlled these, was set fair to win the war. Fortunately, Diocletian had an ally in the governor of Dalmatia, Constantius, who had been a comrade in the *Protectores*.[39] If enough troops could be rushed into Thrace, Moesia and Dacia, Diocletian could link up with him and seize the Danube provinces before Carinus did.

With the loyalties of so many provinces still uncertain, there was great scope for intrigue and propaganda. Part of Constantius' task was to do whatever he could to detach from Carinus the central Danube forces, especially in Pannonia. Carinus publicly proclaimed Diocletian a jumped-up usurper who was only supported by a third of the army.[40] Diocletian's propaganda retaliated, and the war of words during these tense months was no doubt one source of the very unflattering portrait of Carinus that has come down to us:

... He slew the Prefect he found in office, and replaced him by Matronianus, a clerk of his and an old procurer who had always served him in his debaucheries ... He wrote arrogant letters to the Senate, and even promised to hand over the Senate's property to the City mob, as if they constituted the Roman people. By frequent marriage and divorce he took nine wives altogether, and threw over some of them

37

while they were still pregnant. He filled the palace with actors, pantomimists, harlots, singers and pimps.[41]

While the two armies were still thousands of miles apart, Carinus' commander in Pannonia, Sabinus Julianus, revolted against him and had himself proclaimed Emperor, promising to 'restore ancient liberties'. This favoured Diocletian's prospects, since it would at least bar Carinus' route into the central Balkans. These two contenders would clash first, and whoever won would hopefully be weakened in the final contest with Diocletian.

But Carinus showed none of the lethargy he was accused of. He was already on the march through Northern Italy, and in a rapid and skilful winter campaign he manoeuvred Julianus into an unfavourable position near Verona, and annihilated him. Then he pushed eastward into Pannonia and Illyricum, preparing to face Diocletian.[42]

The two great armies finally made contact with one another in the region of Belgrade, in the spring of 285. Despite Carinus' winter campaign, it soon became clear that he still commanded a very formidable force. After a number of preliminary engagements, the main battle was joined at Margus, near Belgrade and the mouth of the Morava at modern Smederovo, probably on the Belgrade–Skopje road. At the crisis of the fighting Diocletian's ranks were broken and his army on the point of being swept away. It seemed everything was lost, all he had hoped and worked for would be thrown to the winds, for the gods had deserted him. Then the miracle happened. Carinus' army did not press home their advantage. In the confusion it was learnt that Carinus had been killed – assassinated, it was said, by one of his own officers whose wife he had seduced. His army had no wish to continue fighting, and were ready to swear allegiance to Diocletian. The war was over. Diocletian was unchallenged ruler of the world.[43]

Years afterwards, he must have reflected on the contrast between all he accomplished and what was nearly his fate at Margus, how he had almost gone down in ruin as just one more adventurer who ruled only a few months. Now, sacrificing in thanksgiving, he had much to brood on. The gods had shown their hand, but their manner of doing it was a reminder – as if he needed it – of how easily their favour could be lost, how precarious the Emperor's position was. Unless he used the time they had given him to prevent new revolts, unless he could somehow master this dangerous, thousand-headed monster of the army, and break the whole bloody cycle – he would go the same way as all the others.

part two

EMERGENCE

chapter three

·JOVE AND HERCULES·

JUPITER RULES HEAVEN AND HERCULES PACIFIES THE EARTH: JUST AS, IN ALL
GREAT ENTERPRISES, IT IS DIOCLETIAN WHO DIRECTS THEM, AND YOU WHO
CARRY THEM OUT.
·PANEGYRIC TO MAXIMIAN, 289·

After receiving the submission of Carinus' old army and incorporating it under his command, the new Emperor was immediately busy making appointments, assembling the nucleus of a court and preparing forces for at least a holding campaign that summer against the tribes on the Danube. But, contrary to tradition, he did not travel to Rome to have his powers solemnly ratified by the Senate.[1] This omission was deliberate, and in keeping with his later policy, which was to remove the seat of government from Rome, to exclude the senatorial class from the administration, and to abolish the very last vestiges of its influence in the business of Emperor-making. He was however quite prepared to concede the Senate a ceremonial role. When the Senate House at Rome was burnt down in 285 he undertook as a matter of course to build a new one – the Curia which still stands today in the Forum. But even the empty symbolism of senatorial partnership in ruling was to be brought to an end. Officially he dated his reign from the day of his elevation by the army at Nicomedia, and it was to be another 20 years before he visited the Eternal City.

But otherwise he did not offend Rome unnecessarily. His emissaries took pains to broadcast that there would be no purges or proscriptions, that their new ruler did not regard Margus as a triumph of East over West or one party over another, but a reconciliation, a new era. Nobody who had served Carinus faithfully and well need fear simply on that account. To demonstrate the point, Carinus' Praetorian Prefect Aristobulus, who had shared the consulship with the Emperor for that year, was allowed to retain both his consulship and prefecture for the rest of 285.[2] 'It was something new and unheard-of,' wrote Aurelius Victor from a later time, 'that after a civil war nobody was disgraced, nobody stripped of their property or dignities. We would usually rejoice at a mild and merciful policy merely if some of the executions, murders and proscriptions could be converted into exile.'[3] According to one source Diocletian repeated the solemn formula which still went down well in senatorial circles, that of all past Emperors he would take the humane Marcus Aurelius as his model.

Very likely his agents had busily prepared some of the ground with secret

41

bargains during the six months' war of nerves. If one seriously supposes that even the turn of the tide at Margus was such a piece of treachery, then of course Carinus' administration would have to have been disloyal through and through, and all this vaunted clemency merely the repayment of debts. But if so, why was a costly battle necessary before his agent struck, and why did Carinus' army come close to winning? Diocletian was shrewd and extremely successful, but such theories, which simply project successes back to deep-laid and ultra-cunning plans, are a travesty of explanation. The government and armies of Carinus knew nothing of him, but were used to such changes. A conciliatory beginning probably seemed a wise investment. Quite possibly he only half-appreciated what the legend of Marcus Aurelius meant to the senatorial class, and was merely following good advice, like a new Tyneside politician addressing the City of London – if indeed he actually made the pronouncement. Carinus' appointees were nearly all highly competent men (contrary to the slanders), and until Diocletian could secure his own grip on the government in the West, one way of forestalling any new usurpers was to allay immediate fears, restore confidence, and hold out the continued promise of careers to the able.

The point was, once again, the awful distances between the real centres of power and the simultaneous military emergencies at different ends of the Empire. Already by the summer grave reports were coming in from several frontiers which for some time had avoided the immediate attentions of Emperors, preoccupied as they were with Persia and with fighting each other. Despite some attempts by his predecessors, the Danube was experiencing fresh invasions of the Sarmatians. Even more alarming was the situation in Gaul. Externally, the invading Alemanni and Burgundians had established themselves in strength across the Southern Rhine, and Franks and Saxons were ravaging the coastal lowlands around the Rhine mouth against little resistance. Internally, order had broken down and communications were all but paralysed. The miseries of invasions, and the cruel cycles of government extortion, followed by rural depopulation, leading to even greater extortion, had long been unbearable to the peasantry and had at last flared up into widespread and desperate revolt. What had been roving, unconnected bands of brigands eluding the authorities had swelled and coalesced into a single great movement of starving rebels, large enough to go where it liked, take what it wanted, and challenge the State's power. Villas were pillaged, towns cut off, and the soldiers immobilised behind fortified walls, deprived of reinforcements or recruits. The chaos was worse than anything since the time of Postumus 20 years before – indeed, it was the culmination of the same economic miseries and chronic insecurity that had helped propel Postumus to power. There was an imminent danger of losing Gaul altogether.[4]

Thus, immediately on becoming sole ruler, Diocletian was confronted with the classic dilemma of control which had faced every one of the Illyrian Emperors. Military crises were breaking out simultaneously, each one serious enough to demand a main field army, which meant it had to be commanded by the Emperor in person. But the Emperor could not be everywhere. Aurelian and Probus had responded to this problem with a demonic energy, ceaselessly travelling with their armies thousands of miles from one war region to another. Political survival had dictated that their military control be centralised: the Emperor dare not be anywhere except in the midst of his army, and this army had to be the largest concentration of force in existence. Moreover, the most capable, hence potentially dangerous, generals had to be placed close to him in the general staff, where they could be both used and watched.

But this could not possibly be the basis of a permanent defensive strategy. Even at its most successful, such frantic movement meant it could be months before major invasions were intercepted in force, by which time they had already caused great destruction. Defeating and expelling them was only a first step, which then had to be consolidated by heavy punitive action, treaties, and strong defensive reorganisation. The undermining of Probus' ambitious defensive policies on the Rhine five years earlier was a frightening reminder of how rapidly the Germans could recover. If they were ever to be shut out, it had to be accepted that nothing less than a continuous, imperial military presence close to the frontier could hope to achieve it.

To restore Gaul would require a great effort lasting years. If Diocletian went himself, it meant not only improvising on the Danube war, but installing himself at the far western end of the world at a time when relations with Persia had not yet been satisfactorily stabilised. If he sent a subordinate to Gaul there were equally great risks. The man would have to be granted very wide powers and considerable forces, and would have to create his own strong administration almost from scratch. If he was completely successful and brought the Gallic provinces firmly under his grip, it was easy to see what his next move might be. However sincere his declarations of loyalty now, it would be a different story after arduous campaigns and hard-won victories achieved under his sole command. He would feel entitled to great rewards, and with a loyal, battle-tempered army behind him the temptation of the purple would be almost irresistible.

Having come to power himself by army intrigue, Diocletian had pondered this first great problem very thoroughly. He was, after all, only one of a group of like-minded generals hovering around the throne, each a potential Emperor. They had supported him but they could equally supplant him at any time, as he had supplanted Carus, and Carus, Probus. The distribution of adequate rewards, the delegation of territorial military command, and the problem of imperial succession, were all inseparable parts of the same great knot. Carus, like others before him, had established his adult son in the junior position of Caesar, with power in the West and the clear title of heir, relying on the stability of the family tie and the dynastic sympathies of the armies. But Diocletian, now over 40, had no son. His solution was bold but rational, a synthesis of the conflicting traditions of imperial legitimacy. It was simply: choose your most reliable man, adopt him legally as son, heir and Caesar (as the Antonine Emperors had done) and make him effective co-ruler. What is lost in the absence of blood relationship can be more than compensated in suitable qualities, and a strong loyal general who has not yet developed treacherous ambitions will receive as a gracious gift what he would sooner or later have coveted as a right.

Everything of course depended on the choice of candidate, and here Diocletian succeeded completely. Maximian, several years his junior, was a fellow-general of long standing who had served with him under Aurelian, Probus and Carus. So suited was he to the role, that it is difficult not to believe Diocletian had carefully cultivated their friendship for some time with this eventual possibility in mind. Some have naturally speculated that Maximian's elevation to Caesar was the result of a pre-arranged deal between them, the pay off for his support in the coup and the civil war. We shall never know what secret bargains Diocletian made with his supporters, but the chronology leaves little doubt that his elevation was premeditated.[5]

Maximian, like so many of the other military grandees, was of obscure Danubian peasant stock, coming from the region of Sirmium (Sremska Mitrovica). He was a fine commander of implacable energy and tough, domineering character, but temperamentally more capable of fierce loyalty than subtle intrigue. Aurelius Victor describes him as 'a colleague trustworthy in friendship, if somewhat boorish, and of great military talents'. Unlike his military peers, who occupied the throne or the prefectures and were becoming more conscious of their educational deficiencies, Maximian had no pretension whatever to culture and no regard for it. In the official panegyric extolling his exploits some years later, Maximian's victories are compared with Scipio's destruction of Hannibal in days of old – heroes whom, the orator suggests, Maximian has perhaps never heard of.[6]

But the difference which really counted was not Maximian's rusticity, but his lack of wider political imagination. In sharp contrast to Diocletian he was very much the blunt, literal-minded soldier, his horizons bounded by battles, triumphs and military order. Certainly he was ambitious, as they all were, but his conceptions of power were quite orthodox, his motives transparent and on the whole honourable. To initiate a careful plot for the purple he would probably require prompting by some more cunning supporter. It was precisely because of these qualities that he was chosen by Diocletian, who was subsequently able to implement his own policies through his colleague without modification. Gibbon, admiring the astuteness of the 'artful Dalmatian', stresses other advantages in the arrangement:

> Nor were the vices of Maximian less useful to his benefactor. Insensible to pity, and fearless of consequences, he was the ready instrument of every act of cruelty which the policy of that artful prince might at once suggest and disclaim. As soon as a bloody sacrifice had been offered to prudence and to revenge, Diocletian, by his seasonable intercession, saved the remaining few whom he had never designed to punish, gently censured the severity of his stern colleague, and enjoyed the comparison of a golden and iron age, which was universally applied to their opposite maxims of government.[7]

That Maximian was cruel on occasions there is no reason to doubt, but some of the charges by Lactantius – that he violated the daughters of senators, that wherever he travelled virgins were torn from the parents to slake his lusts – are of such a classic kind, and come from such a hostile source, that they must be treated with scepticism.[8] Most important, it would be mistaken to think of Diocletian simply manipulating his guileless comrade. Had that been so, Maximian's fierce sensibilities would sooner or later have yielded to the poisonous suggestions of some crafty courtier. Maximian certainly needed proper handling, but their true relationship does seem to have been mutually acknowledged to a remarkable degree. Maximian recognised Diocletian's political wisdom and his own relative ignorance of the mysteries of statecraft, and was content to defer to his advice in all major matters. In return, Diocletian did not stint his colleague in all the military and imperial honours appropriate to him, nor did he ever reveal a hint of intellectual superiority towards him. The soundness of this adjustment was to be revealed only many years later, when Maximian rashly embarked on fresh power struggles without Diocletian to guide him, and was quickly outmanoeuvred by his enemies.

Another, less flattering reason has been suggested for Diocletian's elevation of Maximian – that he knew himself to be a mediocre general, and needed a good one to do the brunt of his fighting for him. The comparison has been made with Augustus and Agrippa. This is perhaps true. Diocletian had enough self-knowledge to realise that his real talent was for organising rather than just fighting. But in any case he was determined once and for all to restore stable frontiers instead of the ravaged war zones of his predecessors, and to do this would still have required a division of command, however great his own individual generalship. For the next five years both co-rulers would be constantly fighting on their respective frontiers.

By our best reckoning it was at Milan in the summer of 285, only months after the decisive battle of Margus, that Maximian was solemnly proclaimed Most Noble Caesar and *Filius Augusti,* and either then or shortly afterwards adopted into Diocletian's family as his son, taking the name Valerius. In itself this was in accord with established tradition. The Caesar was normally the natural son of the Augustus, as Carinus had been, whose exact powers were undefined but who clearly carried the imperial title and the legitimate right of succession. Diocletian's legal 'son', Maximian, was both close to him in age, and promptly invested with all the authority and forces needed to retrieve the situation in Gaul.

In normal times the provinces of Gaul comprised one of the richest regions of the Empire, an exporter of agricultural and industrial produce whose output had long overshadowed Italy. Given only peace and internal order it could hardly fail to yield a surplus of wealth. It was a measure of the times that over several decades they had managed to wreck even this fertile country. In the frontier areas, the main invasion corridors such as the Rhône valley, and many other districts, the once fertile fields were reduced to abandoned scrub and forest, the villas and farms ruined and silent. The proud towns were in a state of dilapidation from barbarian sack, financial exhaustion, and the need for building stone to construct protective walls. To an inhabitant of the prosperous, sophisticated Gallic cities of 50 years earlier, the picture now would have seemed something out of a nightmare – akin to the post-Disaster science fiction horrors which have fascinated the public in our time. Fearful, depleted communities huddle inside cramped walled towns in precarious contact with each other, using the roads only warily, growing what they can in the deserted fields, anxious for news and prone to rumour. Bands of armed strangers governed by no magistrates or soldiers arrive without warning, demanding shelter, threatening to burn the town, telling stories of other parts where everyone has fled the terrible Germans, and some have even taken to living in caves.

Maximian's first tasks were to restore some semblance of order out of this turmoil, and then prepare a fresh effort against the barbarians around the Rhine mouth. The brigand movement was an assortment of peasants, shepherds, *coloni* and others going by the name of *Bagaudae* ('the fighters') and led by two figures Aelianus and Amandus, both of whom had adopted the imperial style. But they had no military organisation or training, and were armed largely in an amateurish way with axes, farm implements and whatever other weapons they could pick up. The products of rage and despair, their morale was uncertain and their aims confused: it is possible that the first of their supposed leaders actually tried to oppose open revolt. Faced with a resolute professional army they soon began to break up, and for several months Maximian's cavalry detachments swept through the countryside, relieving the isolated towns and putting fresh heart into the garrisons, cutting up the clumsy forces of the rebels and reducing them piecemeal. By early 286 the revolt was mastered sufficiently for Maximian to concentrate his forces for a Rhine campaign. However necessary, this war against Roman subjects whom the government and the barbarians between them had driven beyond endurance was a cruel, sordid affair, and the State recognised it. It was not recorded in the official victories, and the later panegyric to Maximian says tactfully 'I pass quickly over this episode, for I see that in your magnanimity you would rather forget this victory than celebrate it'.[9] The rebels who were not caught in arms trickled back to their homes, but for the moment the government could do little for them beyond freeing Gaul from the invaders and restraining the plundering of its own soldiers.

Maximian had established his headquarters at Mainz. From here his mobile troops were despatched against the rebels, and from here he prepared his main campaign against the Germans. The wars of Maximian against the Heruli, Chaibones, Franks, Alemanni and Burgundians occupied the next five years, and are best described together. But in 286, soon after the Bagaudae had been quelled and while Maximian was engaged against the Franks, a new political crisis arose, centred on Britain and the Channel.[10] Added to the existing woes, Frankish and Saxon raiders had for many years infested the Channel, preying on merchant shipping and mounting damaging attacks on both coasts. Partly due to its insular position, Britain had suffered far less than Gaul in the third century, and was now needed more than ever as a supplier of minerals, manufactured goods and skilled labour. The main menace to Britain was from the sea raiders, who would swoop down without warning anywhere on the long coastline from the Wash to the Isle of Wight, sack and plunder settlements, and escape with very little risk of interception. The bolder of them were penetrating far up the estuary and other navigable rivers to attack undefended targets well inland. There are several sites of burnt villas from the period in Sussex, as well as coin hoards throughout Kent, Essex, Suffolk and East Anglia.

The old Roman fleet, the *Classis Britannica* based on Dover and Boulogne, had been unable to cope with the fast tactics of these raiding ships, and work had begun under Probus and Carinus on chains of fortified bases along both coasts, from which a reorganised fleet would operate. Accordingly, Maximian had made an important appointment. Mausaeus Carausius was a Menapian of barbarian origin from the Low Countries who had risen to a high military command, and assisted Maximian against the Bagaudae; he also had close relations with several Frankish tribes. Most important, he had valuable skills as a shipmaster in the difficult northern seas. As early as 285 he was given the important task of clearing the Channel of raiders. Since this meant taking over the newly constructed Channel defence system it involved command of several bodies of troops – perhaps whole legions – as well as the fleet. He set about the task with great efficiency, and before the year was out was capturing raiding ships in great numbers. Diocletian was impressed by such rapid results, to the extent of announcing an official victory in Britain in 285.

But early in 286 reports of a more suspicious kind began to reach Maximian's headquarters. It is claimed that Carausius was taking care to intercept the raiders only after they had done their plundering, and large amounts of the booty were not being accounted for. Rumours were that he was using it to undermine the legions in Britain, even that he had formed a lucrative partnership with his Frankish friends. However, our sources for this are anti-Carausian, and if he really was engaged in secondary plundering to that extent, it is hard to see how he enjoyed his undoubted popularity among the British merchants. But that he was cultivating support among the troops there is no doubt; by the time he was discovered his preparations were well advanced.

Enraged by the reports, Maximian ordered him arrested and executed, but the nimble Carausius moved too quickly. Taking the whole fleet with him he crossed to Britain, where at least two legions, II Augusta and XX Valeria Victrix, promptly came over to his side, as well as all or part of a Continental legion in the Boulogne area (probably XXX Ulpia Victrix) giving him a base on both Channel coasts. The resistance of a few loyal units was quickly broken, and Carausius was declared Augustus.

Now that the blow had fallen Maximian could rage and fulminate, but his hands were tied in every way, and Carausius knew it. Busy with the Heruli and the Franks, he had assigned to Carausius control of most of the coast, and in any case he had no other warships of his own, the Rhine fleet having been destroyed by the Germans a few years earlier. Carausius quickly set about strengthening his position. He paid his troops generously, enlarged his fleet with converted merchant vessels, engaged Frankish mercenaries, and quickly brought the whole coast firmly under his control, from the Rhine mouth to Brittany. In addition to his naval skills, his assets were a good supply of precious metal, which enabled him to buy military support, and the goodwill of merchants and land-owners who had suffered badly from the long years of piracy and government neglect, and saw him as their deliverer. Shortly afterwards this astute character, ruling a considerable territory, proclaimed an independent British state, *Imperium Britanniarum,* on the model of Postumus' Gallic Empire. His first coins assert the solidarity of the British legions, with the Virgilian quotation *Expectate Veni* ('Come, expected one') recalling Aeneas' escape from Troy to found a new empire.

To Diocletian in the East, the news of this successful separatist revolt so early in his reign was a severe shock, which struck at the roots of his authority. Particularly worrying was the ease with which whole legions had gone over en bloc, corrupted by gold and silver. In short, he experienced for a moment the same cold lurch of insecurity that every one of his predecessors had felt when a large body of troops calmly announced that they had deserted him for another, and already delivered several stategic bases into the rebel's hands. The event clearly confirmed his wisdom in appointing a Caesar in the West, but even this had apparently not been enough. Did he have to have a Caesar in every corner? Was the Empire breaking up again as it did in the time of Gallienus? If Carausius got away with it, who would be next?

The bitter fact was that Carausius held all the advantages for the moment, and no military measures could be taken to crush him until an army could be spared and a new fleet built. Worse, he was a threat to Maximian's back, and might be tempted to increase his Continental territories while the latter was fully engaged on the Rhine. Having put down one revolt, Maximian was now faced with a second which could force him to fight on two fronts. We do not know what correspondence passed between him and Diocletian at this time, but the end result emerges, I think, from the pace of events. Maximian faced military crisis, in which the imperial power in Gaul was struggling for its existence, and had to be supported in every way. Even if Carausius made no move there would at least be a propaganda war for the loyalties of the soldiers and provincials. The legions, the tribes and mercenary units whose support would be needed to retake Britain, were vulnerable to Carausius' money and proclamations. He styled himself Augustus, and was already circulating handsome coins calling himself Restorer of Britain. How could Maximian's position be strengthened in this contest?

There was one way. Legitimate imperial authority had long had only a precarious foothold in war-torn Gaul; and it made a difference that Carausius was Augustus whereas Maximian was only Caesar, subordinate to an Augustus on the other side of the world whom nobody had seen. The implication was plain. Under the plea of necessity Maximian could have himself declared Augustus by his army, and might even be sensible to do so. Events were pushing Diocletian faster than he had anticipated, but he came quickly to the only realistic decision. Having shared power so far, he was not going to baulk at going further. Maximian would have to be equal in men's eyes to the usurper.

Accordingly, with as much ceremony as possible, the solemn enactment was made in April 286. Marcus Aurelius Valerius Maximianus was now raised legitimately to share in the sovereignty as Augustus. Together the two united *brothers* in the purple (no longer father and son) would purge the state of all enemies within and without. In particular, implied the panegyric, they would sweep the pirate Carausius from the seas and restore Britain to its due obedience.[11] Most important, the act which bestowed this authority was not the election of the soldiers, but solely the free transmission of powers from the reigning sovereign: legitimacy was carefully underlined and contrasted with Carausius' military usurpation.[12]

The dual imperium was an innovation, but its constitutional form was not as strange as it would have seemed, say, to Medieval traditions of monarchy. Rome had customarily done things in twos, ever since its legendary foundation by two brothers. The Republic had elected two consuls; Emperors had frequently appointed two Prefects; and a century before, Marcus Aurelius had shared the title and powers of Augustus with his adoptive brother Lucius Verus. All the same, a perceptive observer could see that this was different. Lucius Verus' rule had been all but nominal, but now there were two strong, equal soldier-Emperors fighting the barbarians in East and West, each with complete command of armies and government. For the moment their fraternal alliance was one of necessity, but when and if the external dangers were overcome, what would happen to their relationship? Would they divide the Empire in two, or would they eventually fight one another, as so many others had done?

Such speculation was natural enough. But, though circumstances had propelled him to it, Diocletian's decision was soundly conceived. Any course entailed great risks: neither he nor any other ruler in these times could exercise real control over a strong military colleague 2,000 miles away. But he could and did exercise a powerful moral influence over Maximian, and it was this attunement of their respective characters, already described, which was to enable their alliance to withstand all strains. Maximian was to be the great Illyrian soldier-Emperor, conquering enemies and covering himself in glory, while Diocletian was to be the supreme paternal governor, carefully directing the restoration of the state. As the originator of the dual monarchy, Diocletian possessed greater *auctoritas* – the barely defined imperial quality which was not enshrined in formal powers but was signalled only obliquely, for example, by his greater number of consulships.

There was no question of them having separate government of two realms of East and West: all the official propaganda from 287 onwards strenuously counteracts any such interpretation. Rome and its embodiment, the imperial power, was one, eternal and indivisible—*patrimonium indivisum*—the two Augusti merely two arms with one head. The apparent territorial division was no more than convenience of command, and either Emperor could and did move within the other's customary domain. All edicts, legal rulings and official pronouncements were published in their joint names throughout the Empire, coins of both were issued in East and West, and every state celebration involved them both, in effigy at least. Unity—of authority, power, aims and will—was the clear message repeated in every available way; hardly ever before had the theme of identical inseparable imperial twins been laboured so heavily in proclamations, coins, portraiture. Despite their geographical distance from each other they shared the consulship for 287. On 1 January simultaneous celebrations were held, and a fine gold medallion was issued among senior army officers and civil officials, showing a consular procession with four elephants and crowds waving palms. The portraits of Diocletian and Maximian, which face one another, are not only symmetrical and of equal size but resemble each other in facial features, like twin brothers. Under the laurel crowns and consular robes, both are shown as tough, heavy-featured with closely cropped military beards.[13]

Diocletian could hardly have known this at the time, but his decision in 286 to create two Augusti was a crucially important milestone in the whole imperial recovery, the first conscious step in the creation of a new imperial system. With hindsight it is reasonable to mark this as the point at which the self-consuming cycle of ephemeral military Emperors which had plagued most of the third century, was eventually broken.

Maximian's barbarian enemies were many, but they were far from united. The main groups were in sharp antagonism with one another, and their overspill into Roman territories partly the result of their own ceaseless warring. The Franks in

49

particular had little overall cohesion, and during 285 Carausius had used his close ties with some of their tribes to help his Channel policy. After his revolt it was even more necessary for Maximian to exploit these internal divisions, since indiscriminate hostility to all the Frankish tribes would play into the hands of his rival. The largest and most formidable of the invaders, however, were the Alemanni and Burgundians who had occupied the Moselle–Vosges region in the south. Unable to mount an offensive immediately, Maximian adopted a scorched earth tactic, laying waste an area around them and reducing them through famine and subsequent disease during 286 and 287.[14]

His first campaign was against the smaller combination of the Heruli and Chaibones, tribes from the Elbe and the Baltic coast who had broken into the Low Countries. The sources tell us Maximian was able to manoeuvre them into a single set battle at which he fought in person, furiously riding back and forth along the whole battle line, until the enemy broke and the fugitives were mercilessly hunted down, the rout becoming a massacre. Only after this enemy had been destroyed could Maximian turn his main attention to the Alemanni.

This required the main weight of his forces, and was to take two stages of campaigning. The Alemanni were fearsome warriors who fought in a dense mass on foot, only their nobles being on horseback. Their initial charge was very dangerous, and Roman tactics used various ways of blunting it, such as a heavy barrage from archers, before the legions received the shock. Having bled these invaders by famine, Maximian launched a great offensive against them, probably in 287, supplementing his frontal attacks by deep thrusts into German territory itself, aimed at spreading havoc in their homelands and unbalancing them from the rear. By the winter of that year he had clearly gained the upper hand, and was driving them from the west bank of the Rhine. At this point he received a visit from Diocletian himself, who was campaigning on the upper Danube. Their meeting, probably at Mainz, was a council of war rather than a state occasion, and its practical outcome was to lay plans for a joint campaign into German territories the following year, and after that, an expedition to unseat Carausius.

Accordingly, Maximian carefully chose those southernmost points where the Rhine is at low water at certain times of the year, and moved large forces across the river quickly in a surprise invasion of the *Agri Decumantes*, the narrow triangle between the upper reaches of the Rhine and Danube in the Black Forest region, then the heartland of enemy territory. The aim was to create as much terror and destruction as possible, and spread the clear message of burning villages and butchered inhabitants throughout the whole people. Diocletian, based in Raetia, launched the southern prong of the invasion. Levered out of their Roman foothold, streaming back to their devastated homelands, the Alemanni were given no respite. The terror continued until the remaining population had fled deep into the forests, leaving large tracts of territory on the east bank of the Rhine entirely in Roman hands. The Gallic population was able once again to occupy the lands between the Rhine and Moselle. The older Rhine forts and towns, abandoned and partly destroyed, were rebuilt, and extensive bridgeheads on the east bank, at Mainz, Cologne and other points, were created and fortified. A medallion of 288 celebrates the victory and shows the two Augusti at Magontiacum (Mainz) with a bridge across the river joining two fortresses. With the Rhine and Moselle securely under Roman control again, the building of a new fleet could proceed on these rivers.

It was in the Low Countries (Germania Inferior) that a divide-and-rule policy offered best chance of success, since it was essential to isolate those Frankish tribes who were in alliance with Carausius. Maximian therefore made his own alliance with the deposed Frankish king Gennobaudes, helping him to recover the territory from which his rivals had driven him. Then, in a ceremony with all his warriors present he was duly installed by Maximian as king and an ally of Rome, and was able to demand and receive the solemn oaths of homage of many lesser chiefs, who would never have felt bound in this way to a direct Roman ruler. A further measure of territorial stabilisation was to permit a settlement of Frisians, Salian Franks, Chamavi and other smaller tribes in a chosen zone of Roman territory between the Rhine and Waal from Nijmegen to Utrecht. They were granted lands on condition they recognised Roman overlordship, supplied soldiers as necessary, and guarded their new territories against other Frankish tribes. This policy of withdrawal behind a buffer, which was repeated on other frontiers, was dictated by the altered needs of defence in the third century, and especially the imperative of using trained military manpower as economically as possible. South-west of this zone, on the lower Rhine, was constructed the military frontier proper: a deep system of forts, roads and fortified towns, supported by a strong military highway through Tournay, Bavay, Tongres, Maastricht and Cologne, linking into the middle Rhine defences.

For Diocletian in the East, the priorities during the years 285 to 290 were likewise to clear the Danube of invaders, and secure the Orient against renewed Persian aggression following the recent war. Restoration and defence of the 1,400-mile Danube line from the Black Sea to Raetia, was a permanent task offering no prospect of final completion, like Sisyphus rolling his rock up the hill. Throughout living memory it had been a threatre of war, and for many years large sections of the frontier had collapsed completely. It was as if a man were trying to keep out the sea by a long wall made of only mud and sand, which is partly demolished by each tide and has to be built up again if it is not to be swept completely away by the next. Eventually, with help from others and at great cost, Diocletian would replace this with a wall of stone. It would not be impregnable, it would need constant maintenance, and it would include judicious lock gates to allow a controlled influx of barbarians into the Empire. But it would be better than anything else achieved in the third century.

In what is now the Hungarian plain a continual upheaval of peoples was going on. Earlier arrivals such as the Quadi, Carpi, Bastarnae and Sarmatians were under growing pressure from the Vandals in the north, and the Goths and Gepids in the north-east and east. Outnumbered and penned into ever smaller areas by the new migrants, they invariably burst into Roman territory whenever its defences were weak, mixing threats with supplication, respectfully seeking living space in the Empire, then warning of desperate invasion if it was not granted. Rome typically responded in like manner, the contingencies reversed: it would not negotiate under threat, and any invasion would be crushed. But, after defeating them, Rome would settle certain numbers under its own conditions.

In late 285 Diocletian was engaged in the first of a series of campaigns against the Sarmatians, a nomadic pastoral nation, seasonally migrating with their great herds down the traditional routes of the plains. Like the Huns, Magyars and Mongols of later centuries they were fine horsemen and formed a powerful cavalry. Now, however, they were being levered out of their customary pasturage by floods of Goths and Vandals. They resisted, often with success, but were steadily losing against great numbers and territorial encroachment, until their position had become desperate. They demanded either pasturage within the Empire, or Roman help in regaining their former territories. Refusal of both meant war, which they were prepared for. We have no details of the campaign of 285, but although recorded as a victory, it gave a respite of only three years on the central Danube. By 289 the Sarmatians had to be fought again.[15]

In 287 Diocletian moved east to the Syrian frontier with a display of strength, aimed at applying maximum diplomatic strength on Persia, following the victory of Carus. At a meeting with Vahram's ambassadors he extracted a peace treaty whose terms were very favourable to Rome. Although Vahram had now overcome the internal rebellion which had paralysed his war effort in 282–3, he relinquished his claims to both Mesopotamia and Armenia, and recognised the establishment of a Roman ally and nominee, Tiridates III, on the Armenian throne. With Persia, unlike the tribal and nomadic enemies, it was possible to conduct diplomacy that would hold over time and distance. The Persian state was quite capable of appreciating the military balance without continually putting it to armed test, and no hostilities would occur without the Great King's knowledge and permission. The Euphrates frontier was secured, and Diocletian freed from the anxiety that he might have to transfer very large forces to the Orient when they were badly needed elswhere.[16]

Having fortified the strategic city of Circesium (Buseire) on the Euphrates and reorganised the Syrian frontier, Diocletian again returned to the Danube. In the following year he campaigned on the frontier of Raetia at the westernmost end, and participated in the joint offensive with Maximian into the territory of the Alemanni.

The demands of war did not prevent him energetically tackling other pressing administrative problems during his first years of power. From the moment an Emperor was invested with the purple, whether in his palace or at a military camp or on the move, he was deluged with incessant correspondence, demands for decisions and for audiences. He had to be accompanied not just by his bodyguard and military staff, but a host of secretaries and legal advisers and their own subordinates, who tried to impose order on this mass of business and who made up the somewhat arbitrary membership of the imperial court. The work of government did not stop just because fighting was going on and it was near-impossible for an Emperor to avoid it even if he wished. As governorships and higher state offices fell vacant, Diocletian nearly always filled them, not by senators but by men of equestrian rank, often of lowly origins, who owed their whole rise to imperial recognition. A separation also began to be made between military and civil posts (*duces* and *iudices*),[17] in contrast to the old governorships which automatically combined both functions.

The trend, repeated in a number of other measures, was towards limiting concentrations of power by separating lines of authority and giving more men smaller areas of jurisdiction. It was motivated by a natural desire for security, but also Diocletian's determination to get a thorough and competent provincial adminstration going again, as shown in his insistence that governors must try all important cases in person. In 286 also, the gold coinage was stabilised by the issue of a very pure *aureus* at the official weight of 60 to the pound; but apart from its propaganda value this made very little difference to a debased currency in which gold transactions were a rarity. He may well have hoped that the *aureus* would at least be the cornerstone of a restored three-metal currency, when it could be reintroduced.[18]

But inevitably the great mass of Diocletian's daily work revolved around his role as the centre of appeals and petitions of every sort, on all kinds of matter and from all grades of person in the Empire. There were requests for advice from governors, decisions referred upwards, deputations from cities and corporate bodies, petitions from individual officeholders or private individuals for favours, for jobs, for confirmation of rights and obligations or for dispensations from them, for rulings on disputed points of law. The volume of judicial and legal work alone was prodigious. This stemmed from the origins of the monarch as a republican magistrate, and was perpetuated by the central importance of law in Roman public life. Not only was he expected to judge lawsuits brought before him, but his authoritative opinion was sought, through the system of rescripts, on endless points of interpretation of the laws, often arising from private legal disputes. This perpetual queue of requests might be delayed, and often was—sometimes for years—but it could not be delegated. Even though the reply might be drafted by a legally trained secretary, he still had to approve each one and subscribe his approval in his own hand, whether briefly or at length; just as he had to read all correspondence in person, and was normally the first person to read it.

Modern statesmen sometimes complain of being drowned in paper, but they at least have efficient filtering mechanisms to ensure that all but substantial matters are handled by subordinates or referred to other proper authorities. Their office organisations are designed to allow them to subdivide and apportion work smoothly to whatever degree necessary. For a Roman Emperor it was virtually impossible to set up delegated authorities to undertake this part of his functions or have lower officials automatically reply on his behalf to all routine correspondence. Tradition laid down that *he* was the proper authority, that an inseparable part of his duty to his subjects was to hear and decide their requests. There were of course the provincial governors and Prefects who dealt with the bulk of these individual matters. But the right to petition direct to the Emperor was basic and sacrosanct. When Hadrian, on his travels, once protested that he was too busy, the petitioner cried: 'Then cease to be a king!'[19]

Of the petitions dealt with by Diocletian during these early years, a typical instance is that of a woman who had travelled to reach the Emperor when he stopped at Heraclea in 286. She wished to end her marriage, but was being browbeaten by her husband who insisted she was not free to do so, and by her mother-in-law who was threatening to take back the marriage gifts. Diocletian's *subscriptio* replied that she was free to end the marriage if she wished, and to retain whatever had been given to her as a gift: and that the provincial governor would certainly uphold her rights in the matter. It illustrates the system in operation, with its clumsiness and uncertainties as well as its value to ordinary citizens. Armed with this rescript, the woman could be confident of winning a future court case if it came to that. She had not been content to go direct to the provincial governor, or to a legal advocate for his paid advice; nor had she simply petitioned the Emperor by letter, which might never have reached him. By travelling in person, and no doubt by great persistence and expense, she had got the most authoritative legal advice possible. Diocletian was not granting her a favour (though such things were also possible) but confirming what the law was: had her case been a bad one, his rescript could have left her empty-handed.

Over the years many officials had naturally grown up around the Emperor who, if they could not actually take the decisions, could at least regulate the flow of paper and the press of people seeking audience. A considerable share of the administrative load was shouldered by the office of the Praetorian Prefect. From being simply the commander of the Praetorian Guards, this figure had slowly accumulated so many civil functions that he had become the head of the expanding imperial administration, wielding powers second only to the Emperor himself. It was not only their command of the Guards, but above all, their control of the government apparatus which had enabled several Prefects to seize the purple itself during the last half century. In the years of dual rule the Emperors were served by at least three Prefects, and possibly four: Afranius Hannibalianus, Julius Asclepiodotus, and Flavius Constantius. (The last-named was to found a family whose name would shine brilliantly through the fourth century.)

By 287 Diocletion had fixed the main centre of his administration at Nicomedia (now Izmit) situated on the rocky shores of the gulf on the eastern side of the Bosporus, strategically placed between East and West on the great military highway connecting the Balkans with Asia and the Orient. Almost nothing is left of the ancient city today—its foundations buried under Izmit's extensive cement, phosphate and petrochemical plants, and their suburbs. There is a second-century fountain, traces of an aqueduct, and ruins of Byzantine fortifications on the citadel hill. It was founded by Nicomedes I in 264 BC and became the capital of the kings of Bithynia until that state passed peacefully under Roman sovereignty. Recently it had been sacked by the Goths together with many other Greek coastal cities. Diocletian had grand plans to develop and adorn Nicomedia with all the magnificence of an imperial residence. For decades there had been very little large public building. The restoration of cities had been mainly a matter of improving their defences, sometimes amateurishly, often at the expense of their other buildings. Not only were cities chronically short of money, but architects, masons and craftsmen were scarce. Only the Emperor could command the resources for such projects, and much of this likewise had to be directed towards military architecture. Towards the 280s the new and far stronger designs of stone fort had begun to appear on some major frontiers, a development which Diocletian extended everywhere in the Empire. The stimulus to building skills helped create the conditions for a revival of public building, and the market was provided by Diocletian's driving architectural ambitions—or, less flatteringly, his 'building mania' (his baths in Rome are the largest ever built). The transformation of Nicomedia is described in a famous passage of Lactantius, who was professor of rhetoric there. The tone is thoroughly hostile to Diocletian, but even he cannot deny the scope and expansiveness of these designs:

> ... he also had an insatiable passion for building, which resulted in endless
> exactions from the provinces to supply the wages for labourers and craftsmen,
> transport, and whatever else was needed for the works he projected. *Here* a basilica,
> *there* a circus, *here* a mint, and *there* an armament factory; in one place a palace for
> his empress, in another one for his daughter. Soon a large part of the city was
> cleared, and all the people shifted with their wives and children, as if it were a city
> captured by enemies. And when the buildings were completed, to the ruin of whole
> provinces, he said : 'They are not right, let them be done again on a different plan.'
> Then they were to be pulled down, or altered, only perhaps to undergo a future
> demolition. By this folly he was continually trying to make Nicomedia equal Rome
> in magnificence.[20]

In the spring of 289, Maximian was at last ready to deal with the British rebel Carausius. By a combination of fighting and counter-alliances he had isolated his enemy's Frankish allies and stabilised his own position in the Low Countries, and now had a newly-built fleet on the Rhine. He now concentrated his troops to attack Carausius' coastal possessions, and began moving his fleet north. He could only reach the sea by the Rhine mouth, where Carausius naturally expected him. It would therefore be difficult to land his troops anywhere on the British coast without first fighting a sea battle, so losing the advantage of surprise. Not only was Maximian tactically cramped in this way, but his forces were less experienced in naval warfare. Roman fleets were simply a branch of the army, and few commanders specialised in sea fighting. The most common warship of the time was the Liburnian, an 80-foot two-banked galley of about 40 oars and a single sail. It carried a large ram and towers fore and aft mounting catapults, and would be packed with armed soldiers. Since one could normally sink an opposing vessel only by ramming, which involved difficult manoeuvering, sea battles often turned into boarding and capture, so that taking a ship would be like taking a defended palisade. Trained steersmen would be needed to handle these ships, but since nearly all the coast was in Carausius' hands, Maximian would have had difficulty finding enough of them who were experienced in the stormy North Sea.

It was an unfamiliar and hazardous undertaking, and although Maximian's land forces appear to have broken through to the coast, his fleet was defeated. The panegyrics, having promised that Carausius would be dealt with, fall embarrassingly silent until later on, when they briefly refer to a naval misfortune as a result of a storm. Maximian's fleet, ironically, may have been intercepted by the new Saxon Shore cross-coastal defence system which was so successful against the Saxon raiders. Since his fleet had to approach Britain from exactly the same direction, it would have fallen into precisely the same prepared trap.[21]

The outcome of this failure was an inevitable truce. Carausius, wisely, did not seek to extend his territories but only to be accepted as ruler of what he held. However galling, Diocletian and Maximian could not dislodge him at present, nor could they be permanently diverted from the tasks on other fronts. A tacit accommodation was therefore arrived at, apparently accepting Carausius' *de facto* control of Britain and the Continental coast as far inland as Rouen. It was equally in Carausius' interest to advertise this agreement, as it was in theirs to conceal it. To him, it was a solemn treaty granting him legitimate imperium side by side with them, as his new coins proudly proclaimed. To them, it was a regrettable and temporary truce to be revoked as soon as convenient; none of their coins or pronouncements ever reciprocated Carausius' sentiments.[22]

Despite the British defeat and a host of other daunting problems, including fresh disturbances in Syria and Egypt, Diocletian cannot have been entirely displeased with the results of the first few hectic years. In an Empire still struggling for its life, they had been dominated by the two primitive essentials of defending the frontiers and maintaining internal unity, which had to be mastered before anything else could be done. Like his predecessors Aurelian and Probus, he was now gaining the upper hand against this new cycle of invasions: the Rhine was secure again, Persia tied down by treaty, the Danube slowly being stabilised. At the very least, he had survived: he had not fallen to a palace assassin or a new officers' plot. He had judiciously distributed rewards to his fellow generals in the shape of new prefectures, governorships and commands, and (again like Aurelian) begun at the same time to distance himself from them, creating a public barrier of formality and ritual around the person of the Emperor. Above all, the experiment of dual Emperorship had succeeded. There was no lack of voices Maximian might have listened to, whispering that he might make himself master of the whole world. But his victories, and perhaps his reverses too, had strengthened their alliance. They had co-operated both in planning and in fighting, Maximian had willingly accepted his senior colleague's advice, and the result had been solid achievements for their arms in East and West. This fortune had to be seized, cultivated, and reinforced in every way.

In the winter of 290–1 therefore, Diocletian staged an elaborate festival. The two Augusti converged in solemn progress through the Cottian and the Julian Alps to Milan, for conference and public celebration of their joint rule. All the traditional devices of rhetoric, ceremony and festival were pressed into the service of proclaiming the unshakeable foundations of this reign. So insistent indeed is the propaganda, that one can detect in it the very fragility of the actual situation, the deep anxieties of the people to whom it is addressed.[23]

Prominent among these propaganda forms was the panegyric, a long public address to the Emperor by a skilled orator. His theme was given to him by the Emperor, and he was expected to develop it using all the stylistic means of traditional rhetoric. For all their stilted adulation, the panegyrics were composed with great care, each episode or mythical allusion contributing to a definite, though coded, political message (a little like the references in a full-page *Pravda* editorial). They tell us with some accuracy how the Roman State at that moment wished to be seen. For example, Diocletian pointedly did not choose Rome as the location for these celebrations: instead, the Senate of Rome had to travel to Milan to greet their

Emperors. The panegyric introduces the distinction between the ancient, revered City, and the present political capital: 'She (the City of Rome) sent the luminaries of her own Senate, gladly sharing with Milan, then a blessed city, the appearance of her own majesty. In consequence the capital of the Empire appeared to be there, where the two Emperors met'.[24] For the first time it is stated that the City on the Tiber need not be the centre of the Empire: the real Rome is where the Emperor is.

The progress by the two into Northern Italy followed an old practice which Diocletian conscientiously revived. Just as the provincial governor was expected to tour the cities under his jurisdiction, so the Emperor was expected to show himself to his people, to honour their towns and districts with his presence, dispense justice and hear their requests great and small. It was a deliberately slow business, and the stopping places along the route would be advertised well in advance. Cities were expected to stage a great ceremony of welcome (*adventus*) in which all came to meet their Emperor – magistrates and notables, trade corporations, priests with images of the gods, music and ovations. Since the imperial retinue would be great, the cost of hospitality could be enormous. But the benefits could be correspondingly great too. Not only could private individuals with their innumerable petitions have direct access to the Emperor – perhaps the only time in their lives – but the city itself could likewise enhance its position. It might improve its municipal status, or its tax obligations, or its boundaries with another city, or some other right. If the Emperor could be persuaded, it might get money to repair or embellish its public buildings, to build baths or a temple in honour of the imperial visit.

The people of all social levels who flocked to meet Diocletian and Maximian therefore did so for many reasons – love of spectacle as much as any. The panegyric of Mamertinus probably does not need to exaggerate the scene:

> The closer you approached, and the more people recognised you, the more the
> fields filled with crowds, not just of men rushing to see, but even with herds of
> beasts, leaving the pastures and woods. The peasants raced to report what they had
> seen to the villages. Fires were lit on the altars, incense thrown on, libations poured,
> victims slain. Everywhere enthusiastic dancing and cheering.[25]

The public reception was stage-managed with some care. The immediate proximity of the two Emperors was turned into a kind of magic circle of ceremony, by which lesser mortals approached the divine beings. But the greatest display of all was of their unity and concord. They are described emerging from the palace and standing side by side in the same gorgeous chariot as it slowly proceeded to the central square of the city, through a sea of spectators: 'It was as if the houses themselves were moving and alive, as everyone, men and women, old people and children, poured out of doors into the streets, or leaned out of all the windows above you'.[26]

The list of the two Emperors' victory titles dropped the earlier mention of Carausius' victory over the Channel raiders, but otherwise rolled on predictably and identically: Germanicus Maximus, Sarmaticus Maximus, Persicus Maximus. The fact that these differed greatly in character and importance, that in some cases they were not won in person or – in the case of the Persian treaty – were diplomatic and not military, did not matter in the least. It was a matter of the Emperors having to appear to their citizens and soldiers as invincible warriors who could overcome every enemy. More distinctive (and frustrating to historians) was the fact that the panegyrics' descriptions of these campaigns were subordinated to the propaganda need to demonstrate perfect accord between the two Augusti, unmarred by rivalry or jealousy – especially jealousy about military victories. Therefore they are forced into a mould of artificial symmetry: Maximian's treaty with Gennobaudes is placed alongside Diocletian's treaty with Vahram, for example, although they were wholly different. Such stylistic devices, though they obscured the truth, were all part of the attempt to reassure the audience that the indefinitely long night of civil strife and insecurity was at last over. These disasters had occurred because somehow, vaguely, the world had grown morally worse, brother had fought brother, leaders were no longer so virtuous, and the gods had withdrawn their favour. Barbarian invasion, famines, ruined farms, soaring prices, were all aspects of an age in which heaven and earth were out of joint. Therefore, Diocletian and Maximian strove to demonstrate by their religious offerings, their piety and fraternity and the consequent success of their enterprises, that they were once again party to divine favour: the *Concordia Augustorum* mirrored the *Concordia Deorum* in heaven.

Since his creation of the dual monarchy, Diocletian had articulated its nature more precisely through his religious policy. He revived everywhere the cults of Jove (Jupiter, Zeus) and Hercules, and associated these two gods intimately with his own and Maximian's respective governments. Jupiter was the wise ruler of the universe who had overthrown the old race of the Titans, and founded the new race of the Olympians. Thus, Diocletian presided supreme over a new age that would replace the cruel, disorderly succession of usurpers. Hercules was the last of Jupiter's earthly sons whom he fathered on the virtuous Alcmene, a hero for whom nothing would be too difficult, strong enough to overcome all the enemies of gods and men. Thus, Maximian was the indefatigable warrior who would rid the State of all invaders and rebels.

The association with the gods was stronger than just rhetorical allegory. Every Emperor was of course already 'divine' in the conventional sense that he (or his genius) was an object of veneration and sacrifice. But more recently, Emperors had laid greater stress on their links with the immortals. They claimed to be favoured companions (*comes*) of particularly prominent or powerful deities, just as the higher military commanders were *comes* of the Emperor. Aurelian had claimed to be the embodiment or spiritual son of the universal, unconquered Sun, *Sol Invictus*. Their motives were not vainglory, but the very serious need to anchor their thrones in something other than the nod of the soldiers: to signal that the right to rule flowed downwards, from the gods to the Emperors, and distinguish 'legitimate' rule from mere successful rebellion. Effective power must take on responsibilities, and must seek justifications for demanding allegiance which distinguish it from its competitors. Often this justification has to be invented, as in any period of revolutionary turmoil. If that regime does succeed in ruling and commanding long-term allegiance, as opposed to cowed resignation, then the justification becomes in time the solemn foundation myth of future generations. But the myth, like the legendary accounts of the foundations of English and American democracy, will embody genuine political values: and this is no less true of autocratic states than libertarian ones.

Unlike Aurelian, Diocletian leaned emphatically on Rome's traditional gods, but he also asserted a more definite doctrine of their relation to the Emperors. It was from these two gods that he and Maximian received their imperial powers, which they proclaimed by adopting the names Jovius and Herculius. In place of an earthly dynastic right (which they did not possess), and in place of election by the army (which Carausius or any other rebel could equally claim) their legitimacy consisted in their *divine* parentage, quite distinct from their ordinary family origins. They were respectively the sons of Jove and Hercules, and their divine birthdays were henceforth celebrated on the same day (*geminis natalis*).

Divine parentage was a familiar idea in Hellenic and Roman culture (Julius Caesar had claimed descent from Venus). Of course people did not literally believe that Diocletian and Maximian had both sprung fully armed from the wombs of mortal consorts of Jove and Hercules on 21 July 287. But, even in a Christian context it is not the biological birth but the second birth, of water and the Holy Ghost, which is important in earth and heaven. Not only were the gods felt to be at work in human affairs, but in the third century especially, education had everywhere retreated before a tide of magic, revelation, miracle, direct communication and manifestation of gods, in which supernatural agencies were in a closer, though more disorderly, contact with the hopes and fears of ordinary peoples' lives. The apparent failure of the State's protective deities had helped dissolve religious life into hundreds of more or less private channels. Out of this plethora of intimacy, Diocletian sought to turn religious devotion outward again, to the rituals and obligations of public life, the cults of the Eternal State. He and Maximian made an ostentatious example in setting up temples, votive inscriptions, making sacrifices and observing all the traditional pieties.

The power of the gods and their special links with the Emperors was a constant theme of the coinage. Only rarely did it repeat the old slogan *Concordia Militum*, which betrayed the near-total dependence of the throne on the armies. Instead it was *Pax, Providentia, Felicitas, Securitas Augustorum*, and the traditional pantheon: Mars, Minerva, Victoria. But always, most prominent on Diocletian's coinage was Jove, sometimes with a thunderbolt, or with orb, sceptre and eagle; and on Maximian's Hercules with a club, struggling with the Nemean lion or the many-headed hydra.[27] A cautious but deliberate change also begun by Diocletian, was the erosion in the influence of the Praetorian Guards cohorts. The numbers of them regularly accompanying the Emperor were greatly reduced, and the remainder became simply the honoured garrison of Rome; and with the permanent removal of the imperial presence from Rome, they were politically neutralised. Instead Diocletian established a new, smaller corps of palace guards, the *Scutarii,* and raised a number of new élite Illyrian legions, the Jovians and the Herculians. These were field troops, consecrated with special marks of favour and precedence through their connection with the two divine houses. Their large oval shields were distinguished by brightly coloured concentric rings with the eagle in the centre, in red for the Jovii and black for the Herculii: they would be the political troops of the new imperium, should it come to confrontation.[28]

The celebration in Milan was a successful propaganda event for the regime's strength and unity. Mamertinus proclaims:

> You rule the State with a single mind, and so great a distance in space does not prevent you steering it, as it were, with linked hands. So by your double spirit you increase the regal majesty, but by your harmony you retain the effectiveness, of a single rule.[29]

The people of Milan go their gladiatorial shows and spectacle, and the city nobility benefited too. Confirming its growing importance as the second city of Italy, Milan was soon to be expanded and embellished with palaces, temples, theatres and fora as one of the new imperial capitals.

However, there were still many new-grown heads of the hydra to cut off. All the solemn celebrations of the new age were not much more than a promise, still to be honoured. What had been achieved, Diocletian knew, was still essentially a breathing space in which fresh efforts had to be prepared.

chapter four

·THE TETRARCHY·

THIS MAN, PARTLY THROUGH GREED AND PARTLY THROUGH INSECURITY,
OVERTURNED THE WHOLE ORDER OF THINGS: FOR HE CHOSE THREE OTHER
MEN TO SHARE THE IMPERIAL GOVERNMENT WITH HIM.
· LACTANTIUS, *De Mortibus Persecutorum* ·

The first five years had been of ceaseless labour, bold improvisation and great risks. The next period, equally turbulent, was to be a vindication of the policy of power sharing, its articulation into a new imperial system, and the beginning of a radical transformation of the whole machinery of government. The stimulus was still the many-headed hydra of revolts and invasions. But these were overcome with increasing power and confidence, culminating in victories on all frontiers and over all enemies, and most important, the consolidation of these gains in a far more formidable scheme of defences, and the return of real military and civil security for the first time in over half a century.

The unmentioned problem that overshadowed the celebrations at Milan and preoccupied all Diocletian's planning was, of course, Britain. While Maximian had successfully stabilised the Rhine frontier, his defeat by Carausius represented a military and political challenge of the first magnitude. So long as Carausius' state was in being it was a clear example of successful secessionist rebellion, at a time when the unity of the Empire was still very precarious. So long as he was not granted formal recognition (or even if he was) he could attempt to extend his domain in Northern Gaul whenever the opportunity offered. Having control of both coasts, he would be very difficult to defeat in a naval campaign – for which both Diocletian and Maximian were frankly inexperienced.

Moreover, it had to be admitted that Carausius was ruling his domain firmly and well. He garrisoned and protected the northern frontier as well as the Channel. He had likewise cemented his alliance with the Franks and other peoples in the coastal territories of the Low Countries, engaged large numbers of mercenaries, and thus secured his north-eastern flank. Having revived the conditions for a profitable Continental trade, he was popular with the merchants of London and Boulogne and could depend on them for money. Most important, his good supply of gold and especially silver allowed him to issue from his mints at London, Colchester and Boulogne currency of a strikingly superior quality to the inevitably debased official coinage, which Diocletian had scarcely begun to reform. He was careful, too, that this should not appear a deviant or rebel currency: it followed exactly the official denominations and values – the two-denarii antoninianus and the reformed 25-denarii nummus – and when Diocletian adjusted their rates, Carausius followed suit. The difference was that Carausius could afford to increase the silver content of his denarii whereas Diocletian could not, so anyone trading in the Gallic markets would inevitably get more for the former. Since no actual silver or good silver alloy coins had been struck for a generation, Carausius' step had a great effect in bolstering both military and mercantile confidence in his new state. The propaganda message on the coins reinforced their fine quality: *three* equal, fraternal Augusti, side by side, ruling in peace and harmony (PAX AVGGG is the abbreviated slogan). Other themes are strongly maritime: Neptune and the navy, galleys, anchors, trident and dolphin, but Jove too is honoured. In the bid for legitimacy he had also changed his name to Marcus Aurelius Mausaeus Carausius, suggesting family ties with Maximian.[1]

However competent his rule, Diocletian and Maximian were adamant in refusing recognition. The shared imperium with Maximian was emphatically an entity of enhanced strength and unity, not weakness and territorial division. To include Carausius in it would be false to its nature, as well as inviting any usurper who could control a province or two, to join an ever-enlarged club of Augusti. Carausius' model for his rump state was not the present dual imperium at all, but the old separatist Gallic Empire of Postumus, and everyone knew it. Despite a necessary truce, Gallienus had never recognised Postumus' state, and Aurelian had eventually crushed it. The same must happen to Carausius.

The military lesson of the reverse was that Carausius would have to be prized out of his possessions on the Continental coast before a new naval expedition could succeed; for only then could the invaders have the choice of direction and the advantage of surprise. This meant thorough preparation, building yet another great fleet, retaking the fortified bases on the Gallic coast, as well as every effort of propaganda to win back or at least undermine the loyalty of the British troops. And this time, it must not fail. These decisions were not just Maximian's regional responsibility but concerned the vital interests of the whole Empire; and here Maximian should be guided by his senior colleague. The nub of the question was: could Maximian conduct this major western war – not just a short campaign – without the Rhine position being once more exposed? Was there not the danger of being caught by new German incursions in his rear while his hands were tied, just as, in reverse, Carausius had caught him? Once hostilities began, Carausius could be expected to use his Frankish friends to destabilise the lower Rhine, added to whatever trouble the Alemanni might cause at its opposite end. German activity was notoriously cyclic, corresponding with Roman preoccupation on other fronts, and what existed now was nothing less than a second main front in Gaul.

There were enough other causes for concern. On the central Danube, opposite Pannonia and Dacia, it was clear that new campaigns would be needed, and the defences reorganised and strengthened over many hundreds of miles if Roman ascendancy in that sector was not to be lost – a task demanding years of effort and devoted attention. Elsewhere, at many distant corners of the Empire, Roman authority and civil life were being dangerously undermined from without and within – barbarian raiding and economic dislocation causing flight from the villages and the slow crumbling of provinces. In Syria, the incessant Saracen incursions into exposed settlements had grown to such proportions that in 290 Diocletian had been forced to mount a mobile campaign to defeat them. Over large areas of Mauretania the Berber tribes, despite their defeat in 289, were again ravaging the townships and farms on a growing scale. In Egypt, discontent was simmering as the trade routes from the Red Sea were being disrupted by Nubian raiders, who terrorised the Thebaid cities. All these situations needed urgent attention: further deterioration, especially in Africa and Egypt, could create the very conditions for new separatist revolts, in the manner of Carausius. Added to all this was the possibility that, sooner or later, the Persian settlement might break down. If that happened before the Danube defences were completed, the whole position would again be critical.[2]

A consideration of a different kind had also arisen for Diocletian. A few years earlier, Maximian had taken his position as Augustus literally enough to bestow on his baby son, Maxentius, the clear promise of an imperial inheritance. The panegyric to him at Trier in 289 had declared: 'When you are victorious, your son will stand on your right hand, thriving and gifted ... Being constantly in your presence will be the surest guarantee of his imperial education'.[3] At the time such an assumption had been quite natural. Every other Emperor had provided for his son to succeed to his throne. But it would be many years yet before Maxentius could lead armies to victory in person – which any Emperor had to do if he was to survive. In the meantime there were multiple dangers threatening the creaking Empire, and plenty of experienced generals whose higher ambitions, though controlled, were still very much alive. Their loyalties had to be bound to the throne by stronger ties.

Successful political expedients naturally tend to reproduce themselves. By the end of 292 or earlier, Diocletian's restless calculations, which sought to anticipate as many problems as possible, had led him to a decision. To hold the State together, pre-empt the dangerous centrifugal movements, and buttress the joint monarchy, the imperial power would have to be multiplied yet again – but in a legitimate, orderly way. Four princes would now wear the purple.

The apparent shape of Diocletian's new Tetrarchic system is easily described. The two Augusti each adopt a Caesar, or junior Emperor, into their family. Thus there is an imperial presence at every corner of the Empire, each bound by ties of mutual support; the two Caesars serving as executors rather than originators of policy. After a period of about ten years the two Augusti retire, yielding their joint thrones to the two Caesars, who in turn adopt junior colleagues. In fact, the Tetrarchy was far less a system than it appeared to some later writers. It derived not from a prior design of Diocletian, but from a series of steps taken in response to pressing problems; and it worked, not because of an inherent logic, but because Diocletian's commanding prestige and managerial abilities compelled it to work.

Nothing could disguise the novelty of the arrangement. Contemporaries asked, as we might, why such a profusion of rulers was necessary, why Diocletian had apparently divested himself of three-fourths of his Empire, and how he hoped to keep such a coalition united? His predecessors Claudius, Aurelius, and Probus had after all coped single-handed, in what were just as perilous times.

The clearest answer is that he was not satisfied to rule as they had done, that he wanted to do more than just cope. All his active life he had watched brave, indefatigable Illyrian Emperors struggle heroically with burdens that were just too much for one man, until they were cut short by assassination, their work uncompleted. It was indeed a measure of their military greatness that they had been able to defeat the Empire's external and internal enemies again and again. But since becoming Emperor and seeing the problems as they had seen them, Diocletian appreciated even more sharply the full costs of these emergencies: the complete abandonment of security in the frontier provinces, the chaotic state of finances and taxation, the decay of civil administration, the depopulation of agricultural lands. It was not enough just to expel invaders and crush usurpers: the frontiers had to be permanently sealed, so that behind them economic life could again go on in security, whose surplus could support the armies in a regular way; rebellion had to be made so hazardous that it did not occur, and the armies' main efforts devoted to their proper task of defence. To achieve this, he needed helpers.

On 1 March 293 at Milan, Maximian duly bestowed the purple cloak and title of Most Noble Caesar on Marcus Flavius Constantius, his Praetorian Prefect, formerly governor of Dalmatia under Carus, and a key supporter of Diocletian in 284–5. Simultaneously at Sirmium, Diocletian gave the identical title to Gaius Galerius, an experienced military commander and colleague, said to have risen under Aurelian and Probus. Both men divorced their wives to marry into the imperial families: Constantius married Maximian's daughter Theodora, and Galerius, Diocletian's daughter Valeria; and both adopted the family name Valerius. The traditional account is that these remarriages took place on their elevation to Caesars, but in fact Constantius had already been Maximian's son-in-law for some years, and the same may be true of Galerius: so that the choice of these two may not have been completely surprising. But, superseding these family ties in ceremonial importance, the two Caesars were publicly received into the *divine* houses of Jove and Hercules. New coin issues of markedly fine quality proclaimed the *Principes Iuventutes,* and *Iovi et Herculi Conservatori Caesares.*[4]

The inventive orator of the panegyric earns his commission in full as he labours the unique role of the number *four* in the eternal constitution of things. There are, he declares, four seasons, four elements, four continents, and equally naturally four rulers jointly uphold the world.[5] The best known symbolic statue group of the Tetrarchy is the porphyry one now in St Mark's Square, Venice. It has nothing of the classical about it; the four stiff figures have identical, masklike faces, and wear merely the uniforms of higher officers, including the distinctive pillbox military cap of the period. But it has a simple, strong message: the four brother generals, back to back, hands on their swords, loyally supporting one another, look out resolutely to the four corners of a threatening world.

Ancient historians' descriptions of these two new men are inextricably mixed with the hindsight and propaganda of later events. The claim that Constantius was connected on his mother's side with the former Emperor Claudius II was a later fabrication from the reign of Constantine. For similar reasons Lactantius and especially Eusebius praise beyond measure the mildness and benevolence of his rule, just as they damn the tyrannies of the other three. But when this distortion is allowed for, the record shows him to have been an experienced and capable politician as well as a strong soldier, able to combine force with patience and hold the affections of his subjects as far as the difficult times allowed. He was supposed to have been nicknamed Chlorus ('the Pale'). He had a son by his first wife Helena, the boy Constantine, who was approaching 20 at the time his father was raised to the purple.[6]

Galerius had been a simple herdsman before joining the army. He was born at Romulianum on the Danube, and his enemies later alleged that his mother Romula was of barbarian origin ('from beyond the Danube'): but this could equally mean she came over with many other Romans when the old province across the Danube was evacuated. He is described as a man of towering physique and rough manner, very much at home among soldiers, and his military exploits showed a daring that was reminiscent of Aurelian. Superficially he perhaps resembled Maximian, but he was of quicker intelligence, more independent and unashamedly ambitious. The portrait of him as a heavy drinker may also be the work of his detractors, but even they admit that, like Kemal Ataturk, he was careful enough to rule that any order he gave in his cups had to be confirmed in the morning. What does seem undeniable is that his religious leanings were distinctly anti-Christian, a trait which found an echo among pagan 'philosophical' circles in the East. Unlike Constantius, he had no son at this time.[7]

It is hardly surprising that there has been considerable argument about the true nature of Diocletian's experimental institution. The Tetrarchy was so novel in its own time that contemporaries and near-contemporaries also differed in their understanding of it. Lactantius, who was hostile, believed it was a more or less literal division of the Empire into four governments: he assumes, for example, that the armies and everything else were just multiplied fourfold, which we know to be false (this would have meant a professional standing army of over a million, which no Roman economy could possibly have supported).[8] Victor, who praised Diocletian but wrote about 50 years later from uncertain sources, assumed there was a precise territorial division of jurisdictions, because in his own day the Empire was divided clearly into four great Prefectures, derived roughly from the older Tetrarchic ones.[9] Other fourth-century writers, living at a time when the Empire and its armies were divided territorially between imperial kinsmen, likewise assumed the original Tetrarchy to have been the same. But there is plenty to suggest that Diocletian imposed no such rigidities, and probably did not intend to lay a basis for fixed territorial divisions. Some modern writers have cursorily assumed that the Tetrarchy was Diocletian's explicit, formal constitution, settled in 293, and determining in advance that the two senior rulers would retire their places to the juniors. Others have seen it essentially as an emergency military junta, put together to meet the twin crises in Britain and the East: once these are mastered, relations between the four become strained and problematic until, eventually, retirement by the Augusti offers an orderly way out that satisfies the ambitions of the two Caesars. (In Lactantius' narrative, Galerius pressurises an old and sick Diocletian into reluctant retirement by threats of an armed coup.)

We do not need to depend simply on conjecture. To take one example, there is clear evidence that Diocletian at least contemplated eventual retirement, in the shape of his great palace at Split, which must have been begun many years before he actually did retire there: on this point Lactantius is just wrong. Even if retirement was a later device, not considered in 293, it is clear from events that Diocletian had rationalised it into an integral element of his system, by the time it was put into effect in 305. By that time too, fourfold collegial rule was accepted as a rational pattern, however ad hoc it might have been originally: both Constantius and Galerius accepted that they should have subordinate Caesars – the problems were only over who these were to be.[10] What is untenable, is the naive notion that Diocletian could somehow lay down a constitution and get it agreed in 293: the whole political background was lacking for any such orderly contracts. The very conditions which called for the Tetrarchy, entailed that he could not easily enforce his will on his colleagues, should they work free of their agreements. The cement had to be in their interdependence, and the astute arrangement of their interests.

Diocletian's primary aims have already been outlined. In an age of soldiers his great gifts were vision and organisation rather than generalship. All his reign confirms that he was willing to have others do the major part of the actual fighting and enjoy their due share of the laurels, provided he had the final voice in the issues of peace or war, and the shape of the victory settlement. He was able always to keep hold of essentials while conceding externals, with an easy touch few other Emperors had possessed. The two Caesars were far from fools, but they were acknowledged subordinates, and soldiers. Since glory is the chief object of soldiers, glory indeed they could have. Since subjects respected the authority of an Emperor, and since both principals and onlookers are alike sensitive to ranks and titles, let them be seen as four near-equal rulers if people wished. But, if they wanted to see one highest ruler, father of the others, then Diocletian automatically filled this role as and when appropriate.

The most consistent theme is always their unity and fraternity, to the point of identical group portraiture on statues and coins. The writer of the *Historia Augusta* expresses the prevalent official image as well as any:

> ... the gods gave us Diocletian and Maximian to be our princes, joining to these
> great men Galerius and Constantius, the one of whom was born to wipe out the
> disgrace of Valerian's capture, the other to bring the province of Gaul once again
> under the laws of Rome. Four rulers of the world they were indeed, brave, wise,
> kindly, generous, respectful to the Senate, friends of the people, moderate, revered,
> devoted, pious.[11]

Here their harmony and their conventionalised virtues are carefully combined with proper acknowledgements of their individual martial exploits. Elsewhere the pattern is the same. This is in strong contrast to the position two generations later, when the Caesar Julian was so publicly subordinate, that he had to endure having the titles of great victories he had won appropriated solely by a distant Augustus in Constantinople who had no part in them at all. And if a man as philosophical as Julian could be deeply wounded by this, what would a more average general feel? Diocletian gave no such causes for grievance. In the Tetrarchy all members routinely shared each other's victory titles after 293, since each had to be seen embodying an indissolubly united state against all enemies. But the individual victor was also accorded his special celebrations, monuments and orations. Subject only to the overriding needs of unity, no one was left in doubt as to who had actually won the individual wars.

According to Victor, Constantius ruled all the land beyond the Gallic Alps; Maximian, Africa and Italy; Galerius, Greece and all the Danube provinces; and Diocletian, Asia, Egypt and the Orient. Others disagree about these boundaries. Although the four, when they were not on the move, had their main residences in these respective regions (Trier, Milan, Salonica, Nicomedia), raised their troops there and mainly attended to those frontiers, we have good reason to doubt any firm geographical partition of rule, of the kind that later came about in the fourth century. Diocletian not only brought Galerius to fight in the Orient, he joined him to fight on the Danube. Field armies were assembled from units all over the Empire, interchanged between the four of them. Diocletian himself travelled several times through the Danube provinces, issued edicts from there, and celebrated his tenth anniversary, his *Decennalia,* in Pannonia. (A great deal of his time was spent at Sirmium, which became a fifth imperial capital.) He also corresponded directly with higher officials outside his own Eastern domain. Edicts, carrying the names of all four, applied to the Empire as a whole, but in practice always originated with Diocletian. Finally the panegyrics, the official mirror of the regime, say a great deal about unity, but barely even hint at separate territorial jurisdictions. Once we break free of this one assumption, a number of previously puzzling facts about the Tetrarchy fall into place.[12]

The very presence of one of the imperial fraternity at some place, stationary or travelling, meant he was automatically the centre of public business, as he was clearly intended to be after the years of neglect throughout the provinces. *Rome was where the Emperor was.* To the great mass of ordinary citizens, that portion of the imperial purple which existed in the flesh in their part of the world *was* the Emperor. As in all pre-industrial societies, authority and power were roughly proportional to the physical proximity of their source. People did not care whether he represented a half or a quarter of imperial power, or whether his domain extended to some distant land or not. He would issue instructions, judge their cases, hear their petitions and grievances, his soldiers would defend them and his officials tax them. None of this entailed that he had to have exclusive sovereign government of their country, as long as he had full imperial authority to deal with the matters affecting their lives, and they had access to him. If, a few years later, another Emperor travelled that way, he would do just as well provided he too would hear their petitions, keep war from their doorsteps, and tax them no more heavily. If, instead of slighting the name of the earlier prince, he proclaimed his brotherhood with him, so much the better.

The abandonment of Rome as the centre of government served several purposes. It was not only to bring the Emperor closer to the frontiers, or escape the last feeble restraining influences of republican tradition. Unlike Constantine a generation later, Diocletian did not replace Rome by a single new supreme capital from which power once more radiated to every part of the world. The Tetrarchic 'capitals', astride the great strategic road systems, were in fact favoured imperial residences rather than stationary seats of government, for all their rich embellishment. For a long time

Emperors had been forced to carry on the business of state on the move, and now this was made a positive virtue: government became peripatetic. By avoiding the firm anchorage of an Emperor in one place, it was easier for them to support and substitute for one another, primarily in war, but also in much of the endless routine of ruling.

The conclusion, then, is that Diocletian intended the Tetrarchy as he had intended the original dyarchy, as four persons ruling a united, ubiquitous *patrimonium indivisum*. If he left their exact powers and domains undefined, this was no accident. The two Caesars, apprentices in ruling, would not expect equal voices with the Augusti in the greatest issues of state. Their important ministers and advisers – certainly their Praetorian Prefects – would be appointed for them; and Maximian continued to defer to his senior Augustus, by temperament as much as formal agreement. The other three were accorded their armies, honours, titles, statues, palaces. They campaigned against enemies, collected and spent taxes, gathered a court around themselves, appointed and dismissed officials, attended to the rebuilding of frontiers and towns, supervised provincial governors and municipal authorities, granted or refused requests great and small, and generally had the executive powers of Emperors. The one thing they did not have, individually or collectively, was a final veto on really major decisions: this was carefully reserved for Diocletian alone, and was implicit in his titles Jovius, and senior Augustus. The others were not his blind instruments but his helpers, and he could only maintain the relationship in reality by constant use of his great governing skill, as the later events of the persecution were to illustrate.

Nothing testifies more eloquently to this skill, than the fact that somehow, some time between 289 and 293, Diocletian brought Maximian to accept that his young son's right to an imperial future had to take second place before the Caesar, Constantius. It called for all the diplomacy and persuasion he could employ on his fellow-Augustus, but accomplish the task he did, without souring their harmonious relationship. The events suggest that considerations of imperial succession were of distinctly subordinate importance in the creation of the Tetrarchy. The overriding priority was maintaining the unity of the Empire in the next forseeable years, and the eventual solution to the problem of succession would have to be grafted on to that. That the two Caesars would in time become Augusti, was implicit in their titles and position. But the questions how and when, and more bluntly, what was to become of Maxentius and Constantine, seem to have been left undecided in 293. Constantine was already a young man when his father received the purple, and could not simply be ignored. Diocletian therefore took him to the East, without any commitment, where he was to be given a promising career in the army and at court, under the eyes of the Emperors.

Diocletian knew very well the strength of dynastic feeling among the soldiers and people, the fact that legal ties of adoption and marriage simply did not command the same instinctive allegiance as blood ties – especially in the more barbarian elements of the army. It was partly for this reason that mere membership of the imperial family was not enough: the *divine* dynasties of Jove and Hercules were made the distinctive and exclusive symbols of imperial identity. Constantius and Galerius had been raised to this special height not by any ordinary legal enactment, but solely by the free grace of their new, divine parents. As a votive inscription expresses it: 'To our Lords Diocletian and Maximian, born of gods and creators of gods'.[13]

But an even stronger reason for this powerful new religious emphasis was the need, once again, to break with the dangerous tradition that it was the armies' right to make Emperors. If legitimacy, and the ability to confer legitimacy, did not derive from the armies, and not from the Senate, there was only one other source: the gods. The special relationship of the two Augusti to the gods therefore took on new dimensions with the Tetrarchy. Diocletian's Olympian theology was perhaps extravagant, but was a very necessary and promising idea. It gave a permanent underpinning to his political solution of the great problems of unity of the Empire, and the ending of military anarchy. In the polytheistic world Jupiter, founder of the Olympian race, was both father and ruler of the other gods. On earth, his son and chosen nominee would generate and rule a team of other rulers in parallel manner. Each of them owed their title entirely to his divine act, conferring on them a divinity and linking them with the first father of the divine house, Diocletian. In time, as new rulers needed to be chosen, this special form of transmission could be extended to others. The parallelism with the community of gods was the logical expression of the special relationship with heaven. In mirroring the Olympians, above all in their *concordia,* they literally participated in the quality of divine government itself, and ensured divine support. Aurelius Victor captures this subtly balanced relationship of the Tetrarchs:

> All these men were natives of Illyria. But although they were comparatively uncultured, they were of the greatest value to the state, being brought up to all the hardships of rural life and war ... Their native abilities and their military skills, which they had acquired under the command of Aurelian and Probus, almost made up for their lack of noble character, as is proved by the harmony that prevailed between them. And they looked up to Valerius [Diocletian] as to a father, or as one would to a mighty god.[14]

In 293 this strange monarchy was put to work by its author. Nor was it any too soon, for in the other world empire across the Euphrates, great changes were also occurring. Vahram had been succeeded by his son Vahram III, but within three months he had been overthrown in his turn. The throne was seized by Narses, who claimed descent from the great Shapur I. Everything hinged on the intentions of the new King of Kings towards Rome. Narses played for time, and in early 294 sent an envoy to Diocletian with the customary presents and diplomatic courtesies. Diocletian responded correctly and exchanged ambassadors, but the signs were not encouraging. Within Persia, Narses did everything to repudiate the previous reigns of Vahram I and II, effacing their names from inscriptions. Instead, he pointedly adopted all the symbolism of the warlike line of Ardashir and Shapur, including investiture by the priests of Ahura Mazda. For, while Vahram had feebly opted for a disadvantageous peace with Rome and signed the treaty of 287, the terrible Shapur had sacked Antioch, shattered the Roman armies at Edessa and made their very

Emperor, Valerian, his footstool. The flayed skin of the dead Valerian had later decorated his war temple.[15]

It is easiest to follow the main wars of the Tetrarchy separately, despite some chronological overlap.

chapter five

·VICTORY AND·
·CONSOLIDATION I·

·BRITAIN, AFRICA, THE DANUBE·

Constantius' main task, indeed, almost his whole *raison d'être,* was to win the long-awaited British war. Since 289 Diocletian had realised that crushing Carausius was not going to be just another campaign in a remote western island, but demanded all the resources and planning of a major war against a formidable enemy in a near-impregnable position. Although Maximian's failure was alluded to only in the discreetest possible way, Constantius was given to understand that he must succeed where Maximian had been rebuffed. If he wanted to be truly lord of anything, then he had to earn his place in the Tetrarchy by retaking the usurped throne and territory of Carausius.

His elevation to Caesar in March 293 was the clearest possible signal to Carausius and the world that the truce was over, and that war was impending. Constantius massed his troops in the north-west of Gaul, and the new mint Maximian had established at Meaux to finance the war issued coins announcing the suppression of a rebellion. *Two* Augusti only, Diocletian and Maximian: and on the reverse, Jove destroying a titan with his thunderbolt, and Hercules lifting and crushing Antaeus.[1]

Constantius had carefully learnt the lessons of the previous débâcle, and planned the war in two distinct stages. The first was to regain control of the whole Continental coast, its forts, harbours, dockyards and maritime population. Carausius had to be cut off from all his Continental bases, as well as his Frankish allies in the Low Countries who could create diversions on the lower Rhine. Once that had been achieved, Carausius would lose his two main advantages. He could then no longer recruit troops from the Franks, and above all, he would not have undisputed control of the Channel and intelligence of all shipping movements. An invasion could then stand a fair chance of success, even if it had to fight at sea.

Constantius began immediately with a thrust towards Boulogne (Gesoriacum), which either bypassed or cut through Carausius' Continental forces, and soon invested the town and harbour. The city was well fortified and garrisoned and, rather than attempt a costly assault, Constantius sat down to a siege, calculating that if this powerful base fell, the rest of the rebel support along the coast would soon crumble. Some elements of the enemy fleet were caught within the harbour, and Constantius methodically built a great mole across the harbour mouth, driving in piles and filling in with enormous volumes of rubble and stones, until it was securely blocked. The defenders could neither be evacuated by sea, nor receive help from across the Channel. The siege of Boulogne is interesting, because at that time the Romans were building fortifications of a new and far stronger type, with higher, thicker walls and projecting bastions. If Boulogne was fortified in this way, which seems very likely, then it would have been very difficult to capture, either by storm or siege, against a trained and determined garrison.[2]

The defenders were probably the legion xxx Ulpia Victrix, which had gone over to Carausius in his original revolt seven years before. They were able to withstand initial attacks by battering rams and siege towers, but the building of the mole, accompanied by generous surrender proposals, finally convinced them that their position was untenable. As in most of the civil wars, they were not disposed to fight to the bitter end once the tide had clearly turned. And Constantius, who needed all the troops he could muster, had no motive for harsh punishment if he could win them over bloodlessly. The garrison therefore surrendered, with the townspeople and the ships. As the news spread, other rebel forces followed suit. Rouen seems to have changed hands without a fight. Except for the Franks around the Rhine mouth, Carausius had lost all his holdings on the Continent.

Constantius now began building large numbers of warships, and moved in force against Carausius' barbarian allies. Despite the very difficult terrain of estuaries, marshes and forest, he was able to inflict on them a punitive defeat which quickly persuaded them to drop their alliance with the rebel. Stage one was now complete, by the winter of 293–4. With the initiative in his hands, Constantius could now afford to take his time making all the preparations for the eventual invasion. With communications interrupted, Carausius would not know where and when the landing would come; and with the loss of the cross-Channel trade route, his support among the British merchant classes would dwindle. Without its Gallic half, his empire was hardly viable.

Carausius' own authority had suffered a severe blow. Shortly afterwards, news came that he had been assassinated, and replaced by Allectus, who had been his finance minister (*rationalis*). Although it was sparked off by the military setback, the reasons for the coup are not clear. Since Allectus was a civilian minister, it was unlikely it was the work of the British army, and the aim was not a more effective military defence. One promising suggestion is that the London merchant classes found Carausius a liability now that he had failed to maintain peace or hold the Continent. Fearing the wreck of their prosperity with civil war and the strangulation of trade, they favoured a final effort at reconciliation and compromise with the Empire. Allectus shared their outlook, and hoped to present a more pacific, acceptable face to the wrath of the Emperors. Such is the theory, supported perhaps by the messages on Allectus' coins, which play down the old Carausian political aims and stress instead the joys of peace.[3]

There was now a lull in the war, which may have encouraged Allectus in these peaceful overtures. But it was solely for the purpose of building ships and raising troops for the final contest. New dockyards had to be established at the main bases, crews recruited and trained, and legionaries and marines likewise trained in sea fighting and landing tactics. In contrast with Maximian's rash attempt in 289, Constantius showed all the care and planning of the 1944 Normandy landings after the disastrous Dieppe raid. It has to be remembered that the general level of naval skill in Roman times made the whole expedition a very hazardous one – more so than William's invasion in 1066, which did not face interception by a patrolling enemy fleet. Even in the tideless Mediterranean, sea voyages simply ceased during the winter months. It was always risky for ships to set sail in poor weather, and a war fleet was just as likely to be lost by storms as by the enemy. If it was not wrecked, it could easily be scattered by the weather, and the frequent fogs could often take it off course. The reckoning of distances was still wildly inaccurate, as we can see from the portrayal of Britain in the Peutinger map, which was in use at that time.[4]

Constantius built two new fleets. While this was going on, he settled many of the recently defeated tribes of the Chamavi and Frisians as *coloni* on vacant lands in Gaul – part of an extensive programme of recultivation and repopulation, using new Germanic peoples, who provided a reservoir of recruits for the next stage of the war. He also found time for a campaign against a troublesome Alemannic king on the Southern Rhine, and initiated the building of a new chain of forts from Basle to Lake Constance.

Not until the spring of 296 was everything ready. While Constantius assumed command of the invasion, Maximian returned from Italy to control the Rhine defences – exactly the kind of co-operation for which the Tetrarchy had been created. These two attempts to crush the separatist state were not the first time the British island had been invaded from the continent of Europe: but they were the first time the invaders had to reckon with a strong defending fleet.

But the naval advantage was now with Constantius. He could attack from whatever direction he chose, and Allectus could not be certain of early warning of his approach, since it was near-impossible for oared ships to maintain constant patrols over such a large sea area. Allectus' main chance was in a naval battle where he would be at least evenly matched; Constantius on the other hand, hoped to avoid interception and get strong forces ashore safely. He therefore launched two expeditions. The main one was commanded by the Prefect, Julius Asclepiodotus, and sailed from the Seine mouth with orders to select a suitable landing place on the south coast. The second, which was essentially a decoy, sailed from Boulogne into the straits of Dover under the command of Constantius himself.

Allectus had scraped together all the troops he could, including a large proportion of Carausius' Frankish mercenaries. He may also have stripped Hadrian's Northern Wall, for soon afterwards Pictish raiders penetrated into Roman territory. His fleet waited off Vectis, the Isle of Wight. But Constantius' diversion succeeded in keeping his land forces concentrated in the south-east, in anticipation of a landing in Kent.

Asclepiodotus took advantage of a fog to slip past Allectus' ships; 'Just at the right moment, a mist covered the surface of the sea, so thick that the enemy, watching in ambush near the island of Vectis, were bypassed without their realising it: so they had no chance of opposing your attack'.[5] The main army was landed safely near Southampton, and Asclepiodotus, we are told, burnt his ships in dedication to Mars for the coming struggle.[6] He then marched immediately towards London.

Constantius still hovered off the coast of Dover, prevented from landing by bad weather. Allectus, who was after all a military amateur, was caught badly off balance, and rushed his troops westward to block the route to London, apparently losing much of their cohesion in the process. The result was that with only a portion of his total force, he met Asclepiodotus' far better commanded army somewhere on the North Downs, possibly near Farnham, and was completely overwhelmed. Allectus himself fled in the general rout, trying to hide his identity, but was killed with thousands of others. His body was later identified, having discarded all insignia of imperial rank. The panegyric to Constantius tells us:

> Terrified, seeing your army bearing down on him, he panicked. He failed to deploy
> his troops properly, or use all the forces he had at his disposal, but instead rushed
> straight into battle, with all the closest allies of his conspiracy, as well as bands of
> German mercenaries, abandoning the earlier defensive preparations he had made. It
> was a further blessing on the Roman Empire, Caesar, that by your own fortune the
> victory was won with barely the death of a single Roman citizen. I have heard it
> said that the plains and hills were strewn with corpses, but only those of our worst
> enemies.[7]

In fact, many of the dead must have been just as 'Roman' as their victorious opponents. And Constantius of course was not there in person. He had meanwhile managed a landing in the south-east and was marching swiftly towards London. At the same time leaderless hordes of Franks, the uncommitted portion of Allectus' forces, were also moving on London, with a view to sacking and plundering it while they could. The alarmed citizens shut the gates and prepared for defence, but Constantius intercepted the Franks and cut them to pieces. The ovation thanks Constantius, not only for delivering London but also for providing its people with the spectacle of the slaughter of the Franks, as if it had been a gladiatorial show. Constantius' propaganda repeatedly stresses the large 'barbarian' element in the rebel regime, but it is a safe assumption that his own forces contained just as many Germanic soldiers.

Constantius made a carefully staged entry into London in the role of liberator. The gold victory medallion, reproduced in the Museum of London, shows London suppliant to Constantius on horseback, supported by a warship, with the legend *Redditor Lucis Aeternae*: Restorer of the eternal light of Rome. The separatist British state had certainly not been an expression of anti-Roman British nationalism. Its outlook had been just as Roman as the separatist Gallic empire of Postumus a decade earlier, of which Britain had been part. The causes of the break were political, not ethnic: a weakened central government had been unable to protect Britain from the barbarians, so it had set up its own. It was just this kind of ill which the Tetrarchy had been created to remedy. Now that the ten-year adventure was over, we can well believe the propertied London citizens were glad enough to surrender peacefully. Constantius carried on many of the policies of Carausius, protecting the Channel from pirates, restoring the Northern Wall, encouraging economic revival in Britain and Gaul and fostering the Continental trade. He thus inherited Carausius' popularity.

The end of the British war and the return of Constantius to the Rhine, allowed Maximian to turn his full attention to the mounting troubles in Mauretania. The Berber tribes, who inhabited the middle Atlas and beginnings of the Sahara, the very edges of the Roman world, had always lived partly by raiding their more settled neighbours. With the weakening of Roman power in the third century they had extended their raids to the settlements and townships of the coast, culminating in a general onslaught on Mauretania, Sitifensis and Numidia. Outlying villages and farms were cut off, ruined and abandoned, and the raiders' easy retreat into inaccessible mountains made pacification difficult. In 289 the Governor of Maure-tania Caesariensis (modern Algeria), Aurelius Litua, had used his mobile units in a concerted effort against the most troublesome tribes, the Bavares and Quinquegen-tiani, driving them southward into the Hodua and Sekel valley areas, but this had purchased only a period of peace. By the 290s they were active again. Finally Maximian decided on a full-scale expeditionary war which he would lead in person – a decision partly prompted by the growth of sea-raiding by Frankish pirates who were penetrating the straits and attacking the coastal towns of Spain and North Africa, just as formerly they had attacked those of Britain and Gaul.[8]

In 297 Maximian collected a considerable force, made up of Praetorian cohorts, contingents from the legions of Aquileia, Egypt and the lower Danube, Gallic and German auxiliaries, and new Thracian recruits. He moved south through Spain, crossed the straits to Tingitania, and quickly closed both coasts to the Franks. He then fell on the three tribal groups, driving them from the Roman hinterland and vigorously pursuing them through the difficult mountain passes deep into their own territory. The terrain was far more favourable to the enemy, who were adept at harassment and guerilla tactics, but Maximian was determined to bring the war to a decisive conclusion. While previous expeditions had remained content to drive the Berbers back into the mountains, from which they would later emerge again, he wanted to inflict such punishment that this would no longer happen. Despite the apparent tactical unwisdom and disproportionate effort (in which on one occasion he narrowly escaped an ambush himself) he devastated their previously secure terri-tories, killing as large a number as possible, and driving the remaining nomad raiders back into the Sahara.

By the spring of the following year he was successful, and on 10 March 298 made a triumphal entry into Carthage. Numerous inscriptions and offerings in the African cities record dutiful thanks to Maximian, and to the Tetrarchs generally for the restoration of peace. Reconstruction of an inscription at Setif suggests an identical formula to the one used by Constantius on his triumphal entry into London: restoration of the 'eternal light' to all the provinces of Africa.

In 293 and 294, while Constantius was despatched to reconquer Britain, Diocle-tian renewed the Danube wars, this time from a position of strength. This was not one war, but a long series of campaigns of fluctuating success, but whose overall outcome was clear Roman ascendancy the whole length of this great river frontier. Because of continually shifting pressures of barbarian peoples, decisive victories, sealed by rational and enduring peace settlements, were rarely attainable. For the last 30 years the pattern had been incursion, followed by expulsion, punitive counter-offensive, and sometimes acceptance of settlers, until the pressure built up again or shifted to another part of the frontier with the burgeoning of some other tribal group. Apart from the provincials, the worst sufferers were often the smaller tribes, squeezed between the Roman frontiers and their more numerous neighbours. It was often politic to help them, either by controlled settlement (*receptio*) or even military assistance; but it was desirable that the bulk of them should remain in their territories to cushion the impact of new migrations: better that Rome's immediate barbarian neighbours be small, if troublesome, tribes such as the Carpi or Sarmatians, than huge nations of Visigoths or Vandals.[9]

In his earlier campaigns Diocletian had begun replanning the fortifications in Pannonia, and also established advance bases across the Danube in the territory of the Sarmatians (in the Hungarian plain), from which tribal movements could be monitored. Along the 200-mile sector of river flowing due south from Aquincum (Budapest), the older forts were systematically converted into the new and stronger type (see Chapter 7), and fortified landing stages established on the opposite bank at Aquincum, Bononia, Ulcisia Vetera, Castra Florentium, Intercisa and Onagrinum: all of which formed the new defence system known as the *Ripa Sarmatica*. Since much of the Danube froze in winter and could be crossed then, warnings of barbarian approach were needed as early as possible. The new installations served to protect the main crossing points, to act as lookout stations and bases for river patrols, and to allow the fast transfer of strong forces across the river, whether to meet an approaching enemy, or even give help to the Sarmatians in a crisis.

It seems that Diocletian and Galerius combined all three methods of military offensive, receptio and limited assistance in their policy towards the Sarmatians and Carpi. In 294 Diocletian launched a fresh offensive against the main body of the Sarmatians. They were adept at cavalry fighting, usually wearing a flexible scale armour made of bone, with the long lance as their main weapon. Their frontal charge was difficult to stop, but once its impetus was halted the Roman cavalry had the advantage in the ensuing mêlée, partly due to the Sarmatians' lack of shields. By the latter half of 294 they had sustained such a defeat that they ceased to be a threat for many more years. Sarmatian warriors were taken into the Roman armies in large numbers, either as mercenaries or under treaty, and later fought well under Galerius against the Persians. At the same time this policy seems to have been combined with calculated assistance to the Sarmatians against their menacing neighbours, including perhaps encouraging them to construct the extensive system of earthworks in North-Eastern Hungary now known as Devil's Dyke. Even if this was not viable as a fortification, it comprised a distinct boundary line against wandering peoples which they might be persuaded to respect if it was backed by a Roman guarantee to the Sarmatians.

During 294–5 Diocletian continued the inspection and reorganisation of the defences, travelling from Sirmium to Ratiaria, then east to Durostorum, before returning to Nicomedia. The lower Danube defences seem to have held for as long as seven or eight years, but eventually intolerable pressures propelled virtually the whole nation of Carpi and Bastarnae to cross the Danube in strength, temporarily wreaking great damage and sacking the city of Tropaeum Traiani (Adamclisi). It took Galerius a series of repeated campaigns over several years to break their power. Eventually the surviving Carpi were settled to the west of their original homeland in the newly created Pannonian province of Valeria (named after Diocletian's daughter), while the Bastarnae were settled in Thrace.

After this prolonged war, serious breaches in the Danube defences were prevented, although periodic campaigns were still necessary against the Sarmatians. As Galerius is said to have complained, the Danube was perhaps the most difficult frontier of all. Apart from its great length, much of it was unsuited to the kind of warfare in which the Romans excelled. Except for the Hungarian plains, the typical terrain was of steep mountain and dense forest, the only communication being by river or the main military road network through valleys and mountain passes. Despite river patrols it was always easy for bands of barbarians to cross, and correspondingly difficult for the defenders to get to grips with an invading force once it was established in Roman territory. Frequently enemies had to be located and defeated in a long drawn out series of small piecemeal engagements rather than a single set battle. The burden on manpower, logistics and morale was great, the results modest. The confident mood of spectacular victory one reads on Trajan's Column was long gone. Diocletian and Galerius' main achievement was just to maintain the frontier securely: to do that demanded an elaborate system of forts, bridgeheads, fast highways, powerfully walled towns, and a great concentration of 15 or more legions and about the same number of cavalry and garrison troops.[10]

chapter six

·VICTORY AND·
·CONSOLIDATION II·

·EGYPT AND PERSIA·

The Empire of Persia was the only neighbouring state in any way comparable to Rome in power, wealth and political organisation, and relations with it had always been a cardinal task of imperial statecraft. With the overthrow of Vahram's line by Narses, Persian policy had begun to change both at home and abroad. Step by step Narses was undermining the treaty with Rome of 287, without yet giving cause for open hostility. Soon after his coronation he toured his westernmost territories in great pomp and strength, receiving the homage of frontier satrapies. Among these were Bedouin and Saracen leaders who were constantly raiding the frontier of Roman Syria, harassing exposed towns and settlements and attacking trade routes, having been severely punished by Diocletian in a military campaign a few years earlier. These petty brigand 'princes' such as Sayido and Amro were accorded the flattering status of client kings of Persia – a gesture that was not lost at Nicomedia. Towards Rome's firm ally Tiridates of Armenia, the kingpin of the whole settlement, Narses was more circumspect. But he paid him a state visit to receive his compliments on his accession, and lost no opportunity of impressing on the nobles of Armenia the new power and strength of Iran and her many subject kingdoms.[1]

Narses' policy probably included another potential anti-Roman element not immediately obvious. Like Shapur I, on whom he modelled his regime, he once more gave special privileges to the new and missionary religion of Mani, which for decades had been filtering into Syria and Egypt. A Parthian nobleman born in 217, Mani had undergone a great religious experience and announced himself the last in the line of great teachers which included Buddha, Zoroaster and Jesus. His rigidly dualist doctrines, which had elements in common with all of them, begin with the absolute opposition of the two principles of Light and Darkness. Creation of the material world and man is an illegitimate mixing of the two, a pollution of light by darkness which resulted in unceasing, chaotic change and conflict between the spirits of either kind: a primeval catastrophe, in fact. It can only be undone by the eventual victory of light and its separation from the dark again. Like Christianity, by which Mani had been influenced, the religion had close-knit, exclusive communities led by apostles, bishops, priests and teachers, confession and ascetic disciplines, and its own sacred scriptures.

Again like Christianity, Manicheanism had both a single-minded missionary fervour and a strong apocalyptic tone. Mani, who died in 276, was the Last, the True Teacher, whose spirit would conquer East and West. The 'cup of anger' would come to the Great Kingdom (variously identified) on the final Day of Desolation. These simple, pacific people were not directly concerned in the power struggle between Rome and Persia, but it can hardly be doubted that their benefactor Narses hoped to use them to sow disaffection in the Roman provinces when it suited his purposes.[2]

While Diocletian and Galerius were anxiously watching developments on the Euphrates, serious disturbances were fermenting in Egypt. Twenty years earlier the country had revolted against Rome during the ascendancy of Palmyra, and since then the imperial hold on Egypt had been experienced as both oppressive and uncertain. Taxes in kind had squeezed the villages mercilessly, while they suffered the added miseries of differential inflation: in 293 at Oxyrhynchus in the Nile valley the price of a donkey or camel was 60 times what it had been in 250, while an *artaba* of wheat fetched only 12 times the old price.[3] Yet at the same time the government, distracted by wars elsewhere, failed to provide security from desert raiders. During the period when the Mauri and Berber tribes were attacking the settlements of North Africa, the Blemmyes – a negro people formerly kept down by the old Nubian kings – were incessantly raiding the caravan routes from the Red Sea ports across the desert to Coptos. Such cities depended on this trade to survive and pay their taxes, but were unable to prevent these raids, and received only occasional help from the Roman Prefect. At length in 294 Galerius seems to have mounted a successful military expedition against the Blemmyes. But it did not lighten the tax burdens: rather, it added to them the cost of maintaining troops now stationed along the Nile.[4]

It is difficult to say how far the Manichean influence was also working on the feelings of the Nile communities in the following tense years. We have tantalising fragments of letters from a certain Paniskos, writing from Coptos in the Thebaid to his wife at Philadelphia in the Fayum to the north, who talks of gathering arms and equipment, and persuading others to come and join the company of the 'Good Men' (the Elect?). In Seston's view Paniskos was a Manichean, but the evidence is inconclusive. By this time Diocletian had begun his monumental reform of the Empire's tax system (described in Chapter 9), and he now began to apply its procedures and rules to Egypt, which had always been an anomalous province fiscally, and even enjoyed its own independent coinage in parallel with Rome's. The old tax system deliberately favoured the Greek urban gentry against the Egyptian peasants – the former had a far lower poll tax and tax on their private lands, while the private lands of Alexandrians were not taxed at all. All these privileges were now to be abolished: the tax on each unit of land of whatever kind was to be assessed on the uniform, equal standard of its productive capacity alone. To accomplish this a new census of land and people was planned for all Egypt, to begin in 297. In theory, this equalising measure should have been welcomed by the peasantry. But either it came too late, or they simply saw the census as a preliminary to yet more exactions. At any event it failed to counterbalance the already deep resentments of the Greek upper classes, especially the Alexandrians, who feared their city was to lose its special status of royal political capital, which it had enjoyed since the Ptolemies.[5]

But by the autumn of 296 Narses had thrown off the last pretence of peaceful coexistence, and invaded Armenia in strength. Tiridates was unable to resist an offensive on this scale, and was defeated. Soon afterwards the Persian vanguard, spearheaded by their élite Medean armoured cavalry, swept south-west from Armenia through Osrhoene and threatened Syria. Diocletian and Galerius gathered their forces to meet the invasion, beyond the Roman frontier if possible. While Diocletian guarded the Syrian frontier, Galerius led a rapid march across the Euphrates into Osrhoene, linking up with Tiridates and what intact forces he still had.[6]

His aim was perhaps to cut the Persian advance in two before the whole of its weight was thrown into Syria. The two armies met on the plain of Callinicum, just south of Carrhae where Crassus had been destroyed by the Parthians over three centuries before. Sassanid tactics deployed in the front line their élite corps of heavy shock cavalry (*clibanarii*) whose horses and riders were covered in plate armour, and whose charging weapon was the 12-foot lance. On the flank and wings were medium and light cavalry armed with missile weapons, and behind them a chain of elephants whose main purpose was to unnerve the enemy in the tense minutes before the engagement began. ('They advanced like walking hills', says Ammianus Marcellinus of a similar battle.)[7] Behind these came the great bulk of the Persian conscript infantry with spears and wicker shields, very much second-rate troops. Unless the Romans could get their legionary infantry engaged with the main enemy forces, they could not use their principal advantage. The Sassanids, even more than the Parthians before them, could prevent this by skilful co-operation between cavalry and archers. The continual threat of a heavy cavalry charge forced the legions to maintain tightly closed ranks, forming a target which could then be slowly bled to death by endless curtains of arrows, without ever allowing them to get to close quarters. To avoid this trap, the Romans needed to win the cavalry fighting.

All we know is that Galerius suffered a defeat. Perhaps he had been too rash in his tactics, and the numerical odds too heavy against him. Armenian legend has their king Tiridates, his horse wounded, in imminent danger of capture and escaping only by heroically swimming the Euphrates in full armour. Galerius was able to retreat in some kind of order, and the approach of high summer, when water supplies were crucial and operation by heavily armoured troops near-impossible, imposed a lull.

Ammianus and Eutropius, writing a century later, recount that on his sorry return to Antioch Galerius was met by Diocletian, who was so displeased at his failure that he demonstrated this in a public humiliation. Galerius, in full imperial purple, was forced to accompany Diocletian's chariot a mile on foot. The incident is not mentioned by the contemporary Lactantius, and is probably a later invention. Setback or not, Galerius was an intrepid general, willing to take bold risks – just the quality Diocletian's more cautious generalship lacked. There are no other cases of tensions between the senior and junior Emperors being publicly displayed in such a fashion: always, Diocletian's way was to assert his will behind closed doors, presenting a harmonious front to the world.[8]

Barely had the fact of the defeat been digested, than a second alarming blow fell.

The new tax edict had been promulgated in Egypt in March by the Prefect, Aristius Optatius. Shortly afterwards, perhaps encouraged by the transfers of troops to the Syrian front, or possibly even receiving signals emanating from Persia – all Egypt erupted. Revolts overthrew Roman authority almost everywhere: in the Thebaid, centred on the trading cities of Coptos and Ptolemais, in the Fayum and the Delta, at Busiris, Caranis, Theadelphia, and finally the great metropolis of Alexandria itself. The population rose, overpowered the Prefect and magistrates and what forces they had, and probably massacred them. To Diocletian in Syria, this double emergency had all the signs of a great conspiracy. The Alexandrian rebels had chosen just the time of the Persian invasion to seize all Egypt – they were doubtless in league with Narses, whose plan was to create a second front that would tie Rome down. The sinister Manicheans, hitherto overlooked by the authorities, had infiltrated from Persia and corrupted the more gullible Egyptians away from their proper loyalties. The whole coalition was aimed at nothing less than taking the Eastern provinces away from Rome, as had happened at the time of Valerian and Zenobia. At all costs it must not succeed this time.

The Egyptian insurgents proclaimed allegiance to a new Emperor, Lucius Domitius Domitianus. His coinage claimed imperial partnership with the two Augusti, just as Carausius and Allectus had done at the other end of the Empire. He also struck coins of the old Ptolemaic pattern which were popular among the Alexandrians, reasserting the essentially Hellenic character of his regime. Beyond this we know nothing of Domitianus, but he seems in any case to have been largely a figurehead in the revolt. The real power was a character called Achilleus who took the title Corrector of Egypt and combined supreme civil and military power in his hands.[9]

Despite Galerius' defeat, the Persians had made only limited headway: their initial thrust had been blunted, and fallen a long way short of taking Antioch. In the breathing space imposed by summer, Galerius strained all his resources to summoning and organising a fresh army from the Danube, while Diocletian detached a proportion of the existing forces and led them in rapid marches to Egypt. Some Roman forces still seem to have been in being there, and with the arrival of the Emperor and a new army, the systematic isolation and reduction of the Thebaid and Fayum cities began. They were besieged and fell one by one during the autumn and early winter of 297: Coptos some time after September, Theadelphia in October, Caranis after November, Tebtunis after December. Diocletian had meanwhile begun the major task of besieging Alexandria itself.

This great metropolis of nearly a million people, second only to Rome in size, and superior in technical and scientific skills, was well prepared for a siege: the inhabitants had all the resources for producing weapons and artillery to resist. Achilleus took command and dismissed all thoughts of surrender. Though Diocletian's forces were superior in open battle, he had been forced to divide them in order to sever communications and subdue the rest of the country, and preferred a slow strangulation to a costly assault. He therefore invested Alexandria closely, cutting off the aqueducts supplying the city.

The defenders held out with stubborn determination. Perhaps they hoped for relief from Persia, if only a fresh campaign that might lift the siege. One account suggests that Achilleus may have attempted to break out, unsuccessfully. At all events, no help came. Galerius was holding Syria and steadily strengthening his position, and meanwhile the revolt in the rest of Egypt was being stamped out. After an unexpectedly prolonged and dogged resistance of eight months, the exhausted Alexandrians finally capitulated in the spring of 298. Diocletian, enraged by their treachery and the length of their defiance, and perhaps fearful for the future security of the East, was in no mood for clemency. A terrible example was to be made of the turbulent Alexandrians that would end their separatist yearnings for a long time to come: all those who had actively supported the rebellion were to be put to the sword. According to one story Diocletian, deaf to all pleas for mercy, vowed that the slaughter would not stop until the blood reached his horses' knees. But his horse unexpectedly collapsed so that its knees were on the ground: at this sign, he finally ordered a halt to the killing. The wry humour of the Alexandrians later caused them to erect in gratitude a bronze statue of Diocletian's horse.[10]

In the rest of Egypt Roman authority was reasserted with an iron hand. According to Eusebius the cities of Coptos and Busiris, which had been at the centre of the revolt, were actually destroyed. The new tax laws and land census went ahead under the direct eye of the Emperor; Egypt lost its traditional right to a separate coinage, and was administratively subdivided. Lower Egypt, the Delta and the Fayum, were formally separated from the new southern province of Thebaid, although a unified fiscal control was retained. As elsewhere in the Empire, civil and military lines of authority were completely separated. Diocletian travelled with his forces up the Nile for a final expedition against the raiding Blemmyes, who had once again taken advantage of the disorders. Having expelled them from Upper Egypt, he rationalised the frontier. The boundary of the Thebaid was withdrawn north to Philae (Elephantine) on the first cataract, and the more amenable Nobades of Libya induced to settle under treaty in the vacant region. They were to be a buffer against the nomadic Blemmyes, buttressed by a Roman garrison in the Thebaid and supported by an annual subsidy. The archaeological remains of Diocletian's Egyptian tour include an arch at Philae, and a stele in the British Museum in the ancient style, showing Diocletian in Pharaonic form sacrificing to the bull-god Apis. Two new settlements were named Diocletianopolis and Maximianopolis, one of which was probably the former Coptos.

Having settled the frontier Diocletian returned north in the latter part of 298. By this time, we know that the new land survey was proceeding systematically in the Fayum, irrigation canals were being cleared and marginal lands on the edge of the desert brought into cultivation. The country was also full of troops and the population in a sullen mood. Surviving receipts of pay and donatives testify to the presence in the Thebaid of military units of many kinds – archers, infantry, dromedary cavalry – drawn from the legions II Traiana, II Herculia, III Diocletiana and others.[11] Their provisions came directly out of the unremitting tax deliveries in grain, wine and other foodstuffs that the newly appointed *nome* officials were demanding from the towns and villages (toparchies) directly under their charges. Diocletian's court and military retinue, amounting to perhaps two or three thousand, placed on the Nile cities the extra burden of providing quarters, food, river transport and a great deal else. Papyri show that this great host was expected at Panopolis, in the upper Thebaid, at the end of September. They reveal a picture of hapless officials anxiously trying to procure all these services from recalcitrant towns and villages barely recovering from the suppression of the revolt. A stream of letters survives from the new *strategos* of the Panopolite *nome* to the city officials below him, meeting with excuses, delays and even blunt retorts telling him what he can do with his demands. He writes back, fearful and apologetic, to his superiors, the Procurator and the Catholicus (finance minister) pleading the great difficulties he is having. The following is typical:

> To the Procurator. Upon your orders, My Lord, that the ships of the Treasury
> requisitioned from the Upper Thebaid should be repaired and refitted for the service
> of the auspiciously impending visit of our ruler the Emperor Diocletian, ever-
> victorious senior Augustus, I commanded the president of the city Aurelius
> Plutogenes, also called Rhodinus, to select a surveyor to supervise honestly the
> aforesaid ships . . . and also to select an overseer for the same ships, to receive the
> money from the public bank and account for the expenditure incurred . . . But he, in
> contempt of this most honourable duty, had the audacity to reply that the city
> ought not to be troubled . . . Not only this, but there is the appointment of
> overseers and receivers of the *annona* who we are ordered must be reviewed in the
> different localities in preparation for those who will accompany our ruler. On all
> these matters I have pressed him as well as commanded him in writing, not once
> but many times . . . If this man begins defying orders others may do the same, and
> through such unparalleled insolence the whole administration be endangered.[12]

Thus did a sulky Egyptian populace receive their Emperor.

The official attitude to the Manicheans underwent a change as a result of their perceived connections with Persia. The distinctive features of the religion – its closed communities, exclusiveness and hostility to Hellenic and Roman State gods, were now all seen in a highly suspicious light, as a subversive Persian influence which had to be eradicated. The radical change of policy from normal toleration to outright repression is expressed a few years later in Diocletian's ferocious instructions to Julianus, proconsul of Africa, concerning the Manicheans there:

> We note that these men . . . have set up new and unheard-of sects in opposition to
> the old established creeds, with the intention of replacing what was formerly our
> divine heritage, by their own depraved doctrines. We learn that these men have only
> recently sprung up, and spread like unexpected portents from our enemy, the
> Persian nation, to our own part of the world, perpetrating outrages, disturbing the
> peace and causing the gravest harm to communities. We fear they may try, in the
> accursed manner of the Persians, to infect men of a more innocent nature among the
> tranquil and moderate Roman people, indeed infect the entire Empire with what can
> only be called their malevolent poison . . .
> . . . Therefore we order that their founders and leaders be subject to most severe
> punishment: they are to be burnt in the flames, together with their abominable

writings. Their followers, and especially the fanatics, shall suffer capital penalty and
their goods confiscated to our fisc. And if any officials or persons of rank or
distinction have gone over to some outlandish, disgraceful and infamous sect,
especially this creed of the Persians, you shall confiscate their estates and deport the
persons themselves to the Phaenensian or Proconnensian mines . . .'[13]

Though prompted by fear of Persia, the persecution of the Manicheans may have
played its part in the changing official attitude towards Christianity also.

With the opening of the campaigning season of 298, Galerius had launched a new
offensive against the Persians. His army was composed of first class troops from the
Danube, supported by Gothic and Sarmatian mercenaries, and according to some
sources amounted to 25,000 men. The growing success of the Tetrarchy's defence
policies are demonstrated by the fact that such large forces could now be drawn off
the Danube without sectors of that frontier giving way under renewed barbarian
pressure, as had happened so often before.

This time, we are told, Galerius avoided the open plains of Mesopotamia, so
favourable to the Persian cavalry, and moved north-east through the mountains of
Armenia. Again accompanied by Tiridates, Galerius was able to add to his strength
with new Armenian levies. Taking full advantage of the terrain, his scouts carefully
shadowed the unwieldy bulk of the Persian army as it moved through the valley of
the upper Araxes. Then, near modern Erzerum, he launched a surprise attack which
must have been a military classic of its kind. It caused maximum confusion in the
cramped Persian army, who were never able to construct their battle order.
Tiridates' horses dealt with the Persian cavalry, and Galerius turned the ensuing
conflict into a bloody and absolutely crushing victory. The King of Kings was
wounded and barely escaped with a bodyguard, but all his magnificent tents,
treasures, his accompanying family and harem were captured. The booty was so
great it became legendary. Its transport posed a respectable logistic problem, as the
long processions of pack animals on the Arch of Salonica illustrate.

Here was revenge at last for the humiliating Persian captivity of a Roman
Emperor 35 years earlier. Narses fled Armenia into the Iranian heartland, perhaps
hoping to organise fresh resistance to what could be an attempt to take the central
core of his Empire. Galerius followed, entering Nisibis, then crossing the Tigris and
capturing the Persian capital, Ctesiphon. The might and splendour of great Iran had
been trampled in the dust: its armoured cavalry, its fearsome elephants, its flame
coloured banners and fire altars that accompanied the King into battle, its gold,
gems, palaces and gorgeous trappings of Oriental kingship, all fallen as spoil to the
valour of the Roman soldier. In the elation of his victory Galerius may well have
envisaged total conquest of Persia, fulfilling for himself the dream that had
captivated and eluded so many Roman generals, of repeating the feat of Alexander.
Some later chroniclers actually relate, wrongly, that he reached the Indus.[14]

However, Diocletian now took a hand, and it was no doubt under his influence
that the Roman forces halted in the region of Adiabene. Galerius' secretary and
adviser, Sicorius Probus, was despatched to Narses, to persuade him to listen to

Roman peace proposals if he wanted to save anything of his Empire. His hostage family were meanwhile being treated with all courtesies proper to their high rank, consequent on his reply. At the beginning of 299 Diocletian and his forces joined Galerius at Nisibis, where he congratulated his Caesar with great ceremony, and together they prepared to receive Narses' plenipotentiaries, Apharban the chief minister, and the head of the army, Barsaborsus.

After the perilous beginning to the war, Diocletian must have been delighted as he realised the full extent of this historic victory, and the possibilities of a permanent settlement in the East. Since the military menace of the new Sassanid kingdom had first arisen, Severus Alexander had barely managed to achieve a stalemate in 233, Gordian and Philip had ceded Osrhoene ten years later, then in 259 Valerian had suffered the great disaster. This time, a Sassanid king had launched carefully planned aggression against Rome, while fomenting a diversionary war in Egypt – and the undeniable issue of arms had been the most shattering defeat the dynasty had ever suffered. Diocletian's statesmanship now had the opportunity of constructing a stable Roman peace which could put an end to the seemingly ungovernable pendulum swings between the two empires.

A lively account of the negotiations with the Persians, authentic or otherwise, is given by the Byzantine chronicler Peter the Patrician. Smoothly, Apharban pays the highest compliments to the valour of Galerius, which he declares is all the greater for having overcome Narses, most illustrious prince of the Sassanid line. He conveys fulsome gratitude and appreciation for the generous treatment of the royal captives, general praise for the virtue of magnanimity towards the vanquished, philosophical reflection on the great swings of fortune in human affairs, how this naturally induced moderation in wise men when they are victorious, and his confident belief that it will do so in the Emperors at the present time. The Roman and Persian monarchies, he says, are the twin eyes of the world, and it would be a sad disfigurement if either of them were ever to be put out. Galerius can hold his temper no longer with this flowery sentiment, and violently retorts that the Persians are fine ones to sermonise about moderation in victory, when it was they who held poor Valerian captive, treated him atrociously until he died, and defiled his body unspeakably afterwards. However, he concludes stiffly, they can be assured that the Romans are, as always, magnanimous to the conquered and need no Persian instructions in it.[11]

The treaty of 299, which was Diocletian's work just as surely as the military victory was Galerius', was a piece of far-sighted construction that made no concessions either to mere revenge or useless territorial aggrandizement. Roman territory was indeed increased, but entirely in the interests of more economically defensible frontiers. The new frontier ran in a north-easterly wedge through Mesopotamia, from Singara across the Tigris to its apex near Lake Van, then due west again, skirting the Armenian mountains in the North and the Syrian desert in the South. Tiridates of course was restored to Armenia, and his daughter married to one of the spare sons of Shapur. To provide the straight north-easterly line to Lake Van, five small satrapies of Armenia, which the Persians had recently overrun, were now annexed to Rome: Ingilene, Sophene, Arzanene, Zabdicene and Corduene. Armenia was well compensated at Persian expense by a large part of Media

Atropatene whose main city, Ecbatana (Hamadan) was subsequently enlarged and embellished by Tiridates. On the north-east flank of Armenia itself the Roman position was carefully buttressed by taking from Persia formal overlordship of the client state of Iberia in the Caucasus, and installing there a new king, Mirham. His function was to control the Caucasus passes for Rome, cutting off the Persians from contact with the Scythians, and closing Asia Minor to new migrations of Goths, whose movements towards the Caucasus Diocletian and Tiridates had been anxiously watching for some years.[16]

In mere territorial terms Narses had come off lightly. But everywhere along his new, withdrawn Western frontiers, points of vulnerability which might be profitably exploited were all firmly closed. Not surprisingly he and his successors preferred to look henceforth towards their other frontiers, India or Bactria, to extend Persian power. The peace of 299 was to last another 40 years.

But it was not without very heavy Roman investment in security. Though Diocletian, like all Emperors before him, made maximum use of client kings to take over the costly burden of policing distant frontiers, his whole new line was heavily fortified according to the dictates of the terrain. From the Lake Van highlands, south across the Tigris to the Jebel Singar ridge, to Circesium on the Euphrates, to Dura, Palmyra, Damascus and Bostra, new defensive works were created. To the other main support establishments for the army – garrison towns, mints, supply depots – Diocletian added the important features of central armament factories (*fabricae*) at Edessa, Antioch, Damascus, Caesarea as well as Nicomedia. They were entirely under State control, managed along military lines and integrated into the overall army commands.

A hero's welcome was arranged for Galerius at Antioch. He was officially hailed in the panegyrics as conqueror of Persia, and the commemorative medallion shows him on horseback crowned by Victory, charging a group of Persians. He may have expected the full ceremony of an individual triumph at Rome, and by all conventional standards his victory certainly merited it. If so he was disappointed, for when the triumph was finally celebrated at Rome, his Persian victory was swallowed in a huge combined festival to all the Tetrarchs, their victories and anniversaries, a few reliefs of which are still in the Forum near the Arch of Severus. In the most prestigious demonstrations, imperial solidarity had to override individual prowess.

But at his own imperial residence of Salonica he was accorded celebrations, and a triumphal arch built, half of which still stands off the Egnatia Odhos. The surviving reliefs tell the story of his victory, and set it in the context of the Tetrarchy's special theology. Galerius is shown addressing his mail-clad cavalry troops in a mountainous region; in battle with elephants in the background; on horseback in the thick of the fighting, with Persians being slain and trampled all around; then receiving the surrender of a city; finally, dictating peace terms to the suppliant Narses. The more damaged lower panels show Galerius in battle dress accompanied by Peace, sacrificing at an altar on which are reliefs of Jove and Hercules. Nearby stands Diocletian in a non-military cloak, graciously conceding that he is not the actual victor. He is, rather, the architect of order, accompanied by Jove whose universal rule is symbolised by a zodiac. Then on a base panel, the four Tetrarchs are surrounded by gods, the two central Augusti enthroned over a heavenly vault, with their Caesars standing to either side.

The Persian victory was not the end of all the Tetrarchy's wars: there were still campaigns to be fought on the Rhine and Danube. But it was a great and unmistakeable symbol – if one was needed – of the new military supremacy of Rome, the fact that the Empire was ready to defeat any level of threat, and could now fight and win on several distant fronts simultaneously. Any lingering centrifugal temptations of remote provinces and generals were extinguished by the recovery of Britain, the crushing of Egypt and the humiliation of great Persia. The frontiers of the Empire were everywhere stabilised and secured, the result not just of the fourfold distribution of power, but also the replanning of the defences into deep fortified zones, adapted to the new scale of global threat which earlier Emperors had been powerless to contain. All this was achieved in a world of inevitably slow communication and movement, without anything like modern maps. Important decisions had to be made on very limited information, and the success or failure of any plan depended to an enormous extent on the quality of local intelligence.

Two years later Diocletian returned to Egypt, where his administrative reforms were now in operation. The longer-term effect of equalising the tax assessments on the single principle of the land's productivity, was to undermine the separate, Ptolemaic categories of land holding – private ownership, crown land under hereditary lease, or land compulsorily assigned to a cultivator. For all important purposes it was the actual cultivator who became the land's owner, a status that was eventually to be confirmed in law. But this was far from being private ownership as we understand it. While the State endorsed a man's customary and hereditary right to till that land, it equally prevented him from leaving it. As in earlier times, the village communities once again became the focal organisations collectively responsible for taxation, cultivation and labour duties, and it was through them that the State kept each peasant to his plot.[17]

In his visits to Egypt, Diocletian may in turn have been influenced in his wider reforms by what he saw of the workings of this ancient bureaucratic state. For thousands of years Egypt had been the model of a precisely regulated State economy, an engine of agricultural production for the temple cities and the Pharoahs which had impressed her later Greek and Roman conquerors almost as much as had her fabulous monuments. All economic life revolved around the annual inundation of the Nile with its rich fertilising silt, which had to be evenly distributed over the land. Unlike a rainfall agriculture, the growing of crops had therefore required active, organised co-operation on a large scale from the earliest times.

The irrigation system required a complex arrangement of settling basins, connected by feeder and drainage canals and operated by weirs and sluices. The whole elaborate network of arteries, veins and capillaries demanded constant maintenance, since the flood level varied each year and the banks could be eroded; above all the canals needed constant clearing of silt, which would otherwise clog them wherever the current was slow. To do all this demanded sophisticated division of labour, and had favoured the growth of strong centralised State power from the beginning. Foremen, engineers, inspectors and surveyors had grown up, as each village was assigned its specific labour services in maintaining its portion of the great system: the original administrative division into *nomes* was based on the organisation of irrigation. Over them had grown up an elaborate bureaucracy, originally employed by the priestly rulers, to gather and record the agricultural produce, assess the tribute, ensure the villagers worked the land and cleared the canals, and supervise the supervisors. So detailed had the machinery become, that simply from the annual readings of the flood gauges the tax administrators were able to predict the crop for that year and make their assessments accordingly. As Pliny explains in his *Natural History,* 'In a rise of 12 cubits (at Memphis) it senses famine; 13, and it is still hungry; but 14 brings security, 16 rejoicing, and 18 luxury'.[18]

A system in which regular labour duties by every individual at some allotted point are as fundamental as tax deliveries themselves, requires a developed machinery not just of coercion, but of information. This too Egypt had evolved millennia before, for it was also the country of the papyrus. The economic organisation of the Nile had also meant a developed survey geometry, arithmetic and writing, and the most meticulous office accounting. There was no sharp division between the private subject and the official of the State, for all were, in a sense, State servants. Administration was a compulsory labour duty (liturgy) demanded of city councils on the same basis as the dyke corvée. Unlike the earlier Roman municipalities, the officials of these councils were never elected volunteers, but men appointed from above, willing or not, to fill in rotation each specified post according to their registered personal wealth which formed the collective surety for their performance. In this way, through the conscripted services of appointed local agencies, the Pharoahs, the Ptolemies, and then the Roman Emperors had extended their fiscal tentacles down to the smallest village and the most menial service.

It is tempting, then, to speculate just how far Diocletian's evolving policies of economic reform were influenced by his direct acquaintance with this ancient, highly organised managerial economy. To defend the frontiers he needed an enlarged military machine, and to pay for it, a far more efficient, comprehensive system of taxation. But if this was to work, it had to include not just money and goods but essential services of all kinds, from labour duties to local government itself. Not just wealth but men had to be registered, had to be kept to their plot of land or their city council, lest desertion once more undermine the economy of town and country alike. The eternal Egyptian liturgy state was one extreme model of such a system: its logic and its durability could not fail to impress an Emperor who was already immersed in these problems on a worldwide scale.[19]

In the next Part, I suspend the chronological narrative, to look at the interlocking pattern of Diocletian's reforms, which affected virtually every area of government and society. The overriding need was for a more effective strategy of frontier defence, from which most of the other profound changes followed.

part three

THE NEW ORDER

chapter seven

·DEFENCE IN DEPTH·

WHO CAN COUNT THE NUMBERS OF FORTS OF CAVALRY AND INFANTRY THAT
HAVE BEEN REBUILT ALONG THE WHOLE LENGTH OF THE RHINE, THE
DANUBE, AND THE EUPHRATES?
·EUMENIUS, PANEGYRIC·

The story goes that Diocletian, reproving some harshness or other of Maximian, remarked that Aurelian had been a fine general, but a poor Emperor. (Aurelian had been their common military mentor, whose ferocity was legendary.) The anecdote reminds us that the Tetrarchs and their supporters, more than any other ruling group in Rome's history, were professional soldiers in outlook: thorough, authoritarian, severe. Diocletian indeed had a larger view, but it had to be translated into the language of the military caste. All were agreed that the needs of the army were paramount. But it was the army as an instrument of the throne for defending the frontiers – not an independent interest for political adventures.[1]

According to Luttwak, the military changes from the 250s to the 290s represent the critical adaptation from the old 'Hadrianic' defence strategy to the very different one of the Late Roman Empire, when the external threat was of a quite different order, and the global balance shifted permanently against Rome. Hadrian's strategy had been of fixed frontier lines (*limes*). Whether built in stone, timber or earthworks, whether consisting of a military highway or river, the whole continuous perimeter of the Empire had been clearly marked out by thin defence and communications arrangements separating those outside from those within, those becoming Romanised from their still barbarous kin. Trade and contact persisted, but it had been geographically channelled through definite customs points and crossings, under the eye of patrolling forces.

These physical barriers had not been intended as an impregnable curtain wall in medieval castle fashion. Their size alone, even where they were built in stone (as in Northumberland) testifies to this. Hadrian's Wall, after all, was for long stretches only 20 feet high; the defensive line in Africa was simply a shallow obstacle ditch and a seven-foot wall. A concentrated attacking force could easily penetrate these barriers. Rather, they had been designed for surveillance and active, forward defence which could anticipate any such attack. They were combined with watchtowers, signal stations, auxiliary troop forts and full legionary forts. Against raiding or low level threats, the troops in the milecastles and fortlets could sally forth and intercept; a more serious attack required the light cavalry and supporting auxiliary cohorts to

91

advance out and meet the enemy, while the slower legions in the rear came up to their support, and if necessary undertook the main battle. These anticipatory tactics had meant that the fighting would take place beyond the *limes,* in the immediate area *outside* Roman frontiers, sparing the provincials the horrors of becoming a battle zone. It was for this reason that Hadrian and his successors had stationed all the legions on the frontiers, as close as possible to potential theatres of war.

This strategy of 'preclusive' defence had worked very successfully for over a century, while the tribal peoples along the Rhine and Danube remained disunited and manipulable by diplomacy, and as long as the Parthian state in the East remained a loose, centrifugal collection of vassals. But with the new scale of invasions beginning in Marcus Aurelius' time, Hadrian's frontier system was shattered, and peaceful undefended cities in the heart of the Empire found that nothing stood between them and destruction. The invaders, having broken through in strength, were conducted by the excellent road system straight to the rich victim cities. Despite its forward, offensive characters at the frontiers themselves, Hadrian's system ultimately suffered the classic drawback of any thin perimeter defence, namely the thin dispersal of forces. There was no central strategic reserve, and the legions, who could only move at infantry marching speed, were largely immobilised on their respective fronts.

The system was therefore quite inadequate for threats of a great dimension occurring simultaneously at different ends of the Empire. Although new legions were indeed raised, the growing need for rapid transfer of forces also led to existing legions being denuded to form smaller *vexillationes*. This meant that the remaining frontier troops were not only numerically weaker, but usually consisted of the older, less fit men, less suited to the aggressive, anticipatory type of defence for which the system had been designed. Added to this, of course, were the suicidal civil wars of succession which repeatedly stripped critical frontiers of their best legions.

With the breakdown of the entire frontier system after the 250s, Gallienus, Claudius and Aurelian fell back on an 'elastic defence' inside the territories they still ruled, which abandoned all attempt to defend fixed frontier lines, and shed their associated encumbrances. Exploiting the new tactical weapons of cavalry and rapid movement, they were now able to concentrate at a similar speed to the invaders and meet them in strength. The armies were based in strategically chosen cities such as Milan and Aquileia, and the greatly expanded cavalry forces could now travel at 50 miles a day on good military roads, intercepting the enemy far more effectively. Infantry too was made as mobile as possible. Since they now travelled and fought deep inside imperial territory, they no longer dug an earthwork encampment at the end of each day's march, nor carried all their rations on their backs, being supplied instead from depots located along the strategic roads, which themselves were now provided with small forts.

But although this mobile, elastic strategy was effective in locating and beating a moving enemy, it did so at terrible cost. The frontier provinces and their populations would be mercilessly ravaged in the meantime, and could expect no regular protection from the Emperor's armies. Their physical security, which it was the State's job to provide, had been sacrificed. Gallienus had only defeated the

Alemanni at Milan, and Aurelian at Fano and Ticinum, deep inside Italy. Cities who could, hastily surrounded themselves with walls (as Aurelian did for Rome itself). But even if these kept out barbarians they did not protect the countryside, and enabled the invaders to live off the lands they passed through. Now that the Tetrarchy's victories had again achieved ascendancy over the external enemy, Diocletian needed a different strategy which would once again protect these territories, instead of turning them into devasted wastelands.

The mobile field armies had been the backbone of the successful defensive wars of the Illyrian Emperors. At the same time another element had appeared, first in the East and then in Gaul and elsewhere: far stronger stone forts of a new design. The conventional legionary and auxiliary forts could obstruct invaders for a limited time, but had not been intended to withstand a serious assault or siege on their own: under the Hadrianic system, it assumed that their troops would take the initiative. In the new conditions all this was obsolete. In the terrible invasions of Gaul in the 270s 60 towns, including Paris, had been sacked. After the successful counter-offensive had driven the Germans back over the Rhine, the towns erected walls and the fort systems were restored, but no longer in the old manner. Higher, thicker and shorter walls, projecting bastions for enfilading fire, moats and heavily defended gateways, all heralded a new phase of military architecture, the early precursor of the medieval castle. Whether large or small in area, whether enclosing a town or merely a small garrison, these new fortifications were built to hold out alone against attack, if necessary for a long time.

These two main elements, mobile field forces and stationary 'hard' defended points capable of prolonged resistance, were synthesised by Diocletian and his colleagues into a new frontier strategy of defence in depth, which both consolidated their hard-won victories *and* provided security once again to the frontier territories and their inhabitants. It involved breaking up the great agglomerations of mobile troops which formed the standing field armies and using their tactical mobility once more in a regional defence role. This was only possible because the Tetrarchy removed the immediate danger of civil war, and with it the need for a permanent concentration of force around the Emperor. The intention now was to redeploy these powerful forces to seal the frontiers against future invasion, not defeat them after they had penetrated the Empire. The strategy also involved raising the total size of the Roman army permanently to far greater levels than before.

It had to be accepted that the happy global conditions before the tempest of the third century, would not return. The German nations remained huge and powerful, the pressures from new migrations unabated. The Empire would be under siege for as long ahead as men could see, and had to plan and organise accordingly. There could be no going back to the anticipatory, thin perimeter defence of Hadrian. That system had assumed superiority of force at the local level, over settled and disunited enemies – and this no longer existed.

To defeat the new level of threat required a minimum time to concentrate adequate field forces, during which time part of the frontier itself would inevitably be violated. But, if there was a properly garrisoned system of hard-point defences, this could impose considerable delay on the invaders and dilute their impetus, without attempting to stop them completely – giving the mobile battle forces well in the rear the time to concentrate and move to the invaded area in force. In this way, fighting would still take place on Roman territory, but could at least be confined to a shallow zone at the outer edge of a province. Away from this zone, civil life might once again be carried on without the perpetual fear of enemy attack.

The hard-point defences included walled towns, large or small forts, road forts, and even well-fortified private farmhouses and granaries. What was important was their ability to resist attack on their own, and their position within a deep network of similar strongholds which could at least communicate, even if they could not necessarily relieve one another. Thus, when an enemy breached the outermost line of roads and watchtowers he no longer found a broad and easy road into undefended territory: but instead an obstacle zone of some depth, with all the obvious routes blocked by forts which he either had to assault, besiege, or leave in his rear as a constant threat to his communications and supplies. Even if he simply bypassed them he would have to make slow detours which exposed his forces to local attacks from their garrisons. At the same time, the strongholds could store all the available food and fodder in the area, denying it to the invaders and keeping it to supply the eventual relief armies, whose mobility was thereby increased. By largely denying the use of the roads to the enemy, they likewise enabled the relief armies to concentrate safely and quickly. And finally, although the mobile armies were expected to fight and win in the open, in the event of a defeat they could use the temporary refuge of the forts to avoid destruction. (On one occasion Constantius himself was cut off by an unexpected raid of the Alemanni and had to flee to the fortified town of Langres, which had shut its gates and was forced to haul the Emperor to safety by rope. The arrival of reinforcements later enabled him to defeat the invaders completely.)[2]

Far in the rear, strategic highways were now provided with strong road forts at intervals, which could both guard these internal communications and, if an enemy did break through, offer a series of barriers along the main invasion routes he had taken in the past. The main field forces which would mount the counter-attack would be based at selected 'hinge' positions, perhaps many miles behind the line, often themselves fortified cities (such as Sirmium or Palmyra) and connected by safe, fast roads to any point on the frontier. On these heavily defended fronts the actual battle zones could be kept shallow (perhaps ten or twenty miles) but the supporting organisation needed for this meant that much of the life of the protected province would be dominated by the needs of the army – road forts, transport, storehouses, billeting and stabling, perhaps factories for clothing and weapons, and all the other civilian activities which cluster around a permanent army presence. What emerged was a much larger, peaceful but militarised province. Together with the new forms of sector command, this often led to the reorganisation of the whole province, typically its bisection into two smaller ones, the outer 'armed', the inner 'unarmed', as described in Chapter 8.

A section of frontier, which as far as practical was made coterminous with one or more of the newly delineated provinces, would be commanded by a military *dux* who controlled all the mobile forces – two or more legions in 'hinge' positions, and many cavalry units based on road forts or walled towns in the vicinity. Scholars have attempted to reconstruct the features of these powerful defence systems in many places. Perhaps the most complete example is Van Berchem's identification of the Diocletianic lines in modern Syria (see map). The Byzantine historian John Malalas tells how Diocletian 'built a chain of forts along the frontier from Egypt to Persia, and posted *limitanei* in them, and appointed commanders to guard each province, with forts and numerous troops on this side as well'.[3] A 120-mile section of this between Palmyra and Deyr Semali near Damascus has been identified from inscriptions as the 'Strata Diocletiana', a military road built after the Persian war, which may have extended from the Red Sea to Dura on the Euphrates.

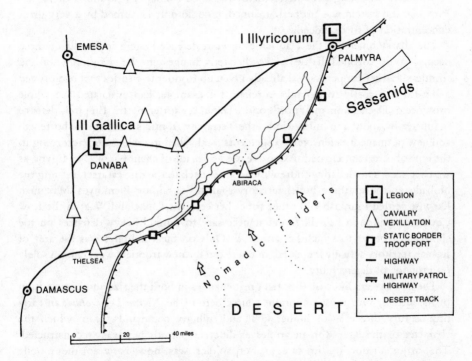

2 The Strata Diocletiana, as reconstructed by Van Berchem and interpreted by Luttwak. The chain of forts along the military highway was manned by static border troops who could obstruct an invader and hamper his mobility in time for the first-class cavalry units and the main legions to reach the area and engage him. Similar systems of defences have been excavated in North Africa.

This was an 'open' (i.e. desert) frontier whose actul boundary was barren and uninhabited. Persistent nomadic raiders would encounter nothing of value until they reached the military patrol road running north-east, backed by the mountains. Along this road were small hard forts containing garrison troops at less than 20-mile intervals, and two, at Thelsea and Abiraca, containing first-class cavalry troops blocking the Damascus highway. These static and mobile troops could defeat nomad raiders, since they commanded both the road and the only route across the mountain ridge to the interior. Against a mobile Sassanid army, which would have to come from the North-East (being unable to travel across desert) they could do no more than impose delaying obstructions. But, depending on which route the invaders took, they would soon be intercepted by the mobile cavalry units from the interior, who could themselves shortly be supported by the legions from their strong, pivotal positions at Palmyra and Danaba. In this way, even a powerful invader would be unable to penetrate deeply or quickly before being met by strong battle forces: the static obstacle system of forts meant that he would have the greatest difficulty moving and deploying large forces in the open, before being intercepted. In the two immediately adjoining provinces, there would be similar distributions of forces. Provided the system was properly manned, it could only be turned by a very great concentration of force indeed.

The abandonment of the Hadrianic forward defence system in favour of these deep, heavily fortified battle zones dictated changes in the geography of the frontiers. Earlier Emperors had already given up frontier territories that had proved awkward and costly to defend: Aurelian, for example, had evacuated the whole province of Dacia (Romania) north of the Danube, shortening the Empire's defence perimeter by about 400 miles. Under the Tetrarchy frontiers were again shortened, and new permanent defensive arrangements established in each sector, according to the type of threat anticipated. Extensive use was made of client peoples. In Egypt, as we have seen, Diocletian withdrew the frontier back to the first cataract, settling the Nobades in the southern buffer territory against the raiding Blemmyes. Maximian likewise settled Frankish and other tribes between the Rhine and Waal in the Low Countries, although he still found it necessary to rebuild heavy defences on the shortened frontier to which he withdrew. Only on the Euphrates was the area of Roman territory actually increased, but here too the new frontiers were chosen solely on grounds of defensibility.[4]

The new system likewise dictated great changes in both the size and composition of the armies.[5] Our most important source here is the *Notitia Dignitatum,* an early fifth-century directory of higher civil and military commands, from which the character of the later Roman armies at different periods has been reconstructed. The major distinction in category of soldier was now between the mobile troops – the legions and cavalry units – and the purely static garrisons of the forts. Most of the fixed, hard-point defences did not need garrisons of first-rate troops, since they were not normally required to fight serious battles in the open. If their forts were strong enough and well-supplied (including a water-supply), troops of second-rate quality (or even citizens) could hold them quite adequately against an enemy who lacked elaborate siege machinery. Provided they had discipline and mastery of limited tactics, the main quality needed was dogged determination to resist.

This meant that static border troops in the forts need not cost the same as the field armies, either in pay, training or equipment. Great initial investment in fortifications would be partly repaid by the lower cost of the garrisons. It was therefore logical, as time went on, to man these strongholds with peasant militia or even barbarian warrior-settlers. Being granted lands in the frontier areas, they would have every incentive to defend what they held, as well as producing sons who would inherit their military responsibilities along with their land.

Thus two general classes of troops were clearly distinguished in fact and in law, as we see from Diocletian's legislation on the privileges of veterans. The legions and cavalry forces formed the first class, serving 20 years before discharge. The second class were the sedentary border troops who manned the forts, and whose service term was 25 years. Though they were still regularly paid and subject to military law, many of them evolved into the hereditary farmer-soldiers of the late Roman Empire, the *Limitanei*.

To create the powerful backbone of first-class forces on which his defence system rested, Diocletian restored the 39 existing legions, many of which had been mere shells of their former selves, and raised an unprecedented number of new ones. Previous Emperors had created two or three new legions: Diocletian and his colleagues raised at least 14, probably more. Many, of course, were made up of the numerous élite infantry units which he dispersed from the central field armies he inherited; but many too were the result of intensive recruitment in the Danube provinces and elsewhere. The new legions we know of include the famous I and II Jovia, II, III and IV Herculia, III Diocletiana and I Maximiana. (If the nomenclature went in pairs as many believe, there would have been a IV Jovia also.) At the very least, the Tetrarchic armies had a grand total of 53 old and new legions, far above any previous reign. Their full strengths were probably smaller than the old level of 5,500 men, but they were modelled on the traditional highly trained heavy infantry legion, and represented a considerable increase in infantry numbers.[6]

Alongside the legions and equal to them in status and quality, were a very large number of cavalry *vexillationes*, probably each 500 strong, who could either fight as an independent force or in combination with the legions. These too had formerly been part of the central field armies, and included many different types of horseman and fighting skill: fast, light cavalry, mounted archers, heavy mailed shock cavalry (*cataphractarii*) armed with lances, and others. Their total numbers were approximately the same as the legionary forces, and they came under the same provincial command structure. When a large expeditionary force was needed, as in the Persian war, it could be drawn off and assembled from among these first-class mobile cavalry and infantry units, and then redistributed on the frontiers again afterwards. After the legions and cavalry, came the second-class static army of the border troops.

At the beginning of the great crisis, the total size of the Roman armies had been about 350,000 men. To meet the new scale of military threat, Diocletian had to raise this to the enormous level of over 500,000 men of all types, and this at a time when the Empire's population and material resources had shrunk. It has been suggested that the late Roman Empire had to produce about 90,000 recruits each year if its armies were to be kept at full strength.[7] Every method had to be used. Tapping the barbarian populations themselves was the most obvious, and it was done in a number of ways. Mercenaries were hired in limited numbers. The Tetrarchs also settled many Germanic colonies on vacant lands (*laeti*) away from their original kin, as a means of easing external pressures and getting the land under cultivation again. They were organised into corporations whose land was surety for providing a fixed quota of taxes and recruits. In Gaul, Constantius settled Germans extensively on deserted lands around Amiens, Beauvais, Troyes and Langres. Similarly, prisoners of war and hostages under treaty formed a natural, if irregular supply: the days were long gone when this valuable source of fighting manpower could be wasted in the slave markets and the amphitheatres. Although growing numbers of them were used in the first-class forces, especially the cavalry, Diocletian remained conservative: German officers were not allowed to reach the upper levels of command. But it was among the second-class, border troops that they appeared abundantly. On the different frontiers were posted units whose names read like a list of Rome's enemies: Saxons, Vandals, Goths, Alemanni, Franks, Sarmatians, Quadi, Juthungi, Sugambri and others.

In practice the Roman army had long been a standing force manned by volunteers, but there existed a theoretical obligation for citizens to serve when required, and this was now invoked for the first time in centuries. It could only have limited use when there was barely enough labour to till the land, but this use was fully exploited within the framework of Diocletian's evolving system of taxation and compulsory services. Direct conscription was applied to those of no definite occupation, especially the idle mobs of Rome, Alexandria, Antioch and other big cities (*otiosi*) who lived on the public dole and circus entertainments. This was very unpopular, and allegedly led to men cutting off their thumbs to avoid service: not a very promising reservoir of brave material. A different kind of conscription was also introduced on rural estates, whereby each tax unit (*caput*) was also annually liable for one recruit, or fractions of the same, or their equivalent in cash or goods. Finally, although it was not enshrined in law until after Diocletian, it is very likely he also instituted the rule that sons of soldiers, whether of the field armies or the frontier troops, had to follow their fathers into the army. (The Christian conscientous objector Maximilianus, who was called up in Africa in 295, seems to have been in this category.)

The new tactics of combined static and mobile defence centred on the new forts. Many sites survive today, and many more were later adapted into medieval castles and towns. The new types of fortification began in the East in response to improved Sassanid siege tactics, but were soon adapted to Western needs also. They became universal under the Tetrarchy and continued, with modifications, into the period of Constantine, and well into the Byzantine era (culminating in the truly massive land walls of Constantinople). Unlike the old legionary and auxiliary forts they were not rigidly standardised in shape or size, although they have easily recognisable common features. Some – especially on the Danube – were reconstructions of earlier forts, while others were sited on defensible high ground, rivers, or water sources. They were greatly reduced in area where possible, sometimes to less than a quarter of the original (as at Vindonissa on the Danube), the main reason for this being the change in function, from a base for large numbers of troops, to a stronghold to be held by a small garrison, which dictated the shortest practical length of wall to defend. As against the spacious, second-century legionary forts of about 400 feet square, some of the Tetrarchic road forts are as small as 70 feet square: on the other hand, forts which were intended as strategic bases, such as the Saxon Shore forts, could be as large as 600 feet square.[8]

The earlier legionary forts certainly had towers, elaborate gates and embattled ramparts, but these were designed primarily for observation, and to impress tribal peoples. The towers did not project from the walls, and the rampart walks were suitable only for sentries, but too low and narrow to serve as serious fighting platforms. In the new forts and town walls, massive square, round, polygonal or fan-shaped towers project far out, capable of covering every part of the wall with archers and artillery (the polygonal tower at York, built by Constantius, is a good example). The old, shallow obstacle ditches were replaced by wider ones (25 to 40 feet wide) and placed much further out, up to 90 feet from the walls. This was intended to stop an enemy bringing ladders, rams or towers close up, and was the obvious origin of the moat.

On top of the towers were installed *ballistae,* a two-man torsion machine like a giant crossbow, which fired a bolt with a lethal range of about 300 yards. Another heavier machine, installed in the large forts was the *onager* ('wild ass'), a catapult that fired either single boulders or a volley of small stones. Fighting tactics required proficiency in these missile weapons, so that the defenders had superior firepower and could keep the more numerous besiegers away from the walls. In some forts, especially in the East, there is also protection against mining operations, in the shape of a raised internal floor level, and even (at Amida and Aquileia) a second, concealed wall of earth or stone. Gateways, of course, were potential weak points. The old four, compass-point gates were often reduced to one or two, with far more serious protection – double portcullis gates, guarded internal courtyards under continuous cover from the walls, or even double pairs of towers, as at Divitia on the Rhine.

One of the best illustrations of these late Roman castles is the chain of great forts covering the English coast from the Wash to the Isle of Wight: the forts of the Saxon Shore, already mentioned in connection with Carausius. They were matched by a similar chain along the French coast from Oudenburg to Brest, but hardly any of these now survive beyond the foundations. They were built not against invasion, but as bases against Saxon, Frisian and Frankish sea-raiders. The only certain way of intercepting these fast vessels was the costly one that was eventually adopted, which amounted to denying them access to this sea area at all.

There were ten forts on the British coast, all on natural harbours or river mouths: moving south from the Wash – Brancaster, Burgh Castle, Walton Castle, Bradwell, Reculver, Richborough, Dover, Lympne, Pevensey and Portchester. Each was large enough to house a considerable military force, and shelter a neighbouring population if need be: but their role was definitely not a passive one. They were permanent bases for a powerful fleet that could operate from either coast. Early intelligence of the raiders' approach was provided by a chain of signal stations down the East Anglian coast. The tactic was to trap and destroy the raiding ships when they sailed into the Channel, or cut off their retreat by sea if they did land anywhere on the coast. In these foggy waters the element of surprise was important, and we learn that the scouting ships had their hulls, sails and even the mens' uniforms camouflaged in blue-green.[9] The Roman line of defence was thus a sea-frontier across the Channel and the narrow neck of the North Sea.

Several of these forts were built on the base of earlier coastal forts (Brancaster,

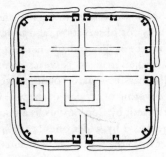

SECOND CENTURY

Spacious area, four gateways. Thin walls. Observation towers. Narrow ditch, close to walls.

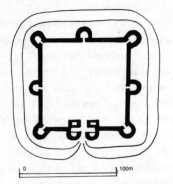

END OF THIRD CENTURY

Smaller area. One, defended gateway. Thick, high walls, artillery bastions. Wide ditch, far from walls.

3 The change in fortress achitecture, from the spacious fortified legionary camp, to the smaller 'hard' fort manned by fewer troops and designed to withstand a siege. The new forts varied greatly in size and shape according to the terrain and their role in the frontier defence system. Adapted from Petrikovits and Luttwak.

Reculver, Richborough). But the main building of the system has been dated to the decade before 285. This would explain the very rapid success of Carausius in clearing the Channel of pirates so soon after taking command: he found all the elements of the system, including a fleet, already in existence. Carausius almost certainly strengthened many of the forts, and brought the system into operation against the Saxons for the first time. The reason he could defeat Maximian's invasion attempt in 289 was no doubt that it came from the same direction as the raiders, against whom the system had been designed.[10] After the restoration of the Tetrarchy's authority, Constantius continued to use the forts and the fleet in the same way.

Of the ten forts, the best preserved are Burgh Castle, Richborough, Pevensey and Portchester, the last two containing Norman and medieval inner castles. Portchester in particular, retains all its walls and most of the original 20 U-shaped bastions. The original 12-foot thickness of wall was greatly reduced by medieval builders. Two gateways remain in slightly altered form. Originally each formed a rectangular entrance courtyard with twin guard towers which commanded the road, and narrowed the entrance to about ten feet. Within the walls were streets, headquarters buildings and living quarters.

It is one thing to describe the forts and their functions: another to record the massive grandeur they still unfailingly convey 17 centuries later. Pevensey and Portchester are impressive not just as superb military architecture, but as concrete expressions of Roman civilisation facing a new, threatening world and determined to resist with all its skills and power. Having been forced slowly back from the spacious, dignified cities of the High Empire when civic life and travel needed no walls, it had to turn its attention to castles: and the castles it built on this coast were so well constructed, and so formidable, that Saxon peoples centuries later believed them to be the work of giants. Normans and Plantagenets adapted them into castles which were still in use a thousand years later (William I used Pevensey as his bridgehead-base; Henry V was based at Portchester for the Agincourt expedition). The reader of this biography who stands on the long sea walls at Portchester will have a more vivid sense of the age of Carausius, Diocletian and Constantius than any of the palaces and official monuments impart, grand though some of them are: a Rome in which defence, not in panic but carefully, resourcefully planned, has become the dominating theme of all its policies and outlook.

Superficially, Diocletian has appeared to some a traditionalist in his military policies. His emphasis on the backbone of strong, single legions, and his return of the armies to the frontiers rather than as a standing force around the Emperor, contrast with Constantine. But his strategy of defence in depth was an original one, which avoided the weaknesses of Hadrianic perimeter defence. Static forces absorbed and mobile forces destroyed invaders before they could penetrate deep into the provinces. When major wars had to be fought, the strategy was strong and flexible enough to allow very large forces to be drawn off without weakening the frontiers dangerously.

This last was a truly great achievement, which had eluded every one of Diocletian's military predecessors. No longer was an Emperor forced to make a choice between a centralised field army or a strong frontier defence – in effect, between protecting the throne, and protecting the provinces. With the new strategy, and the fourfold division of power, both could be done. As Zosimus wrote nearly two centuries later:

> By the foresight of Diocletian the frontiers were everywhere studded with cities and
> forts and towers, and the whole army stationed along them. It was thus impossible
> for the barbarians to break through, since at every point they encountered an
> opposing force strong enough to repel them.[11]

chapter eight

·THE RECASTING·
·OF GOVERNMENT·

HE MULTIPLIED THE WHEELS OF THE MACHINE OF GOVERNMENT, AND
RENDERED ITS OPERATIONS LESS RAPID BUT MORE SECURE. WHATEVER
ADVANTAGES AND WHATEVER DEFECTS MIGHT ATTEND THESE INNOVATIONS,
THEY MUST BE ASCRIBED IN A VERY GREAT DEGREE TO THE FIRST INVENTOR.
·GIBBON, CHAPTER XIII·

The Tetrarchy was Diocletian's novel solution to the overriding problem of imperial stability, but it was still only the topmost facet of his political reconstruction. Below the four palaces, the whole apparatus of government was to be expanded and reorganised down to the outermost details of provincial administration, into a rigidly hierarchical, closely supervised set of mechanisms. The adjective 'Byzantine' universally connotes labyrinthine bureaucracy, slow-moving and ritualised in its subdivisions of departments, grades and titles. For good and ill it was Diocletian who was responsible for creating, deliberately, all the foundations of Byzantinism:

> The number of those being paid by the state was so much larger than the number
> of taxpayers, that because of the enormous size of the assessments the resources of
> the tenant farmers were exhausted, fields were abandoned, and cultivated land
> turned into wilderness. And to instil fear into everyone, the provinces were also
> chopped up into small pieces, many governors and even more minor officials
> fastened like incubi on each region and almost every single municipality, as well as a
> multitude of tax officials, administrators and vice-Prefects. Very few civil cases were
> heard by them, but only condemnations, confiscations, endless exactions of
> innumerable kinds of goods, and intolerable wrongs in the process . . .'

The writer is Lactantius, who is bitterly hostile to Diocletian and all his works. But, leaving aside his extreme bias, his polemic describes the most conspicuous features of the reorganisation. Its main innovations were, the careful separation of military and civil lines of authority (a change not completed until after Diocletian's reign); the division of the provinces into much smaller areas; and the creation of an extra tier of authority, the vice-Prefects or *vicarii* between the Emperor and the provincial governors. Italy lost its privileged position, and the old quasi-independent status of senatorial provinces was likewise abolished. As far as practical, the whole Empire was brought into a uniform system of government with the same channels of control from the centre. The traditional machine of Augustus which had served for three centuries, but was now obsolete, was finally dismantled and replaced by a new one that was openly autocratic.[2]

The keynote of Augustus' original system had been the attempt to preserve a partnership in ruling between Emperor and Senate, while at the same time preventing the provinces being irresponsibly plundered, as in the days of the Republic. The position of a Roman governor was inevitably that of a minor monarch over the province he ruled, and the senatorial aristocracy had always considered these proconsular posts as their exclusive birthright. Augustus successfully compromised by dividing the Empire into senatorial and Imperial provinces. The former, where few troops were stationed, continued to be administered by the Senate as in earlier times. The Imperial provinces were ruled by the Emperor himself, through appointed legates, men of junior senatorial rank. Most important, financial affairs in the Imperial provinces were placed in the hands of separate procurators, answerable directly to the Emperor. These were not senators at all but salaried, career officials drawn from the inferior equestrian order.

This social distinction was of great significance. As citizenship spread and the provinces evolved from being mere conquered nations towards something like equality with Italy, administration changed considerably. The small number of top jobs continued to be reserved for senators, as always; but below and alongside them, there grew up a far larger professional civil service – procurators, heads of bureaux and all the middle levels of advisers and functionaries – which favoured able men of the equestrian class. At the apex was the unique figure of the Praetorian Prefect, who had gradually become the nearest thing to a Chief Minister. It was this great body of equestrian administrators who effectively ran the successful High Empire of the Flavians and the Antonines. This was not just because of their greater professionalism, but primarily because of their far greater numbers. Since the equestrian order was entered by property qualifications, not birth, it offered an incomparably greater pool of educated, competent and ambitious men. Like the full-time military tribunes and *Primipilarii* in the army, they were excluded from the uppermost rungs of responsibility. But they did the real work, held the hands of their noble superiors, and waited for their day to come.

We have already seen how the wars of the third century brought to power a professional military class of low social origins, and led Gallienus to displace senators from legionary commands – which automatically meant that proconsuls and legates no longer commanded the troops in their provinces. In the crisis and ad hoc militarisation of government, anything that stood in the way of efficiency was likely to be swept away. Governors would be appointed for loyalty and ability, and this meant equestrians, often military men. In the perpetually threatening civil war they would be key pieces on the board, as Constantius had been in Dalmatia during 285. Already the supposedly distinct judicial and financial powers had often become reunited in one man, and this became even more necessary as the frantic demands of war taxation required governors who could extort even greater amounts from the populations under the flimsiest of legal pretexts. The sheer needs of the army frequently dominated the governor's whole task, to the exclusion of others. Supplies of all kinds had to be raised and delivered to the depots at the required time, labour and transport had to be provided, recruits raised and often forces commanded in person, for in the frequent emergencies the securing of this or that city or highway could be crucial. Much judicial work was neglected, lawsuits and appeals went unheard, systematic assessment of tax resources was abandoned, non-military public building ceased. In Egypt after about 260, the regular registration of land and population simply petered out, and in provinces on the war fronts the position must have been far worse.[3] Wishing to escape the attention of the authorities, most of the population fended for itself as best it could.

This was the distorted state of affairs inherited by Diocletian as peace and civil order slowly returned. Some provinces were full of troops and little more than war zones, the agricultural populations and the civil officials completely geared to the work of defence. Others were empty of troops and unscarred by war, but economically disrupted, with the administration only half functioning. Some were still ruled by proconsuls, some by senatorial legates, most by equestrians or soldiers. A few governors still had no legal control over finances, but many had military powers. Accountability and supervision were heterogeneous and weak, and in the emergencies every kind of abuse of authority had naturally blossomed. Even in more normal centuries, Emperors had felt the need to watch the behaviour of governors, and had used certain officials of the postal system, the *frumentarii,* who became in effect political agents of 'the centre. But the remedy had grown worse than the disease, and the very name become synonymous with false accusation and extortion.[4]

The problems facing Diocletian were quite different from those that had faced Augustus. First, they were strategic. The heavily armed frontier defence zones had to be constantly maintained and supplied, and the enlarged armies paid. This meant a far more efficient and total mobilisation of the Empire's taxable resources, which required a revitalised civil administration. Second, they were political. A distant governor or general must not be allowed to gather all the threads of power into his hands, so that he could thwart the demands of the centre or even break away from it during a temporary period of weakness. And third, they were problems of good government and public order. Diocletian was concerned not just to squeeze the necessary taxes out of the population, but to put taxation on a systematic, viable basis of proper assessments and accountability. He was equally concerned to get the lawcourts functioning again and make them available to everyone.

He had never been a believer in giving officials a loose rein. For him, good government was closely supervised government. The kind of governor he wanted was a legally trained and expert man, but not the senatorial viceroy of the earlier Empire – rather, the conscientious functionary who carries out his assigned duties according to the rulebook.[5] His chosen way to achieve all these aims was to multiply the number of governors while reducing their functions, scope, and territories.

Various provinces had been divided before, but nothing as radical as Diocletian's boundary changes had occurred since the beginning of the Empire. With the creation of the Tetrarchy in 293 and proceeding rapidly thereafter, the whole Empire was turned into a veritable mosaic of just over a hundred provinces, virtually double their previous number.[6] Many of the subdivisions were dictated by military needs.

Following Aurelian's original example in the new Dacia, the typical pattern is of an inner, protected, 'unarmed' province, and an outer militarised one, encompassing the permanent stations of the legions, and the forts and battle zones of the frontier troops. On the Danube both Noricum and Pannonia were divided in this fashion, while in Gaul, Belgica and Lugdunensis were likewise bisected. Elsewhere we find a province elongated to give unified control on a vital military road. Of these small, outer militarised provinces, one writer has observed that the older order of things was reversed: instead of the frontier being designed to protect an existing province, a new province was created to sustain a frontier.[7]

But military needs were not the only reason for chopping up the provinces. The old, unarmed senatorial provinces such as Africa and Asia were divided just as finely. Africa was split into three new provinces, and Asia into no less than six. We can appreciate the purpose of this by considering the very wide civil tasks a governor now had to perform. He was responsible for supervising the city councils and ensuring they performed their municipal obligations; for judging the civil cases in the cities and dealing with the endless queues of petitions and appeals; for public order and crime suppression, for maintaining roads, postal communications, waterways and harbours, granaries and army supply dumps. With the decay of the procurator system, all the taxation of the province came into his hands again, in addition to the military duties he still retained. In the late 290s Diocletian embarked on the most thorough overhaul of the tax system ever undertaken, beginning with a detailed census of all resources in the Empire, in which provincial governors were closely involved. Not only this, but he also insisted that governors try all legal cases in person, and no longer delegate: or at least, that they only delegate the lesser cases, and only after they have ruled on questions of law, leaving their deputies merely to decide matters of fact.[8] It was clearly impossible for one man to carry out all these duties effectively in territories of the old size. The old proconsul of Asia, for example, had no less than 250 cities, great and small, under his jurisdiction. He had only been able to cope at all, because city magistrates themselves decided many of the lawsuits which now came direct to the government. Like the imperial power itself, provincial government had to be divided if it was to be revived and put on an efficient basis in the harsher conditions now prevailing.

The number of distinct new provinces was too great for real control, even by four Praetorian Prefects, and so they were grouped into 12 administrative *dioceses*, each headed by a new, equestrian vice-Prefect, the *vicarius,* and corresponding roughly in area with many of the nation states of modern Europe. From West to East they were: Britain, Gaul, Viennensis (Southern France), Spain, Italy, Africa, Pannonia, Moesia, Thrace, Asiana, Pontus and the Orient. (The full list of all the new provinces, based on the Verona List, is given in Appendix I.) As an illustration, Britain since the second century had comprised two Imperial provinces, Britannia Superior and Inferior, based respectively on London and York, and governed by senators having the ranks of consul and praetor. After the recovery of Britain by Constantius, it was divided into four new provinces. Britannia Prima comprised Wales and the West, with its capital at Cirencester; Britannia Secunda the North, based on York; Maxima Caesariensis (named after Galerius) the South-East, based on London; and Flavia

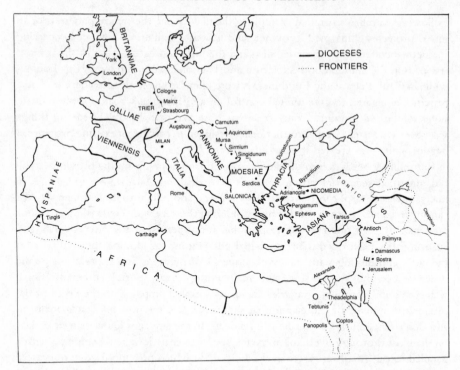

4 Diocletian's reorganised Empire with its 12 Dioceses, each of which was divided into a large number of small provinces (see Appendix I). The territorial withdrawals have been minor. The important cities are now the strategically placed military-imperial strongpoints, especially along the Danube highway and the reconstructed frontier system in the East.

Caesariensis (named after Constantius) the East Midlands and East Anglia, based on Lincoln. All four had equestrian governors, and together formed one diocese under the vicar of Britain with his headquarters in London.[9] The four vicars of Britain, Spain, Gaul and Viennensis were responsible in turn to Constantius and his Praetorian Prefect at the imperial capital at Trier. It was not a simple hierarchical chain of authority from the Emperor down to individual governors, but apparently contained certain mutual checks. The vicars took over many of the duties of the Prefects, but were appointed and removed by the Emperor alone, and their legal decisions could only be overturned by him. The governors could also appeal for directives over the heads of the vicars, direct to the Praetorian Prefect, and it seems they were positively expected to make use of this right.[10]

Most striking was the change in social composition of these officials. Just as Gallienus had removed the senatorial class from army commands, now Diocletian squeezed them out of provincial governorships. When earlier Illyrian Emperors had wanted to bypass the senatorial class, they had deliberately left vacant governorships unfilled, and ruled instead through equestrian deputy governors or vice-presidents. Diocletian made this practice official in all the new and smaller provinces he created.

By 305 senatorial governors had all but disappeared. The only senatorial provinces remaining were Asia and Africa, and these had been truncated to a seventh and a third of their former size. The normal pattern was the small province governed by an equestrian president (*praeses*), and answerable to the vicar and the Prefect. The vicars, in particular, were men of the type Diocletian and his colleagues could trust, equestrians of lower origins who had risen entirely in the imperial service, not senators who expected high positions as their birthright. The old senatorial class was now reduced to political impotence, while an equestrian career was the path to the highest rungs in the imperial government.[11]

A radical change was in Italy itself, which had never been a province nor paid taxes: Diocletian had firmly decided to put an end to this special position and have Italy on an equal footing with the rest of the Empire. This development, as well as the permanent removal of the imperial capital from Rome, was the logical culmination of the long process whereby citizenship had become universal, the provinces achieved legal and political equality with what had once been the conqueror nation, and the Empire became a truly supra-national world state whose boundaries were defined by common laws and a common Roman-Hellenic culture. Tradition of course remained, and here Diocletian was more than willing to make concessions. The district of Rome, up to the old hundredth milestone, was exempted from the provincial system and the new tax system: it was after all a consumer of revenue, not a producer. It continued to be governed by a senatorial City Prefect, responsible direct to the Emperor in Milan rather than through any of the Praetorian Prefects. But outside Rome the whole peninsula, including Sicily, became one entire diocese (later two) comprising 16 new provinces.[12]

The pill was also sugared by distinguishing the Italian provinces by the name of 'districts' and allowing most of them to be governed by senators with the old Roman title of *corrector,* together with the *Correctores Italiae.* In sharp contrast to the other provincial governors of Diocletian's reign, we find noble senatorial family names among them: Volusianus, Titianus, Clarus. But the new vicar of Italy, Caecilianus, was an equestrian.[13] The old *correctores* had been magistrates with powers to investigate financial abuses in the Italian cities; the new ones were in effect governors by another name, whose unpopular duty would be to carry out the census of taxable resources for the whole of Italy. It was typical of Diocletian to present this exception as a concession to the senatorial traditions: in fact, it was as much a cushioning device to neutralise possible trouble from Italy, where the senatorial nobility were still the natural leaders. As much later events would show, the taxation of Italy nonetheless caused deep resentment, which was to fuel a revolt once the firm hand of Diocletian was removed.

The third vital element in Diocletian's new system was the separation of military and civil authority all down the line. The early panegyrics make the new distinctions between *duces* and *iudices,* that is, military commanders and civil governors.[14] But the process was a gradual one, which had to await the ending of the great military emergencies, and be carried out as suitable candidates became available. In 298 for example, the governor of Britannia Secunda, Aurelius Arpagius, still had military responsibilities, as did many others.[15] The Praetorian Prefects, such as Julius

Asclepiodotus were still trained generals: it was too early for Diocletian to displace these pivotal supports. Although complete separation was not achieved until Constantine's period, there is no reason to doubt it was Diocletian's long term aim. It meshed logically with his constant policy of giving officials carefully defined, more manageable areas of responsibility, and of avoiding wide discretionary powers.

But he was determined this should not be done at the expense of military efficiency. Because supreme military command was now divided among the four Emperors, Diocletian could afford to allow a regional commander the control of considerable forces. A military *dux* on an important frontier had a command spanning several provinces and containing far more troops than an old provincial governor. But he was now to be a purely professional soldier, with military powers only. The supply and pay of his troops, the raising of taxes and jurisdiction over cities and civilians, were to be placed in the quite separate hands of the presidents and vicars, who were responsible to the Praetorian Prefect. The military and civil branches of course had to co-operate, but they were not to take over one another's duties in the way that had been unavoidable during the years of crisis. In particular, the raising of taxes ought no longer to involve the menacing presence of regular soldiers. This separation of the lines of authority meant that if a military *dux* contemplated rebellion as did Carausius or Domitianus, he would have to make complex horizontal alliances with the civil officials before his plot stood much of a chance.

It also meant a steady separation of professional ladders. Lack of education and culture was no longer a handicap in a purely military career, and the logical result was that it became easier for officers of German, 'barbarian' origin to climb the promotion ladder. Conversely, the new generation of educated equestrians eager for government jobs had no need to master the science of war, but relied solely on their training in rhetoric and law as they queued up for appointments in the expanded staffs of the governors, vicars, Prefects and departments of the Court. The cleavage was to have very profound consequences, both good and bad, during the next two centuries.

In a civilization where every high public official was a form of magistrate, a very great deal of the state's relations with its citizens resolved itself into the procedures of law. At every level administrators had to give legal decisions, often in court in the presence of advocates; they had to express and publish the will of the Emperor in all kinds of subordinate legislation and instructions, and represent the state's interests in legal appeals and disputes, especially over tax assessments. It is not surprising that the Prefects and vicars needed many trained advocates on their staffs, and that these jobs were seen as the first step in a successful career in the bureaucracy. The law schools underwent a boom throughout the East, especially the famous school of Beirut. In the West, Constantius endowed a chair of rhetoric at Autun; it went to the imperial secretary Eumenius, who praised his benefactor lavishly, not just for fostering the revival of learning, but for offering so many students access to the higher government service.[16]

These new men entered into an elaborate hierarchy of ranks and titles, designed to match not just their functions but to express a new kind of social rank. One need not go into the subtle differences between *Eminentissimi, Perfectissimi* and *Egregii* (let alone the more ornate styles that blossomed later) to see the intention of all this ritualisation. Since the days of crisis, when a great amount of routine office work had been by soldiers detached for that purpose, their organisation had inevitably been a quasi-military affair. Now that he was separating the two, Diocletian wished to retain similar routines of obedience and deference in his civil service, and to make the detailed operations of the machine as automatic as possible. Staffs of the higher officials had been organised into cohorts, and military cloaks worn instead of the civilian toga. All this was retained, even while soldiers were replaced by lawyers. The civil service was still known as the *militia* (as distinct from the armed service, the *militia armata*) with corresponding emphasis on military discipline and loyalty.

The system was certainly successful in reviving firm and effective provincial government and the administration of justice, maintaining the strong frontier defences, and discouraging centrifugal tendencies in the great unwieldy Empire. The fact that it was now possible to reform the whole system of taxation so effectively, testifies to a new power in the long arm of government, reaching from the centre down to every province, city and village. But, like the other types of bureaucratic State apparatus in Egypt or China, it was achieved only by a huge multiplication of officials, which was correspondingly costly. Even though the salaries, owing to inflation, were far lower than those of second-century civil servants, the total cost of the new officialdom has been estimated at the equivalent of two or three new legions. And before long the other inevitable accompaniments of great bureaucracies began to appear – corruption and above all, self-proliferation. Diocletian must have foreseen the danger of these organs of government fattening themselves at the expense of the treasury and taxpayers, yet from early on we hear official complaints that dishonest men are taking advantage of their official positions – naive attempts to stem the developments whose seeds his own policies are everywhere sowing. This rebuke to an Egyptian strategus from his superior is typical:

> It is apparent from the accounts alone, that many persons wishing to batten on to the estates of the treasury have devised titles for themselves, such as administrators, secretaries, or superintendents, whereby they procure no advantage to the treasury but only eat up the revenues. I must therefore instruct you to have just one competent superintendent chosen for each estate on the responsibility of the council concerned, and to put an end to all the other offices; although the superintendent chosen shall be empowered to choose two, or at most three, others to assist him...[17]

These great changes were steadily laying the foundations of an explicit absolutism, replacing the old constitutional partnership of Augustus. The abolition of the senatorial provinces finally terminated the pious fiction of the Senate as a separate governing body in the Empire. The exclusion of senators from top posts confirmed the point that henceforth, a career in public life meant promotion by merit (or favour) through the salaried professional civil service of the Emperor, and nowhere else. The decay of city life and the bankrupting of the local propertied classes had all but extinguished local self-government, especially local lawcourts. As provincial government was reorganised the new governors everywhere stepped into this vacuum and performed many of these functions – but now, as the direct agents of the State, not elected municipalities. And, for all the increase in the size of the army, its separation from civil functions was intended to turn it into a corps of specialists, not a distinct, politically conscious estate of the realm. Both civil service and armed service were designed to be joint departments carrying out the orders of the Emperor.

At the centre of the whole machine, several factors therefore pointed to the need for changes in Court organisation: the separation of military and civil powers, the new financial controls and provincial organisation, and not least, the great increase in Diocletian's judicial work, instructions and correspondence. The result was the beginning of functional ministries, though this was not brought to completion until Constantine's reign. The advisers and officials around the Emperor formed the council which now came to be known as the Consistory. Separate departments (*scrinia*) were now distinguished, the name deriving from the boxes used to hold the masses of documents on the incessant travels of Diocletian's court through the provinces. There emerged different *magistri* with their secretariats: dealing with petitions and favours, with all Latin and Greek correspondence, foreign embassies, and with the more complex legal questions. The Consistory included a permanent body of legal advisers, some of whom, like Hermogenianus[18] achieved very considerable influence. There were the two finance ministers (of the public treasury, and the imperial private domains), and overshadowing the whole court, the powerful figure of the Praetorian Prefect.[19]

His position was something between deputy Emperor, Secretary of State and grand vizier, an official with a staff of hundreds and duties in every sphere of government.[20] He had somehow to help shoulder the gigantic workload of a monarch who, like earlier kings and city magistrates, was still expected to deal in person with all the affairs of his country. The Prefect had ultimate responsibility under the Emperor for the whole apparatus of civil administration, including taxation; he had judicial powers second only to the Emperor; and he had military commands also, since his original office was commander of the Praetorian Guard. But, with Diocletian's reduction of the Guards to a mere city garrison of Rome, his military functions in practice gradually gave way to civil ones. The new tax system and governorships placed even greater financial powers in his hands, although he was now able to delegate much of the detailed work to the 12 vicars with their attached fiscal departments. A major demand on him was the prodigious growth in petitions and legal work, despite the extra legal advisers and secretaries. The burden, as always, was shared between Emperor and Prefect. An example of this was Diocletian's ruling that either of them could constitute the final authority of appeal from the courts. An appellant could go to the Prefect or direct to the Emperor, but not both: there was no longer any appeal from the Prefect's decision to the Emperor. Even so, we get a glimpse of Diocletian struggling under the deluge of work. 'The channels for petitioning cannot just be granted to anyone, unreservedly and indiscriminately,'[21] he says, trying to put some limits on the volume of requests that might be placed on a hard-working Emperor in a period of civil recovery.

A great deal of Diocletian's time was thus spent dealing with legal queries and private supplications from humble citizens. But at the same time, he deliberately changed the way in which the Emperor appeared to his subjects in public – whether in the judges' seat, in procession, or in the formal receptions at the palace, an elaborate circle of ceremony now separated the mere citizen of whatever rank, from the sacred being of the ruler. To many contemporaries, this was the most conspicuous of changes Diocletian introduced into the form of government: the symbolism of imperial power. It was no longer quasi-republican but oriental, proclaiming the unlimited powers of absolute kingship; no longer *Princeps*, but *Dominus*.

Under the careful double standard of Augustus, the First Magistrate in his lifetime was only accorded divine honours in the provinces. In Rome and Italy, with their traditions of liberty, religious veneration was paid not to him, but to his *genius* or tutelary spirit – a typically Roman distinction and Roman compromise. But with the steady provincialisation of the Empire the balance had swung in favour of the first version, and the subtle distinction became harder to see. Not only was the Emperor's effigy required in every place where valid legal enactments were made, but an oath by his *genius* in its presence (the symbolic witness) was more binding than an oath by the gods. In the armies, the *imagines* of the Emperors carried on the sacred legionary standards had long possessed an iconic quality: men made salutation and obeisance to them with all the ceremony proper to the Emperor's physical presence. During the third century a non-Italian, even oriental element begins to appear: Emperors adopt the radiate crown, and later, on triumphal occasions, the use of gold embroidered robes and jewels.[22]

All these theatrical devices were now used by Diocletian to elevate the four rulers permanently into towering, godlike monarchs, beings of a different order from their subjects. Though the theology of Jove and Hercules was Roman in inspiration, the new imperial style was far more reminiscent of Eastern Hellenistic, not to say Pharoanic, concepts of monarchy. Gone were the days when an Emperor such as Marcus Aurelius would deliberately mix and converse with senators in an informal public atmosphere of near-equality. At his great palace at Nicomedia, Diocletian's throne and person were carefully secluded from the ordinary public world, both by architectural design and by a fixed order of ritual – the only means by which this profane world could be connected with the sacred presence. Delegations, for example, would be ceremonially conducted through long, vast marble halls by successive grades of priestly officials, past rows of glittering, motionless guards, through huge emblazoned doors, and finally to an inner sanctum. There, was the enthroned, impassive godlike source of all earthly power: the Lord of the World with a crown of the sun's rays, robed in purple and gold, and encrusted with precious stones down to his very shoes, holding the emblems of absolute power.

To such quasi-divinity the proper gesture was no longer salutation, but prostration, *adoratio, proskynesis*. At the meeting of the two Augusti in 290 the panegyric describes this as 'an act of adoration, like that performed in the holy of holies, which filled with wonder those to whom the dignity of their rank gave the right of admission to the ruler'.[23] To be one of the circle of *admissionales,* who regularly came into the sacred presence, was itself an honour and a symbol of high office in its own right. On their reception, such people would kneel and kiss the hem of the Emperor's robe. And when the *Sacred* council met formally for imperial decisions to be taken, the Emperor alone would be seated while all the others would stand in their appointed places around the throne, like decorated figures in a tableau. The stiff, otherworldly groupings of saints and soldiers, so common in Byzantine mosaics, merely reproduce faithfully the stage directions imposed by Diocletian at the Tetrarch's courts.

Similarly, on the many occasions when this mighty Emperor showed himself to his people or addressed his soldiers, it was automatically a form of festival, an epiphany in which the god-king imparted grace by his very appearance to them. His litter or chariot, his soldiers, retinue and banners would be as magnificent as possible, blazing in purple and gold, and his slow, measured progress and reception by a city, for example, would be met by rhythmic chanting of hymns, incense, torches and other gestures appropriate not just to the head of the Roman state but to the kinsmen and representative of Jupiter or Hercules. At Diocletian's palace at Split, all the lines of the arcade and peristyle lead the attention to the one elevated central arch, towering over the raised portals from which the Emperor will make his appearance. Later reigns were to continue this institution, even when the Emperors were devout Christians: witness the colossal head of Constantine in the Palazzo dei Conservatori, the giant imperial statue at Barletta, or the enthroned Theodosius in the silver dish at Madrid, his head crowned with the diadem and surrounded by the heavenly *nimbus*.

Aurelius Victor shakes his head deprecatingly, and puts it down to Diocletian's humble social origins which drove him to crave adulation: 'Just as one who has fasted then gorges himself gluttonously, so one who has never held rank and power will later display it quite immoderately'.[24] But the Emperor who shared power and glory with three colleagues knew what he was doing. His motives had nothing in common with the *folies de grandeur* of Caligula or Commodus, who had outraged responsible opinion and ended by being assassinated. On the contrary, his adoption of this mummery was necessary for survival.

Aurelian had given one essential reason for the change, when he lectured the soldiers that the Emperor's power and term depended not on them, but the gods. It was not enough for him to claim divine legitimacy in place of military election; not enough to improve his bodyguard and personal security. The more the Emperor in fact depended on the army, the more necessary it was to create a psychological barrier between himself and them, to awe them into habits of absolute obedience. They had to be made to feel that assassination of the Emperor was not just treason (which could and did prosper) but sacrilege of the most horrendous kind. The familiar, popular general among his soldiers was quite the wrong imperial style for one who wished to reign a long time and introduce painful but necessary changes. Since the conventional oath of loyalty to the Emperor's person had been progressively devalued, the soldiers' deepest religious taboos and outright superstitions had to be worked on. The very men who had raised him from one of themselves to this height, now had to be bound by a miraculous spell to forget what they had done.

1 Imperial bust of Diocletian, found at
Nicomedia. National Museum, Istanbul.
(Photo courtesy Max Hirmer)

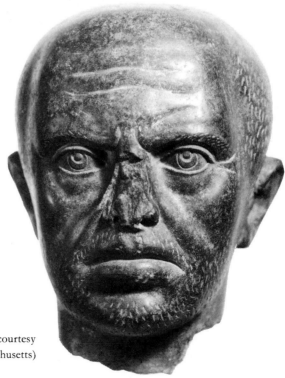

2 Porphyry bust of Diocletian. (Photo courtesy
Worcester Art Museum, Massachusetts)

(a)

(b)

3 Consular gold medallion issued in 287 to higher officers. (a) *Obverse*, Diocletian and Maximian, joint Augusti. (b) *Reverse*, a consular procession with elephants and crowds waving palms. (Photo courtesy Hirmer Verlag, Munich)

4 The Tetrarchy. Four united soldier-Emperors face a threatening world. The new stylised sculpture deliberately portrays them not as persons but as identical types. Porphyry statue in St Mark's Square, Venice, probably looted from Constantinople in 1204. (Photo courtesy Peter Clayton)

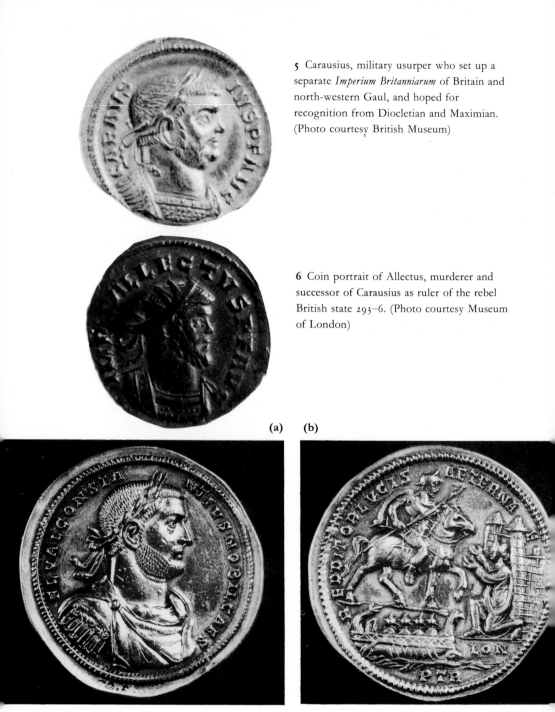

5 Carausius, military usurper who set up a separate *Imperium Britanniarum* of Britain and north-western Gaul, and hoped for recognition from Diocletian and Maximian. (Photo courtesy British Museum)

6 Coin portrait of Allectus, murderer and successor of Carausius as ruler of the rebel British state 293–6. (Photo courtesy Museum of London)

(a)   (b)

7 The Arras medallion celebrating Constantius' reconquest of Britain. (a) *Obverse*, Constantius Caesar. (b) *Reverse*, a suppliant London welcoming its liberator as 'restorer of the eternal light'. (Photo courtesy Museum of London)

8 Panels from the Triumphal Arch of Galerius, Salonica. *Top*, Galerius entering a city. *Centre*, Galerius in battle, trampling down the Persians. *Below*, much worn, the four Tetrarchs among the Olympians. (Photo courtesy École Française d'Archéologie, Athens)

(a)

(b)

9 Galerius, who achieved the great victory over Persia, and later was the leading advocate of the persecution of Christians. (a) *Obverse*, a typically stylised portrait, after his elevation to full Augustus. (b) *Reverse*, the standard figure of Jove, the preserver. (Photo courtesy British Museum)

10 *Below* The new Roman fortress architecture. Portchester Castle, one of the best preserved of the Saxon Shore forts, probably built by Carausius. On other frontiers the new forts were generally far smaller in area but with the same high walls and projecting bastions. (Photo courtesy Department of the Environment)

11 Diocletian's anti-inflation policy. A fragment of the famous Edict on Maximum Prices, recently excavated at Aphrodisias in Turkey. (Photo courtesy M Ali Döğenci)

12 Peristyle of Diocletian's Palace at Split. All the lines of the arcade converge on the great arched portals separating the private from the public spheres, through which the divine Emperor makes his appearance. (Photo courtesy Yugotourist, Belgrade)

13 The new architecture of an Empire on the defensive, massive and defiant, combining civil and military elements. The Porta Nigra at Trier, imperial capital of Constantius in the West. (Photo courtesy Max Hirmer)

14 *Below* The new imperial cult. Diocletian deliberately raised the figure of the Emperor to godlike proportions, using all the devices of oriental ceremonial, and the conversion of the Empire to Christianity did nothing to diminish this. This silver missorium shows the Catholic Emperor Theodosius (378–395) surrounded by his two sons and German bodyguard. (Photo courtesy Max Hirmer)

The need went well beyond mastery of the armies. The cataclysms society had been through had shaken mens' deepest faith in the whole world order of things. Their causes might be ill-comprehended, but everyone concurred in seeing them as cosmic in scale, far greater than the mere human and political. In a hundred different ways, people's imaginations had begun to suppose the unthinkable: could it be possible that Rome was not eternal, that the gods had deserted it, that the world was facing its end? Eschatological visions were vividly recalled – Jewish, Christian, Mazdean, Manichean: history would culminate in unimaginable calamities, the sun be stayed in its course, the oceans erupt in smoke, kingdoms and empires would pass away, the armies of light and darkness would gather for the final battle, and a saviour would appear.

Men were convinced even less than before by argument and demonstration, but by signs, oracles, divinations and all kinds of magical meanings that gave expression and answer to their fears and longings. Against this dark background, the Emperors who aspired to the role of Saviour of the World had to be larger than human, invincible *colossi* on whose power every enemy would break itself, and who would protect their people from all harm: Our Refuge and Our Strength. Now as never before, the Emperor was the one object of loyalty that gave identity to the diverse peoples with their particular cultures and religions. To an Egyptian peasant, a British merchant or a new Frankish warrior-settler, the traditions and legends of the Republic, the Senate, the Capitol, meant very little. The great struggle with Hannibal, Rome's finest hour, was as remote from their time as Agincourt is from us, and in any case had no intrinsic connection with their homelands and people. But the names Caesar and Augustus were everywhere understood as the central, immortal embodiments of Rome. He might be vaguely thought of as a supreme War Chieftain, as Pharoah kinsmen of Osiris, as lawgiver, *Basileus,* or the Great King of Kings in the West, but he was the common focus of allegiance; and if any symbol of the Empire was to be magnified, it was this.

It must be stressed that this change was in the public image of monarchy rather than its substance. It is true there was a shift in the absolutist direction. But his formal constitutional position changed much less than the presentation of it. It was psychological, not legal, authority which was transformed. Gibbon puts it eloquently:

> Like the modesty affected by Augustus, the state maintained by Diocletian was a
> theatrical representation; but it must be confessed that, of the two comedies, the
> former was of a more liberal and manly character than the latter. It was the aim of
> the one to disguise, and the object of the other to display, the unbounded power
> which the Emperors possessed over the Roman world.[25]

The early imperial symbolism was of the supreme civilian magistrate ruling in partnership with the Senate, combining in his person the republican offices that were formerly separate. The third century wars had militarised the Emperor's public style: he became the supreme and victorious commander, unashamedly chosen to rule by the Noble Soldiers on whom all public safety depended. Diocletian's new iconism ended this exclusive identification with army rule. While still showing every mark of regard for the military, his image was now that of divinely appointed Lord (*Dominus*) towering over soldiers and citizens alike, each of whom have their proper functions only as he commands them.

We may therefore wonder what Diocletian the man, the stage manager, thought of all this. He was not just astute and practical, but strongly religious, believing that he and his colleagues were directly favoured by the gods. As founders of a new order and regainers of divine protection, they and their successors were assuming greater burdens and should rightly demand greater honours. Necessary and calculated it all may have been, but as Gibbon testifies, we, whose political roots are Western, cannot find it admirable in comparison with what went before. For all his policy, one strongly suspects Diocletian did not find the task of distancing himself from his soldiers and subjects at all uncongenial. There is in him a distinct vein of aloofness and sensitive pride, which shows in his reluctance to expose his prestige to risks, and is captured in Lactantius' observation that 'he always wanted to appear shrewd and clever in everything he did'.[26] It is as if his brittle sense of dignity cannot tolerate that anything he undertakes be seen to fail. One cannot picture Diocletian making some public faux pas and easily laughing it off. Contrast with this the later Emperor Julian, who found all the ceremony oppressive and deliberately adopted the simpler informality of Marcus Aurelius: Julian is a far more human, attractive figure, whose very mistakes stem from a fine open spirit. But unfortunately he misjudged the age, and his attempt to return to old Roman manners was as dismal a failure as his attempt to return to paganism. Subjects saw it as weakness and immaturity that he failed to adopt the full despotic regalia they now expected of their sovereign.

chapter nine

·FINANCE, TAXATION,· ·INFLATION·

WHEREAS THE BANKERS STAND PUBLICLY ACCUSED OF CLOSING THE MONEY
EXCHANGES BECAUSE THEY WILL NOT ACCEPT THE DIVINE COIN OF THE
EMPERORS, IT HAS BECOME NECESSARY TO ISSUE THIS ORDER TO THEM TO
OPEN AGAIN, AND EXCHANGE ALL COIN EXCEPT THE TRULY SPURIOUS AND
COUNTERFEIT . . .
·ORDER OF AN EGYPTIAN STRATEGUS, 260·

In a population accustomed for generations to fixed prices, wages and rents, the experience of uncontrolled money inflation has profoundly disturbing effects, on the State no less than its taxpayers, in the shock to general confidence and particular expectations no less than in the concrete loss of wealth. When a salary or a loan can lose half its value, savings evaporate and next year's prices become utterly unpredictable, all kinds of other social bonds and practices begin to be broken, and more brutal or elementary relationships take their place. Uncertainty about the future is compounded with loss of understanding at what is happening, the mistaking of causes and effects. The greater part of the third-century inflation did not result, as some contemporaries liked to think, from ignoble acts such as bribing the threatening barbarians or the insolent soldiery. The soaring costs of war ('the father of taxes') and the shrinkage of cultivated land were far more relevant; but these too were combined with an extraordinarily rigid and weak system of taxation for a world state.[1]

The corollary of the notion that everything had its proper price, was that taxes too were traditionally fixed, and often remained unchanged for centuries. To raise them, or worse, to introduce new taxes, provoked great popular resentment, not least among the propertied classes whose support the government needed in so many ways. At a time of record prosperity, the mere one per cent tax on auction sales had been so unpopular that even Tiberius had found it expedient to halve it. If governments were to build up any reserve to meet emergencies such as wars, they had to balance their books extremely carefully: fiscal management was synonymous with cheese-paring. Even so, the resources attainable in this way were quite puny by modern standards; 20 years of peace and the most thrifty stewardship could barely pay for a couple of years of war. When this ran out, the State had to resort to irregular expedients, legal or illegal. It could sell off imperial property: Marcus

Aurelius publicly auctioned the palace wardrobe and furniture. It could request the customary 'free gifts' of gold from the cities for some celebration such as a victory: Caracalla was continually inventing victories for this purpose. He also extended full citizenship to every free inhabitant of the Empire, thus making them taxable.[2] It could confiscate the estates of nobles after contrived treason trials, as many Emperors did. Such iniquities were condemned by every senator, yet their indignation would have been little less towards a general increase in the taxes on their estates. Or finally, it could debase the coinage, which for a time proved most productive of all. The most common currency of the Empire was the silver denarius (later accompanied by the antoninianus, twice its value), and from Marcus Aurelius onwards the imperial mints began issuing new denarii with progressively smaller silver content, imperceptibly as they hoped: first 75 per cent, then 50. As the wars grew worse, the State was not expected to charge any more for the one commodity whose price was escalating faster than any other, namely its own military protection. It did at length levy special emergency taxes, the *indictio extraordinare,* but these too proved insufficient for an emergency that had become permanent. To pay its soldiers, recruits, officials and all the other war costs, there was little else it could do but go on multiplying the ever-diluted silver coinage over and over again, and for a time this seemed to work – that is, the effects were slow in working through. Prices certainly rose and the silver lost its relation with the purer gold coinage, but while a coin was still shiny, clear and the proper weight, its purchasing power did not fall as rapidly as its actual silver content. As MacMullen puts it, the financial advisers of the time must have believed they had opened the door to virtually limitless wealth.[3]

By the time of Gallienus, when the Empire was all but engulfed by its enemies, it was also being deluged by floods of near-worthless coinage of tatty appearance and a mere thin wash of silver over a copper base, but still at the old denominations. The price of wheat had risen over a hundred times, yet a soldier's cash pay had barely doubled.[4] Moreover this rotten 'silver' coinage was playing havoc with the regular copper currency that men had needed for small transactions and which had been produced quite legally by local mints for local use. It too had to reduce its weight and quality against the plummetting official silver, until eventually the local mints were driven out of operation. The State might still pay for its supplies by compulsion at the old prices, but not surprisingly, neither contractors nor soldiers would any longer accept payment in the useless denarii and antoniniani. Since soldiers urgently needed to be paid with something, the State in turn became reluctant to accept its own debased coinage in taxes. The silver currency had collapsed, and the government fell back on taxation and pay in kind.

Aurelian, unable to debase further and faced with monetary confusion, experimented with a new device. A great deal of the rotten coinage of varying weights and styles was reminted, being replaced by two new denominations, still only silver-washed, but of regular weight and finer design, intended to raise confidence. The first was marked xx.i, that is, it was set at 20 sesterces or five denarii, while the second was half the weight and marked vsv (usualis), that is, a standard antoninianus of two denarii. They were quickly accepted. The innovation was that instead of manipulating the silver content, the government had simply announced an official value, and advertised its own support for this currency. It had stumbled on a new way of increasing its resources, by a form of fiduciary issue. In effect, it was printing money.[5]

Diocletian absorbed this valuable lesson, but with the return of what he hoped was stability, he wanted to go further and get a genuine silver currency circulating once again, in a regular relation to gold. During the first eight years no silver was struck, and the xx.i silver-wash coin (now known as the *nummus* and officially revalued by five times) was the most common token of exchange. But in 286 he did issue a very pure gold *aureus* at the new weight of 60 to the pound, perhaps intending this as the stable basis of the future, post-inflationary three-metal currency. But, being rare and of handsome quality, it was virtually confined to donatives to troops or similar prestigious uses. Only the very top generals and officials could normally be paid in gold. The rest continued to be paid mainly in goods with small additions of money, and this still had to be the coin accepted in the marketplace, namely the washed *nummi* or copper. Like it or not, the State had to go on using this currency insofar as it needed to use money at all. Not only that, but whatever gold existed in private hands had by now largely disappeared from the market, not even into hoards but into plate and jewellery. There was not enough gold about even for genuinely large purchases. For these, the time bankers would take counting the colossal heaps of petty coins, led to the treasury having to issue sealed bags (*folles*) guaranteed to contain 1,000 nummi.

It was Carausius, unacknowledged British Emperor, who began issuing good quality silver from his London mint for the first time in decades. He was in possession of a healthy stock of silver and the appearance of these superior, impressive coins, showing the three fraternal Augusti, was excellent propaganda for his regime. It was equally galling for Diocletian and Maximian in the earlier years, observing the circulation and demand for these constant reminders of the successful rebel. Accordingly the creation of the Tetrarchy, and all the ambitious hopes invested in it, was the occasion for a new reform of the currency. Its prominent feature was to out-do Carausius with the issue of a new and very pure silver coin, the *argenteus,* fixed at the old Empire standard of 96 to the pound and (perhaps) 20 to the gold *aureus*. This was of course a relatively rare coin, and it was accompanied by a concerted attempt to introduce order into the everyday currency. The *nummus* was retained, but most of the varying provincial copper types were replaced by a single uniform coin, the *follis,* whose value was fixed against gold and silver. There is disagreement about the new official ratios of these coins to the pure silver. But whatever it was, their market values relative to silver soon drifted down again. Precious metals were simply too scarce, too thinly spread, to make the difference. All the same, debasement had definitely ceased, and the government's financial ministers now expected that the inflation would level off somewhere.[6]

Even if these monetary reforms had succeeded, Diocletian could not depend on them for the urgently needed overhaul of taxation. During the emergencies the instrument for supplying the armies had been the *annona militaris,* originally the compulsory purchase of provisions. But as money became worthless it became simply an arbitrary requisitioning. The armies had to be paid in something of real value, rather than cash. The ordinary soldier had long ceased to have deductions made from his miserable pay for rations, uniform and weapons; now this was reversed, and additional rations or clothing became instead the substitute for money. Among higher officers, their traditional pay entitlements were reflected in their equestrian service grades – *sexagenarius, centenarius, ducenarius* and so on, in theory receiving many times the soldier's pay. They too, where they could not be paid in gold, got multiples of rations which could be exchanged, or were paid in horses, cloaks, or decorated weapons and armour. (All the same, the real value of these salaries in kind was far below the pre-inflation levels, and were often supplemented by other means.) In this way, the *annona* was turned into an ad hoc device of taxation in kind, gathered by the armies in the manner of near-plunder. Unlike the old money taxes it specified no fixed percentage (since officially it was not a regular tax at all) but just the infinitely extending 'needs' of the army. As one campaign or civil war followed another, the Prefect and the generals, the governors and their agents, met these needs from whatever property was within reach. Although Aurelian attempted to curb its most oppressive aspects, there was little plan or method beyond the immediate emergency. It weighed most heavily on those whose goods could be easily seized, whose lands were on the line of march, who possessed those things the army happened to want at that time – or who were simply too weak to bribe or bargain. Flight, concealment, corruption of all kinds were near universal.

Nonetheless the *annona* was absolutely indispensable, as Diocletian knew very well. The military recoveries would have been impossible without it, and his own grand plans would require more wealth, not less, to be raised from the population. The old, creaking system of money taxation had broken down irretrievably in times of emergency, and with the Empire in a state of perpetual siege, emergency was now permanent as far as fiscal matters went. It was here, especially, that Diocletian displayed his rare talent for innovation and systematizing, his ability to take existing practices and older traditions and turn them into something essentially new. His policy was to develop and regularise the haphazard principles of the *annona* to cover all the land and wealth in the Empire: but in such a way that goods, services and produce became as far as possible interchangeable by a single standard, everyone's capacity to pay was assessed on a common, equitable basis, and the more productive areas subsidised the less. The starting point was no longer any fixed percentage or tariff, but an annual budget of the state's global requirements, which was then matched up against a vast register of the Empire's total resources, broken down province by province, city by city, field by field.[7]

This was the ideal, but one which actually came to be realised to a very considerable degree, and introduced immeasurably greater rationality into the State's exploitation of resources than anything other Emperors had ever done. Instead of the separate, unrelated poll tax and land tax, with all their regional variants, what his new taxes did for the first time was to unite in a coherent, workable way the two permanent elements of taxability – land and population. It classified land not just as area but as a productive resource, and people as units who could work it and be supported by it, and it made its calculations accordingly. It was in fact the virtual uselessness of the money system and the old fixed taxes which cleared the way for this fundamental rethinking. Diocletian looked at the problem not from the point of view of a banker or financial adviser, but of an army quartermaster. The administrators of the *annona* had long worked with the simple standard of how much grain, oil, wine, pork, olives, and salt were needed to feed one soldier for a year. This could be multiplied up for officers or in lieu of pay, or converted into equivalents in other goods. They could calculate accurately enough what a unit of any size and type would need in horses, transport, clothing, equipment, billeting and manual labour, and express this as a theoretical total of *annonae* units if necessary. Just this approach, ignoring the vagaries of money prices and calculating only usable goods and tasks, was now applied to the needs of the State as a whole, for which everyone had to pay.

The two main traditional money taxes throughout the Mediterranean were the poll tax, levied on persons as such, and the land tax. There was also a customs toll, a sales tax and various taxes on manufacture. The percentages varied considerably, there were different bases of calculation, and all manner of privileges and exemptions. Italy, the imperial heartland, paid no taxes at all. The poll tax in particular was inequitable, imposing the same burden on rich and poor alike. Most of these anomalies resulted from the fact that the Roman conquerors had usually just taken over the customary tax systems of the states they displaced, especially in Greece and the Hellenic East. Being careful of expenditure and seeing no reason to put all the provincials on a common footing, Rome had preferred to farm out the privilege of collection, tolerate traditional diversities and abuses, and get as much as possible for the minimum outlay.

Introduction of the new system inevitably proceeded at a different pace in different provinces, but the important years are 298 onwards, after the suppression of the Egyptian revolt.[8] At long last, Italy lost its old privilege of exemption, and was made subject to taxation like any other diocese. One after another, most of the obsolete traditional money taxes which had become scarcely worth collecting, were abolished or allowed to die out. By about 290, documents first stress the important notion of *Capitatio*.[9] Originally this just meant common people's tax liability in general; now it came to express, roughly, the absolutist principle behind the budgetary estimates, namely that the State has the right to demand whatever it needs from its citizens in whatever form, provided it is done legally and correctly. In effect, Diocletian asserted that the terrible burden of past exactions had all been necessary, but had been done in a most unequal and illegal manner, which would henceforth be remedied. Thus the Edict of 16 March, 297 by the Prefect of Egypt, Aristius Optatius (which was shortly followed by the national revolt) represents the new census as a measure of equity:

Our most provident Emperors [followed by their titles] have learnt that the public taxes are being levied most unevenly, some taxpayers being excused while others are overcharged. They have decided to root out this detestable and pernicious practice, and therefore publish a salutary regulation to which all must conform. I have set forth, so it may be known to all, the levy on each *aroura* of land according to the quality of the soil, the quota on each head of the agrarian population and the minimum and maximum ages of liability, according to the recent divine edict and the attached schedule, copies of which I have prefaced for promulgation with the edict. Accordingly, as a result of this great benefaction, the provincials should now resolve to pay their taxes with all speed, and not wait until they are compelled by the collector . . .

The magistrates and heads of each city council have been ordered to send to every village and locality a copy of the recent edict and the schedule and of this present edict also, so that the munificence of our Augusti and Caesars is known to all. The collectors of each kind of tax are warned to uphold this regulation to the best of their power, for transgression of which they risk death. Year 13, 12 and 6 of our Lords Diocletian and Maximian Augusti, and Constantius and Maximian [Galerius] Most Noble Caesars, Phamenoth 20.[10]

Although Diocletian's device of *caput* contained elements of the old poll tax and clearly shaded into it, it was concerned not just with persons in themselves, but also with them as labour power, with what a man could produce from the land he held, and what he himself needed. The new census began in 296 and for the first time united people and wealth. It was a gigantic, tireless cataloguing of all resources, every field, orchard, vineyard, every labourer, slave and child, every horse, ox and pig, and their expression, as far as possible, in a coherent scale of values. Surviving fragments of the tax rolls from Thera, Lesbos and other islands show the careful lists of cattle, sheep, asses, slaves and *coloni*. Papyri from Egypt contain declarations made in 298 under oath, that a certain person from Caranis possesses 24 olive trees, and that one in Theadelphia has two *aroura* of private land under cultivation. The following year, similar declarations are recorded for the month Thoth, when the lands are hidden under the Nile flood, and these have to be attested by a number of surveyors, jurors and other officials.[11]

The two basic units, inspired by the principle of the *annona*, were the *iugum* and the *caput*. The first derived its name simply from the Roman square measure of land, the *iugerum* ($\frac{1}{8}$ acre), and was theoretically the acreage that could be cultivated by one man and support his household. It therefore varied systematically according to the productivity of the land. In the Syrian regulations, the unit of one *iugum* equalled five *iugera* of vineyard, 20 of best arable land, 40 or 60 of poorer quality arable, 225 *perticae* of old olive trees, and 450 of mountain olive trees. Generally, mountainous land was assessed not by area at all, but simply how much was needed to yeild a given measure of wheat or barley. The *caput* theoretically stood for the one man, with additions for his household. Women were commonly rated at half a *caput*, and in most cases slaves, tenants and their families, all went into the total of *capita*. Children were counted into the total at the ages of 12 or 14, and people over 65 (where they existed) were exempt.[12]

In the Thera records there is the assessment of the total estate of one Paregorius, now deceased, which has been divided among his four heirs, his daughter Euphrosyne receiving the greater share. It consists of eight scattered farms and two smallholdings, and includes arable, vineyard and olive trees, plus some livestock. The largest farm has 138 *iugera* of arable, 30 of vineyard and 286 olive trees, while the smallest holding is merely six *iugera* of arable. All ten plots of land are added together and assessed according to appropriate scales, with vineyard naturally rated the richest. Two oxen, one ass and eight sheep merely make up one-seventh of a *caput*. With some rather cumbersome fractions, the whole estate adds up to just over ten *iuga* (or *capita*).

If a household was very poor, it might be grouped together with another similar household to make up just one *caput*. Conversely, a wealthy household might be rated at many *capita*. Thus a city and its attributed lands and people represent many thousand *capita,* but the figure would bear hardly any relation to its actual numbers of inhabitants. It was precisely this flexibility that proved such a useful innovation. Beyond providing a base of calibration, the actual acreage and heads did not correspond to *iuga* and *capita*. These became just abstract, universal units of liability, which could be used to capture all forms of taxable wealth in a single scale of values. For the first time, taxability itself was made as consistently measurable as weight or length. It was, of course, the hopeless instability of money prices, and the refusal to use money for many exchanges, which made this practical device necessary. But it was an opportunity to clear away an ancient thicket of anomalies, privileges, overlapping practices and gross inequalities, which would never have arisen if money had remained stable. The new State needed to tap every source of wealth, and it saw no reason to respect class or regional differences. It was a pragmatic soldier's reasoning: rough, fair, and above all workable.

In the standard case, *iuga* and *capita* would be totalled according to some formula, using fractions and multiples as necessary, to express the full tax liability of a person, his village, and his city. There have been lengthy discussions about the way the formula worked, and it is near-certain that there was no single, rigorous formula of the kind modern students might expect. The Empire was too diverse. All kinds of concessions had to be made to local custom if peoples' compliance was to be depended on. The *iugum* measures vary between Syria and Crete; in Dalmatia women were rated as equal *capita* with men, while in Egypt they were not rated at all. In some documents a person's *capita* includes his land, and conversely the iugum sometimes has not only land but men included in it. In short, the two were not independent units, but interchangeable. This is confirmed in the case of Paregorius and his estate, and by fourth-century laws which talk indifferently of a person's *iuga* or *capita*. A strictly logical system could have reduced them to a single unit. The fact that this did not happen was due to the limits of innovation and enforcement, the tenacity of tradition. The two things that had always been taxed, back to the Seleucids or the Pharoahs, were land and heads. To a villager, this was as inevitable as the weather or the Nile floods. He might try to evade taxation, and might succeed, just as he sometimes avoided other ills by cunning and determination. Every self-respecting Egyptian peasant could show the honourable scars, not of war, but of floggings for tax evasion. The quite routine mention of the death penalty in the Edict, and many similar documents, betrays how difficult strict enforcement really was. But tradition told him that it was in these two ways that the authorities would always try, relentlessly, to take goods from him. They were accepted evils: that is to say, he had no external vantage point from which to conceive of them as unjust, or alterable.[13]

The global survey of resources was to be five-yearly (this was later changed to a 15-year cycle). Then, each year on 1 September, the State's total requirements would be published in the form of an *indictio,* which would be apportioned to the vicars of the dioceses and thence down to each province according to its recorded resources, where the governor would be responsible for supervising the cities' assessments and the collections in kind, or occasionally cash. It was paid in three instalments during the year, and to allow for emergencies the State could revise it upward by a *superindictio.* (Even more rarely, as an ultimate appeal against unjust assessment, special inspectors might be sent to revise the amount demanded of a city or village.) Jones has suggested, very plausibly, that it was once again the flight from money that led to the annual estimate and annual collection – in effect, to a modern fiscal year. Because most of it was paid in kind, mainly foodstuffs which were perishable and demanded considerable storage space, it was far more necessary to estimate requirements accurately.[14] The total annual tax burden of the new State is near-impossible to estimate, but it must have been greater than that of Diocletian's predecessors for an average year of minor wars. Bury suggests that the State's annual revenue during the fourth century, when a money economy had largely returned, would have been at least 50 million gold solidi: perhaps £800 million at 1980 prices.[15]

The *annona* already provided a stable reckonable unit of the State's requirements. One soldier's theoretical maintenance equalled so much in cloth, leather, weapons, horses or whatever else was needed. The *iuga* and *capita* totals recorded in the survey now allowed the same to be done for taxable resources. A quantity of produce would have its equivalent in a transport charge, labour duty, billeting for troops, or anything else that might be supplied. Each year, in the central bureaux of the prefects, and in each individual city, the two had to be matched up. If the State's estimated needs had risen since the previous year, the bureaux would use a higher ratio of *annona* per *iuga/capita,* spreading the load as before.

The assessment having been made, it was for the civil chain of authority, rather than the army, to collect it in. The city councils – the decurionate – had to publish the demands and appoint officials to do the collecting, with councillors' own collective property as surety. Here the machinery was often at its weakest. In much of the Empire these councillors were few in number. The *curiales,* the local propertied class who were expected to fill these posts and administer the cities, had been all but ruined in the crisis years: men sought to evade these responsibilities where they could. Since the State could not dispense with their unpaid services in tax collection, it encountered here a bedrock of resistance to which it had to adjust. Having exhorted and threatened, it knew that in the end it had to settle for what it could get. This is graphically illustrated in the stream of correspondence from the Procurator of the Lower Thebaid, Aurelius Isidorus, to lower officials, in 300:

> I command you to make a comparison of the returns, under each *nome* and locality, with the records compiled by the census, in order that those who neglected to make returns, either in whole or part, may be detected. From whom, without delay, you should demand the wine due for the first and second indictions ... and they should be well satisfied with having escaped a greater penalty.[16]

The letters complain repeatedly of false returns, tardy deliveries, produce being sold off on its journey down the Nile. The new survey also reveals for the first time that the *whole* city council of Panopolis has been in collusion for many years to falsify its accounts: the furious Isidorus orders all the councillors locked up to await trial before the Catholicus, the fiscal head of Egypt. Thus the government had to discover empirically, in each city, just how much of its due taxes it could realistically expect, and so it is not surprising to find the methods and rates of assessment varying considerably with local conditions.

A different kind of tax adjustment is illustrated early in the fourth century when Constantine remitted the tax obligations of Autun, not by lowering the demand per unit, but by reducing the total number of units represented by the city in the survey – in this case Autun lost 7,000 *capita*. Each remaining *caput* then represented a larger proportion of the whole, more real wealth out of which the annual tax had to be found. Since people's properties remained unchanged, the number of lost units could be absorbed either by amalgamations, or by crediting citizens with fractions of a former *caput* as if the tax on them had been paid. Since the remissions were not just for that year but for the whole survey cycle, Autun's relative advantage was retained whatever the annual assessment. Similarly, in 311 a constitution states that soldiers and veterans who have served their full time are excused four *capita* from the census and the regular payments of *annona*. By the mid-fourth century, *iuga* were being sold by auction.[17]

What did the changes actually mean, say, to a Pannonian or Asian peasant and his household? Taxes had always borne heavily on the poor and they continued to do so; and Diocletian's dominant motives were not philanthropy but sound economic support of government and defence. The advantages to the ordinary taxpayer came not so much in any immediate easing of his burdens, as in the categories of freedom from fear, predictability and greater fairness of sacrifice. When all allowance is made for the many gaps between plan and reality, the regular experience of being treated like conquered territory by armed men who are supposed to be one's protectors really was made a thing of the past for millions of people. They no longer just had to pay up resignedly every time a soldier appeared on the scene. This ending of violent extortion was made possible by the separation of administrative powers in the provinces, and the exclusion of military authority from the fiscal machinery. People's *iuga* and *capita* were known to them and the basis of their assessments published. They could present proper evidence of having paid their taxes, and appeal to the authorities if more were demanded by anyone. The smaller, more closely supervised governorships brought the State's coercive powers closer to them, but by the same means it offered a better hope of appeal and redress of injustices. Alongside Aurelius Isidorus' fulminations over tax evasions are equally strong warnings about extortion by the tax collectors. In a public notice he declared:

> I had supposed every pretext for extortion had now been completely removed, since
> the divine decree has limited to a stated figure the amount of each tax liability ...
> but ... in the Hermopolite *nome* I learnt that certain collectors of military supplies
> ... had dared, against the orders of their superiors, to accept money in lieu of the

meat which should have been supplied, and that too not the equivalent to the amount laid down in the divine regulation, but many times greater, and completely intolerable to taxpayers. Others, in the case of barley and chaff, have been using not the authorised measures but greater ones, inflicting no small loss on the proprietors ... I enjoin the collectors that ... should they be detected in such enormities, they will suffer not merely financial penalties but risk capital punishment. The taxpayers should not submit to such demands, but merely furnish the provisions precisely as laid down in the regulation.[18]

Accordingly he orders the *nome* officials to ensure that meat is only delivered in the city itself. The baskets for chaff and barley deliveries are to be standardised to hold 25 lb each, and proper measuring scales, sealed with the official seal, kept locked up in each toparchy and each village so that taxpayers can all use them.

As the Edict and this notice indicate, the government really was concerned that its citizens should understand the common basis on which everyone's liability was worked out, and that the calculations and comparisons should be as public as possible. The poor should be able to see what their rich neighbours owed, and whether it was paid. All these things must have been at least partly achieved, if by Constantine's time a city or a deputation of veterans could petition for, and be credited with, so many purely notional tax units, and if *iuga* could actually be auctioned. For these would have been not just worthless, but wholly meaningless, unless there existed a generally respected public tally of who owed what and whether they had paid. The ancient writers were generally ready to describe almost any level of taxation as extortionate and intolerable, so that there can be little reliance on their unsupported accounts, even when these descriptions happen to be true. Lactantius, as we saw, states that Diocletain's taxation produced 'exhaustion and ruin', which is difficult to reconcile with the new lease of life which his overall reforms undoubtedly gave the Empire. Against this is the complimentary report of his reign by Aurelius Victor, which states that the new tax system was endurable and not excessive during the Tetrarchy, although later it grew into a scourge.[19]

From the State's point of view it was an unequivocal success. At first sight *iuga* and *capita* look crude and makeshift devices; but their great utility to a government devoted to reconstruction but inheriting a debased currency, lay in the fact that they were purely abstract units of value in which could be expressed any kind of wealth that people could offer, and the State needed. In a hypothetical transaction, suppose a small land-owner owes so much tax on his *iuga,* which he pays in grain. The city official must supply most of it to an army depot, so he remits a portion of it in exchange for the land-owner transporting it. At the receiving end, a centurion is paid with so much of the grain, which he gets as tallies redeemable from the quartermaster in any suitable form; he pays these to a tailor for cutting and finishing a cloak, who repays them to civil officials in lieu of his taxes or municipal labour obligations. The device of a purely contrived unit, divorced from gold or silver, had not been consciously thought of before, and it took the experience of uncontrolled inflation to bring it into use. Certainly, official rates of conversion from one commodity to another could be manipulated like money prices; and in any case, it was impossible to maintain more than rough equivalents, in an economy that was largely local. And the ordinary citizen at market still had to haggle with the dubious coinage for the small daily transactions on which he depended. *Iuga* and *capita* were never intended to replace money by a barter economy, but to bypass its temporary uselessness as a means of financing army and government, and in their flexibility they did this admirably.

By making the *indictio* a regular, integral feature of the tax system instead of an occasional emergency resort, Diocletian introduced, for the very first time, a modern annual budget whereby tax rates were automatically adjusted to the government's requirements. This was an invention of the very greatest importance for the Roman State and its Byzantine successor. In place of the makeshift fiscal expedients of the old Empire, the confiscations, fines, debasements of silver and arbitrary plundering, he provided a machine for acquiring, legally and regularly, the resources the government needed, rather than being ruled by what it could get. In place of the motley variety of traditional taxes, all at rigid percentages and allowing every kind of inequality and avoidance, he spread the burden in a uniform way by the comprehensive quinquennial census and the standardisation of tax units.

Not surprisingly, wealth poured into the coffers of the Tetrarchy as it had never done in mens' lifetimes. No longer living from hand to mouth, the four rulers could plan their grand palaces, capitals and other ambitious designs free from the shadow of bankruptcy. Lactantius attributes this new accumulation of wealth to Diocletian's 'insatiable avarice, which would never permit the treasury to be diminished; he was constantly accumulating extraordinary resources and funds, so as to preserve what he had already stored untouched and inviolate'.[20] Elsewhere he accuses him of the old tyrannical device of trumping up treason charges against the wealthy: 'This was peculiar to him, that whenever he saw a remarkably fertile field or an unusually elegant house, a false capital charge was immediately prepared against the owner, so it seemed that he could never plunder people without also shedding blood'.[21] But, despite the great care that the educated nobility took in every age to record these unforgiveable crimes, there is no other evidence of Diocletian committing them: he did not need to.

Also not surprisingly, the successors who inherited this wonderful instrument of the annual budget nearly all used it during the next century to revise the State's 'needs' ever upwards. We can easily see how, between the time of its introduction and when Aurelius Victor was writing, it did become more oppressive. The efficiency of this machinery of exploitation, as well as the layers of the officialdom itself, insulated later Emperors from the warnings that should have reached them when the economic base was being inexorably eroded.

chapter ten

·A COMMAND ECONOMY·

THE ASSESSMENT OF SPECIAL PUBLIC SERVICES SHALL NOT BE LEFT UP TO
CHIEF DECURIONS. GOVERNORS OF THE PROVINCES WILL BE REQUIRED TO
PERFORM THIS ASSESSMENT THEMSELVES, AND IN THEIR OWN HANDS COMPILE
THE LISTS AND ANNEX THE NAMES, OBSERVING THE GENERAL RULE THAT THE
SERVICES ALLOTTED SHALL BE PERFORMED FIRST BY THOSE OF HIGHEST
PROPERTY RANK, AND THEN BY THOSE OF MIDDLE AND LOWEST STATION.
·LAW OF CONSTANTINE, 328·

When the stilted prose of later Tetrarchic pronouncements talks of 'this happy age of ours', the official formula actually bears some relation to the truth. By about 300 there really was an end to the continual invasions and civil wars that Emperors and soldiers had known all their lives. The frontiers were largely secure, the armies obedient, the peasants' produce no longer plundered. Towns were being restored, land brought back into cultivation. As any of the princes travelled with their retinue along the main highways from city to city they could look on their realm and find it, on the whole, good. There were of course contradicting reports from some regions but the overall picture, as far as they could form one, was of improvement, the return of blessed stability. Why, then, did prices continue their alarming upward rise?

In our days of a managed currency, manipulated bank rates and the Treasury computer, government still has at best an insecure understanding of money's behaviour. It is too easy for modern historians to point out what Emperors should have seen and should have done. As we struggle with one recipe after another we are conscious of nothing so much as producing material for future economic treatises pointing out what we failed to see and do. As our illusion of control fades, so perhaps does the sense of distance between the Romans and ourselves.

There can be no single estimate of the extent of the inflation because it clearly varied geographically, and there was no single standard such as gold to which money values were anchored. The universal money unit in which the price of anything (including gold) was expressed, was the denarius, which itself had depreciated so drastically. Expressed in denarii, the average price of wheat had risen about 200 times since the Antonine period, but the quantity of denarii and their multiples in circulation had also increased over 100 times. Both agricultural production and population had also fallen. Cash had been converted wherever possible into gold, ornaments, land or property, and state salaries into goods. The main losers were small creditors, long-term mortgagees, and the higher officials, whose pay in kind was still far below what their second-century salaries would have purchased. Ordinary soldiers, once their pay was primarily in kind, suffered less. Peasant leaseholders paying in cash obviously gained, while land-owners naturally tried to convert rents into kind. Loans and leases became for short terms only. Others who still used cash simply raised their prices and wages into hundreds of cheap coins as best they could.

There was no theory of economics in the ancient world, beyond the mere precepts of sound estate management and careful accounting, and it is almost a definition of an inflationary crisis that these kinds of maxim are found to break down. The State understood well that wheat prices, for example, would rise sharply with famine or by hoarding, and fall once again with abundance. It was, after all, its customary duty to intervene and relieve excessively high prices by releasing grain on to the market, if necessary by compulsory purchase from the merchants for this purpose. It also understood that interest rates varied with the demand for money and its availability, and again, certain rates were considered extortionate and might be curbed by law. What it did not recognise at least not clearly and steadily, was that currency itself could vary in price just like any other commodity. Through its own expedient of stipulating higher values, the State had half-grasped that money values might be arbitrarily fixed. But this was still felt to be almost a fortunate sleight of hand, just as debasing the silver had been. All the pull of tradition taught that the 'real' value of a coin was in its precious metal content, and only by varying this could its proper purchasing power be permanently changed. This was still a long way from recognising that mere volume of currency and its rate of circulation directly affected the price of goods.[1]

The Emperors might perhaps have seen, as they built their great palaces and capitals and bid for the scarce labour to embellish them, that their own demands were pushing up prices. Certainly, given the deep attachment to the idea of value as metal content, they should have expected prices to rise as they remorselessly lowered the silver content to a tiny fraction of the original. Perhaps they did. But for a long time the dilution had kept ahead of price rises, and even after that, the issue of handsome new coins at much higher denominations had seemed to accomplish the same trick. And while measures still more or less work, governments are slow to see their theoretical weaknesses. At any rate, it seems Diocletian's advisers, whoever they were, had at last learnt the lesson, for in his currency reforms both these techniques were deliberately used in reverse, as *deflationary* instruments in terms of silver content. A new silver-washed 25-denarius piece was issued of superior weight and metal content. And the earlier poorer *nummus* which it replaced, perhaps the most common coin then in circulation, was officially retariffed downwards, to half its value. The sudden effects of this move are graphically illustrated by a letter from an official, with inside knowledge of the devaluation, to his steward:

Dionysius to Apio, greeting. The divine fortune of our masters has decreed that the Italian coinage be reduced to half a *nummus*. So make haste and spend all the money you have, buy for me any kind of goods at whatever prices you find them ... But I warn you not to try any sharp practice with me, because i won't let you get away with it. May you continue long in health, my brother.[2]

According to the State's view, then, price inflation should now have ended. Harvests were good. It had reintroduced a proper three-metal currency, and markedly improved the quality and silver content of the common denarii coinage. The fact that it had opened many more mints, which were now churning out oceans of the new coins far in excess of what was being called in and reminted, would not have seemed an objection. And yet, all the voices that were reaching Diocletian's court were of merchants charging unheard-of prices for all kinds of goods, and labour demanding far higher wages.

Lactantius simply puts the cause down to Diocletian's own 'extortions'. He would have been nearer the mark to blame his excessive spending. It is fairly clear that the information reached Diocletian mainly through the complaints of officials and soldiers in his retinue, and his armies on their travels. Multitudes of men with money to spend would converge on a city or town, urgently demanding billets, provisions and services of every kind. Was it really so surprising that vendors put their prices up? Had not this always been the experience of Emperors on progress? Admittedly the excessive money supply made the rises many times steeper: and there is at least a hint in Diocletian's Edict that a certain rise in profiteering might have been more or less tolerable, but the actual extent of it breaks all bounds. 'If the excesses of unlimited, furious avarice could be checked by some self-restraint . . . then perhaps there would be some room for dissimulation and silence . . .'[3]

But his dominant tone of righteous indignation leaves no doubt that Diocletian saw the cause as the insatiable greed of merchants. He has the stock image of the hoarder and speculator who profits by misery and hates abundant harvests, which is contrasted with that of the honest soldier, stripped of all his hard-earned pay by these vultures. Is it for this that toiling people have payed their taxes? Soldiers have been forbidden to seize what they need, and must pay properly for their purchases, and what is the result? The soldiers simply become victims of extortion in their turn.

Baffled by several years' fruitless attack on the inflation, having tried different devices to no effect, Diocletian concluded, as so many other rulers have done, that his efforts were being frustrated by mercantile villainy. Like many dictatorial governments in our own time, he now sought to prevent this by law. As with his other measures, this was far bolder, more complete and rigidly detailed than anything Romans had known before. The famous Edict De Pretiis, published in early 301, laid down compulsory maximum prices for most common articles and services, as well as maximum wage rates. It is an enormous document, listing about a thousand different items in 32 sections. In the custom of major Edicts, in addition to the papyrus copies and the painted wooden display boards, it was laboriously engraved on stone in both Greek and Latin, many fragments of which have turned up at Eastern sites. How the information was gathered, how long it took to compile and how many people it occupied, can only be guessed at. It shows only a limited economic wisdom, but it bears all the marks of thoroughness and system, of leaving as little as possible to chance, which is characteristic of an essentially military approach to the state's problems.

The didactic preamble is worth quoting at some length, setting out as it does the compelling reasons for the measure. Conscious that it is a piece of unprecedented intervention, Diocletian does everything to enlist considerations of fairness, common sense, and humanity on the State's side, and turn people against the wicked profiteers. In its appeal to gods, ancestors, duty, patriotism and the concern of the Emperors for the general good, it is a specimen of his propaganda at its most concentrated. After the long recital of the four rulers' titles and victories, it begins by setting the idealised scene:

> As we recall the wars we have successfully fought, we must be grateful for a tranquil world, reclining in the embrace of the most profound calm, and for the blessings of a peace won with great effort. It is demanded, both by right-thinking public opinion and by the dignity and majesty of Rome that this fortune of our State, second only to the immortal gods, be faithfully established and suitably adorned. Therefore we, who by the gracious favour of the gods, stemmed the former ravaging tide of the barbarians by destroying them, must guard this peace, established for eternity, with the due defences of justice.

Then comes the note of exhausted forbearance already quoted. If the avaricious only showed some limits to their appetites it might have been possible to ignore it; but

> Since the only desire of these uncontrolled madmen is to have no thought for the common welfare, for with the immoderate and unscrupulous it is almost a creed ... not to curb their plunderings until forcibly compelled, and since others, in their extreme need, have become aware of their unfortunate position and can no longer close their eyes to it. We—protectors of the human race—are agreed that justice must intervene, so that the long-hoped solution which men could not supply for themselves may, by our foresight, be applied to the general betterment of all ... There can be no complaints that our intervention is untimely or unnecessary or unimportant, for the unscrupulous have perceived in our silence over so many years a lesson in restraint, but have been unwilling to imitate it.

Then follows a recitation of the evidence of the evil, and a lurid portrait of its perpetrators:

> Who is so insensitive and devoid of human feeling that is unaware or has not perceived that immoderate prices are widespread in the commerce of the markets and the daily life of cities, and that uncontrolled lust for gain is not lessened by abundant supplies or fruitful years? Truly, the evil men engaged in business actually try to predict the wind and weather by watching the movements of the stars; for they cannot endure the rains nourishing the fertile fields and promising rich future harvests, since they only reckon good weather and plenty as their own loss ...
> These men use a poor year to speculate in the losses of the harvest and agents' services, and have amassed personal fortunes enough for whole nations, yet still try to capture smaller fortunes and charge ruinous interest rates ...
> Who does not know that wherever the public safety requires our armies to be sent, the profiteers insolently and covertly attack the public welfare, not only in villages and towns but on every road? They extort prices for merchandise not fourfold, not eightfold, but so great that human speech cannnot describe it.

Sometimes a soldier in a single purchase is stripped of both his pay and his donative. The contributions of the whole world to support the armies falls to the profits of thieves, so that our soldiers seem to be handing over the rewards of their service and their veterans' payments to the profiteers, and these pillagers of the State daily seize more than they know how to hold.

Finally, the new law, its application, penalties, and warnings about evasion:

We have decreed that maximum prices for sale must be established. We have not set down fixed prices, for we do not think it just to do this, since many provinces occasionally rejoice in the good fortune of low prices and the privilege of prosperity ... Every man may know that while permission to exceed (the maxima) is denied him, the blessings of low prices have in no way been restricted in those places where supplies are seen to abound ... Since it is agreed that in the time of our ancestors it was customary in passing laws to prescribe a penalty, since a situation beneficial to humanity is rarely accepted spontaneously, and since experience teaches that fear is the most effective guide and regulator for the performance of duty – it is our pleasure that anyone who violates the measures of this statute shall, for his daring, be subject to capital punishment. And let no one consider this penalty harsh, since there is a ready protection from danger in the observance of moderation. The same penalty applies to him who, in the desire to buy, conspires against the State with the greed of the seller; and to him who, though in business and possessing commodities that are needed, attempts to withdraw them from the general market – for a penalty should be severer for him who introduces poverty than for him who illegally accentuates it.

Then follow the long lists, which are not only a mine of economic information, but also interesting social documents, giving a picture of trades and their relative pay and status, the varieties of goods on the market and their places of origin, types of dress, culinary tastes, and techniques of manufacture.

The main categories are foods, raw materials, clothing, transport, wages and various services charges. All prices are in *denarii communis,* indicating that whatever Diocletian's hope of popularising his better quality currency, the baser coins were still the most common. The stipulated ratios between gold, silver and the common denarius, whatever they were, appear to have drifted by 301, since both gold and silver are priced in denarii. The gold *aureus* has now risen to 833 denarii, against the second-century rate of 25. The price of silver is missing, but an official transaction six years later would put the pure *argenteus* at 86.5 denarii.

It is fairly certain that the prices quoted, however they were arrived at, are below the then market rates, and in transactions where the State had a special interest, such as freight charges, they are deliberately lowered.[4] At the same time there appears a certain equalising tendency compared with the great wage differences of previous centuries. The impression is that, had these wages and prices actually prevailed, both peasants and proletarians would have had a bearable standard of living. For example, labourers, herdsmen, mule-drivers, sewer cleaners get 20–25 denarii a day, enough to buy two pounds of pork, or three pints of plain wine, or 0.25 *modii* of wheat (the volume equivalent of about half a gallon). Three days' work would buy a cheap pair of shoes, nearly a month, a shirt. A carpenter, baker, plasterer and worker in tessellated floors all get double this, about the same as an elementary schoolteacher, who is paid 50 a month per pupil. A scribe of the best writing gets 25 per 100 lines. With rarer skills and higher education the rates rise considerably. A figure painter earns 150 a day, a teacher of rhetoric 250 per month and pupil, an advocate 1,000 for pleading a case. In fact, it is most likely a herdsman would be paid below his maximum, whereas the tessellated floor worker or figure painter could probably expect (illegally) to exceed theirs.

We find the cheapest meats are mutton, goat and beef (the latter presumably being old draught animals rather than bred livestock). Poultry and prepared meats such as Menapic ham are costlier. The cheapest cereals are barley, rye, millet, the dearest rice. For the better-off there is wide variety in price and quality among meat and fish, less in wine. There is pheasant, boar, gazelle, quail, dormice, francolin, oysters, mussels, sea urchin. Almost the only significant price difference in wine seems to be between the plain (*rustici*) and the rest. Tiburtine, Falernian, Sabine, Picene and others are all 30 denarii a pint, with reductions for wine a year old, confirming that storage and maturation had not yet been generally mastered. Three kinds of beer are mentioned, Celtic, Pannonian and Egyptian, the latter an inferior brew at only two denarii.

Not surprisingly silk is by far the costliest textile, followed by various wools and linens, down to 'coarser linen for the use of common people and slaves'. Finished garments such as the hooded cloak (*birrus*) or dalmatic sleeved tunic are classified by weight, style and people of origin. Cloaks from the Nervii appear to be the best quality (about 10,000 denarii), those from Africa the cheapest (1,500). For cutting and finishing one of the former a tailor received 60 denarii, for a pair of trousers 20. A long list of skins and furs is mentioned, ranging in price from tanned badger and deerskin, to luxuries such as leopard or sealskin. Despite the State's depression of the charges, the list confirms how costly was overland transport in the ancient world. To travel 20 miles cost a man a day's skilled wage, and to transport a 1,200 lb load that distance by wagon, 400 denarii.

The Edict is something of an idealised measure, bearing some relation to observed market prices, but trying to see through them to some presumed normal, fair, 'proper' price. It is not just an anti-inflation weapon but an attempt to legislate what are considered socially just ratios between wages and prices, necessities and luxuries. The antecedents are in the government's traditional duty to intervene occasionally in an otherwise unregulated market economy. But Diocletian's policy is a huge step away from that tradition. It aims at generalised permanent control, and in forbidding merchants to withdraw their goods from sale at the stipulated price it has a distinct totalitarian ring, proclaiming in effect the State's primary claim on the use and direction of the material resources of society, private ownership notwithstanding.

In fact, however, unless the maxima had broadly coincided with actual price movements at the time, the law was all but unenforceable. It had to depend on individual complaints, or on inspectors of markets employed by the municipal councils, who were themselves owners and vendors of property. State officials, who were involved in so many transactions, would only show zeal in enforcing prices to their own advantage, and the existence of an economy in kind side by side with the money economy made evasion especially easy. According to Lactantius, 'Much blood was shed for the merest trifles. Men were afraid to display anything for sale, and the scarcity became more grievous and excessive than ever – until in the end, having proved ruinous to so many, the law was abrogated out of sheer necessity.' Apart from this charge we have no idea how many violators of the Edict were punished, but proof of guilt must have been difficult. And it is clear, in any case, that men were *not* afraid to withdraw their wares from the market.

Within a few years the whole elaborate Edict was a dead letter. As prices continued their upward rise it became common knowledge among the government that it could not be enforced, and it was quietly allowed to lapse. Diocletian's ambition of re-establishing a stable silver currency which would once again be the universal medium of exchange, was never achieved. Monetary stability of a kind was only to be attained many years later, with Constantine's gold *solidus*.[6]

Diocletian's failure to enforce what he saw as equitable conditions, and the sheer clumsiness of his law as an instrument for controlling commerce, did not deter him (or his successors) from intervening in the economy on a growing scale. In his view, he had no option. Even had he and his advisers a sophisticated grasp of economics – which of course they had not – they would hardly have attempted to return to the old, minimal economic role of the State which had existed before the great crisis. The complex web of relationships that had made up the diverse economy of the old Empire, had been broken in too many places. The human bases of confidence, healthy institutions, readiness to work and cultivate and invest, were no longer there.[7]

As his new tax system forcefully illustrates, he saw economic activity essentially in strategic terms. Its legal foundation was unquestionably private property, but its function was to yield a large enough taxable margin to supply the State with soldiers to defend it and civil government to administer it. If land was idle, the State had to settle cultivators on it; if the cities would not govern themselves voluntarily, their propertied classes had to be compelled to perform their duties. Like the other Illyrian Emperors, Diocletian easily tended to think of land-owners, craftsmen, and peasants, in terms of so many officers and soldiers with their assigned positions in the system. Perhaps more consciously, he had observed in Egypt the workings of a different kind of economic machine – the liturgy State of compulsory services – and it had implications for the Empire as a whole.

The basis of the Empire's economy was of course agriculture, but it was focussed on cities in a way that was unique among ancient civilisations. All land was formally attached to some city, in which its owner normally formed part of the local governing aristocracy. Out of those whose property qualified them as *decuriones* or *curiales*, magistrates were usually elected annually, often on a rotating basis. A committee of ten, or sometimes twenty, of the city's wealthiest members would be directly liable for the duty of tax collection, with their own property as surety for any shortfall. As far as the State was concerned, this had long been their most important function. It was absolutely dependent on this unpaid service: to have done the job with its own salaried officials would have been unthinkably costly, and to return to the old system of tax farmers (*publicani*) was a recipe for abuses and unrest.

But the *decuriones* had many other duties towards their native cities: representing it in legal cases and petitions; ensuring an adequate food and water supply; maintaining public buildings, streets, highways, managing the baths, theatres, temples and providing public festivals – in short, an indefinite list of municipal and State services, all unpaid. In more prosperous times there had been no lack of wealthy citizens willing to shoulder these duties, and to achieve civic distinction in this way: the adornment and very life of the cities of the High Empire depended on the social aspirations of this rising bourgeoisie. The civic obligation accompanying private wealth – the *munus personale* and *munus patrimonii* – had become so sanctified by custom that it had increasingly passed into law. It had been a highly civilised custom, which took the edge off inequality and competition by making wealth socially acceptable only when it was seen to be publicly shared. It became difficult for the rich man to set himself completely above and apart from his peers.

This natural connection between wealth and civic office was not just an expression of the 'stake in the country' view, but conversely the more practical consideration that wealth – pre-eminently land – provided a surety for dutiful public service, especially tax collection. The whole functioning of the cities – the lifeblood of Roman and Hellenic civilisation—depended on a thriving land-owning class; and the chaos of the third century had sapped this lifeblood almost beyond recovery. The wealthy, threatened by soaring taxation and seizures as much as by barbarian invasions and civil wars, retreated from the cities to their lands, or even sold up and fled. The cities decayed, potentially taxable land was abandoned. Men sought to conceal their remaining property, *decuriones* went to extreme lengths to avoid election to the magistracies, and others to avoid being enrolled in the list of *decuriones*. What had once been an honour for which they had competed, was now a crushing burden that spelt bankruptcy.

For years the government had hypocritically kept up the old official attitude that magistracies were a civic honour which men should be glad to have bestowed on them. With Diocletian, finally, the outworn mask was discarded. His laws and pronouncements acknowleged civic office as the unrelieved burden everyone knew it to be. Instead of insisting on the proper social qualifications for enrolment in the decurionate, he systematically lowered them to catch as many people as possible in the net. Anyone owning as little as 25 *iugera* of land was compelled to enrol and to serve, and his sons after him. Only when he had filled every municipal office in turn was he considered to have discharged his obligation. Earlier grounds for exclusion were swept away. Men of illegitimate or slave birth, illiterates, even those who had suffered public disgrace (*infamia*) were liable to serve merely by possessing the minimum amount of property. Nor were they permitted to leave their city of birth to avoid these duties. Abandoned land was to be forfeit, and granted to others willing to till it.

In this way, these civic duties ceased to be regarded as voluntary gifts of a man to his city, and became rather compulsory unpaid services to the city and the State. *Munera patrimonii* became the gentlemanly counterpart of labour corvées, *munera sordida.* The forerunner once again was the Egyptian liturgy system, where in addition to manual work on the dykes (which could be done by a substitute) a man was liable for a whole number of other State services, according to his station. Thus, under Diocletian and after him, a nominated magistrate might have to perform not just his municipal duties but also, say, provide horses and waggons for the imperial post, or billets for soldiers and officials. It was useless for him to protest that he could not afford it. If he defaulted, his colleagues on the council who knew his property and were probably no better off themselves, had to pay. If for some reason he could not supply that particular service, why, let him do or supply the equivalent in some other form. *Munera* thus fitted in easily with Diocletian's new tax system, as he intended they should. A unit of service, in whatever form was required, might be demanded and credited just like *iuga* and *capita,* and calculated into an enlarged tax liability for a city. And, instead of the near-impossible task of pursuing and punishing every individual defaulter, the State relied increasingly on communal sanctions. Behind each *decurion* stood his fellow councillors who had to stand surety for his payment. Armed now with the much more exact information of the city's total resources, the State was determined to exact its due one way or another, and would brook no evasion. Short of mass exodus, the propertied class had a collective incentive, imposed from above, to keep each of their individual members in his place.[8]

This principle of compulsory organisation became the cornerstone of the new State policy towards manufacturing and trade. It developed gradually, utilising older precedents and custom wherever possible, but the trend was unmistakable: conscripted service and collective liability for its delivery. It began with Aurelian or earlier, was developed into a coherent, general policy under Diocletian, and was completed and enshrined in specific laws under Constantine. Innumerable customary unpaid services which had traditionally been rendered to assist the State in different ways, now became frozen into compulsory duties. The voluntary associations of businessmen and artisans (*collegia, corpora*) were transformed one by one into obligatory organisations like the city councils, geared to the larger State machinery.

Among the first functions to change in this way was the onerous, traditional task of feeding the swarming, idle proletariat of Rome itself which had always required the organisation of large grain convoys from Africa and Egypt. For centuries the Emperors had hired private shipowners (*navicularii*) for this task, and their trade associations were granted special recognition and privileges. The State had found it more convenient to contract with a corporate body than with so many individual shippers, and for its part the association undertook that, between its members, the City's supplies would be maintained. But soaring price inflation confronted Emperors with the possibility that they would be unable to pay for these absolutely necessary supplies. The shipowners' associations therefore came under tighter State controls, eventually embodied in law, which fixed the duties of their members, and their corresponding exemptions from taxes and municipal service. Membership was to become compulsory and hereditary, their property was held as surety for the delivery of the cargoes, and transfer of capital out of the trade forbidden.[9]

The same happened to the guilds of bakers and millers. (In the latter case, a later law even required men marrying the daughters of millers to take up the trade themselves.) Similarly, the State placed controls on beef and mutton merchants, wood merchants, dyers, weavers, and transport merchants. The detailed controls varied, and were experienced in a creeping form over many decades, as a result of tax and service demands, petitions, or specific legal decisions, but the pattern was everywhere the same. Compulsory organisation began with the trades directly supplying the great cities, or the armies, or some other strategic lifeline, and slowly extended to the whole of industry. The State could not rely on unfettered private enterprise to deliver the goods, because it could not pay the inflated market prices. Many industries had declined to the point where they no longer traded their wares in distant markets, but produced for local needs only. The flight of wealth from the towns to the rural estates accentuated the problem, as the villas became more self-sufficient in most manufactured goods. The one way for the State to be sure of the supplies it needed was to organise essential trade on the same basis as tax and *munera*.

Where it could offer incentives, it did so. But these were within a growing framework of compulsion, and typically consisted of exemptions from other compulsory duties, a trade-off of one obligation for another. Exemptions from *munera* could be offered in lieu of wages or dubious cash payments, just as favoured cities might be credited with so many *iuga* or *capita*. The guilds and corporations were to become the instruments of indirect State control of production. Their members, and their heirs after them, were to be prevented from leaving their occupations. Their property was recognised and to an extent protected, but only provided it was at the corporate service of the association, which underwrote its members' public obligations. Like the attempt to control prices and wages, the free movement of capital and labour, the freedom of contract and exchange, even the free choice of occupation now became circumscribed.

The system was undeniably hard. But to Diocletian and his new generation of administrators it was simply part of the higher price every citizen now had to pay for security, public order, and even survival. He probably had little sympathy for the merchants, who had brought increased coercion on themselves by their refusal – as he saw it – to co-operate in stabilising prices. As for the *decuriones,* the Emperors had always depended absolutely on their help in good times and bad, if civil society was to be kept functioning. The fact that everyone was poorer and they no longer offered their services voluntarily, did not in any way diminish this need. The burden was being shared fairly and openly; they were no longer being dragooned by military violence, or intimidated by spies and agents. The soldiers and officers who defended them likewise had to accept sacrifices in pay, yet they no longer mutinied and plundered as in the past. All the civic duties were after all regularly recorded and reckoned in the total balance sheet of work, produce, resources, taxes and military service by which he had to plan for the Empire's survival.

Labour, skilled and unskilled, was systematically drafted in a variety of ways. The corvée of city plebs for roadbuilding, fortification, haulage, cleaning of streets and sewers and similar heavy labour, had been extended and regularised on something like the Egyptian model, thus reclaiming something from the *otiosi*, the idle mob supported by the corn dole. Aurelian's great defensive wall around Rome was built with conscript labour in this way. By contrast, individual craftsmen, who were in high demand everywhere, were far better treated. Generous payment in kind and exemption from taxes and *munera* were frequently offered to attract them where they were needed. But if this was not enough, the government had no hesitation in simply directing them, as when Constantius drafted metalworkers and other artisans from Britain for the restoration of Gallic towns. Like the small manufacturers and traders, all workers with a definite skill were gradually compelled to join a corporation, to remain in their trade and teach their skill to their sons, who automatically inherited their place and obligations.[10]

Where the State's vital supplies were directly concerned, something like military regimentation of labour was adopted. Among Diocletian's strategic reforms was the innovation of new State arsenals (*fabricae*), managed by army personnel and worked by skilled craftsmen conscripted as for military service. About a dozen arsenals were established by Diocletian, more by his successors. Those in Asia Minor were generally located near iron ore deposits, and each tended to specialise in mass production of particular items. The works at Nicomedia produced shields and swords, at Caesarea, armour, and in Cilicia, spears and lances. Others were located at strategic military cities such as Edessa, Antioch and Damascus in the East, and later at Sirmium, Salona, Ticinum in the West.[11] Parallel with the arsenals were other new imperial factories turning out cloaks, headgear, and textiles for army use, where the labour organisation was probably similar, but the working conditions inferior. Textile works, State and private, were sited in Asia Minor, in the Danube provinces at Aquincum, Sirmium, Siscia, and in Northern Italy at Milan and Ravenna. In the private works the weavers and their employers were alike grouped into compulsory associations and obliged to deliver a fixed quota of produce to the State. The State was also a monopoly owner of the silk works, dye works and associated clothing factories that produced high quality garments for use by the palaces and higher officials. Mint workers were also subject to conscription and direct State management, since the ready supply of coinage was seen as a strategic item almost on a par with weapons or clothing. Finally, there were the traditional heavy industries such as brickworks and especially mining and quarrying, which had always included a large measure of State control, which was now extended until, by the fourth century, nearly all of the sites came under direct imperial operation. The labour here was provided largely by convicts and to a lesser extent slaves, although working conditions varied. Other industries more peripheral to the State's interests – glassware, pottery, furniture, ornaments—gradually came to be grouped into compulsory corporations in the fourth century.

The new conditions produced a modest revival of cities in both East and West, although they could not regain their former extent and prosperity. The pattern of revival was in any case significantly different. In the earlier Empire city growth had reflected commercial and economic life, rich estates and the new settlements of a rising propertied class. Now it was determined more by the strategic needs of government. The more prominent cities to emerge out of the third-century decline were the administrative capitals close to the frontiers – Trier, Milan, Salonica, Sirmium, Nicomedia; the vital communication points such as Aquileia, Mursa,

Singidunum, Serdica, Adrianople; the defensive strongpoints on the Rhine such as Cologne, Mainz, Strasbourg, Bonn; and those manufacturing centres of direct interest to the State machine, such as Arles, Lyons, Ravenna. Whereas the Flavian cities had been self-sustaining municipalities, the cities of the Tetrarchy and after were rebuilt mainly by direction from above.

The great crisis had produced a steady migration of this class out of the cities and back to their rural estates, as far away as possible from invaders, soldiers and tax collectors. Of necessity, they had fallen back on a rural self-sufficiency which bypassed the chaotic conditions of money and trade. Absentee landlords became occupiers and managers of their lands again. With the return of security those who had created viable economic units of their estates had no inclination to return to an expensive and onerous life in the cities. Parallel with the stagnation of cities was therefore a growth of expensive and luxurious country villas. In Britain, while Verulamium and Silchester were in a dilapidated state, flourishing villas were springing up throughout Oxfordshire, Wiltshire, Hampshire and the South-East, many of which are still being excavated. True, these new rural aristocrats could not avoid the tentacles of the new tax machinery, or their liability for *munera*. But in the country they minimised their overheads, had far less frequent contact with the authorities, and in any case were in a better position to strike bargains when they did.

These estates were no longer slave-operated *latifundia*. For centuries now slave labour had become scarce and expensive (since the end of Roman military conquests) and it was cheaper for a landlord to lease out plots of land to free tenant farmers (*coloni*). A typical pattern consisted of the bulk of an estate parcelled out to *coloni*, while the owner kept a portion for himself which he still cultivated directly with slaves. The *colonus* traditionally enjoyed freedom of movement and contract, and during the crisis years many had abandoned their rented lands. Nonetheless, various pressures were slowly accumulating to tie him to the land, and make him more dependent on the large estate. In difficult times he easily fell into rent arrears and debts of every kind to his landlord, whose interest therefore coincided with the State's in holding him to his plot, and producing a taxable yield.

Similarly, the independent smallholder was at a great disadvantage towards the large estate owner, which drove him into something like tenant status. He might own his few acres of land, but other facilities such as mills, presses, draught animals or periodic extra labour all might have to be hired from the estate, at rates determined by the owner. The small man could not sustain a bad harvest without falling into debt which might force him to offer part of his labour in payment, or to rent part of the estate land in addition to his own (the two began to lose their difference). In threatening times, the arrangement sometimes offered a peasant and his family the protection of a rich and more influential patron; but the landlord could still treat it as a purely commercial relationship which he would exploit to the full. Whatever protection it did confer – over lawsuits and boundary disputes, or the depredations of the military, perhaps – was purchased only at a price which amounted to servitude.[12]

Whatever legal or traditional reservations Diocletian's government may have had about all this, from a fiscal point of view it offered very great advantages. Derelict land and rural depopulation was probably the greatest single economic ill the State had to grapple with, and it used every device it knew. Aurelian's policy was vigorously continued of offering a three-year tax exemption and hereditary ownership to anyone who took over vacant land. In Pannonia, Galerius launched large State schemes of land drainage and reclamation. In Gaul, Constantius settled many new communities of Alemanni and Franks in the vacant lands, and they farmed their lands as hereditary communities with corporate tax obligations – which could be commuted into recruits for the army. The State itself was the largest single land-owner, traditionally letting its lands to *coloni,* encouraging cultivators and penalising those who gave up their holdings. The Emperors fully exerted their right to confiscate deserted lands, but were still faced with the problem of how to get them back under the plough. Rather than multiply individual tenancies, they began simply to assign these new lands to a city council, who were then forced by the automatic tax liability to find them a cultivator.

These being the State's priorities, a class of large private land-owners who effectively bound their tenants to the land and prevented them leaving it, meshed into them very well. The large estates farmed efficiently for profit, raised production, reclaimed land, and acted as tax collectors for their tenants just as they might have done as city magistrates. They might neglect their municipal services, but they could readily substitute others. In this manner the late Roman State came into implicit alliance with the class of great landed *possessores,* against the *coloni.*

It was not the conscious intention either of Diocletian or Constantine to blur the distinction between slave and free status. But the decline in the economic importance of slaves, and the underlying logic of a liturgy system with its very different definitions of property rights, combined to bring slaves and landless *coloni* together in a single condition of unfreedom. To a tenant farmer with no independent land of his own, his rented plot represented all he had. Unless his rent was impossibly oppressive he would cling to it, especially if he had improved it through his own efforts. His landlord had every reason to keep him there, since he had to pay the tax on the plot, and new tenants were not easy to find. Thus, a hereditary security of tenure – which the law recognised – easily blended into an obligatory tie to that estate. The fact that he would routinely be counted in with the slaves for census purposes, and that his landlord would customarily answer for him in dealing with authority, gradually led jurists to think of him, for many purposes, as similar to a slave.

By Diocletian, most slaves in law and fact were no longer the brute chattels of earlier times. Their economic value had risen with scarcity, and their owners' treatment of them and right to dispose of them were restricted by a thicket of laws. Diocletian merely continued the trend when he prohibited the exposure of slave infants, and ruled that an owner killing his slave could face capital punishment: Constantine forbade splitting of slave families on sale.[13]

On the other side of the coin, the government's overriding interest in holding peasants to the land in communities brought the notion of the semi-slave (Inquilini) into general use. The landless tenant (though not those who still owned their few acres) was regarded as part and parcel of the estate. A series of legal decisions by

Constantine confirmed what was already common practice, that *coloni* and slaves alike were bound to their landlords in a hereditary unfree condition which we would compare to serfdom. Land-owners who shelter a *colonus* belonging to another must return him and pay his capitation tax for the period of absence:

> And as for the *coloni* themselves, it will be proper for such as contemplate flight, to be bound to a servile status, so that by virtue of this servitude they shall be compelled to fulfil the duties that befit free men.[14]

This, then, was the 'command' economy laboriously created by Aurelian, Diocletian and Constantine. The State's interest in the eonomy was what it had always been – as a source of taxes and a reservoir of resources to help it defend and govern. The emergencies and exhaustion inherited by Diocletian demanded far greater organisation, control and compulsion than before. The key to this was his vastly improved tax machine which netted all productive resources in its scope. But his tireless cataloguing of all wealth and manpower was little use as a tool of control, unless that labour stayed put. Since money was unstable, he had to purchase what he needed in other ways, demanding from each person whatever they could provide, trading goods and services, concessions and privileges according to a rough rule of equity, spreading the burdens as widely as possible. All had to serve, in their particular stations: the *decurion*, the manufacturer, the craftsman, proletarian, barbarian settler, *colonus* and even land-owner. Where law or custom did not already secure their service, then their property or labour had to be deposited in some organised public community which ensured them a place, but went surety for their performance. In theory, at least, every acre of usable land, and every trained pair of hands was put to work; and behind every man was some palpable guarantor who held him in his place.

In practice, the system was subject to all the clumsiness and approximation inherent in ancient government. Mobility of labour was sluggish, and most trades were near-hereditary anyway. The law was not concerned with an individual changing his trade, so much as deserting it altogether without providing a substitute; hence the responsibilities placed on the associations. The imbalance of incentives led to distortions of the State's own making. In lieu of money, State officials were granted immunity from municipal services, with the result that the bureaucracy later became swollen by *decuriones* bribing their way into even minor posts.

The policy was pragmatic, not ideological.[15] It adopted practices from Egypt and the Eastern Hellenic economies, but it grafted these on to Roman traditions wherever it could, and disguised rather than displayed the real scale of the change. Roman law still took property rights and personal liberty very seriously, at least among men of social rank. It is not as if there was some coherent, alternative, non-interventionist economic policy which Emperors of a different class and persuasion might have adopted. The Illyrian Emperors, certainly, did not believe in leaving things to work themselves out – that would mean abandoned fields, worthless money, greedy merchants fattening themselves while the towns starved and unpaid soldiers mutinied, as surely as night followed day. But in that respect, their outlook was only the natural, responsible view of any Roman ruler.

chapter eleven

·THE NEW ORDER·

THE WORK OF DIOCLETIAN WAS DECISIVE, HEROIC, AND RUTHLESS. ALMOST BY
AN ACT OF WILL HE STABILISED THE EMPIRE, TRUNCATED THE AGE OF
ANARCHY, AND INSTALLED THE MONARCHY THAT DID NOT END UNTIL 1453.
·MORTIMER CHAMBERS, IN *The Transformation of the Roman World*·

There are some things no ruler, however despotic, can command, and one of them is
public confidence in his state. He may issue fine coins with gods and cornucopia
proclaiming Prosperitas, Felicitas, Concordia, give lavish games and celebrations,
receive extravagant eulogies, or represent dubious treaties as immortal victories
meriting triumphal processions. But if his realm is actually crumbling, no gestures or
edicts of his will prevent men perceiving it, and making shift accordingly, even while
they flatter and cheer him. No ferocious laws or punishments will stop them burying
their gold, leaving their lands or deserting the old gods, if the times are indeed felt to
be without hope.

It had taken nearly 20 years of unceasing toil by Diocletian, his fellow Emperors
and his growing armies of soldiers and officials to produce conditions in which the
spiral of fear, emergency, ruin and despair could be reversed, and men could
cautiously lift their heads again. Even so, the work was far from complete; and the
State had to accompany it with unceasing propaganda of all kinds to capture and
hold the loyalty of its subjects, buttressed by various attempts at compulsion where
this failed. But there was now palpable substance in its claims. Compared with the
terrors men could recall and the prospect of universal desolation that had stared
them in the face, it seemed that Fate could after all be mastered; the worst was over;
the gods whose altars were everywhere burning again had not deserted Rome.

One did not need to be a soldier or strategist to be convinced that the Emperor's
victory titles were real enough. The great Persian victory in particular had become
legendary, with the capture of the Great King's family and quite fabulous quantities
of treasure. A citizen of one of the towns near to the Rhine or Danube no longer
lived under the perpetual shadow of barbarian sack and the prospect of having to
flee and abandon all he had. No longer did every other year bring another new name
on the coins, another new effigy hastily erected in every market-place, to be followed
inevitably by the clash of armies, whose predatory troops would seize his goods
whichever side won. He might see deserted acres of farmland slowly being settled
again, or drained for cultivation, new and strange-looking castles being built, his
own town walls strengthened, roads repaired, a new altar or temple dedicated. All

this he and his household would have to pay for one way or another, but it was properly registered and not just stolen from him, and others paid their share too. He would still encounter the bright dress and ornaments of the barbarians and hear their guttural tongue, but they would be new settlers or soldiers who, if they were alien, at least were not a direct threat.

Enclosing and underlying these signs of renewal was a driving spirit of innovation and a truly great plan. Men, far more conservative than today, observed different aspect of the change around them, but few comprehended all its inner connections. Just as Augustus three centuries before had 'restored the Republic' but in reality replaced the power of Senate and People with a subtly contrived form of monarchy, so Diocletian's restoration of the State was in fact a half-perceptible reconstruction of a new one, a fortress Empire in which each person was assigned his place and secured to it by new bonds.

Such a State was the logical culmination of decades of piecemeal experimentation by vigorous military Emperors struggling with intractable problems: the new fighting tactics and forts, the *annona,* compulsory services, the attempted currency reforms, the imperial style. But with Diocletian all these half-articulate trends become abruptly conscious and deliberate. He understood their implications and connections with a steady clarity that few Emperors had possessed. More than all the others, he knew what he was doing, as he drew their disparate threads together, carried them further, and added sweeping new reforms of his own. Nothing is more expressive of his cast of mind than the sheer coherence with which his different reforms intermeshed. Central to everything were imperial stability and frontier defence. The first was solved by rationalising the distant military power centres into a college of Emperors: strong men, so chosen that Diocletian could lead them without dominating. This gave regional military control, which both discouraged usurpers, and allowed the frontiers once more to be sealed by provincial field armies backing up the new chains of forts. To pay for this, State revenue was totally overhauled with the extraordinarily detailed census of all wealth in *iuga* and *capita*. This bypassed the inflated currency, produced a comprehensive and workable tax system in kind and services, ended outright military seizures, and allowed an adjustable annual budget to be calculated and published. To run the tax system, to restore proper civil administration, to service the defence zones, and to supervise all these functions, the provinces were sliced into more manageable units and placed under vicars. To limit the scope for separatist revolts and encourage a habitually obedient bureaucracy, these civil officials lost their military powers and became a separate establishment. To ensure that the economy continued to support this great burden, every kind of service from weaving to military conscription was counted as a tax obligation, and each man registered in an organisation responsible for delivery. Exemption from such obligations could itself serve as salary for the officials who exacted it.

It was a work of several decades, which is why he needed helpers. It proceeded by trial and error as conditions allowed, and there were of course failures, some of them all the greater for the scope of the attempt – witness the monumental folly of the Price Edict, and later, the drive to coerce the Christians once and for all into worshipping the State gods. But never did he slacken the impetus, or lose the overall sense of direction, or allow easy corners to be cut. In an age that depended far less than ours on central instructions, and far more on the discretion of the man on the spot, it took Diocletian's infinite capacity for detail and unflagging energies to translate the plans into physical operation. We find him always on the move, inspecting the Danube defences and new building, supervising the land survey and the tax measures, overseeing the reorganisation of a province – at Sirmium, Durostorum, Ratiaria, Viminacium, Serdica, Adrianople, Antioch, or the Nile cities.[1] If the route maps are faulty, get to work drawing up accurate ones; if the land survey is out of date, or the citizen roll unreliable, then appoint men to start counting and measuring from scratch; if the mass of laws and imperial decisions is confusing, then get the best jurists to sort them out into an intelligible compilation. Traditional methods and vague assurances would not do: as little as possible was to be left to chance. Everything had to be weighed and judged by results, and this meant proper records, figures, reports. The habits of military thoroughness and regulation were to be consciously applied in every department of administration. But in contrast to others who are dominated by detail or slaves to the rulebook, Diocletian saw every element steadily as a part of the whole, and was prepared to mobilise them all in imaginative new schemes. Rarely had such a combination of qualities been so matched to the needs of the age: he was indeed, as the historian says, 'vir necessitatem rei publicae'.[2] A modern writer on the period, Ramsay MacMullen, expresses it:

> He was a man of ideas, for historical stature fully the equal of Augustus.
>   But how different, since the times demanded it! Where Augustus proceeded gingerly in his rebuilding of a riven nation and had fifty years to do it, Diocletian must act abruptly, placing or displacing all the resources of his realm like little chessmen: here a castle, there a knight; here a pawn, there (in a mine, a quarry, a *fabrica*) a bishop. All must serve his purposes. When Constantine had added his own measures, then indeed all his subjects not actually administering the system, and even some of its ranks, were meant to move about and have their being only as he directed them.[3]

This leads finally to consideration of the whole Absolute character of the monarchy which Diocletian erected over the remains of the civil Principate, and which was to continue for a millennium. It has been described in many terms – as an Oriental Despotism[4] or as 'an autocracy tempered by the legal right of revolution'.[5] But to approach the issue, we need first to look at one more institution that underwent important development under Diocletian, and which was essential to the way monarchical power operated and was defined: the institution of Roman law.

Other great civilisations of course had their law codes and judges, but none had the same deeply legalistic ideology as Rome, none accorded such importance to public, explicit legal decisions in their daily affairs from the earliest times. Thus there had evolved unique traditions of advocacy and adjudication, and a highly sophisticated, self-conscious civil jurisprudence. Roman concepts of political authority had grown out of their concepts of legal authority: their leaders were essentially magistrates long before they were generals, dictators or Emperors. Though rival factions murdered one another in the Forum, generals intimidated the Senate with their soldiers, or Emperors gathered all the strings of power into their hands, Romans always discriminated sharply between legal and illegal acts: law might be violated, but it could not be blurred. The same careful distinctions they had always made in their arguments concerning leases or marriages or inheritance, they carried over to defining the proper powers of their rulers. A law might be a bad one, its application cruel or iniquitous, but there was still all the difference between a law made by the competent authority and applied by regular process, and mere despotic arbitrariness. Emperors were expected to observe and apply the law essentially as they found it, including the laws of their predecessors. Despite the Senate's executive impotence it still possessed a final spiritual sanction over the Emperor after his death, if he was judged to have ruled unjustly or tyrannically: a vote of *damnatio memoriae* entailed not just refusal of divine honours but cancellation of all his edicts – tearing him out of the book of law which was perhaps his most important form of survival.

The great pattern in all this was that the institution of civil, private law governing property, status, individual rights, predated the political authority which Emperors gradually accumulated to themselves. They had to adapt to it and rule through it. Their own general edicts or mandates of good government were superimposed on the great body of private law and required to be consistent with its principles and spirit. Over tax disputes, for example, the imperial State was a party before the courts, with its own advocates; and down to the very last days of the Empire, professional legal advice was an essential part of the imperial court.

The early third century brought classical jurisprudence to its peak with such great jurists as Papinian, Ulpian and Paul. It also brought legal order to the various expressions of the imperial will, establishing clearly that not only his general pronouncements but also his many decisions on points of private law – the rescript system – were an authentic source of law. But with the convulsions that overtook the Empire, the operation of law was disrupted like every other department of life. Governors' courts became infrequent or simply ceased as city life suffered and the educated classes dwindled. Emperors, fighting for their existence, were unable to reply to the stream of legal requests reaching them: the output of rescripts became erratic after the 240s, and almost ceased after 260.

Diocletian, as we have seen, was concerned to put the legal system back into working order after decades of neglect, and ensure that all citizens had access to it. Governors, now multiplied, were instructed to hear all important cases in person, and he himself tirelessly replied to the hundreds of petitions and queries from great and small. His output of rescripts was prodigious: over 1,000 still survive, and this is only a portion of the total. But he did more than just revive the earlier system. With the help of two exceptional jurists, Gregorius and Hermogenianus, he evolved a distinct policy which would, he hoped, give greater finality and clarity to the law, and make its fixed principles better understood by his subjects.[6]

For all his innovation in government, Diocletian – again like Augustus – was profoundly traditional in morality, culture and religion. Despite the instruments of Hellenistic kingship which he adopted, his own fundamental values were self-consciously Roman, not Greek or Oriental. To him, Roman law was a sacred inheritance whose pure principles had to be preserved, and this placed a special responsibility on the rescript office. It was this accumulation of imperial decisions which lawyers had increasingly come to treat as a standard. Private collections were made of them, and they were used in the law schools. Diocletian therefore aimed to make his rescripts the vehicle for reaffirmation of pure Roman law, which, as conservative jurists saw it, was in danger of distortion from Greek and Eastern influences. Unlike imperial correspondence, rescripts were issued in Latin only, so that the law schools now growing up in the Greek East, such as Beirut, had to teach and think in the Latin tongue – a trend Diocletian approved and fostered.

His legal decisions emphatically breathe the traditional Roman mores. Non-Roman family institutions such as polygamy, adoption of brothers, or consanguinous marriages, are all rejected. *Patria Potestas* is upheld. Sons may not testify against their fathers. Contracts are sacred. Personal status is fixed by law, not custom or opinion. Sometimes the tone of the rescripts is factual and logical:

> In respect of a contract of sale, once the transaction has been properly concluded, one party may not at any time withdraw his agreement. This is contrary to our rescript, which is the law our treasury is determined to uphold.[7]

Elsewhere, it is more didactic:

> It is common knowledge that nobody living under the authority and name of Rome is permitted two wives. A praetor's edict has singled out such men as meriting public disgrace, and no qualified magistrate will allow such behaviour to go unpunished.[8]

The wording was normally drafted by the imperial secretary *a libellis,* though the Emperor had to read, approve and subscribe it in his own hand. By analysis of the style of rescripts between 282 and 305, Honoré has identified the two prominent secretaries to Diocletian, whose traditionalist attitudes he approved and whose talents he put to use. Gregorius held the secretaryship for two periods, from 284 to 287, and 289 to 290. He was conservative, patriotic, religious, a lawyer of plain style and orthodox grammar, who not only answered petitioners but strove to educate them in the underlying principles of the law, as instanced by their particular cases. In furtherance of this aim he compiled and published, probably with Diocletian's support, a collection of legal enactments and decisions of Emperors from Hadrian down to his own time, 291. This was the *Codex Gregorianus,* intended to propagate knowledge of the law and its unchanging rational principles.

But the programme went further. In 293, with the creation of the Tetrarchy with all its hopes of a new era, Diocletian appointed another eminent jurist, Hermogenianus, as secretary. He has been described as 'one of the leading Roman lawyers ... (who) ... deserves to be called the last classical lawyer and the first legal theorist'.[9] His rescripts were of outstanding quality, and carefully compiled into a collection which was intended to serve as a model of legal reasoning. Hermogenianus did not just state or explain Roman law, but typically deduced the particular decision from some general principle by logical inference: he was in effect demonstrating to the petitioner how a grasp of legal principles, carefully applied to the facts in hand, will yield the answer he seeks. Law is systematic, rational and, in principle, intelligible to all civilised men:

> If he (your master) gave you to his wife before their marriage and afterwards, having left a legacy, expressed the wish in his will or codicil that you should be freed by his heirs, then there is no doubt that they were obliged to purchase you and free you (since they accepted the inheritance and with it, the obligations due to the deceased). Therefore a fideicommissary freedom is due to you.[10]

> No one is compelled to remain in a state of joint ownership against their will. Therefore the governor, when he has been approached, will ensure that those goods he ascertains to be held in common by you and your sister, are divided.[11]

The complete collection of rescripts for the two busy years 293–4 was published as the *Codex Hermogenianus*. Diocletian's purpose, through his secretary, was both to establish a standard, and to give a certain finality to these interpretations. Since essentially the same problems would continually recur, this exemplary work would be an authoritative reference to their solutions, which might relieve governors (and Emperors) of a purely repetitive burden, and also protect the essential character of the law from drift through continual new interpretation. Roman law would become the property of all. Like his predecessors Sulla and Caesar, Diocletian envisaged a comprehensive codification of the main body of law, which henceforth would change only marginally, and no longer be the sole property of lawyers. It was an ideal that was to recur in the fifth century and again in the sixth, when it was brought to fulfilment. The Codes of Gregorius and Hermogenianus were in large part incorporated in the great Code of Justinian, published in 529, which, together with the Digest of 533, remains the most comprehensive monument of Roman legal thought and its profound legacy to European civilisation.

So, while Diocletian was steadily bringing every department of life under imperial control, and amplifying the Emperor's position from *Princeps* to *Dominus,* he was simultaneously strengthening the foundations of law and promoting respect for it. Numerous rescripts affirm the principle, deeply ingrained in Roman political tradition, that nobody, including the Emperor, is above the law. A fifth-century edict states clearly: 'The truth is that Our authority depends on the authority of law. To submit Our sovereignty to the laws is something greater than the imperial power'.[12]

Modern attitudes are apt to conflate Absolutism with Despotism, and even Totalitarianism. The new monarchy was overtly absolute, but it was certainly not arbitrary. Its style had strong Oriental elements; but it was far removed from the Asiatic despotisms which Romans so abhorred, where (as they supposed) individual rights had no meaning, and each subject high or low was merely the slave of the monarch, his property and security entirely subject to the monarch's pleasure. As Romans saw it, they were ruled by a sole monarch, but they were still free citizens within the law. The body of laws and the spirit of law (*ius*) existed independently of the Emperor's will and constrained, through tradition and practice, his method of ruling and his powers. But this was an implicit, inertial constraint. There was no way in which a law could be condemned as 'unconstitutional'. However, since change was the exception, it was required to be minimally consistent with existing law, just as it was required to be competently drafted. (A Byzantine lawbook firmly rules that an Emperor's rescripts, at least, must not contradict existing general laws.)[13] As for his edicts, these were expected to be broadly consistent with existing law, if only because there was no certain way of repealing earlier laws, short of *damnatio*. An edict could supersede an earlier law, at least in the Emperor's lifetime, but it did not wholly eradicate it. Edicts operated not as detailed instructions but as general expressions of the imperial will, which governors of necessity had to adapt to their actual circumstances. Hence, an edict which was unworkable or highly unpopular or in flat contradiction to established law would tend to be diluted in proportion to the physical distance from the Emperor's presence.

There was no political check to stop an Emperor carrying out private murders or holding his own secret treason trials. But since justice essentially required public conviction by proper standards of proof, such measures were invariably looked on as shameful perversions of it. Of course, he could ignore public opinion, with impunity in the short run. But this included the opinion of his own educated bureaucracy which he needed to rule. If he outraged it entirely, they would be the more willing to support a rebel, should one arise. And here is the point of the paradoxical description of the monarchy as an autocracy tempered by the legal right of revolution. Unlike Medieval kingdoms where the blood royal was an overriding requirement for legitimate succession, Rome and Byzantium never entirely lost the tradition of military 'election', despite Diocletian's efforts to weaken it. No Emperor could ever just rest complacent in a divine hereditary right. If a section of the army elevated their own candidate and he defeated the Emperor, he automatically became Emperor both de facto and de jure, and the civil bureaucracy transferred their allegiance to him with a clear conscience.

There was no separation of supreme powers, no obligation on the Emperor to consult the wishes of any other established body, and no legal, peaceful way of opposing his will. All this had been true for a very long time. Diocletian legitimised absolutism, making explicit the Emperor's position as sole source of political authority, abolishing the last veils which had suggested otherwise. In none of the official formalities was it even suggested that the Senate was consulted about anything; as Gibbon says, the mortal wound he dealt the Senate was to ignore it.[14] More pointedly, he abruptly ended the Augustan tradition of 'partnership', which in practice had long meant mainly that the top appointments were reserved for the senatorial class. This did not destroy a separate estate of the realm, but it did alter considerably the social composition of the government. It buried for good the old *civilitas,* the 'special relationship' of the Emperor with senatorial, sentimentally republican manners.

To us, the apparently natural trend of progress in modern Europe since the seventeenth century has been from absolute monarchy to constitutional pluralism and representative government. From the time Rome acquired a world empire, the trend was in the opposite direction, from the narrow elective senatorial oligarchy and turbulent demagoguery of a City State, to a universal monarchy on which all real power devolved. The 'liberty' that Brutus fought for had been to a large extent the privilege of a few senators to exploit the provinces. To millions of provincials, by contrast, it was the Augustan Empire that set them free, by the steady extension of citizenship and the equality of provincials with Italians. The final stage, the new absolutism, amounted to this: that the Emperor no longer pretended, even in the most tenuous way, to be *primus inter pares* of any other broad ruling group – neither the old senatorial aristocracy nor the new military grandees. His position was that of a monarch entirely in his own right, over and above them all. After three centuries the last shreds of traditional embarrassment about monarchy were disgorged.

The suggestion that the new order was in some sense totalitarian arises out of the increasing compulsory State organisation of what were previously voluntary guilds and municipalities.[15] This was a great contrast with the past, and made the new Empire a more oppressive place to live in. In the second century the profusion of prosperous, self-governing cities had been the glory of Rome's achievement in the Mediterranean. They had seemed concrete proof that the free life of the citizen in the *polis* could be combined with a monarchy. But this great vitality of the urban gentry had been destroyed in the crisis and never really returned. For the most part, cities were of smaller size and population, and in more straitened circumstances: men of property either could not or would not supply their native cities with the municipal services they once had done. With the middle-sized land-owners this was due to hardship, but with the wealthier, who had benefited from the return of security, it was a more atomistic self-interest, a turning inward to cultivate one's villa. Hence men had to be compelled to do what they had previously done willingly, and the municipal councils survived as peripheral instruments of the State, rather than self-sustaining bodies. It was not because the new Emperors were hostile to independent cities (or trade associations), but precisely because they recognised how indispensable they were, that compulsion was resorted to: the encroachment was an unfortunate necessity, not a violation.

But the effect nonetheless was bleak. In place of a thriving civic life on which the Emperor's hand had rested lightly, there was fragmentation and inertia. Town life was kept going not spontaneously but by pressures from the centre: the public spirited citizen was replaced by the uniformed bureaucrat, whose cloaked figure looks out from the Byzantine mosaics.

A very different picture was provided by the many strategic cities, especially along the Danube highway, through which Emperors frequently passed, and which had acquired imperial residences. Here, with generous money and patronage from the treasuries, splendid public buildings were going up, and the mood was of expansion, activity and prosperity. Here, the New Order was apparent in grand visible expression in new styles, stimulated by Diocletian's passion for building, which his colleagues imitated. His reign began the last great period of Roman architecture, many of whose forms were later adapted into Christian and Byzantine building. As Vogt puts it, 'Absolutism stimulated Roman public architecture to its final flowering'.[16]

The most noticeable change from the classical style is a deliberately massive quality in the new architecture. In the long period of emergencies, civic building had come to a halt. The resources of architects and masons had been dragooned into building military walls and fortifications on an unprecedented scale. Towns had become strongpoints, enveloped with high walls and bastions, and defensive tactics had dictated the shortest practical wall circuits. Ornament, and the generous layout of space were naturally sacrificed, and indeed became most incongruous with these grim reminders of the times. The curtain walls built by Aurelian around Rome itself ('that great but melancholy labour') are abruptly military and utilitarian, contrasting sharply with the gracious temples and porticoes they enclose and defend.[17]

Since this was the permanent condition of things, the spirit of fortification-architecture entered the styles of the new public buildings the victorious military rulers commissioned: but they were combined skilfully with civic forms. A natural meeting point was the design of gateways, fortified yet also expressive and monumental. Compare the stark military gates in Aurelian's wall, with the Porta Nigra at Trier, built under Constantius. The latter combines a great defended city gate with the imposing dominance of the triumphal arch. Its projecting towers and severe engaged colonnades have a heavy, defiant grandeur, an embodiment of defensive strength which is new in Roman civic buildings. A similar transformation can be seen in the Porta Aurea of Diocletian's palace at Split. This too is a defended courtyard gateway, overtly military in inspiration; but its strong arcades with niches for overlooking statues still proclaim a civilised, protective spirit.

In fact the whole plan of Diocletian's palace illustrates the change well. Compared with the relaxed serenity of Hadrian's villa at Tivoli, for example, it appears a blocklike, rectangular fortress, capable of resisting an enemy if need be (as in later centuries it did). The layout of buildings is no longer free and open but firmly symmetrical, divided by axial cruciform streets in the manner of a legionary camp, each sector having its properly allotted function: gardens, private apartments, public square, temples. Here as elsewhere, the main palace building came to be known as the *praetorium,* or headquarters. Yet, it is not a true fortress either: we can immediately see that by comparing it with a real fort of similar size, such as Portchester. At Split the colonnaded streets, the generous arched window apertures in walls and towers, the long arcade facing the sea with its series of loggias, are all integral civil elements. It is an expression of unified power and authority, but not a functioning military bastion.

Another obvious feature of the new architecture is its size, and the use of forms which emphasise this from the interior – high barrel vaulting, and especially domes. Even when an architect deliberately follows earlier styles, as in Diocletian's public baths in Rome, he does so on a larger scale. These baths, in the north-east of the City, were designed to counterbalance Caracalla's baths, built a century earlier, whose plan they mirror faithfully – three great rooms, palatial central hall, columned vestibules, and square plan. But this time each side measured well over 3,000 feet: the most extensive and magnificent public leisure facilities in the Roman world. Today its great shell faces the Piazza Repubblica, easily enclosing the National Museum of Rome. The magnificent central hall of the baths forms the church of S. Maria degli

Angeli. The new Imperial baths at Trier, done on a different plan, are on a similar grand scale by the standard of most Gallic cities. Its composition skilfully combined dome, cross-vaulting and barrel vaulting. It was in bath complexes such as these that architects confidently experimented with these forms, which were soon repeated in the imperial basilicas and later, in the new Christian churches. The huge basilica begun in Rome by Maxentius shortly after Diocletian's retirement, and later completed by Constantine, is a striking case. Here the visitor was overawed by a series of gorgeously coffered half-domes high above him, leading finally to the great apse in which the Emperor – or his gigantic effigy – was enthroned. At Trier, the basilica is longitudinal like a cathedral, its rhythm of columns again focussing all on to the imperial end apse. Diocletian's mausoleum at Split is a domed interior, still with classical columns and entablature, but already suggestive of the early domed church: and its octagonal exterior a clear anticipation of the Byzantine.[18]

The blocklike, explicit symmetries of the new architecture resulted from more subtle influences than just the military Emperors' liking for forts. Among later third-century architects there was a reaction against the free arrangement of buildings of classical Hellenism; against the interflow of open and enclosed spaces by means of colonnades and porticoes, against traditional wall decoration, detail and the use of naturalistic sculpture. Instead, everything had to be clearly subordinated to the total plan of the building or complex of buildings. Individual detail must not distract the eye from the dominant controlling forces of mass and dimension: where ornament had formerly rescued a building from uniformity and monotony, now it was dispensed with for the very same reason. Spaces too had to be firmly enclosed and separated from the area outside, so that a building was to be experienced primarily from the interior.

The reasons for this profound change lay only partly in the new spirit of absolutism in government and society, embodied in the heavy symmetry, uniformity and enclosing character of these buildings. In particular, it was the hieratic character of the new, Eastern Emperor-worship that promoted the strict separation of profane, outer, from sacred, inner spaces. The person entering the throne room of one of the palaces or the aisles of a great basilica had to feel he was in a mysterious area of divine power, different in kind from the open square he had come from. Hence too, the move away from statues and high relief in favour of the subtle use of light, separating brilliant illumination from shadow, or playing on to shimmering mosaics. Columns gradually disappear into smooth walls, which cease to obtrude and are mere enclosures for the manipulation of space, light and colour: we are already half way to Byzantine Christendom.

This 'spiritualising' of interior space was also the result of new religious undercurrents of the times, which were eventually synthesised in fourth-century Christianity. Neoplatonism and its offshoots stressed not the harmony, but the conflict between soul and body, pure spirit and base imprisoning matter. The true goal of man was no longer civic virtue in the Just City, but the freeing of the soul from such imprisonments. Such an attitude dealt a slow but mortal wound to the inspiration of classical art with its harmonious bodily forms and its insistence on organic proportion. In sculpture, the natural unity of composition is replaced by a rigidly abstract, imposed arrangement. Concrete individual elements become stereo-types, symbols of a higher meaning.

All this was very serviceable to the new type of monarchy Diocletian had established. Of course, his architects and sculptors might have just resurrected the styles of the High Empire and repeated the buildings of Trajan or Hadrian, in a rather hollow gesture of continuity – just as his legal and religious policies were guided by a rather forced Roman traditionalism. Instead, the materials were already there to give appropriate expression to the new order. The trend in portraiture was away from individual likeness towards the simplified, iconic type – a trend which had spread from the East, especially Egypt, in the second half of the third century. It allowed Diocletian, on his coins and official statues, to present himself and Maximian as inseparable and identical brother-rulers. Later, in the Venice group, all four Tetrarchs are shown in this way. Emperors thus ceased to be individual persons and became instances of an eternal superhuman type, the Basileus or Pharoah.

Even more significant is the composition of groups. In earlier monuments the grouping of figures (soldiers in battle, or citizens in procession) is always natural, flowing and relaxed, according to classical canons dating from the fifth century BC, with sensitive rendering of individual detail. On the Arch of Galerius we first begin to see a change. The Emperor is larger than life, the dwarflike soldiers grouped hieratically around him. By the time of the Arch of Constantine, barely 20 years later, the change is almost complete. Instead of the natural unity of the figures there is a mechanical ordering in horizontal rows, as straight and rhythmic as a colonnade or a rank of guards, all strictly subordinated to the dominant figure of the Emperor. At the same time naturalistic detail, such as the folds of draperies, becomes stiff and impressionistic, the lines no longer shaped by a chisel, but merely suggested by quick use of a running drill. In this dramatic change, the freezing of figures according to an imposed order, we already sense a distinct anticipation of the art of the Middle Ages and Byzantium. The traditional groupings of high relief figures in natural poses and typically in profile, were beginning their transformation into the flat ethereal mosaics and frescoes of saints, looking down full-face with the eyes of the spirit.

The energies of the new architecture were to provide the elements of the new Christian architecture, which spoke not of a social but a transcendental order. The long colonnaded basilicas whose lines all led to the place of imperial authority, evolved naturally into the basic nave church whose early examples are still to be seen in S. Sabina, S. Maria Maggiore and a host of others. The domed or octagonal tombs of the Emperors were the precursor of the early round church, Baptistery or shrine. The colossal vaulted bath complexes and basilicas paved the way, technically and aesthetically, to more ambitious combinations of the domed form, which culminated in the unsurpassed achievements of the great Byzantine churches.

But all this was in the future. Diocletian's conservatism about Roman values was nowhere more pronounced than in his devotion to the old gods of the State. His New Order was to be one which would reaffirm and celebrate the ancestral pieties, and in which Christianity was an alien body. Nobody could have forseen that within a generation the new religion would be victorious and dominant, and impart a quite different spiritual character to the reconstructed Roman State.

part four

TRIUMPHS AND DEFEATS

chapter twelve

·THE GODS ARE ALIVE·

THE IMMORTAL GODS IN THEIR PROVIDENCE HAVE SO DESIGNED THINGS
THAT GOOD AND TRUE PRINCIPLES HAVE BEEN ESTABLISHED BY THE WISDOM
AND DELIBERATIONS OF EMINENT, WISE, AND UPRIGHT MEN. IT IS WRONG TO
OPPOSE THESE PRINCIPLES, OR DESERT THE ANCIENT RELIGION FOR SOME
NEW ONE, FOR IT IS THE HEIGHT OF CRIMINALITY TO TRY AND REVISE
DOCTRINES THAT WERE SETTLED ONCE AND FOR ALL BY THE ANCIENTS, AND
WHOSE POSITION IS FIXED AND ACKNOWLEDGED.

Thus speaks Diocletian in 302, in his instructions to Julianus, proconsul of Africa, concerning the Manicheans.[1] Despite the xenophobic atmosphere which prompted that ferocious ruling, his emphatic traditionalism is a faithful echo of Eternal Rome as seen through the eyes of the soldier-Emperors, self-conscious inheritors of its spiritual legacy. This traditionalism provides as good a starting point as any to the understanding of Diocletian's fervent revival of the old Roman cults, and his eventual bloody conflict with the new phenomenon of organised Christianity.

The apparent horror of all change and questioning, which seems more appropriate to a nineteenth-century pope than a reforming, pragmatic Roman Emperor, was neither an unusual nor an extreme attitude. The historian Cassius Dio puts the same advice, approvingly, into the mouth of one of Augustus' councillors: 'Everywhere worship the gods according to the customs of the fathers, and compel others to do likewise. Those who import anything alien into their worship must be condemned and punished, not just because that is the will of the gods, whose contemners have no respect for anyone, but also because men who wilfully introduce new gods seduce many others into an alien habit. So are conspiracies, factions and secret societies born.'[2]

And yet, of course, official religion could and did coexist quite amicably with a great variety of other individual cults, often having secret and arcane rites, whose gods were outside the traditional Graeco-Roman Pantheon. Also, the worship and very identities of many of the Roman deities themselves were continually being modified by assimilation of various local, national gods among the distant peoples of the Empire. The Punic Baal was identified with Zeus-Jupiter, the Celtic Maponus with Apollo, and likewise for numberless others. To a great extent 'alien' things were being imported into the worship of the gods all the time, without causing any political tensions. This seeming paradox is lessened by appreciating the very different nature of traditional Roman religion from the religion we are familiar with at the latter end of the Christian era. In modern Europe, for example, official religious toleration has largely come about through the exhaustion of fanaticisms and the slow decline in the importance of religion altogether. Some have been inclined to think of Roman government's toleration in a similar way, as a more or less secular preoccupation with statecraft which did not deeply care what or how people worshipped, provided they kept the law and respected conventional propriety. Had this been so, the specific persecution of Christianity at a time when it had long since ceased to be regarded as politically subversive, would not have made sense. Roman imperial governments always took religion seriously, and were quite foreign to a polite ruling-class agnosticism or indifference which is some-times found among the Greeks. But it was not religion as we are accustomed to think of it.[3]

The old gods of the Mediterranean were all at bottom particular deities, in contrast to the unqualified universality of the great monotheisms. They were originally gods of peoples, places, cities or aspects of the world with which their identities were bound up. Even when their worship had spread over continents, their titles still tied them to some special place: Capitoline Jove, Paphian Venus, Ephesian Diana and so on. However powerful they were, however great their domains, they were still a proper part of the cosmos, not above and distinct from it. Even Zeus had a birth and a history at a particular place and time. It was as natural to acknowledge a people's gods, with their finite but legitimate sphere of influence, as to acknowledge their customs and country: there was no contradiction at all in worshipping them as well as one's own, and indeed it was required by diplomatic etiquette. The Olympian gods were dominant and universal mainly in the sense that Rome had made one fatherland out of the nations of the Mediterranean, and wherever Roman magistrates ruled and Roman soldiers were stationed, Jupiter, Minerva, Mars, Hermes and the others would be worshipped. But this dominance was neither exclusive, nor missionary. Among a recently conquered people, such as Diocletian's remote ancestors, acceptance of the Olympian cults was merely part of the slow Romanisation of the local aristocracies and the acknowledgement of Roman authority.

The gods were divine rulers and governors rather than transcendental beings: immortal, and more powerful than men, but not of an utterly different order. They could control the forces of the natural world and the fortunes of mortals, and were entitled to the reverence due to any wise, benevolent overlord; but hardly the unqualified awe and self-abnegation demanded by Jehovah or Allah. They were represented everywhere in statues, on pottery, mosaic floors and other public or private ornaments in familiar classical dress without any sense of irreverence. People's relations to them were of a piece with their other relations in their earthly life, bound up with their social identities and all the rituals which gave expression to them. A person needed the help of the gods to steer him satisfactorily through the world; religious observance was inseparable from an upright life, and priesthoods a public office like any other magistracy. Traditional religion was not a separate and profound dimension in a person's life distinct from his social existence, and there was little stress on salvation in an afterlife. Having one's name perpetuated and one's memory revered by later generations in this world was the only real, desirable form of survival for most old Romans.[4]

Devotion was thus barely separable from one's other loyalties and one's civic position: it was only through a religious act that these loyalties could be sincerely and adequately expressed. Whatever the defects of Durkheim's general thesis that the 'real' object of religious veneration is (in some sense) Society,[5] it is probably more appropriate to ancient Roman religion than any other. Their interest in the gods was not in the least speculative, but centred on the gods' relation to social life, its sacred bonds and duties, and the cohesion and moral health of the State. When Lucan in the *Pharsalia* adopts a stark atheism its grounds are entirely moral ones – how can there be any provident gods when Romans are allowed to massacre one another and victory go to the Caesarean forces of crime?[6] In a certain sense, the old gods of Rome had no existence independently of the City. Cicero and especially Varro, come closest to saying that the gods are human institutions – this in a spirit of reverence, not cynicism. If the City cannot survive without the favour of the gods, then conversely, without the City and its continued worship of them, the gods would dwindle into a most shadowy and dubious existence.[7]

Central to the social-religious attitudes was the concept of *Pietas* which embodied, in a way we have lost since the rise of liberal individualism, the deep obligations which tie a person to their social roots, more basic than any contract. It encompassed the things one owed to one's parents, to one's city and country, to the ancestors who had built and handed on what existed and whose culture one inherited, and to the gods who protected all these. The god or the genius of a city represented all that was precious and permanent, that distinguished a homeland from just a collection of buildings, and its way of life from the arrangements of a passing tenant. Another such concept was *Felicitas*: not personal happiness or random good luck, but the healthy thriving proper to a person who lives and acts well, indicating that the gods are on his side. It included the notions of success, influence and fortune: not a chance condition to be envied, but a virtue to be admired. The righteousness and fitness of a ruler was to be inferred from his *felicitas* as much as from the wisdom and justice of his acts. The deep connection between *pietas* and *felicitas* was not purely a contingent one, a casual exchange whereby a person or city bought the god's favours by sacrifice: both were aspects of the same broad attitude which was entailed in having the right kind of relationship to the gods.

It can be seen how different is the strong traditionalism expressed by Diocletian and Cassius Dio, from the later orthodoxies of the great monotheisms, which demanded uniformity and authority in belief, ritual and religious organisation. For the Romans, to revere the gods at all, *was* to revere them in the manner of the ancestors in an unbroken continuity of relationships, according to rites believed to be as old as mankind. Customs could be combined, but deliberate *innovation* in worship was almost self-contradictory. Other gods could not displace the Olympians, but they too could and should be honoured: it was right for a provincial to revere his own national, ancestral gods in just the same way, and for a traveller in that country to do likewise. As Celsus said of the Jewish religion, it may have seemed weird, but at least it was in the manner of their ancestors. On the other side atheism, denial of the gods, was not so much heretical opinion as an act of impiety, like rejecting one's parents or people.[8]

As subjects and citizens of the Roman State, everyone was expected to demonstrate their common loyalty by participating in the appropriate festivals and honouring the gods of Rome and the genius of the Emperor. The form of this demonstration, however, was not just conventional, in the sense that it could equally be accomplished by some other expressive gesture: sacrifice was what the gods had always required, and what would therefore ensure their protection for the Empire. In Horace's words, 'So long as you obey the gods, you will rule'.[9] This ancient verity is similarly expressed in the Sibylline verses, which Zosimus quotes in his description of the Secular Games, traditionally celebrated in Rome every 110-year cycle:

Whenever man's longest span of life
Comes round its cycle of one hundred and ten years,
Remember, Roman, however forgetful,
Remember to do all these things
In honour of the gods undying
On the plain washed by Tiber's wave ...

... Then do you make offerings
To the procreant Fates, both lambs and dark she-goats.
Gratify the goddesses of childbirth
With incense fit. Next, for Tellus,
Teeming everywhere, slaughter a black sow.
Let bulls, all white, be led to Jupiter's altar
By day, not night. For the heavenly gods
Daytime sacrifices alone are pleasing ...

... Both day and night, let a vast throng
Continually attend the gods' chairs.
Mix solemnity with laughter.
May these things always be in your hearts and minds,
And all the land of Italy and Latium
Will ever submit to your sovereignty.[10]

Such a religion was a strong social and political cement in the unique Roman achievement of extending the culture of the City State to World Empire. Its acceptance in lands as different as Britain, Africa, and Dalmatia was because of its inherent respect for traditional gods and toleration of local diversity, not in spite of it. Because it was particular, ancestral, and had no interest in theology (unlike the great universal religions of the Near East), it served the interests of political harmony without imposing orthodoxy. In the long period of consolidation in which provincials achieved social equality with Latins and Italians, it offered a powerful expression of civic pride, Roman patriotism, continuity and membership of something far greater than one's own individual life, especially if one occupied or aspired to a recognised social position. Through it, a man whose ancestors were perhaps obscure tribesmen or slaves, could become not only the respected dignitary of his own proud native city, but inheritor of a mighty eternal civilisation, repeating the same sacred ceremonies, occupying the same offices and entering the direct line of the fabulous, long dead Romans whose matchless virtues had given them mastery over the whole earth. Its rituals were dignified and impressive, containing little or nothing of emotional mass enthusiasm: a mood that would meet the approval of an Enlightenment gentleman or a Confucian mandarin.

But it held out no satisfaction at all to men's deeper, more personal and intellectual religious longings: the sense of the holy and ineffable, the mysteries of creation and existence, the individual's cosmic loneliness and fear of extinction, his yearning for surrender and ecstatic communion with his god. To supply these things, men turned to the very different mystery cults, with their ancient roots in Thrace, Syria, Egypt, Persia, and Phrygia.

Many of these had been accepted among Romans from an early time and achieved great respectability. The mysteries of Eleusis, into which several Emperors had been initiated, was one of the most prominent. Although the nature of the rites remained a close secret, its central archaic myth was the abduction and rape of the maid Persephone by the god of the underworld, and the consequent dark blight laid on the world by her grieving, wandering mother Demeter, goddess of fertility: finally her daughter was restored to her and living things resurrected again, but she had to return to the underworld for six months every year. The ceremony in the Hall of the Mysteries seems to have involved vivid re-enactment of the story, the dark journey through death, then finally the brilliant entry into blinding light with the revelation of the sacred objects, including the symbolic ear of corn. Afterwards came a communion of cereal and barleywine:

> Happy among men on earth is he who has seen these things. But he who is
> uninitiate, and has no share in them, will not share in like things when in death he
> lies beneath the broad-spreading darkness.[11]

Secrecy, dramatic effects, holy objects, sometimes initiation ordeals were the common repertoire. The mysteries of Dionysus similarly celebrated the growth, death and rebirth of the god, the eternal potency and wild energy of primal nature, its peaceful reconciliation in man, and the hope of renewal. In the frescoes at the villa of Istacidia women go through the stages, which involve creating a heightened atmosphere of terror, figures representing Pan, Silenus and satyrs, the unveiling of a great phallus, the flagellation of the initiate, then the triumphant emergence from this ordeal and the Bacchic dance. The greatly respected Phrygian cult of the Great Mother Cybele included the *taurobolium,* in which the neophyte stood in a pit below the sacrificial bull and had his face and body drenched in its hot blood as it was killed by a spear; after which he was welcomed among the reborn in a sacramental meal. The public processions of the Great Mother (including the eunuch priests who had castrated themselves in orgiastic frenzy), are described by Lucretius:

> The taut drums thunder under the open palm, cymbals clash, the horse-echoing
> blare of horns startles, hollow flutes rouse the spirits with their Phrygian cadences,

martial arms make a display of fury to amaze the ungrateful minds and impious hearts of the vulgar with awe of her majesty. As soon as she rides through mighty cities, silently blessing mankind with benediction, they strew all her route with silver and bronze and shower roses down on her.[12]

The Persian cult of the hero-saviour Mithras, extremely popular in the later Roman armies, was celebrated in cavernous underground temples, such as the one excavated in the City of London and visible in Queen Victoria Street. It included such ordeals as branding, fasting, and scourging. There were seven grades of initiate corresponding to the seven planetary spheres, and the main mystery enacted the journey of man's immortal soul through life, at the seven stages of which he is given knowledge, and the chance to shed, one by one, the vices of anger (Mars), sloth (Saturn), greed (Mercury), lust (Venus), ambition (Jupiter) and so on, until after death the soul is fought over by the opposing forces of darkness and light, and the predominantly good soul returns to the home of Light and the Sun.

Most of the cults had long been popular, and did not see themselves as in any way rivalling the official state cults. Although they had select memberships they did not demand exclusive allegiance, and a person could be initiated into several cults. But they did gradually introduce a new emphasis, in the promise of personal immortality. Whether seen as a reward or a release, a recompense for this life's suffering, a serene tranquillity or an ecstatic union, whether the escape was from a fiery Gehenna or merely dusty oblivion, in one sense or another the real and important life of the individual was no longer this one. All the cults offered the initiate a new, inward, spiritual identity: he was born again, cleansed, transformed, healed, enlightened, *not* through public actions but more usually by ascetic disciplines, a lonely and private therapy of the soul.

This was now a purely personal type of religion in the modern sense, having no particular connection with his observance of the state and municipal cults, his national traditions or social identity. Indeed, the fellowship of initiates forged different links which cut across all these. An alternative and far more important distinction was now between the once-born and the reborn, the saved and the damned, the awakened and those still walking in darkness. For the Gnostic or Christian, especially, his 'real' life was one of direct personal relation to God which owed nothing to society. A slow loosening of the public social distinctions, and the obligations and ties associated with them, had begun.

Against the catastrophic realities of the third century it is tempting to see the great popularity of the mystery religions as people's flight from civic insecurity into otherworldly promises and esoteric secret societies. But, however they may have been accelerated by the prolonged sense of disaster and decline, these religious currents were already well under way in the second century; at the height of peace and prosperity people were already flocking to the mysteries, as Marcus Aurelius' initiation at Eleusis illustrates. What is true, however, is that during the calamities the old protective gods of State and city seemed, somehow, to have failed. A religion whose main province is the benign protection of the human race, in concrete terms the *felicitas* of an actual society and State, cannot long survive their palpable deterioration (which is doubtless why Augustine later located his imperishable City of God in a safely immaterial realm).

As the cities declined under invasion, civil war and financial bankruptcy, their cults naturally declined with them. Few of the propertied classes could afford to fill priesthoods or pay for public festivals, let alone restore temples, which fell into disrepair together with theatres, fora and basilicas: stripped of their statues, burnt in the sack of cities, or pulled down to build emergency walls. Though the gods still received offerings, prayers, modest sacrifices and votive inscriptions, the great, generous collective festivals were far more difficult to maintain. The physical destruction of altars and temples demonstrated that the gods, like the cities they lived in and protected, were weakening. All the dominant themes of traditional state religion, *Pax, Pietas, Felicitas, Prosperitas, Victoria, Concordia,* became for most people as doubtful as the trashy coins on which they were proclaimed. Men did of course confuse cause with effect, linking the ill-fortune of a murdered Emperor with the coming of famine, or the omission of some costly festival with a military disaster; but the overall conclusion was inescapable: the heavens, if not empty, were silent.

All these experiences combined to produce a charged atmosphere of heightened religious sensibility among all grades of men, statesman and soldier, educated and rustic, which the mere civic cults could not satisfy. To sum it up very simply, it was a profound shift in focus away from the Hellenic emphasis on living, natural gods to transcendental spiritual realities beyond it: the shift which Nietzsche identified and so hated, and which is very visible in the art of the late third and fourth centuries: from body to soul, from natural form to abstract symbol. It existed at many levels. Philosophy, in its dominant form of Neoplatonism, slowly but steadily developed a far closer association with religion than hitherto. The influential Plotinus, who died in 270, taught that the goal of man is the soul's liberation from the lower, material world of illusion and change, back to its original state of pure contemplation, union with the changeless One, the principle of Pure Being. In his unified, ultimately unchanging cosmos, this perceptible world of matter and man is the lower, baser one compared with the detachment and stasis of the purely intellectual realm. Plotinus' pupil Porphyry, a contemporary of Diocletian, extended the doctrines to justify oracles, astrology and theurgy, and reconcile them with virtually all the beliefs of the traditional cults. No longer was philosophy confined to its concern with the rational pursuit of wisdom: its goals and increasingly its methods appeared to be similar to those of religion – not the virtuous, fulfilled, whole life in this world, but recipes for escape from it.

Thoughtful pagans increasingly sought greater order and unity in their polytheism, in the broad trend known as syncretism. The many gods were not denied but, as their identities merged so readily, attention was directed more at the one hidden, highest god (Summus Deus) believed to be above and behind them, of whom they were felt to be lesser companions or even aspects. Names were not important but a unifying principle was. A Supreme God, known by many symbols, whose essence was more mysterious than the familiar Olympians yet embraced them too, answered the need of growing numbers of people at such a time. This new mood did not weaken traditional tolerance – rather the opposite. It was not towards exclusive monotheism, but towards more explicit unification of the many objects of worship. The most prominent official step in this direction had been taken by Aurelian, who established among the older gods at Rome the cult of *Sol Invictus,* the Unconquered Sun as the highest deity, protector of Emperor and State. In addition to being identified with the Mithraic Helios, *Sol Invictus* was readily acceptable to Greek and Roman worshippers of Apollo, source of Light. But his role of Highest God was even more important than his identity. The more conservative could consider the deity whose different aspects were *Sol Invictus* and Jupiter, as one and the same being.

But in the longer run, the total spiritualisation of philosophy fatally damaged the controls of rationality and whatever shreds were left of the Aristotelian scientific spirit. Despite all Plotinus' disclaimers and Porphyry's logic, if philosophy, like religion, was really the direct experience of divinity and the soul's escape from earthly existence, who was to say that it could only be approached by the educated intellect? That revelation, dream or magic were inferior paths? The 'philosophy' of Iamblichus, one of Porphyry's pupils, was a popular mishmash, sprinkled with mysticism and number lore; Iamblichus was also credited with powers of levitation. Any magician, wizard or occultist could now claim to be a 'philosopher'; and the popular image of the philosopher slowly shifted from the self-conscious intellectual, to the saint or holy man through whom divine forces worked; from what he taught, to the powers he was in contact with. If, in our own time, many of the educated have succumbed to a fascination with the occult, rejecting rationality for the easier thrills of short cuts to wisdom, how much easier was it in this ominous time, when education had everywhere declined with the decay of city life.[13]

To all this, however, was added a quite new element, external to the Hellenistic spirit and ultimately destructive to it. Its origins were in Persian Zoroastrianism and it diffused westward in various forms into Judaism, Mithraism, Christianity and above all, Manicheanism. This was a view of the meaning of the universe as an all-pervading struggle between opposite forces of good and evil, light and darkness, in which human life is the eternal battlefield. It was originally enshrined in the Avesta, the sacred sayings of Zoroaster concerning the cosmic war between Ahura Mazda and Ahriman, and the duty of men to fight for the eventual victory of Light. A religious outlook of this kind naturally leads to a tension towards other cults. For if everything is a war between these two forces, other gods and beliefs must have a place in the war, in the ranks of one army or the other: there can be no neutrals. As in any ideological war, comparatively innocent and trivial actions and events were now discovered to have a larger significance. Christianity especially saw in the motley, largely mundane confusion of spirits and demiurges which people casually accepted, an unseen daily struggle between the rival legions of God and the devil. All such beings had to belong to one host or the other, and if it was difficult to be sure, that was because the devil's followers could assume many insidious guises for the ruin of souls. For the Christian, a more satisfying explanatory system was thus introduced into the untidy congestion of polytheism, and it was a sinister one. Grace and sin were no longer right and wrong actions or dispositions, but rather a kind of spiritual captivity, perhaps unconscious, by the angelic or demonic. Rather than deny the existence or properties of the pagan gods, Christians regarded them as evil demons.

And, when faced with the obvious resemblances between pagan religions and their own – especially Mithraism – this was explained as the insidious counterfeiting of the divine by its demonic mirror-counterpart.[14]

The Balkan soldier-Emperors were indeed religious men, which is a reflection on the age as much as their personal characters. Nothing is clearer than that in a world battling painfully for survival the State needed all the divine help it could get. Unlike Aurelian, Diocletian's bent was markedly conservative. It was the Olympian gods and heroes who had made Rome great and would restore her again, provided they were served in the true ancestral manner. Jupiter was the father and supreme ruler of gods and men, under whose intimate care Diocletian had placed himself and his whole Tetrarchic system of government: he ruled with Jupiter's power, in his name, and in his manner. To Jupiter he had built innumerable temples and altars and made abundant sacrifices, and the reciprocity of Jupiter towards him had been plainly manifest to everyone. If, in the years of disasters, the gods seemed to have withdrawn, the years of victories and restoration of security had surely demonstrated the reverse. It was therefore the duty of all men to co-operate in renewed religious observation.

But, however fervent in belief and punctilious in ritual, he could not of course just 'restore' the religious climate of traditional Rome, any more than any cultural revival is a return to its original. This was a new age of altered needs and longing, spiritualisation and escape from the world; as well as a State where the old civic institutions and feeling had been permanently replaced by those of centralised imperial power. Diocletian's insistent old Roman-ness was, if not artificial, at least only one spirit among many in this new world – not unlike the attempt to 'restore' an unchanging ancient Catholic Spain after 1936.

Neither he nor his predecessors had failed to observe how the Persian State had made Mazdean religion into a powerful centralising force, imposing uniformity and repressing most of its rivals. But Diocletian's reassertion of traditional religion involved no such intolerance towards its many bedfellows, provided they were respectably established and did not clash with the traditional observances. This was entirely consistent with the essence of the old Roman traditionalism, as already discussed. Only at the very edges did toleration end. His furious policy towards the Manicheans was untypical: this was a new, innovatory sect being manipulated by the Persian enemy. But with Mithraism, which was also Persian in origin, there was no question of any hostility.

Thus, Diocletian did not need a theistic revolution, but merely a firm shifting of the accepted scenery, in order to place Jupiter, rather than *Sol Invictus,* in the highest place. Jupiter's statue was placed on the highest column, on the hill outside Nicomedia and again in the Forum at Rome. But *Sol* was also celebrated on the coins, a Sun-temple was built in Italy by Diocletian, and at Aquileia there is a dedication to *Sol* by himself and Maximian. The same went for the other well-known cults, and for local gods. Temples to Isis and Sarapis were erected by him at Rome, and as the Emperors were frequently on the move, he and his colleagues were careful to worship the dominant gods of the places they visited. The aim was to encourage all inhabitants of the Empire once again to pay full honours both to their own traditional gods and those of the State; to involve as many people as possible in revived festivals. The panegyric to Maximian declares:

> You have heaped the gods with altars and statues, temples and offerings, which you dedicated with your own name and your own image, whose sanctity is increased by the example you set, of veneration for the gods. Surely, men will now understand what power resides in the gods, when you worship them so fervently.[15]

In the main, however, the great majority of Tetrarchic coinage and inscriptions concentrate centrally on the Olympians, and show a certain ingathering tendency which reflects the syncretist background.[16] Diocletian's appeal to tradition combined a genuine piety with a new, heavy emphasis on public order, traditional morality and duty, accepted rules – all that supposedly united Romans with their past and one another. As Emperor and *Pontifex Maximus* these components were for him barely distinct. He expresses this concern most clearly in a law against consanguinous marriages, which lays down the traditional Roman rules defining which marriages are incestuous: rules far stricter than contemporary practice and ancient custom in many provinces, especially the East. (Egyptian brother-and-sister marriages were firmly suppressed.) This was because, 'To our pious and religious disposition, it is clear that what Roman law prescribes as chaste and holy is especially valuable, and should be preserved with eternal religious veneration'. And because

> There is no doubt that the immortal gods, as always friendly towards Rome, will be reconciled to us only if we have ensured that everyone within our empire pursues a pious, religious, peaceful life, and one thoroughly pure in all regards . . .
> For our laws safeguard only what is holy and venerable; and it is in this way that the majesty of Rome, by the favour of all the divine powers, has attained its greatness.[17]

The new religious approach met a deep, genuine response in the citizens of the Empire. As Eternal Rome visibly righted itself and the Emperors were everywhere seen restoring the forms of worship, people followed their example. Dedications and votive inscriptions from private individuals became more numerous. Among soldiers, alongside the powerful cults and rituals of the military standards, there appeared a new ceremonial respect paid to military *genii*; not only to the well-established *Genius Illyrici,* but to the *genius* of a fort, of a legion, or a cohort. This was a distinctly old Roman concept. The *genius* was a companion *geist* to some enduring entity such as a person, an institution, a city, a family, a house: not so much a deity as the essence of the thing, over and above its transient components, to which reverence could be directed.[18] And there was abundant proof – the only kind men recognised – that this renewed reverence was answered by the gods. The striking success of the Tetrarchy in restoring the Roman State was not just accident. These men really were the specially favoured sons of Jove and Hercules. When the panegyrist proclaims, 'Best of Emperors, you have deserved your good fortune (*felicitatem*) by your piety',[19] he was not just referring to religious observances, but to the larger virtues of Diocletian and Maximian, especially the trust and harmony between them.

chapter thirteen

·POLITEIA CHRISTI·

NEAR AT HAND
IS THE END OF THE WORLD, AND THE LAST DAY
AND THE JUDGEMENT OF IMMORTAL GOD, FOR SUCH
AS ARE BOTH CALLED AND CHOSEN. FIRST OF ALL
INEXORABLE WRATH SHALL FALL ON ROME;
A TIME OF BLOOD AND WRETCHED LIFE SHALL COME.
WOE, WOE TO THEE, O LAND OF ITALY,
GREAT, BARBAROUS NATION.
·SYBILLINE ORACLES·[1]

But the revival of traditional paganism had another accompaniment. As the festivals and priesthoods flourished again under generous imperial patronage, their leaders realised to their dismay just how much ground had been occupied by the Christians, especially in the East, during the dark years. While the vitality of the older civic cults had dwindled, the mystery religions had been more successful at holding their devotees; but none had grown so spectacularly as Christianity. There were now Christian churches, supported by increasingly wealthy communities, in virtually every Eastern city, whose bishops were in close communication and met regularly in councils. Worse still, this sect had attracted growing numbers of the educated and influential, and now openly boasted members among lawyers, soldiers, magistrates and even some high Government officials. Opposite Diocletian's very palace at Nicomedia stood a new Christian church; among the teachers and writers in the city were Christians who openly attacked the gods and called on men to abandon them.

Against this threatening growth, many pagans now felt the need to organise. Since the truce of Gallienus 40 years before, there had been no lack of anti-Christian advocacy, but it had been confined to an intellectual war of words, most prominent in which had been Porphyry's 15 books *Against the Christians,* an exhaustive catalogue of arguments written from a sound knowledge of Christianity and the Bible. Porphyry was concerned not only with the truth and falsity of Christianity, but primarily its revolutionary threat to traditional culture. In offering the support of philosophy to pagan polytheism, he was deliberately trying to create a sense of unity among 'Hellenists', that is, all who accepted the traditional outlook, the mutual compatibility of the cults and the full civic pieties of Roman society – a unity that would exclude and oppose the Christians. In the following generation of the Tetrarchy and its religious revival this movement gathered momentum, at the expense of intellectual clarity. Iamblichus had neither the temperament nor philosophical ability to confine the effort to sober persuasion. In many ways a pagan counterpart of the zealous Church fathers, he stressed the need to match the Christians with a similar organisation, and to compete with them for the hearts of the uneducated. United Hellenism had to become militant and conversionist too, and this meant blurring over the sharp divisions between the philosophical schools which the ordinary man could not understand. In Iamblichus' hands, 'philosophy' became all one: Plato, Aristotle, Democritus were served up in a single dog's breakfast with the revelations of Hermes Trismegistus, Gnosticism and Chaldean Astrology. 'Neoplatonist' teachers became Hierophants who initiated their pupils into the mysteries. The drive was to create a common religious community and organisation embracing all the mysteries, pooling their stock of wisdom, revelations, salvation and all other spiritual benefits.[2]

Whatever the subtleties inspiring the earlier thinkers, this late pagan ecumenical campaign bears all the marks of rushed expedience in the face of a common threat, to the point of trying to copy the very features of the enemy which had proved so effective. It is of course difficult to assess this movement since we know it failed; and most of its records, like Porphyry's books, were subsequently destroyed under the victorious religion whose distant children we all are. But it is hard not to see it as extremely strained. To preserve paganism and 'Hellenism' it had to be forced into a mould that was sharply alien to its nature: an organised, united polytheistic church where all interesting distinctions are suppressed, variety blurred, traditions and ritual promiscuously mixed, and a simple missionary appeal made to all classes of society. (Imagine today's ecumenism trying to bring about a merger between High Anglicanism and the pentecostal snake-handlers of Tennessee.) These standardising features were as natural to the Christian Church as they were foreign to its adversaries, and so long as the battle remained one for hearts and minds, it seems most unlikely that pagan adoption of them would reverse the tide.

What the pagan cults had in common, after all, was not so much their content, as a shared attitude to culture, society and State. It is not surprising, then, that the more active leaders of the revival began to look to the powers of the State for more positive aid in resisting Christianity. Diocletian was well aware of the mood and strongly sympathetic to it, but for most of his reign he turned a deaf ear to any suggestion of renewed persecution. But the petitioners discovered a more receptive prince in Galerius. One of the leading advocates was the Neoplatonist philosopher Hierocles, who was successively governor of Phoenicia and then Bithynia, and probably the author of two books attacking Christianity. He and his circle bent their skills to convincing the semi-educated Galerius, whose prestige was enhanced by his great Persian victory, of the need for action.

The Christians themselves were anything but united in their attitudes towards the Roman State or Hellenic cultural traditions. Of course, the whole world was soon due to end and the Kingdom of God established. But the less simple had perceived that the growing organisation of the Church, its multiplying communities and increasing wealth, demanded some minimal attention to the political order it lived in. Yet perhaps the most conspicuous feature to the reader is the ultimate *irrelevance* of political matters for the church. This intensely active religion, which insisted like none of the others on doctrinal correctness and thrashing out disagreements on all theological, scriptural and organisational issues, still had no clear official doctrine about its relation to the State, beyond the demonic nature of the State's gods and the sinfulness of sacrificing to them.

There were a few, like Hippolytus, who saw the Empire as the fourth beast of Daniel, come out of the sea with iron teeth and nails of brass, which had achieved a promiscuous mixing of races and tongues, whose Emperor demanded that all fall and worship him in the manner foretold of the Antichrist. And there were the so-called Sybilline oracles, in which Jewish and Christian hatred of Rome was poured forth in bloodthirsty prophecies of its fall. Others, like Tertullian in his more militant moods, also considered the Roman State an enemy, but one to be fought by infiltration and passive resistance: 'We would take up the fight against you without arms or commotion . . . With our numbers, the defection of so many citizens in the far corners of the earth would suffice to undermine your Empire . . . You would look in vain for your subjects, and the enemies at your gate would outnumber your own population.'³ The view of Christianity as a state within a state was by no means confined to suspicious governments. It was enthusiastically shared by Christians themselves. Many apologists talked of the spiritual community in Christ as the *Politeia Christi,* and the earthly Church as its non-violent *militia,* whose military oath is baptism, whose officers are the clergy, whose wars the persecutions, and battle decorations the martyr's crown.⁴

All the same, despite the persistent emphasis on loyalty to Christ against Caesar which led many to refuse military service, there were more who did not think the two incompatible. Tertullian at one point boasts of the numbers of Christians in the legions. By the third century Christians were also to be found serving faithfully in magistracies and the bureaucracy, even as provincial governors: their well-known reservations about sacrifice being accommodated by one compromise or another. In an earlier time, when nearly all Christians were people of very low social position, it was easier to reject a worldly power which was quite out of reach anyway. But when substantial converts were made in the higher social levels, it was only natural that the Church should become more tolerant of the individual adjustments of conscience made by these confident, influential brethren. For every fanatic who deliberately provoked the authorities into martyring him, there were a dozen more responsible Christians who no doubt hoped to prove steadfast should the day of battle come, but saw no virtue in drawing it upon their congregations, and sincerely sought some *modus vivendi* with the civil power. And, whatever individuals might preach, it was now common knowledge among the authorities that the Christian community as a whole was quiet and law-abiding, except in the one matter of honouring the State gods. Unlike the Jews they were not prone to rioting, and avoided the circuses and theatres. Their only aggressive side seemed to be in their fierce doctrinal quarrels, but these were their own affair.

Against Tertullian's earlier rejection of Hellenic culture ('What has Athens to do with Jerusalem?') many Church fathers had absorbed the Greek intellectual heritage and tried to reconcile it with Christianity. Clement had evolved a new theology, following John, in which Christ's incarnation was the Divine Logos (Mind, Reason, the first principle of things), which complemented and completed the earlier Human Logos of Plato and the philosophers. Origen, a considerable intellect who studied under the same teacher as Plotinus, developed a comprehensive theology whose elements – God, the fall of the soul from the spiritual to the material world, its need for purification and redemption – are counterparts of those of Neoplatonism. To him, the Roman Empire was not so much the fourth beast, as a providential preparation for the eventual unity of all nations under Christ, since its communications had made possible the spread of the Gospel throughout the world.[5]

Christianity, in short, had undergone great changes since the days when the Second Coming was expected in men's lifetimes. Most impressive to friend and foe alike had been its sudden expansion throughout the world, despite great obstacles and opposition. This had occurred within the same long chain of upheavals that had eclipsed the old political aristocracies, provincialised the Empire, diffused the mystery cults, undermined city life, and brought a Balkan military class to power. From being a despised sect of the humble and dispossessed, Christianity had come into its own in the long imperial peace, as great numbers of the lower orders everywhere began to climb the intermediate rungs of property and status, but without adopting the cultural outlook of the older élites. The new classes who were slowly rising were no longer local city notables but true cosmopolitans of the Empire – merchants, freedmen, shopkeepers, lesser functionaries who had prospered above all from the great opportunities for trade, travel and emigration in the High Empire. To them, without deep religious or civic roots, Christianity offered the strong, simple message of universality, One God, One Church, One equal brotherhood in Christ: and also a concrete social community which gave them a home wherever they travelled or settled. As the great cities became more amorphous, the Christian communities in them grew steadily. In place of the anomie of being just a wandering citizen of the great impersonal world, a Christian knew he would find hospitality, meetings for prayer and the common meal, alms if he needed them, and companionship as a fellow in Christ irrespective of his race, language or social rank. The Christian communities thus became alternatives to the hierarchic, *localised* civil communities. And when the upper crust of the city aristocracies crumbled together with their gods in the crisis of the third century, this alternative community was well placed to survive and receive many of the refugees.[6]

Of course, the Christians were not alone in offering to the anxious and they lost an alternative kind of spiritual belonging. The other mystery cults such as Cybele and Isis had also become near-universal, and attracted masses of converts. But Christianity excelled in at least two main things. First, it democratised the mystery cults, and went much further than any rival in ignoring outer social distinctions, some of which were becoming increasingly empty. Just as Buddhism had swept India partly by offering the hope of Nirvana to other castes than the Brahmins, Christianity in these troubled times offered personal salvation not just to soldiers, or men, or Greek speakers, but everyone: slave and free, men and women, Greek and barbarian. And such were the great social shifts and fragmentations of the epoch, that what had been a handicap in the aristocratic first century, was an advantage in the socially mobile third. The very humblest still flocked to Christianity in the absence of alternative havens, but they were no longer predominant, and hence their presence no longer deterred those of higher status as it once had done. Men who were already ruled by Emperors and governors of lowly origin and military manners, were less likely to mind being preached to by bishops who were perhaps their social inferiors. The Church had in any case managed to equip itself with an intellectual appeal to the educated without abandoning its broad democratic base.

At the same time as it welcomed all types of convert, Christianity maintained a strong wall separating those inside the faith from those outside. Its particular monotheistic exclusiveness, derived from Judaism, had led to an unrivalled concern with organisation. The very concept of a *Church* was unique to it, as was its systematic, dynamic missionary activity. While the community in each city was closely-knit, inward-looking and defensive, it derived moral strength through its carefully fostered links with other communities, new and old. Its bishops travelled, met and corresponded ceaselessly. The result was that, by about 200, there was almost everywhere a uniform governing structure of bishop, presbyter, deacon and layman, with the bishops of the mother church ordaining ministers in the new foundations. And, though achieved through painful controversies and schisms, there was increasing uniformity of doctrine, ritual, and discipline.

As a result, religion exerted more constraints on the life of the average Christian than on his pagan counterpart. He might be no deeper in religious feeling than a devotee of Isis, but unlike him, he could not easily drift away or try other cults, and to modify or reject part of his religion ran more risk of losing all the other parts too – God, Christ, salvation, eucharist, communion and the very community in which he lived. The lapsed Christian had a far greater sense of being cast out alone in an alien world. It is no accident that his baptismal allegiance was represented as his *faith* (*fides*), analogous to the Roman sacredness of an oath, especially the military oath.

While other cults offered personal survival after death but left this world broadly as they found it, Christianity (like Judaism in modern Europe) offered a distinct discipline of living in this world too. In its positive aspects it could be very impressive to outsiders. Galen remarked how the Christians' naively simple parables enabled them to live to the highest ethical standards. In the ravages of the third century virtually all churches set aside part of their revenue for the sick and the poor, and were ready to help the dispossessed and the desperate in a way nobody else did. Impressive too was the courage of many of them under torture and threat of death during the sporadic persecutions. The strong, exclusive group links the Church had forged among its members were partly designed to meet just this challenge, and courageous martyrdoms were used to maximum propaganda effect to stiffen the faithful and impress potential converts. As Arnobius says, 'Do you really believe this happens by blind chance, that such courage comes from accidental influences? Is it not far more likely to be God-given and holy?'[7]

For all these reasons, the growth of the Church was not a steady upward curve but a series of spurts and setbacks, with something like an explosion in the third century. Even so, its unexpectedness should not prompt exaggerated estimates. Despite all its special mass appeal, by Diocletian's time well under a fifth of the Empire's population were Christians, mainly in the Greek East, Syria, North Africa and the far fewer great cities in the West.

The State, for its part, was generally more concerned with avoiding civil conflict than with religious consistency. It did not understand or like the Christians, but it had come to recognise that most of the lurid traditional accusations against them were groundless. While it had no hesitation in crushing a religious sect that was a focus for rebellion (such as Druidism in the first century and Manicheanism at the end of the third), it was difficult to see Christianity in this light. True, denial of the gods was always a crime, as was refusal to make the proper gestures of loyalty to the Emperor when demanded by a court, and any magistrate would have no option but to punish such acts with exile or death, if clearly proven. But in peaceful times most of them were not disposed to hunt out quiet, law-abiding folk merely on that account. Anti-Christian enthusiasts, of whom there were many, could be deterred by the wise law against false accusations: if a Christian before the magistrate decided to compromise, and offer his pinch of incense, it could be his accuser who was punished.

For most of the time, therefore, Christians would not be oppressed who did not ask to be, even though their religion remained officially proscribed. Hence in Trajan's time there is the celebrated puzzlement expressed in Pliny's letters: this sect was illegal, but just what specific offences were individual Christians to be charged with? Tertullian in the *Apology* was scornful of this inconsistency. Trajan's ruling, he said, amounted to this: Don't look for Christians, but punish them if you find them. But if they are guilty, surely they should be hunted down; if innocent, why punished?[8] Literally speaking, however, public denial of the gods *was* a crime, and therefore in strict logic the whole religion was an organised incitement to break the law. But the machinery of the law hesitated, for all kinds of reasons. It put a premium on public peace, and an onslaught on this sect would cause disorders, especially among pagan mobs who might well instigate riots and pogroms. The law had plenty of other things to do than devote most of its energies to what was only a peripheral nuisance. Not knowing what to do, it generally did nothing, unless strongly pressed.

The fact was, the underlying spirit of Christianity was essentially alien to Roman tradition, and between it and the State was a gulf of incomprehension. At best there could be truce between them, but never harmony or genuine toleration, given the quite different meanings that each attached to this notion. There were too many aspects of this religion that were profoundly deviant. Had it just been the one matter of the form of a gesture of loyalty, a blind eye could perhaps have been turned: Mithraists, after all, had religious qualms about wearing the crown at public festivals, and this did not lead to trouble. But it was far more than that.

The Christians were secretive and held themselves apart: was it surprising they were periodically accused of conspiracies? They were atheistic, regarding the gods of Rome and of everyone else except their own as evil demons: was it surprising popular feeling was outraged, and blamed them for every calamity? They claimed that the Roman State was against their God, when it was they alone who had declared spiritual war. Rome could accept their version of the Supreme God, whom others called Jupiter or *Sol*; it could accept Christ together with other heroes and divinities (the eclectic Emperor Alexander Severus honoured Christ in his temple alongside Orpheus, Abraham and others). But what was preposterous was the Christians' arrogant insistence that *no* gods had ever walked the earth until an obscure Jewish teacher who was executed in the reign of Tiberius. This was insulting, not just to Rome but to a thousand years of Hellenic culture, even though educated Christians wrapped it up in Plato. The gulf was not bridged but widened, as the argument was conducted at a higher intellectual level, as Porphyry's theses indicate. Say what you will, he concludes, when all misunderstanding and foolish prejudice is removed, the fact remains that the Christians' central beliefs are incompatible with the Roman idea.

It was scarcely enough for Bishop Dionysius to protest that Christians were loyal citizens who prayed for the health of the Emperors. What could the most reasonable magistrate reply except to ask why, in that case, they could not demonstrate their loyalty in the proper way like everyone else? Rome was tolerant, but it was not a modern secular liberal state which demands very little of its citizens beyond passive compliance with the law. Genuine loyalty could hardly be divorced from worship of the genius of the Emperor in the way that was laid down. To a modern liberal it might seem (as it seemed to John Stuart Mill over atheist jurors) that legally compelling early Christians to sacrifice was not just coercive, but absurd: for of what possible value could their offering be, if in their hearts they repudiated it? But much of this chapter has tried to show that Roman religious conceptions were not at all like this. What mattered to gods and men was not a person's belief but its expression in acts, not his private silent vows but his public oaths and commitments: Jupiter saw your actions, not your thoughts. And in their different way, the Christians too saw the offering of sacrifice not just as an embarrassing convention, but aiding the demonic forces and polluting oneself with evil.

As the times ceased to be tranquil, some Christians indeed saw the signs that had been prophesied: nation against nation, plagues and famines, the approach of the Last Days. Paganism, frightened, blamed events on the impieties of this sect of atheists, which deeply displeased the gods. By 250 popular anti-Christian feeling had broken out in riots at Alexandria. Under Decius a far more determined attempt was made to regain the favour of the gods. He ordered an offering to the gods *en masse*, with commissioners appointed to see that everyone took part, and issue certificates that they had done so. This was the most thorough onslaught on the Christians yet. Many were executed, including the Bishops of Rome, Antioch and Jerusalem; many others succumbed and sacrificed. A lucrative market in certificates grew up among the wealthy.

Decius' successor Valerian continued the persecution, this time directing it far more specifically against the clergy and organisation of the Church, but leaving individual lay Christians alone. But the very emergencies and fragmentation of the Empire obstructed this policy, and it was officially ended by Gallienus in 260. For the next 40 years this truce continued – Aurelian's intended move against the Christians being prevented by his death. The main legacy for the Church itself was the reopening of the old controversy over whether, and how, Christians who had weakened into apostasy under pressure, might be readmitted. This led to a fierce dispute in which Stephen, Bishop of Rome, went so far as to denounce Cyprian of Carthage as the Antichrist, and the split between the two sees became near-permanent.[9]

Preoccupation with other matters diverted imperial attention from the Christians throughout most of Diocletian's rule, as it had done for decades previously. Christians continued to occupy honourable posts in the bureaucracy, the army, and even the palace staff at Nicomedia. In the late 290s we first hear of incidents which, though recorded as glorious martyrdoms, were peripheral brushes with the law and can in no sense be called persecution. Their significance is rather that they occurred in the army, and may first have raised the question of the compatibility of Christianity with full military discipline. In 295 at Tebessa in North Africa a Christian youth, Maximilian, was put forward as a recruit by his father under the new conscription system.[10] He persistently refused to take the military oath, declaring that his conscience did not permit him to serve as a soldier, and was consequently executed. In 298 at a public festival at Tingis (Tangier) the senior centurion Marcellus loudly renounced his oath of allegiance to the Emperor, threw away his arms and insignia, exclaiming that he obeyed none but Christ, and would have no part in the weapons of this world or the service of idolatrous rulers. The immediate reaction to this extraordinary demonstration was one of astonishment:

> When the report was read out, Agricolanus asked: Did you say what appears in the official records of the governor?
> Marcellus: I did.
> Agricolanus: Were you in service with the rank of centurion of the first class?
> M: I was.
> A: What madness possessed you to renounce your oath and speak as you did?
> M: There is no madness in those who fear God.
> A: Did you say all those things which appear in the official records of the governor?
> M: I did.
> A: Did you throw away your arms?
> M: I did. A Christian who is in the service of the Lord Christ should not serve the affairs of this world.
> A: The acts of Marcellus are such as to merit disciplinary punishment. Accordingly, Marcellus, formerly in service with the rank of centurion of the first class, having declared that he had degraded himself by publicly renouncing his oath of allegiance, and having moreover put on record insane statements, it is my pleasure that he be put to death by the sword.

> As he was being led away to execution, Marcellus said: Agricolanus, may God be kind to you! And after he had said this he was slain with the sword, and so obtained the martyrdom he desired.[11]

Whether or not it was prompted by incidents like this, there appears to have been in either 298 or 299 a military order concerning religious observance which bore directly on the position of Christians in the armies. It may have been a reinforcement of the requirement to sacrifice, as part of the general policy of religious revival in the armies; or perhaps the order requiring *adoratio* to the Emperor's image on appointment, promotion or transfer. It seems to have been initiated in Galerius' Danube armies. The Christian historian Eusebius, surprisingly, does not record the content of the order, but merely says: 'The Master of Soldiers (Veturius) first began persecuting the troops, classifying those in the legions and offering them the choice: either obey orders and retain their present rank, or be stripped of it if they refused to obey the edict. A great many soldiers of Christ's kingdom chose without hesitation to confess him, rather than cling to the mere outward glory and position they enjoyed.'[12]

It is difficult to decide whether this army purge (if indeed it occurred in 298 and not later) was deliberately aimed at the Christians. Just as, during the long period of truce it was not so much mere Christian membership that got people punished, but more usually the refusal to sacrifice when ordered, so here the crux may have simply been disobedience of military law. Eusebius is quite definite that it was in the army alone that the persecution began, implying that it was a stealthy attempt by Galerius to prepare the ground for a wider offensive. Lactantius tells a different story, describing the purge as the outcome of Diocletian's wrath when the auspices were repeatedly thwarted by the Christians:

> While in the East Diocletian, always fearfully anxious to know the future, sacrificed victims and sought to read events in their livers. And some of the servants who knew the Lord were present at the sacrifice, and put the *immortal sign* [of the Cross] on the pieces. The demons therefore fled and the sacrifice was spoiled. The Haruspices were filled with fear when they saw no signs in the entrails at all, for it seemed as if their sacrifices were unacceptable. They offered fresh victims but again and again saw nothing.

> Finally the Chief Haruspex, Tagis, whether out of suspicion or because of something he had seen, declared that the sacrifices were producing no response because sacrilegious men were participating in sacred things.

> Diocletian became so furiously angry at this, that he ordered not only all those who had attended the sacrifice, but everyone else in the palace to offer sacrifice themselves; and that those who hung back should be beaten with rods. He also had orders sent out to all the army commands, that the soldiers should sacrifice, or face dismissal.[13]

Diocletian's wrath could be terrible when thoroughly provoked, as the Alexandrians knew to their cost. But it seems unlikely a burst of anger alone accounted for the systematic religious purge of the armies. The general policy of reviving traditional cults and symbolisms, and calling men back to the old religious ways, would be sufficient to account for it. In view of later events, Eusebius' view is certainly plausible, that it was intended by Galerius as the first move in the larger war with Christianity.

The Christian narrators are agreed that it was largely bloodless. Since the penalty was merely dismissal from the army – a disgrace enough for men of that social rank – the handful of martyrs mentioned at this time may well have been guilty of further offences against military law, like Marcellus. In the Danube armies five are mentioned: Valentinian, Pansecratius, Heschyias, Marcion and Nicandor, plus the retired veteran Julius, and a reserve soldier in Africa Tipasius, who ignored his recall to active service.[14] The purge having been carried out, things rested there. Whatever Galerius may have wanted, Diocletian took no further action against the Christians at that time. It was another four years before this decision was changed.

chapter fourteen

·THE GREAT·
·PERSECUTION·

ALL HAS BEEN FULFILLED IN MY OWN TIME: WITH MY OWN EYES I SAW THE
PLACES OF WORSHIP THROWN DOWN TO THEIR FOUNDATIONS, THE HOLY
SCRIPTURES COMMITTED TO THE FLAMES IN THE PUBLIC SQUARES, AND THE
PASTORS OF THE CHURCH COWERING SHAMEFULLY IN ONE REFUGE OR
ANOTHER, WHILE OTHERS WERE REVILED AND RIDICULED BY THEIR ENEMIES.
·EUSEBIUS, *Historia Ecclesia*·

For several years the argument went on.[1] Our main sources agree that Galerius was a
driving force for persecution, whereas Diocletian had misgivings about the policy, if
not the principle, of a general war against Christianity. But eventually he was
persuaded, and set in motion a series of Edicts, culminating in the last and most
ferocious persecution in Rome's history.[2]

Some modern writers have sought to mitigate Diocletian's responsibility for these
horrors. It is argued that he was browbeaten and manipulated by Galerius – of
whom Lactantius claims he was secretly afraid. But it is preposterous to suppose that
the Senior Augustus, the man 'at whose nod everything happened',[3] who had
recently dominated Galerius so firmly in the Persian peace treaty, should have been
intimidated by him. A slightly more plausible suggestion is that Diocletian, who was
seriously ill when the last and bloodiest Edict was issued, was not by then in
complete control. Possibly, this final measure went further than he would have
wished to go in the absence of Galerius, or would have consented to going in full
health. But by then he had already gone well down this path of his own accord: the
final Edict was in Diocletian's name and on his authority, and he must surely bear the
responsibility.[4]

The anti-Christian fanaticism of the 'wild beast' Galerius was supposed to have
been imbibed from his mother Romula, augmented by his own savage temperament.
These stories of course explain nothing. His attitude reflected the growing concern
of influential circles of pagans, especially in the East, that the State should stop the
spread of the Christian impiety before it was too late. Rather than Galerius' zeal, it is
Diocletian's passivity towards Christianity for 18 years, and his reservations even
then, that need explaining. The improbable idea that he was inhibited because his
wife Prisca and daughter Valeria (wife of Galerius!) were secret Christians, certainly
will not do.[5]

All the logic of his time and his policies pointed to the need to face the challenge of the Christian church. The growth of this organisation was like a tenacious, insidious ivy that was loosening the mortar and foundations of the edifice he had spent so much labour in building. The terrible crisis the world had passed through had shown to everyone that had eyes to see the need to regain the gods' favour and protection. And the gods had indeed responded. Yet all this was being jeopardised by the desertion of their shrines and altars in ever-increasing numbers by this deluded sect. How long would heaven be patient?

It was not a matter of the new autocratic State imposing a more uniform religion in the manner of Persia, but of demanding renewed reverence for the established gods in all their diversity. Since these were so intimately linked with the State, their worship was part of the duties of a loyal citizen: and since the Christians so pointedly denied them this worship, the antagonism inevitably became a political matter. The church which demanded these people's first loyalties was a rival state within the Empire. Things could not just remain as they were, if the Roman renewal was to be secure.

One might illustrate the concern of the pagan rulers by means of a modern parable. A small state, brave and resourceful, is permanently surrounded by powerful enemies who threaten to destroy it. By great efforts it had succeeded in repelling them again and again. But its government soberly realises that, in the long run, it can only be sure of surviving if it retains the friendship (and ultimate protection) of a certain Superpower. Should this be forfeit, no amount of bravery can guarantee it against being eventually engulfed. But in this state is a noisy radical minority violently opposed to the Superpower, whose activities threaten the vital relationship. The government tries to persuade them to keep their views to themselves and show at least outward respect for the Superpower, for the sake of their country's safety. But the radicals utterly refuse such a compromise, and their movement is growing in numbers. Finally, the government's supporters urge that it has no option but to suppress this movement before irreparable damage is done. In this parable, the small state is Rome; the Superpower is Jupiter and the gods; and the radical minority, the Christians. It was this remorseless argument, rather than any bullying by Galerius, that shifted Diocletian.

His initial reluctance was over the practical measures. We are told that in private conference with Galerius at Nicomedia during the winter of 302–3, Diocletian agreed to a more thorough purge of Christians in the courts and the armies. But he argued that a total persecution of the kind that earlier Emperors had practised would inevitably mean widespread disorders and a great deal of bloodshed. Everyone knew how the Christians thrived on martyrdom: was that the most effective way to deal with them? This account is a plausible reconstruction of the arguments.[6]

In his whole work of rebuilding Diocletian placed a very high priority indeed on public order, tranquillity, settled custom, and habits of obedience. The last thing he wanted was the fanaticisms and commotions of an all-out religious war with such a stubborn enemy. Against the offence of Christian impieties, was balanced his own conception of Jupiter – not at all the libidinous Zeus of Greek myth, but in every sense *Cosmocrator,* the Architect and Lord of Order, Government, Law. Chaos and unruliness were also offensive to Jupiter, especially if they were let loose by his earthly viceroy.

The outcome was to consult more widely. It seems likely Diocletian was now committed to action, but still undecided about the form it should take.

> He decided therefore to sound out the opinions of his friends and advisers ... He called in a number of civil officials and military commanders to give their views. The question was put to each of them in turn, according to their rank. Some, out of personal malice towards the Christians, answered that they ought to be extirpated as enemies of the gods and of the established religious ceremonies. Others did not share this opinion but, knowing the will of Galerius and either fearing him or wishing to oblige him, concurred in damning the Christians.[7]

Again, the direct leverage of Galerius is perhaps exaggerated. At this conference was Hierocles, Governor of Bithynia, a leader of the 'Hellenist' movement and a vigorous supporter of strong measures. If ever the advocates of general persecution had their chance, this conference was surely it. Nonetheless, the account goes on to say that Diocletian still looked for further guidance, and sent an envoy to consult the oracle of Apollo at Didyme, near Miletus, one of the holiest shrines of the Hellenic world. According to Constantine, who was then at the court of Nicomedia, the reply had very little of the oracle's usual ambiguity:

> It is said that Apollo spoke from a deep and gloomy cavern, through a medium that was not any human voice. He declared that the Righteous Ones on Earth were preventing him speaking the truth, and that therefore the oracles that issued from his tripod were worthless. This was why he hung down his hair in grief, mourning all the evils that would result for mankind from the loss of the prophet spirit. [When this was reported] I heard the Senior Augustus ... enquire of his advisers: Who are these Righteous Ones on Earth? And one of the pagan priests replied: The Christians, of course. This was received like a honeyed draught, and unsheathed the sword which should have been reserved only for criminals, against those whose holiness was beyond reproach.[8]

A new persecution was therefore agreed on: perhaps it had already been decided. Even so, Diocletian did not accept the advice of the root-and-branch party, but 'attempted to maintain sufficient moderation to carry through the policy without bloodshed: whereas Galerius would have had everyone who refused to sacrifice, burnt alive'.[9] The policy was to attack the organisation of the Church and the civil status of Christians, especially those in the upper classes.

The persecution was launched at Nicomedia on the Kalends of March, festival of the god Terminus (23 February 303). Lactantius, who was present, says it began with a symbolic act of demolition. The newly built church of Nicomedia, which stood in full view of the imperial palace, was surrounded by the Prefect, accompanied by military commanders and treasury officials. The doors were forced, and guards seized the ornaments, church furniture, and whatever else could be removed. Volumes of the scriptures were burnt. Then a guards unit advanced in battle order with all the equipment for besieging a city, and within a matter of hours had pulled the whole building to the ground. Diocletian and Galerius watched the operation personally from the palace.

Next day an Edict was published in the city. Throughout the Empire churches were to be demolished, sacred vessels confiscated, Bibles and liturgical books surrendered to the authorities and publicly burnt, assemblies for worship prohibited. Christians who refused to sacrifice would be expelled from all civil offices and lose their civil rights. They could no longer bring cases in the courts, but could still be accused. Christians of rank accused of crimes could be put to judicial torture just like the lower orders. Slaves could not be freed.

The Edict, displayed on a painted wooden board in the centre of the city, was immediately pulled down and torn to pieces by a Christian fanatic, Euethius, shouting tauntingly, 'Here are your Gothic and Sarmatian triumphs!' For this treasonable insolence he was arrested, tortured, and executed by burning the same day, becoming the first martyr of the new persecution.[10]

The Edict, stern enough, reflected Diocletian's tactical approach to the task. The Christians' central rites and meetings would be broken up. But he was not going to give them the excitement of glorious martyrdoms unless, like Euethius and other zealots, they openly challenged the law. Rather, the broad mass of middle-of-the-road, lay Christians would gradually find life so onerous they would eventually make their peace with the State. Since they were parasitical on Roman institutions, claiming the rights yet refusing the central religious duties, let them return to proper reverence for the gods and make their sacrifices, and their civil status would be restored. Meanwhile, altars would be placed in the lawcourts so that each litigant would be required to offer his incense before his case was heard.[11]

It met with some success. There were few arrests and even fewer executions, and then only as a result of obstinate refusal to comply with the law. Considerable numbers of Christians made their compromise with the State and regained their rights, as Eusebius complains. Others laid low. But as a whole, the organisation of the Church stood firm. Within its ranks there were disagreements, which were to grow into fierce conflicts, over the point at which compliance with the law became apostasy. To sacrifice, of course, was to forfeit one's salvation. But should one flatly refuse to hand over church plate, or scriptures, thus defying the law and inviting punishment? We find these uncertainties in the dialogue between the City Prefect of Cirta in North Africa, and Paul, the local bishop. The subdeacons hand over the church plate and other property, including large amounts of male and female clothing. There is equivocation when the scriptures are demanded. Catullinus, a subdeacon, hands over one very large volume.

The Prefect: Why have you given only one volume? Produce the others that you
       have.
Marcuclius and Catullinus: We have no more, because we are subdeacons. The
       readers have the books.
Prefect: Then show me the readers.
M and C: We don't know where they live.

Prefect: In that case, tell me their names.

M and C: We are not traitors! Here we are – order us to be killed!

Prefect: Arrest them!

They did however reveal one reader, for the Prefect then moved on to the house of Eugenius, who produced four books. After this, resistance ceased, and the clerks Edusius and Junius showed the Prefect to the houses of the other six readers. Four produced their books without demur. One was out but his wife produced the books, and the Prefect had the public slave search the house to make sure none had been overlooked. One declared he had no books, and the Prefect merely entered his statement on the record.[12]

As before, the moderate Christians faced the extremists in a dispute which was to split the Church for centuries. In most of the East, surrender of church vessels and books was considered permissible. The Bishop of Rome, Marcellinus, surrendered the scriptures. Mensurius, Bishop of Carthage, complied in suspending public worship, and satisfied the lenient authorities by handing over heretical volumes. (One bishop actually handed over medical treatises.) But in Numidia this was regarded as rank apostasy: the Christian's clear duty was to defy the laws and face death – even handing over worthless books was cowardly evasion. Anything less than this was a betrayal of those heroic fighters for Christ who had already won the martyr's crown. The compromisers were branded as *Traditors* (Those who surrendered).[13]

Within months of the Edict, the Christians at Nicomedia (or so their enemies thought) hit back. The imperial palace at Nicomedia caught fire and was seriously damaged, not once but twice in the space of 15 days: Diocletian's own bedchamber was destroyed in the flames. Lactantius, most implausibly, blames the fires on the agents of Galerius, who wanted some way to push Diocletian into stronger measures. (Galerius would have had to be very adroit to deceive Diocletian in his own capital and palace, where Diocletian's servants and spies outnumbered his own: and he would have been risking all his fortunes by discovery.) Years later Constantine, who claims to have been an eyewitness, blamed the second fire on a bolt of lightning sent by God to frighten Diocletian. Suspicion, naturally, fell on the Christians. Diocletian, thoroughly aroused and determined to crush all opposition, instituted a grim inquisition to discover the arsonists. Galerius is supposed to have withdrawn ostentatiously from Nicomedia, declaring that he had no wish to be roasted alive.[14]

The fires were the first point at which persecution intensified, and significant bloodshed began. Hitherto, Diocletian had wanted to keep the repression within certain bounds and under the regular controls of the law, and slowly drive a wedge between the Christian fanatics, and what he hoped would be the more malleable majority. Now coercion increasingly gained the upper hand. This of course was what many others eagerly wanted: the long-awaited theomachy, the unrestricted war to the finish between the gods of Rome and the god of the Christians. On the other side too, zealous Christians saw the Day of Battle, the final Armageddon surely approaching, which after unspeakable calamities would usher in Christ's kingdom.

Lactantius, with that distinct streak of Christian sadism that delights in contemplating the agonies of God's enemies, complacently predicts that in these great convulsions nine-tenths of mankind will perish; and even of the worshippers of the true God, only a third will survive.[15]

The imperial palace and household of Diocletian had been an insidious nest of Christian influence for too long, despite recent purges. Suspect members of the palace were questioned under torture to discover the origin of the fires – a regular judicial proceeding, in which Diocletian himself sometimes presided. At the same time everyone in the palace without exception was ordered to sacrifice, including Diocletian's wife Prisca, and daughter, Valeria. Sacrifice was an obvious loyalty test, and anyone who refused put themself under suspicion of implication in the fires. Two of Diocletian's most trusted personal servants, Dorotheus and Gorgonius, would not sacrifice and were tortured, then executed. Another Christian in the palace is described by Eusebius undergoing a vile succession of torments – scourging with loaded whips, then slow burning – to make him sacrifice. But the arsonists were never discovered.[16]

The screws of persecution now tightened. Magistrates were enjoined to greater severity, and torture more freely used. A number of executions occurred in Nicomedia. Presbyters and other clergy were often arrested without waiting for an accuser, and summarily condemned to death. News came of minor revolts by Christians, perhaps in reaction to the repression, in the Eastern provinces of Syria, and Melitene in Armenia. They were easily quelled, but the juggernaut gathered momentum. Church discipline and organisation had proved stubborn, and incited Christians to resist. A new Edict was therefore issued in the summer of 303, striking at the head of Christianity. All clergy were to be imprisoned.

> The spectacle of what happened next beggars description. In every town great
> numbers were locked up, and everywhere the prisons built long ago to house
> murderers and grave-robbers were crowded with bishops, presbyters, deacons and
> exorcists, so that there was no room left for those convicted of crimes.[17]

The error of this step was soon realised, as in many Eastern cities the prisons proved quite incapable of holding so many, and much of the ordinary machinery of apprehending criminals became clogged. It was therefore replaced by a third Edict, purporting to be an amnesty. Clergy would be released: but there was a catch. In return for release, they were required to sacrifice. This was the first time compulsory sacrifice was included in a general Edict. Refusal made clergy liable to torture. The State probably knew many would still refuse, but it found it more practical to force matters in this way, than have the prisons crammed indefinitely.[18]

It was now that the horrors began: racks, burnings, flayings, pincers. Gibbon treats many of these stories with some scepticism, coming as they do from highly coloured Christian sources bent on glorifying the martyrs and edifying the faithful. There is no doubt exaggeration in writers who easily turn a few deaths into 'multitudes', who make no distinction between unsolicited martyrdoms and those resulting from deliberate provocation; and who relate how wild beasts in the amphitheatres furiously mangled all other criminals but were stopped by a 'super-natural power' from touching the Christians. But, even allowing a margin for invention, what remains is terrible enough. Unlike Gibbon, we live in an age which has experienced similar things, and knows how unsound is that civilised smile of incredulity at such reports. Things can be, have been, every bit as bad as our worst imaginings.

The burden of persecution was by no means the same in all areas. Indeed, it illustrates well the practical limits of Roman administrative law; and incidentally was the first public example of discord among the Tetrarchs. Just as Christians varied in their defiance, so the authorities differed widely in implementing the Edicts. A zealous persecutor like Hierocles in Bithynia could easily contrive to arrest not just clergy but laity too, and recruit extra squads of hardy sadists to torture them. But other governors and magistrates behaved otherwise. They could not all afford the labour and equipment to demolish churches, nor had they the prison capacity to lock up more than a fraction of the clergy. Some were simply humane, or did not want all the commotion and bloodshed that increased persecution would entail. Especially in a small town it was very difficult to regard these reserved but inoffensive people, and so many of them, too, in the same light as real criminals. Often the magistrates would take their cue from the local church. They would take token measures, shutting the churches and confiscating books, but might not be too diligent in hunting down clergy, provided the latter co-operated by keeping inconspicuous.

Only the first Edict seems to have applied throughout the West as well. Maximian carried it out faithfully, but since it was precisely intended to put pressure on Christians without bloodshed, there were far fewer martyrdoms and brutalities. These were mostly in Africa, where churches were more fanatical. Felix, Bishop of Thibiuca, resolutely refused to hand over the scriptures and after careful warning was arrested and sent to the proconsul at Carthage, where he maintained his attitude, and after examination was finally beheaded a month later. At Abitinae there were people who continued to hold services in private houses and admitted as much, declaring that they would defy the ban.[19]

In the Gallic provinces, Constantius hardly complied even with the first Edict. He did not share his imperial colleagues' antipathy towards the Christians, nor did he see them as a threat to the State. His moderation has been subject to great historical distortion: the later propaganda of Constantine, after his conversion, includes the myth that his revered father was not just a friend to the Christians, but one himself. Therefore Eusebius tells us that Constantius 'dedicated his entire household ... to the One Supreme God, so that the company within the palace hardly differed from a church of God'. The truth seems to be that Constantius prudently took nominal measures, but in practice went little further than purging his court of Christians, and demolishing some churches ('mere walls, capable of being rebuilt'). Unlike Max-imian, he did not interpret the demand for surrender of scriptures and suspension of worship as enforceable by capital punishment, and so nobody under his jurisdiction was executed.[20] This relative lenience in the West made the plight of the Eastern churches increasingly bitter.

In the East, where Galerius was influential, the whole policy was becoming rapidly bloodier. Diocletian might have reflected, in a sober moment, the prediction that Christians would be eager for martyrdom, and their examples steel the fanatical resolve of the others. But there were now few sober moments. The Emperors and the State had been challenged, and the conflict had gone too far for them to draw back. This stubborn sect had to be broken, by sheer force if necessary. It was no longer a matter of public worship or handing over books: increasingly, both sides fought to capture the one vital battle line between them – sacrifice to the gods. In calmer times this had been the one complaint against the Christians to which Roman government had returned again and again. Now that things had come at last to a head, it saw what an absolute sticking-point this act was with Christians, and therefore concentrated all its pressure here, in the tense feeling that this was a struggle it could not afford to lose.

Timid or wavering minor clergy could not now (if they ever could) take refuge in the excuse that offering a pinch of incense was only an empty outward gesture – and that God, knowing their hearts, might after due penance forgive their weakness. The heroic examples of those who stood firm under torture, the ignominy and anathemas of their brethren if they gave in, the fear of total rejection on earth and eternal hellfire afterwards, made such a compromise very difficult indeed – unless they severed all their links with the Christian community. The Church took its stand on the clear command in Exodus: 'He who sacrifices to other gods shall be destroyed'.

Yet here, perhaps, the Christian was caught between differing religious conceptions, and had the worst of both of them. On the one hand was the newer idea of faith as inward, spiritual, and unworldly, not to be imprisoned in mere social rituals. On the other was the older, simple, jealous god of a national people fighting other peoples, who demanded exclusive loyalty and sacrifice. The Roman State cults, for all their urbanity, still had residues of the older concept. They demanded political allegiance. In his long polemic against paganism Lactantius argued, as many Greeks had argued before him, that it was now absurd for educated men to believe that the Olympian gods literally ate the sacrifical offerings and drank the libations. Logically, this should perhaps have tempered the central significance of the act of sacrifice, allowing Christians to see it more as a civic loyalty gesture, than as giving nourishment to the tribal gods of the Hebrews' enemies.

But the beleaguered Christians naturally did not see it this way, Lactantius least of all. Anyone who burnt incense to these filthy demons had cut themselves off from Christ, like the rotten branch that is cast into the fire. He urged the faithful to remain steadfast in the mighty tempests which were about to strike the earth, tribulations which had never been seen since the creation of the world; for at the end of a fixed time the evil one and all his followers would be destroyed. All this, he said, was prophesied from ancient times and is now marvellously coming to pass. A mighty king come out of the East, who would try to destroy the temple of God and persecute the righteous, ordering that he himself be worshipped as the son of God:

> As many as believe him and support him shall be marked by him as sheep, but
> those who refuse his mark shall either flee into the mountains or be seized and slain

with exquisite tortures. He will burn righteous men amidst the books of the prophets, and power shall be given him to desolate the earth for forty-two months ... The righteous shall separate themselves from the wicked, and flee into the wilderness. When he hears of this, the impious king, inflamed with anger, will come with a great army and surround the mountain on which the righteous are all gathered. They, besieged on all sides, will call on God with a loud voice; and He shall hear them, and send from Heaven a Great King to rescue them, and destroy all the wicked with fire and sword.[21]

Lactantius' apocalyptic prediction involved, if not actually the physical destruction of the world, then at least the end of Rome and the consummation of a whole historical epoch. 'No field, nor tree, nor vine shall produce anything ... the sun will darken, the moon will fail, overspread with continual blood ... the stars will fall in great numbers and the heavens be deprived of their light. The highest mountains will be thrown down on to the plain, and the seas made unnavigable.'[22] He drew on a great mine of Jewish and Gnostic prophecies, as well as Roman superstition itself, to establish his argument that the Last Days were indeed come. The Sybilline books and related traditions foretold a fixed succession of ages through which Rome would pass before meeting its inevitable end, and Lactantius readily saw them as confirming the prophecies of the Bible: 'That it shall come to pass, the predictions of the prophets announce, though in cryptic form. But the sybils openly foretell that Rome is doomed to perish, and by the judgement of God, because it held His name in hatred'.[23]

This kind of propaganda was the very opposite of what Diocletian's government was proclaiming. Their consistent message was that the time of world catastrophe was past, that the four saviour-Emperors had regained the favour of the gods and thereby ushered in a new era of tranquillity and security: against this, the Christians were preaching cosmic revolution. But the very efforts to suppress Christianity of course brought home to the Christians, in their mounting ordeals, the truth of these prophecies. The host of the righteous were being separated from the wicked.

Philieas, Bishop of Thmuis in Lower Egypt, describes the horrific ordeals of his fellow clerics at Alexandria:

All those who wanted were invited to insult them, and some beat them with cudgels, some with rods, straps or rope-ends. The spectacle of these outrages was constantly changing, and thoroughly abominable. Some had their hands tied behind them and were hung from gibbets, and their limbs stretched by machines ... Some died under torture, shaming their enemies by their determination. Others were thrown back into prison half-dead, and a few days later succumbed, and found release. The rest recovered, and their stay in prison restored their spirit. So, when they were asked yet again to choose between touching the abominable sacrifice (whereupon they would receive that freedom that brought a curse with it), and refusing to sacrifice, and incurring the supreme penalty, without a moment's hesitation they went gladly to their deaths.[24]

All the tightening pressure of the first three Edicts had taken place in a single year. There is no doubt that the pace was being forced, partly as a result of the fires at the palace in Nicomedia and the disturbances in the Eastern provinces, partly through the defiance and 'provocations' of the Christians, the growing number of spectacular martyrdoms and immolations; and partly, perhaps, through the daunting discovery of just how numerous the Christians really were. To all these obstacles, Galerius and his partisans had only one response – even more rigorous repression. In the background of all this was, inevitably, the gravitational effect of the rising over the setting sun. Diocletian was still in control, but he was about to enter his twentieth year as Emperor. He was now nearing 60, and although in good health, by Roman standards he was an old man. If and when he might leave the scene, the domineering Galerius, conqueror of Persia, looked set to become unchallenged ruler in the East. Possibly, in inner court circles, the wish of Diocletian eventually to retire was already discreetly known. All this as well as Galerius' somewhat choleric temperament, made it natural that the cautious and the ambitious should incline to him.

It might have been prudent, if that is the right expression, to give existing measures a chance to work before going further. From the State's point of view the results even of the first Edict alone were by no means a complete failure. There is no doubt from Christian sources themselves that very many of the flock did apostasize, and without the extreme threats of death or torture. Instead, the fanaticism of Galerius drove even faster. At the beginning of 304, during his journey through the Danube provinces, Diocletian suddenly fell ill, rallied, then grew worse. For the whole year his health was in doubt. However great and unchallenged the authority of an old ruler may be, there is nothing like sickness to diminish his *mana* dramatically. Loyal ministers and intimate advisers who would normally support Diocletian's wishes against the more extreme counsels of Galerius' party could hardly help thinking of their own futures. One way or another, Galerius managed to take full advantage of the old Emperor's lowered resistance. The upshot was his agreement to yet a fourth Edict, issued from Pannonia in April 304.[25]

This went much further, indeed to the very limits it was practical for the law to go. It revived the Decian policy of total persecution, aimed not just at the clergy, but the whole Christian population in the East. For the first time since Decius, Christianity was flatly declared a *religio illicita*, as Manicheanism and Druidism had been – no longer a permissible religion of the Roman Empire. Under this Edict everyone in the East without exception, was required to sacrifice. The penalty for refusal was death. And so, Eusebius relates:

> Some of the victims suffered death by beheading, some by fire. So many were killed
> in a single day that the axe, blunted and worn out with slaughter, was broken in
> pieces and the executioners periodically relieved one another. But always I observed
> a wonderful, truly divine enthusiasm in those who put their trust in Christ. No
> sooner had the first batch been sentenced, than others from every side would jump
> up to the platform in front of the judge and proclaim themselves Christians.[26]

In theory the fourth Edict was a suspended death sentence on millions of Christians throughout the East. In practice, of course, it was nothing like that. The worst affected provinces, where Christians were numerous and the persecutors zealous, seem to have been Bithynia, Syria, Egypt, Palestine, and Phrygia. The total number executed cannot have exceeded a few thousand. But the number of deaths is not a fair measure of the suffering inflicted. The Roman State was out to compel Christians to sacrifice, not exterminate them. Many clergy, for example, endured the cat-and-mouse ordeals of being imprisoned, taken out and tortured, then thrown back into prison again, never knowing when and what agonies would be applied to them next. The torturers came into their own:

> Things were done in Pontus that would make the hearer shudder. Pointed reeds
> were driven under the fingernails of both hands. Lead was melted over a fire and
> the boiling, seething mass poured down their backs, roasting the vital parts of their
> bodies. Others endured in their bowels and private parts sufferings shameful,
> merciless and unmentionable, which these fine and noble judges, upholders of the
> law, had ingeniously devised, vying with each other as if in a competition in the
> invention of new outrages.[27]

But contrasted with these judges were others, described by the same author, who went out of their way to avoid brutality and disorders, despite provocation by Christians. They would simply record that Christians in their city had sacrificed whether they had or not, or accept the mere hearsay reports of sacrifice as sufficient: so long as the records were in order, that would do. By an artfully equivocal formula, one judge accepted a Christian sacrifice to 'the Only God', without further inquiry about the identity of that deity. Some had Christians forcibly dragged to the altars and made to drop their pinch of incense, like a reluctant child being given its vaccination jab. Often it was only the very noisy Christians, who shouted at the tops of their voices that they had never sacrificed and never would, who were maltreated – and then only to silence them and drive them away as if they had sacrificed.[28]

Elsewhere, the atrocities reached a climax in acts such as this:

> A little Christian town in Phrygia was surrounded by soldiers, who set it on fire and
> completely destroyed it, with its whole population – men, women and children – as
> they called on Almighty God. Why? Because every one of the inhabitants, including
> the town prefect himself and the magistrates, all declared that they were Christians
> and that they utterly refused to commit idolatry.[29]

Diocletian was nominally responsible for the fourth Edict which resulted in such things, but during 304 he was laid low and in no position to exert his influence, and Galerius had things very much his own way. Even after Diocletian recovered, he never regained the dominant control of events he had previously enjoyed. From this point on, both religious and secular decisions bear a stronger mark of Galerius' personality, as events in the next chapter will show.

These events can still arouse partisanship, and it is natural for us to want to pass judgement on the actors. There is no doubt that Diocletian had control of every major policy in the Empire until 304, and has the major responsibility for the persecution until that date. I believe he was guilty both of great cruelty, and of a political error comparable in some ways with that of the Prices Edict. As a responsible Emperor dedicated to saving the State, he cannot be blamed for opposing Christianity and attempting to counteract its influence, using the instrument of the law if necessary. Indeed, given his deep attachment to the traditional Roman gods, and the intransigent attitude of the Christians towards almost everything the gods stood for, he would have been negligent not to act. But he did not allow the first, bloodless Edict an opportunity to work. It would not, of course, have broken the church, but it might well have driven it underground and curtailed its overt influence. If the policy of avoiding martyrdoms could have been maintained, then a stalemate might have been reached in which the State gods were no longer offended by the open celebration of these atheistic ceremonies. And this was probably as much as Diocletian sought. But instead, against his own better judgement, he allowed himself to be provoked into increasing torture and martyrdoms, and thus drawn into a spiral of violence and resistance which became very difficult to halt, and which only steeled Christian fanaticism just as he feared it would. This repression was to continue well after Diocletian's reign and still fail to achieve its goal, as even Galerius was eventually forced to admit. The same end result might have been reached with far less suffering.

Diocletian was not a cruel or arbitrary ruler in comparison with most of those who preceded and followed him. He had a very high regard for legality, and would always use persuasion or guile in preference to force; there are no reliable records of him resorting to widespread political killings, for example. Only when the imperial will was stubbornly defied, as at Alexandria, was he roused to break resistance by fire and sword. It was a cruel age, when the lower orders, the *humiliores,* could be legally tortured, and the normal forms of capital punishment for them (incurred for numerous offences) including burning, crucifixion, and being thrown to the beasts. But even by the standards of this age, not ours, the later stages of the persecution were shameful.

Whatever the law might say, many pagans who had no religious leanings towards Christianity could not accept that these people should be treated in the same manner as murderers and felons. They might keep themselves apart and object to offering sacrifice, but in the last resort they were ordinary people whom they met in the markets and public squares and they behaved decently enough. Except for the one peculiarity of their god, they harmed no one, yet the price they were paying for their religion was a very bloody one. More people came to feel that it was wrong. At Alexandria, despite the warnings of the authorities, pagans sheltered Christians from the law.

The impetus of persecution slackened by 306, partly as a result of other great political changes that were then taking place. But it also marks the point at which the initiative in this struggle passed to the Christians. The mood of State and society was altering. It ranged from the weariness of torturers who no longer had enthusiasm for their work; the growing feeling of magistrates that enough was enough, that the effort was becoming disproportionate to the goal; pity for the Christians, and awe for their god who put such courage in them; to simple disgust that Roman citizens who were neither criminals nor barbarians should be treated in this way. There would still be new trials for the Christians to bear, but they had already endured the worst their enemies could do to them, and the church had stood firm. Sooner or later, as God willed, it must end.

Meanwhile profound shifts were beginning in the imperial order, which must now be described. The eventual failure and final abandonment of the persecution was reserved for a later date.

·ABORTIVE RENEWAL·

By the year 303 Diocletian had other things on his mind than the Christians. He was about to enter his twentieth year as Augustus, in itself a remarkable achievement. He had already ruled longer than any Emperor since Marcus Aurelius, and turned a tottering, chronically insecure throne into a strong, stable inheritance. He had done it by an extraordinary balancing act, of dominating while conciliating, of delegating freely yet remaining in supreme command. Just as in the early days, he was under no illusions that the Empire could ever again be satisfactorily ruled by one man alone. The time was perhaps approaching for a cyclical renewal of the joint imperium.

The whole logic of the Tetrarchy and the divine houses of Jove and Hercules entailed that one day, Galerius and Constantius must succeed to the rank of full Augusti. Diocletian, typically, seems to have been wary of announcing too widely just how and when this would come about. But nothing could disguise the fact that among several other of his great building projects, was a magnificent new palace at his own native Salona on the Adriatic, which had been under construction for several years.[1] This could have no other meaning than his own eventual retirement, since Salona was geographically unsuitable as a centre of government. Of course, that might not mean actual abdication. After all, Tiberius in his old age had retired to Capri (and his sexual orgies) without relinquishing power, allowing things to go badly at Rome. But when Diocletian finally chose to take up residence on the tranquil Adriatic, Galerius would surely inherit the power that now emanated from Nicomedia. But what about Maximian in the West?

It was about this time that Diocletian's decision took its final shape.[2] He and Maximian would abdicate together, Galerius and Constantius simultaneously take over their powers, and younger men be appointed as Caesars. The two heirs were as fit for full imperial rule as they ever would be, and expected their inheritance. The plan would have to be carefully explained to Maximian, and his agreement secured: just as he had raised him up and given him a long and glorious reign, so his benefactor would at last require him to lay aside the purple and join him in a peaceful retirement, laden with honours.

The twentieth anniversary of his own reign and the tenth of the Caesars', both fell within the same period, 303–304. Already the building of a grand new circus at Nicomedia, to mark the occasion, was under way. Petitions were made to him that he should celebrate this great and glorious event at Rome itself, with festivities equal to his unparalleled fortune and achievements. This time, Diocletian agreed. He would combine the solemn commencement of his *Vicennalia* with the *Decennalia* of the Caesars, and a grand Triumphal procession for the combined victories of the four Tetrarchs. As of old, he decided, he would share the celebrations with Maximian; and also as of old, he would use the occasion to obtain his colleague's acceptance of his future constitutional plans.

The City made lavish preparations for the events, including erection of a triumphal arch and separate columns to each of the four Emperors. Not since Probus had the Roman Senate and people enjoyed the spectacle of a Triumph, and they were determined to make the most of it. The senators had reason to fear and dislike Maximian, both for his rough manner, and for a number of executions for treason which, they considered, had more to do with the wealth of the accused than his offence. But the most salient feature of Diocletian had been simply his remoteness, and now this was to be amended. They would impress on this Dalmatian Emperor the unforgettable magnificence of a great festival in the Mother of Cities. The *Vicennalia* was fixed for 20 November 303, 19 years to the day since Diocles had been proclaimed Augustus by the army at Nicomedia. Celebrations would continue until the New Year, when the Senate would solemnly confer on Diocletian his ninth consulship, and on Maximian his eighth.

There was every reason for Diocletian to welcome this as a fitting occasion to visit the Eternal City at long last. Against the background of the Christian troubles in the East, he would embody all the ancient virtues and pieties that had made Rome great, presiding as Pontifex Maximus over the sacred rites of the Capitol, and proclaiming in his Triumph the New Era he had so successfully ushered in. To one with his enthusiasm for grand buildings, what could be more satisfying than to view for the first time the splendours of the monuments of his predecessors – and to inspect the building of his own gigantic baths, whose size surpassed even the baths of Nero and Trajan?

He had seen many imposing cities – Alexandria, Antioch, the temple cities and colossal monuments of the Nile – and had himself erected a splendid new capital at Nicomedia. But, however hostile he was politically to the gravitational pull of Rome, neither he nor anyone else of any sensibility could be immune to its physical presence. Then, even more than now, Rome was a symbol articulated in an architectural grandeur, order and variety which had no equal: a vast metropolis of seemingly endless, interconnecting public places, temples, squares, basilicas, theatres, baths, circuses, markets, amphitheatres, all of grand and spacious dimensions. Between them, wide avenues, porticoes, colonnades and the countless maze of smaller streets and districts all leading in geometrical regularity to the long straight thoroughfares and thence into the central places. A city of over a million people of all nations, of the great and the humble, the old and the new, and with dwelling places for every one of the gods of the Mediterranean.

The great Triumphal procession of Diocletian and Maximian passed through the sea of cheering citizens, followed by gaudy representations of all the major victories of the Tetrarchs: Britain, the Rhine, Africa, Egypt, the Danube, and with painted images of the family, harem and household of Narses, decked in every fabulous trapping of Oriental display that the designers could contrive. A great portable map of the conquered nations preceded the trophies by way of explanation. Several monuments still survive from this occasion. To the north-west of the Forum are several column bases, which once supported the statues of the four Emperors and, dominating them all, the figure of Jupiter. One shows a sacrificial procession of bull, goats and sheep, and the priest ready with the knife. In another, an Emperor makes offering at an altar, accompanied by gods and companions. In a third panel is celebrated the tenth anniversary of the two Caesars: a cartouche bears the legend *Caesarum Decennalia Feliciter*, supported by winged figures and victory trophies. Having provided all these glories, Diocletian exacted from his faithful imperial colleague an oath, at the altar of Capitoline Jupiter, that he would respect the constitutional settlement of the new order of Jove and Hercules, and that they would both retire from imperial power together when the time came.[3]

Despite it all, Diocletian increasingly disliked Rome. The sheer extravagance and frivolity of the city's celebrations jarred on his puritan taste. Gladiatorial fights and chariot races were all very well, but the Roman populace seemed to have unlimited appetites for every kind of drunken revelry and buffoonery. The whole thing was becoming more like an endless vulgar comedy than a dignified, religious State ceremony. Diocletian's idea of a great celebration was something far more controlled, reverential, a solemn ritual expressing the bonds of duty and piety linking the people to the Emperor and to the gods – rather than the excitement of the shouting rabble at the races. This idle, riotous, rudely familiar multitude offended his sense of authority and order, all the traditions of *gravitas* and propriety he understood and upheld.[4] As so often happens, Diocletian was made suddenly aware of the great contrast between the Roman Idea as he and his Illyrian officer background had received it, and the concrete fact of the turbulent city on the Tiber. If this was the much-vaunted ancient liberty, then Caesar and Augustus had done well to make an end to it, and he himself was fully justified in completing their work. Finally, unable to endure the thought of a further 13 days of banqueting and riot, he announced that he was cutting short his stay, and that he would receive his ninth consulship on the Kalends of January in Ravenna.

The whole court prepared for the journey north, in a severe winter accompanied by incessant rains. From Ravenna, Diocletian planned another progress along the old familiar route through the Danube provinces which he had traversed so many times before, among populations he was at home with, cities who knew how to welcome him, and whom in return he had generously endowed with public buildings.

During the winter he contracted a slight feverish illness, possibly brought on by the weather. He was unable to throw it off, even with spring, so that for much of the journey he had to be carried in a litter. Still, he determined to press on with the progress, to arrive at Nicomedia by the autumn. But the attentions of doctors and his own driving will did not succeed in conquering the disease. It was in April, in Pannonia, that among other public business he assented to the fourth and most drastic Edict against the Christians, requiring general sacrifice – in just what state of mind, we do not know. The whole summer of 304 was increasingly painful and apprehensive, as the Emperor's health fluctuated, then deteriorated, and members of the court could not help exchange the mute glances which expressed their one shared thought.

Nonetheless, Diocletian insisted on carrying on to Nicomedia, to dedicate the circus marking his twentieth year of rule. Perhaps he too had the same thought, and had decided that he would at least die in his capital, if he had to die. He arrived at the end of the summer, and with a great effort publicly dedicated the new circus. But the festivities were marred by the all too obvious sickness which had almost prostrated him. Immediately after the ceremony he retired to his bed, while public prayers and sacrifices were ordered for the health of the Augustus. For months he did not appear in public. Then on the Ides of December 304, he fell into a coma. The atmosphere in the palace was one of shock, which quickly communicated itself to people outside. Court officials ran about, without trying to hide their agitation; it was said that the sounds of weeping and lamentation had been heard in the palace. The whole city was silent, awaiting the fateful news. Word had been sent to Galerius to come to Nicomedia. Rumour quickly spread that Diocletian was dead, and even that he had already been buried.

Early next morning the news among the waiting crowds changed. The Emperor was still living after all. The officials and guards had lost their long faces, and again expressed hopes of a recovery. But who really knew? Only the doctors, and a few intimate members of the court among the huge palace staff, had actually seen the Emperor for months. As the tense waiting dragged on, some voices put about the theory that Diocletian had died, but the truth was being carefully concealed for fear of a military coup by the units stationed in Nicomedia, before Galerius arrived. The rumour gained credence as week after week passed, with no definite news of improvement, and no public view of Diocletian.

It was only dispelled at the beginning of March when, like a man back from the dead, their Emperor made a ceremonial public appearance. He had recovered at last after over a year of illness: the prayers and sacrifices had once more been answered. Yet the toll his illness had taken was painfully evident to everyone. His face was so pale and emaciated he seemed to have aged many years. After an ordeal of this kind, in which he had hovered on the brink of death for so long, he could not avoid recognising that it was time to put his retirement plan into effect. When Galerius arrived at Nicomedia shortly afterwards, congratulating him on his recovery, Diocletian gave him good reason to hope that he could now prepare for full power, as the Tetrarchic system renewed itself.[5]

In Lactantius' narrative it is the violent, overbearing Galerius who actually suggests to Diocletian the idea of abdication and retirement. He complains that he has been campaigning for years against the barbarians on the Danube, the most laborious and thankless frontier of all, while others rule easier, more tranquil portions of the Empire. When is his reward to come? Either Diocletian resigns to him the authority of full Augustus voluntarily and regularly, or, he says menacingly, he will have to look to his armies and consult his own interests. The cowed old Emperor submits.

This is mere invention. First, Lactantius could not of course have been privy to any such conversation. Second, there is independent evidence that Diocletian had contemplated retirement for some time. And third, Lactantius almost contradicts himself, by making Galerius in the course of his arguments allude to something very like a prior plan for the succession. 'Galerius . . . replied that the settlement made by Diocletian should be inviolate: this provided that there should be two of higher rank vested with supreme power, and two others of lower rank to assist them.'[6]

If Galerius did exert pressure, it was only to hasten the implementation of a step that had already been carefully planned. It does seem that Diocletian had come increasingly under his influence, and that after his grave illness he never fully recovered his grip on affairs. More than ever, Diocletian now thought of retirement, and was rushed into decisions which, for the first time, showed weakness and lack of judgement.

Maximian had none of Diocletian's longing for the peace of retirement, and had consented to the plan only very reluctantly. If the complicated Tetrarchic system was to be renewed, prudence surely suggested to Diocletian that whoever was appointed Caesar in the West should be acceptable to Constantius and to the armies there. Maximian's son Maxentius was now nearly 20 and his father, it seemed, had still not despaired of an imperial future for him: he had married him to Galerius' daughter, Valeria Maximilla.[7] But both Diocletian and Galerius had a low opinion of the youth, and it was decided once again to pass him over. This made it even more imperative that the new Caesar should have strong and assured authority in the West.

The sad fact was that growing antipathy and distrust existed between Constantius and Galerius, the two who were now to become supreme heads of the Herculian and Jovian dynasties. It was not merely over the widening religious split, although the sharpening contrast between the fate of Christians in East and West was certainly an inauspicious atmosphere in which to effect a smooth transfer of power. Only the firm hand of Diocletian had kept this rift under control, and now this was to be removed. Even so, the difference need not have been fatal, provided each respected one another's domains. But Galerius' unsubtle notions of imperial stability meant in practice, maximal power for himself and his nominees. The whole settlement was heavily weighted towards the East, and Galerius. When the two new Caesars were finally decided on, it was by Diocletian and Galerius alone at Nicomedia, and both turned out to be Galerius' creatures:

> Alas, said Diocletian with a deep sigh: the men you propose are not fit for high positions.
>
> – I have tried them.
>
> – In that case, be it on your own head, since you are about to take over government of the State. As for me, so long as I was Augustus I spared no pains to keep the Empire on a secure footing. If there are new disasters, the responsibility will not be mine! (Lactantius)[8]

In fact, there is no evidence of such misgivings at the time, and the two new men were probably capable enough. The Caesar in the East was a nephew of Galerius, Maximinus Daza (or Daia), who had originally been a *Scutarius* in the imperial guards, then a legionary tribune. More significantly, he shared Galerius' fanatical anti-Christian attitudes, and was no doubt an active persecutor during 303–4. The Western Caesar, Severus, was an older, experienced commander from Pannonia, a long-standing military colleague of Galerius. Another man whose hopes were to be disappointed (and doubtless his father's hopes too) was, of course, Constantine: an error which in hindsight was to have the gravest consequences. Indeed, from about this point on, our major sources treat ensuing events not as a Roman power struggle, but an unfolding religious drama whose culmination is the victory of Christ's Church, and whose hero is Constantine.[9]

At the time he was in his early thirties, a tribune first class in the army. He had been brought to the courts of Diocletian and Galerius many years earlier to acquire a military education, and because he was his father's son. To describe him as an imperial 'hostage' as some have done, is quite untrue. But it seems Diocletian, unsure about the succession question, did not quite know what to do with him. He had served with distinction against the Sarmatians under Galerius, and accompanied Diocletian on his Egyptian war. But apart from being an able and popular officer, he had never commanded an army nor actually administered anything. The fact that he was passed over for imperial rank, like Maxentius, does not prove that Diocletian dogmatically excluded dynastic succession; only that there were better qualified candidates – or so it seemed.

Nonetheless, there are signs that Constantine might not have been discouraged from imperial hopes, at least before Galerius' ascendancy. His position was a frustrating and confusing one. Once it had leaked out that new Caesars were to be chosen, a certain faction did expect him to be promoted to Caesar. The mint at Alexandria most rashly anticipated the event by striking an *aureus* inscribed *Constantinus Caesar*. Coin messages in the Roman world were of extreme political sensitivity and it put him in a difficult position.[10]

On 1 May 305, 20 years after the battle of Margus, Diocletian and Maximian both retired the purple simultaneously at their capitals of Nicomedia and Milan, transmitting their imperium to the new Caesars in front of their assembled armies, and thus producing a new generation of the Jovian and Herculian houses. Lactantius describes the scene at Nicomedia:

> Three miles outside Nicomedia is the hill on which Galerius had received the
> purple. On its summit stood the high pillar with the statue of Jupiter on top. The
> procession went up to this spot, while a great assembly of the army was drawn up
> around it. Tearfully, Diocletian addressed the soldiers, saying that he was now
> infirm after his years of ceaseless toil, and that he had earned a rest from his labours.
> He was therefore going to resign the Empire into younger and more vigorous
> hands, and at the same time appoint new Caesars.
>
> The assembly waited in tense anticipation for the names to be announced. He
> then said that the Caesars were to be Severus, and Maximinus. There was general

amazement. Constantine stood prominently nearby, and men began to wonder whether he had not changed his name to Maximinus. But then, in the full view of everyone, Galerius reached back his hand, brushing Constantine aside, and drew Daza forward; he relieved him of his ordinary cloak he wore as a private man, and put him in the most prominent position. Everyone wondered who he could be, and where he came from. But none raised any objections, they were so taken aback. Then Diocletian took off his purple robe, and put it on Daza: while he resumed his original private name of Diocles. He descended the tribunal, and passed out of Nicomedia in a chariot. Then this old Emperor, like a veteran soldier finally discharged from military service, retired into his own country.[11]

Thus it was; except that Lactantius probably exaggerates the army's surprise. Maximian, still unable to bring himself to defy his older colleague, likewise retired from Milan to his estate in Lucania. For a short time the weaknesses in the new regime remained latent. The smouldering disappointments of Constantine, of Maxentius, and before long the restless old Maximian too, were controlled. The provinces were divided anew between the four rulers. Constantius retained Gaul and Britain and acquired Spain; Severus, Pannonia, Italy and Africa; Galerius the whole Eastern Danube and Asia Minor; and Maximinus Daza, the Orient. Soon afterwards, Galerius began the second great census of resources, which Diocletian's new tax system had stipulated for every five-year cycle, and Severus followed suit in Italy.

Everyone observed the letter of Diocletian's settlement. Constantius loyally accepted Severus without demur. The political atmosphere was not unlike that of the passing of Oliver Cromwell. It took a certain time to sink into mens' minds that the mighty hand that had ruled them unchallenged for so long, was actually gone. When it did, the mould that had confined them began to crack, then shattered completely with a relapse into seven years of new civil wars and confusion. Aurelius Victor says of Diocletian that he was like a father to the Roman people: soon his heirs were to be squabbling again like unruly children.[12]

Like so many other things he did, Diocletian's retirement from power was almost without precedent. Except for the caretaker Nerva in 96, no Emperor had ever abdicated before. Victor suggests that Diocletian foresaw the onset of new civil troubles which he was unable to prevent, and so, disdaining to take part in yet another crude power struggle, he withdrew himself from the scene with his reputation secure. Another tradition is that he was getting a bad conscience about the Christian persecutions (perhaps even regarding his illness as a punishment), and wanted to dissociate himself from them.[13] But the attested facts seem straightforward enough, without these suppositions: he had contemplated retirement for some time, probably as part of the imperial renewal, and his illness, possibly aided by Galerius' persuasion, provided the occasion.

Retirement certainly improved his health, for he had chosen the site of his retreat with great care. The climate along this part of the Adriatic coast is one of the most attractive in the Mediterranean: a dry heat, lush vegetation, brilliant sunlight and translucent waters. The palace is still one of the best preserved Roman monuments, and a deservedly famous tourist attraction. Sited at a secluded point on the peninsula separating the bay of Salona from the sea, it was built very much as an imperial palace, not a private villa (such as Hadrian's villa at Tivoli). Diocletian had hardly learned how to live as a private citizen, so perhaps it is not surprising the palace was still a place of outward ritual and formality, with sentries reassuringly patrolling the walls, and a clear divide between the private apartments and the public spaces. Still, it was a serene enough atmosphere, and as his spirits recovered he set to work enthusiastically drawing up plans for extensive planting, gardening and building in the palace and the surrounding acres. His natural bent towards construction, order and supervised detail was now absorbed in horticulture. On a nearby island, marine excavation has also revealed remains of enclosed fish pens which probably served the palace.

The plan of the palace is essentially that of a military fort, a great walled rectangle with projecting towers and straight cruciform streets linking the four compass-point gates, the whole enclosing a total area of seven and a half acres. The long southern façade, which now overlooks the main thoroughfare and harbour, was an arcaded gallery broken by three loggias, and opening directly on to the sea, the lower gateway opening on to a jetty. The walls provided a continuous walk around the perimeter of the palace. The main gate, called the Golden Gate by the Medievals, was an impressive courtyarded entrance to the north, which is still well preserved. Above the entrance are a series of niches crowned with arches, in which were probably statues of the Emperor and his family, while on the cornice above that are four pedestals which may well have supported the images of the Tetrarchs. The corbels supporting the former pilasters are decorated with minotaur heads that look down on the visitor as he approaches the gate.

Once through the courtyard, the visitor's gaze would be immediately captured by the long rhythmic colonnades either side of the main street, which led to the central public square, and peristyle. Here all the architectural lines culminated in the imposing raised portals which were the entrance to the imperial reception area, and through which the Emperor and favoured friends would make their public entrance. They were dominated by the arched pediment resting on four great red granite columns, and topped by a four-horse chariot group. To the west of the peristyle was a temple, probably to Jupiter, which now survives as a baptistery, plus two smaller circular religious buildings whose foundations have only recently been excavated. To the east was the great octagonal mausoleum of Diocletian (now the church of St. Duje), whose form anticipated the later rotunda of Byzantine architects.

The private apartments were confined to the southern part of the palace overlooking the sea, so that the only chance a curious observer had of glimpsing the retired Emperor, was by taking a boat around the southern façade. The different suites of halls, vestibules, baths, corridors and private rooms that made up this area were largely demolished by the medievals for building stone, but below the raised floor level the lower plan is intact, and excavation is revealing the whole arrangement of the upper storey. So far one of the most prominent results is the elaborate *triclinium* or dining quarters on the south-east, with its cruciform arrangement of chambers around the central hall.[14]

Overall, the first impression of the palace is still that of a fortress. (Had its later

Croatian inhabitants not been able to use it in this way, it would hardly have survived to the present.) But the remaining colonnades nonetheless recall a place of spacious, sunlit walks among fine buildings and imposing gardens. In fact it was to a real fourth-century fort what Tudor palaces were to real medieval castles – a softened, mannered version of a war citadel. In these surroundings Diocletian took his ease, enjoying universal respect and honours. If he did not actually forget the outside world of government, at least he was personally free of its burdens and anxieties. The *Historia Augusta* attributes to him the reminiscence on the difficulties an Emperor faced in trying to govern justly:

> Diocletian, while a private citizen, said that nothing was more difficult than ruling well. It is so easy for four of five advisers to concoct a plan for deceiving the Emperor, and then persuade him of the need for some particular decision. From within his palace he cannot know the true situation, and is forced to see through their eyes. So it happens that he appoints to high office men who should not be appointed, and removes those who should be retained. In this way the favours of even the most wise and upright Emperor are often bought and sold.[15]

But outside, events were moving quickly in the power vacuum created by his withdrawal from affairs. Constantine's position at Galerius' court was now embarrassing and dangerous. Sensing the situation, his father, Constantius Augustus, lost no time in requesting his fraternal imperial colleague to send his son to him in Gaul. Galerius prevaricated and delayed, but finally – in a mellow mood after dinner, it is said – consented. The young Constantine seized the opportunity before it could be withdrawn, and travelled non-stop across the world using the imperial post horses. He eventually joined his father at Boulogne and accompanied him to Britain for a brief campaign against the Picts in the North.

Perhaps, as some writers suggest, Constantius already knew himself to be ill when he sent for his son. But, after his victory over the Picts, he died at York in July 306, suddenly removing a cornerstone of the still untried second Tetrarchy. He had been a popular ruler north of the Alps, healing many of the civic wounds inflicted by previous Emperors and usurpers. (He is said by Eusebius to have remarked that the best place to keep his treasury was in his subjects' purses; and to demonstrate the frugality of his court, he was supposed to borrow silver plate when he gave a banquet.) At the same time his efforts to promote economic recovery included settling very large colonies of Germans in Gaul, whose recruits were slowly constituting an alternative, rival army élite to the Danubian legions. It was with such soldiers that his son Constantine now took the first step in demolishing the settlement of Diocletian.

Perhaps he had no choice, now that his father and protector was dead. Constantius had apparently accepted Severus as his Caesar, but as he sensed death approaching he either engineered, or at least acquiesced in, his son's seizure of power. Frankish soldiers at York led the army in proclaiming the young Constantine Augustus in succession to his father. Constantine tried to clothe this with as much legitimacy as he could. He wrote to Galerius explaining the position, protesting that the armies had literally compelled him, and would serve no one else. Galerius realised he had been outwitted: anyone who held all Gaul and Britain with loyal armies would be extremely difficult to dislodge. He therefore swallowed his anger and agreed to recognise Constantine, not as Augustus, but merely as *Caesar* of the Herculian dynasty in the West: Severus was automatically raised to the senior position. Constantine, biding his time, accepted.[16]

But his example of a successful rebellion, recalling that of Carausius 20 years earlier, was soon copied, and from then on the collapse began. Severus was quite unknown in Italy and increasingly unpopular, as the second great tax census sharply reminded Italians of the ancient privileges of exemption which they had lost at the hand of these Illyrians. At Rome the Senate and the Praetorians, both of whom resented their eclipse under the Tetrarchy, plotted with the young Maxentius to alter this state of things. At a suitable opportunity they proclaimed Maxentius Emperor in Rome, as protector and restorer of 'ancient liberties'. The City Prefect and other appointees of Severus were isolated and massacred. Maxentius' next shrewd move was to approach his father Maximian, with much flattery, to come out of retirement and resume his former throne: the old man, already chafing at his loss of power, needed no second bidding. When Severus marched on Rome to chastise the usurper, he found it skilfully defended: worse still, his own troops, who had formerly been Maximian's, began deserting back to their old Emperor, helped by lavish promises of gold. Severus retreated to Ravenna, where Maximian besieged him. He was persuaded into an unwise capitulation on conditions which Maximian then betrayed. Promised his life in return for abdicating the purple, he was then forced to commit suicide and given an imperial funeral by way of recompense.

This was too much for Galerius, who marched into Italy himself with his loyal veterans. But he too failed to eject the old Maximian, who fought a brilliant delaying campaign to wear him down and deprive him of supplies. Baffled, advancing to within a few miles of Rome but unable to take it, Galerius offered negotiation but was rebuffed. He eventually withdrew from Italy having achieved nothing, his frustrated armies plundering and ravaging the territories along their retreat. Meanwhile there had begun a poker game of alliances and counter-alliances, in which Constantine was to prove himself the most patient and astute. To cover his northern flank while he dealt with invasion, Maximian had made an alliance with Constantine. He offered him his daughter Fausta in marriage, legitimate connection with the Herculian dynasty, and promotion to the rank of full Augustus. In return, Constantine offered no concession beyond military neutrality: he carefully did nothing further to offend Galerius. He divorced his wife Minervina, and married Fausta in March 307.[17]

Maximian's military skills contrasted sadly with his political ineptitude. With Galerius expelled from Italy, hostility soon broke out between him and his son. Maxentius had found the old man indispensable as a general and a figurehead, but now no longer needed him, and had no intention of letting him actually rule. Maximian indignantly tried to force the issue, denounced his ungrateful son in front of the army and stripped the purple from him. But then he had the unpleasant shock to find that the troops favoured his son, who knew how to bribe them if not lead them in war. Maximian was allowed to leave Italy, and sought solace and refuge with

Galerius, feigning repentance for ever having opposed him. Meanwhile, Africa revolted against Maxentius and set up a usurper called Domitius Alexander.[18]

In this shambles to which the collegiate government of the Empire had been reduced barely three years after Diocletian's retirement, it was hardly surprising that the older men who had served with him, should sooner or later come to seek his advice. In the Autumn of 308 the secluded residence on the Adriatic received an important messenger. Galerius, no longer overweeningly confident but now an anxious and perplexed man, wanted his father-in-law's help. Diocletian was determined not to enter the political arena again, but otherwise agreed to be of what help he could. His experienced advice, his influence over Maximian, and perhaps his prestige, were what Galerius now sought. It was agreed that Galerius, Diocletian and Maximian would all meet for conference at Carnutum on the Danube, in November. Many of the soldiers must have wondered at the sight of this venerable old grandfather of the Jovians and Herculians being trundled back again into imperial counsels.

It was at this meeting that Maximian, outmanoeuvred and impotent but with greed for his old power virtually written on his face, appealed to Diocletian to reassume the reigns of power, for the good of the Empire. There are many things Diocletian could have replied to this. He might have pointed out that just 'reassuming' the purple after abdicating was not as easy as it sounded, as Maximian had discovered. He could have charged that it was precisely Maximian's own folly that had caused most of the troubles, by preventing first Severus and then Galerius from crushing the perfidious rebel, his ungrateful son Maxentius. Did he, Maximian, really expect Diocletian to come and pull his chestnuts out of the fire for him? But instead, we are told, Diocletian dwelt on the pastoral joys of retirement. If Maximian could only see the fine cabbages he had planted with his own hands at Salona, he said, he would not want for him to exchange this true happiness for the illusory promises of pomp and power. No doubt he sincerely meant it.[19]

The conference agreed at least the shape of a settlement, provided the parties could achieve it and would respect it. Maximian was to return into retirement. Constantine was acknowledged, as before, as Caesar (not Augustus) in Gaul and Britain. Maxentius and Alexander were treated as usurpers. In place of the dead Severus a new, legitimate Augustus would be appointed to the Herculian dynasty. This was Licinius, another military colleague of Galerius. He would rule in Pannonia until he was able to recover Italy and Africa.

The immediate sequel was that Maximian, Lear-like, took up residence with his son-in-law Constantine, the only court that was now prepared to receive him. The latter still found him a useful symbol and treated him with all honours, but was very careful not to let him get his hands on the one thing he wanted, which was real power. In the Orient, Maximinus Daza objected that Licinius should be appointed Augustus, and after months of complex wrangling Galerius gave way and was forced to cede the title of Augustus to both him *and* Constantine. Diocletian had meanwhile returned to his cabbages.

But he could hardly fail to have been disappointed in the apparent ruin of his imperial system. He had failed, after all, to solve the great problem of orderly succession. What had been a genuine fourfold monarchy was now simply an armed truce between distant power centres, in which Emperors had proliferated until now there was the absurd and unwieldy number of *six* Augusti. All the dignity of the Jovian and Herculian houses now seemed increasingly just a brittle veneer over the old carve-up of the Empire between rival generals. What was to prevent things sliding back into the military anarchy of a generation ago?

This gloomy prospect was underlined when, a year later, the incorrigible old Maximian made a last desperate bid for power. Constantine no longer needed him, and may well have expected some such move. Maximian quite underestimated his rival's cunning, generalship and support among the army. While Constantine was away campaigning on the Rhine, he seized Arles, put out news of Constantine's death, assumed full powers and with the treasury of that city made a generous donation to the garrison. Then he summoned other army units to his standard. The response was tardy, while by very rapid marches from Cologne, Constantine was upon him almost immediately. Maximian fled to Marseilles, was besieged there, forced into surrender, stripped of the purple, then ordered to take his own life. Constantine later gave out the story that Maximian had actually attempted to assassinate him. Maximian's daughter Fausta either could not or would not intercede for him. Instead of the honourable retirement, after a glorious reign of nearly 20 years that Diocletian had made possible for him, Maximian died unsuccessful and disgraced, without allies or sympathisers, a dangerous, wild old man who had to be put out of the way.[20] Constantine subsequently secured his *damnatio memoriae,* wiping him out of the role of Emperors. Despite its complexity, Diocletian's Tetrarchy had been less of a system than it looked. It had been a skilful rationalisation of endemic military rivalries, and reflected the particular personal strengths of its chief rather than an inherently sound constitutional design. It had worked, not so much because the rulers had been really weaned into co-operation, but because Diocletian had been able to manage them, and exert to the full his extraordinary gifts of delegating. But a system that depends on the rare abilities of one man is no system at all, since it cannot be perpetuated. (Here again, one thinks of Oliver Cromwell.) Galerius, it is true, did make a brave attempt to keep the Tetrarchy working. He was a strong man with many qualities (leaving aside the uniformly black picture of him which Christian sources naturally portray), but they were not of the same type, or the same order, as those of his father-in-law. He was better at using force than diplomacy, at commanding than persuading, and he had no great gift for penetrating the minds of his enemies or allies. The other rulers felt no such sense of obligation towards Diocletian's government or memory, and their use of the old Tetrarchic symbols of legitimacy went no further than opportunism.

It has often been said that Diocletian's grave mistake was in ignoring hereditary claims to the purple: this is a fair criticism as far as it goes. In the third-century anarchy, the appeal of dynastic loyalties had not been very effective, except where the heir was strong and an able ruler in his own right. At the creation of the Tetrarchy in 293 the dynastic option had not been open: at its renewal in 305, it was. The pattern of eventual succession had not been fixed in 293 and could easily have been adapted to fit the later circumstances. The error in 305 was not in the competence of the new

Caesars, but in the fact that *two* of Diocletian's colleagues, Constantius and Maximian, quite naturally harboured dynastic ambitions themselves, for all their professed loyalty to his settlement. These two each enjoyed a secure power base and loyal armies in the West, far away from Nicomedia. These two were not consulted, nor placated, nor their influences counteracted – indeed, the intelligence about political feelings in the West seems to have been inexplicably poor at Nicomedia. Yet these two, and their sons, were expected to bow completely to the political will of Diocletian long after he had retired from the scene. Such shortsightedness is so glaring, and so untypical of Diocletian, that it may indeed reflect his state of health and the consequent influence of Galerius.

The house of Constantine was later to have the problem of too many male heirs, which would lead to a bloody round of family murders. And imperial kinsmen were just as capable of making civil war on one another as unrelated Emperors. But for all this, a far more stable imperial system was eventually achieved in the fourth century, around the twin principles of dynastic succession and collegial rule. That stability was due, in part, to the deep foundations Diocletian himself had laid, which had been quite absent in the third century: the long practice of joint Emperors in East and West, the change to an absolute, 'Oriental' style of monarchy, and the careful separation between civil and military authority.

Thus, the years of breakdown following Diocletian's retirement seemed more destructive to imperial government than they actually were. Later generations were forced to appreciate that his underlying construction was, after all, surprisingly sound, and outlasted the cumbersome fourfold division of rule. But all this would not become apparent until well after his death. The very last period of his life was embittered by what seemed the failure of so much of his work, as well as the insults of the new rulers. He, who had founded the Tetrarchy, was to be its last surviving member.

So long as Galerius lived and ruled, Diocletian's memory and his surviving family were assured of proper treatment. But in 310 Galerius was suddenly struck down by illness. He and Maximinus Daza had continued the policy of persecution with plenty of cruelty but no great success. All except the most dedicated anti-Christians were becoming wearied and often repelled by these futile measures. And Christians themselves now looked with envy and hope to the West, where persecution had been ended by both Maxentius and Constantine, the latter inclining towards Christianity himself. So, when Galerius fell ill in the eighteenth year of his reign and at least his sixth decade of life, Christians had no difficulty in regarding it as a righteous punishment from God. Lactantius, whose whole theme is to show what befalls God's enemies, gloats disgustingly over the details of Galerius' terminal illness, for the edification of the faithful. Surgery was attempted, more and more of his flesh cut away to no avail. 'His bowels came out, his whole anus putrefied . . . the stench filled not just the palace but the whole city . . . his body, in intolerable tortures, dissolved into one mass of corruption.'[21]

Galerius' last important act before his death was to end the persecution of Christianity. Perhaps, as the Christians claimed, he recognised the victory and power of their God. But his Edict, issued in April 311 from Serdica, expresses not so much repentance, as an admission of bafflement and defeat. The Christians, he says, have remained utterly obdurate, and the result is that they are publicly worshipping no gods at all, neither the ancestral ones nor the Christian god. Such a state of affairs cannot go on, and so the Emperors in their clemency have finally decided to permit Christian worship once again. Christians are henceforth enjoined to pray to their own god for the welfare of the Emperors and the State.

This did not just return to the position before the persecution had begun. It finally acknowledged Christianity as a fully legitimate religion of the Empire, and the Christian god as a powerful deity. Throughout the East, great numbers of clergy and laity returned again from the prisons and the mines to open the churches and celebrate their worship publicly. It was a time of rejoicing and of victory for them, after the long purgatory they had endured. For the arch-persecutor publicly to admit his own failure and the strength of God's church, meant that the Great Battle, the theomachy, had at last been won.

By the time the Edict was published in the main cities of the East, Galerius was dead. He was buried at his own birthplace, the city of Romulianum, a short distance up the Danube from Bononia. The great mausoleum he had built for himself at Salonica was never used. It was a considerable building, a rotunda in the new style which was later converted into an internally domed church by Theodosius (with what purification rites we do not know), and stands today, with accompanying minaret, as St. George in Salonica.

With Galerius dead, it was not long before Diocletian experienced the cold indifference of his successors, and was made to realise just how little his own prestige now counted with the new generation of rival rulers. His daughter Valeria joined the court of Daza after the death of her husband Galerius. The ambitions of Daza, it seems, led him almost immediately to propose marriage with her, a proposal she refused. As a result he deprived her of her household and banished both her and her mother Prisca from Nicomedia. She later arrived in Syria, from where she got word to her father Diocletian of her plight. He therefore sent a messenger to Daza with the request that his daughter be allowed to return to him at Salona: it was ignored. Repeated requests likewise produced no response. Finally he, Diocletian, the creator of all the Emperors, who six years earlier had raised Daza himself to the purple, was obliged to ask one of his own relations who was now a powerful general in Daza's court, to intercede for him with this one petition. The man did so, but regretfully reported that he had been unsuccessful. This was what his glorious memory had now come to. This was the ingratitude of a ruler who no longer feared him and therefore cynically dropped any pretence of respect or even courtesy. To these new men he was just a nuisance, a useless and barely tolerated relic. When Constantine demolished the statues of the disgraced Maximian in Gaul, the statues of Diocletian which were normally joined to them, were smashed too.[22]

These then were the bitter fruits of abdication. Perhaps Maximian had been right after all to want to live and die in the purple? Perhaps Diocletian's own misfortune had simply been to outlive the Caesars? But the wheel of fortune had almost come full circle now, and he had clearly lived too long. Though he still resided in a magnificent palace, he had seen his great political work (apparently) come to nothing, his statues overturned, and he finally endured the pain and humiliation of being unable even to protect his family from the depredations of the mighty. Whether we accept the suggestions that he chose a voluntary death, it remains that (on the best reckoning) Diocletian died in 312 – disappointed, weary, ready for his exit. This was on the eve of another round of civil wars, which would leave the world divided between Constantine in the West and Licinius in the East. After Daza had been crushed, Licinius conducted a bloody purge of all the remnants of his family and that of Galerius. In it perished Candidianus, the young natural son of Galerius, the son and daughter of Daza, and Prisca and Valeria, wife and daughter of Diocletian.

Diocletian was buried in the fine mausoleum he had constructed for himself in his palace, which is now the church of St. Duje in Split. Apart from a small nave later crudely added to the eastern side, the building is still remarkably intact. Externally it is an octagon, surrounded by its own colonnade, its gate facing the peristyle arcade and flanked by two black Egyptian lions. Internally it is a circular domed building, whose Christianization has not altered the fundamentally pagan classic character. The circular space is defined by an internal Corinthian colonnade at two levels, the upper columns rising from the elaborately decorated cornice projections of the lower. High above pulpit and altar, on the wall below the upper cornice, runs a continuous frieze of animals, gods, *putti* figures of the funerary style of the day, in which are enclosed the rather weathered portraits of Diocletian and Prisca. He was probably interred in a porphyry sarcophagus. It is reported that about 50 years later a robber stole the rich purple shroud from the mausoleum, for which he was put to death.[23]

part five

AFTERMATH

chapter sixteen

·CONSTANTINE'S·
·COMPLETION·

THUS ALL TYRANNY HAD BEEN PURGED AWAY, AND THE KINGDOM THAT WAS
RIGHTLY THEIRS WAS PRESERVED UNDISPUTED AND SECURE FOR
CONSTANTINE AND HIS SONS ALONE. HAVING MADE IT THEIR FIRST TASK TO
CLEANSE THE WORLD OF HOSTILITY TO GOD, THEY REJOICED IN THE
BLESSINGS HE HAD CONFERRED UPON THEM
·EUSEBIUS, *Historia Ecclesia*·¹

Within the year of Diocletian's lonely death, the long expected rupture occurred in the West between Constantine, who ruled the Gallic provinces, and Maxentius, who held Italy and had recently recovered Africa. The war was short and decisive, and revealed Constantine's military skills to the full. Forestalling his rival, he marched across the Alps and into Italy at great speed, with a highly trained mobile army containing a high proportion of Germans. Two attempts by Maxentius to halt him, at Turin and then Brescia, were defeated, and in record time he was approaching Rome itself.

But most significant of all in this age of religious revolution, this was to be a battle between the old gods and the new. Constantine's expanding ambition, conceived as a sense of divine mission, had long been searching beyond traditional polytheism for the Supreme God who would give him victory and dominion. He had already tried the sun god of Aurelian, *Sol Invictus*. But now he turned to the god of the Christians, and before the walls of Rome he received a sign, as those who seek for signs usually do. In a dream, we are told, he was commanded to have painted on his leading soldiers' shields the Chi-Rho monogram of Christ (☧). Meanwhile Maxentius was seeking aid of the pagan gods and consulting the Sybilline books. The two armies faced each other with the Tiber to Maxentius' rear, on 28 October 312. In what became known as the Battle of the Milvian Bridge, Maxentius' army was routed and he himself drowned in the general flight. It was also the last stand of the Praetorians, who preserved their order and died where they stood: one of Constantine's first acts after entering Rome as liberator, was to abolish the Guards for good and pull down their camp.²

From then on, Constantine showed conspicuous favour towards the Christians. The Lateran palace was given to the Bishop of Rome. The following year he and

Licinius, who had now entered into an alliance, issued from Milan a joint programme of toleration which inclined towards Christianity, and went much further than Galerius' Edict two years before. 'The Christians and all others should be free to follow that mode of religion which seems best to them ... No man should be denied the right to devote himself to the rites of the Christians, or to whatever other religion his mind directs him; so that the one Supreme God, to whose worship we freely dedicate ourselves, shall continue His favour and beneficence to us.' Not only was all persecution at an end, but confiscated property and meeting places were to be restored to the Church, and its communities recognised as corporations with legal rights. In the following years these privileges were increased, raising Christianity to a clear position above other religions. Clergy were exempt from municipal obligations, bishops could adjudicate in civil as well as ecclesiastical cases, and Sunday was declared a public holiday. While traditional paganism was not (yet) interfered with, it received no such State support, and was expected to wither away of its own accord.[3]

From the Church's point of view, which most surviving sources take, Constantine's ascendancy was of course a major turning point in history. Not only was the whole Christian community henceforth assured of imperial protection and patronage, but it was drawn into an entirely new alliance with the Roman State, in which Emperors would actually use their power to decide between rival factions and impose unity. In this respect, Constantine's attitude was that of a traditional Roman Emperor, concerned to secure the protection of the most powerful god for the State, by ensuring proper piety and worship. His own Christian leaning was no doubt genuine, but hardly orthodox: he was barely concerned with Christ at all, but only with the great God whose power he could enlist as world ruler. Despite the appearance of a radical break with Diocletian, naturally heightened by the religious change, Constantine was to develop and complete nearly all the great reforms Diocletian had instituted. Whatever his attitude to the man and the persecutor, the edifice of the new Absolutism enclosed them both, greater than any individual: it forced them to co-operate in the great plan of survival, spanning the generations.

All Constantine's recorded references to Diocletian are derogatory, and he took pains to distance himself officially from the Tetrarchy. He claimed legitimacy, not through his original connection with the Herculian dynasty but by the Divine Will of the Lord and, more concretely, because he was his father's son: his father Constantius in turn was now supplied with a bogus lineage tracing his family back to the Emperor Claudius II, conqueror of the Goths. At Salonica, Rome and elsewhere, surviving reliefs of the other Tetrarchs usually have their faces mutilated – acts which could only be done with official approval. Lactantius crowed with triumph that the dynasties of Jove and Hercules were eclipsed. Only in the army were the identities of the Jovian and Herculian legions preserved.[4]

In the East, Licinius had defeated and supplanted Maximinus Daza (with full approval of Constantine, for as well as his connections with Galerius, Daza had attempted to revive the policy of persecuting the Christians). After initial hostilities the two Augusti ruled their separate halves of the Empire in peace for nearly ten more years. But Constantine's great ambition, fortified by his earlier success and no doubt his sense of religious destiny, did not sit easy with sharing dominion of the world. In the final great clash in 323, a war prodigiously costly in resources, Licinius was defeated twice, then after capitulation, murdered. Thereafter Constantine ruled the whole Empire alone until his death.[5]

Unlike Diocletian he was prolific in sons, and in later years associated his three sons Constantine, Constantius and Constans with him as Caesars, but without permitting them independent power. In all, from his elevation by the army at York in 306, Constantine reigned a remarkable 31 years, and proved as vigorous and far-sighted in administration as in war. Despite the great diversion of forces in the civil wars, they did not lead to major new incursions by Rome's external enemies, thanks largely to the soundness of the frontier defence system which Constantine inherited. His reign was a further period of stability and far-reaching construction, and his House was to occupy the imperial throne for over half the fourth century, inculcating strong habits of loyalty to his line, and through this, to the dynastic principle.

More than a generation of crisis had driven home the lesson that an Emperor's effective capital must be located according to strict military and strategic needs. The Tetrarchs had erected and embellished their own capitals close to the frontiers, and Constantine himself had ruled and defended the Rhine from Trier. Having fought his way to undivided rule, he was now determined to establish yet another, final imperial capital that would outshine all its predecessors. His war with Licinius had impressed him with the unique position of the peninsula of Byzantium, controlling the straits between Europe and Asia, and athwart the main highways from one end of the Empire to the other. It was an optimal position from which the Emperor could quickly reach the Danube or the Euphrates. Similar considerations had weighed with Diocletian in the choice of Nicomedia, but Byzantium was in addition eminently defensible, being surrounded on three sides by sea. The new capital of Constantinople was dedicated in 330 and given the artificial identity of New Rome, with 14 districts, seven 'hills' and a ceremonial Senate. Constantinople was the culmination of a long period of migratory imperial government, which had begun when Gallienus had been forced to establish his base at Milan. The city was also a natural trading port, and within two generations had expanded well beyond its originally projected size. From here, the new bureaucratic machinery of government extended its web over the Empire.

With a fixed capital went a single imperial court, no longer frequently on the move as the Tetrarchs' courts had been. The departmentalisation of the central government, which Diocletian had begun, was now given its definitive shape. Thus all legal matters – the drafting of laws and rescripts, legal advice, and the whole traffic of petitions and decisions to and from the Emperor – were now grouped under a supreme legal minister, the Quaestor of the Sacred Palace. As before, two separate finance ministers were responsible respectively for all public finances, and for the Emperor's private domains. The whole civil administration down to governors and town councils was headed by several regional Praetorian Prefects, who now shed their former military functions. Supreme military direction, under the Emperor, was vested in two newly created commanders, the Master of Cavalry and

Master of Infantry. Staffing and appointments to the Palace and the lower grades of the great bureaucracy, as well as State postal communications and the network of political agents (*agentes in rebus*) were controlled by a new and powerful service minister, the Master of Offices – who also managed audiences, and the now highly elaborate Court ceremonial.

It might be thought that Constantine's adoption of Christianity would cause deep difficulties for the exalted Emperor-worship that was an integral part of the new State system. It did not. In deference to Christianity he dropped the formal claim to divinity and no longer demanded the pagan act of sacrifice as part of the cult. But in every other way he elevated the imperial figure to godlike proportions. He was no humble Christian penitent, but a universal monarch who had entered into alliance with the Supreme God. The close, exclusive relationship which Diocletian had claimed with Jupiter, Constantine claimed with the God of Abraham. Just as every lawcourt displayed his iconic effigy, so too did each church in which the bishop conducted the liturgy.

The Oriental rituals of the Court and public epiphany were developed even further: the diadem, kissing the hem of the robe, prostration, the gorgeous clockwork pageant of palace ceremonial. At Rome the Palazzo Conservatori still contains the giant head of the 40-foot statue of Constantine which once surveyed the world from the great apse of his basilica: *Dominus, Autokrator*. The cult of the superhuman Emperor crystallised into both Byzantine ruler worship and later, Western Caesaropapism.[6]

Separation of military and civil authority reached its logical completion. With the abolition of the Praetorian Guard, the Prefect became supreme civil magistrate under the Emperor, outranking any general. The Empire was normally governed by four Prefects, their territories divided in the manner of the Tetrarchy: the Gallic provinces, Italy, the Balkans and the East. Below them, the vicars of dioceses and governors of provinces continued in the pattern laid down by Diocletian. Each Prefect acted as supreme judge of appeal, and issued minor edicts himself; he had his own treasury and a vast staff, divided into functional bureaux and co-ordinated by his own permanent secretary or *princeps*. Down the line, these bureaux were reproduced at vicar and governor levels, staffed by fixed complements of permanent civil servants with standard office routines, who advanced gradually according to seniority (in contrast to the vicars and governors who, like modern government ministers, changed frequently).

Thus the old Roman method of delegated rule by a few personally picked men, was finally replaced by something like a Chinese bureaucracy. With it went a mandarinate. Whereas Diocletian had squeezed out the senatorial nobility from his provincial governorships in favour of equestrians and former military men, Constantine opened these posts to senators again. But this was no restoration of the old privileges. 'Senatorial' rank was attached to the top jobs, and was automatically attained by anyone who rose high enough. For the purpose of the imperial service, equestrian and senatorial ranks were merged into a single order. A new 'aristocratic' class, the *Clarissimi*, arose to share the duties of governing, but it was not one of birth or independent landed wealth: it was an aristocracy of salaried state service, dependent for its distinctions entirely on the Emperor and his machine.

The army career ladder, now divorced from all connections with civil office, demanded no culture or education at all, only ability. Inevitably this meant not just a widening gulf between soldier and civilian in the upper strata of society, but a creeping 'barbarisation', as more and more Germanic conscripts and mercenaries were raised. But Constantine accelerated the process, favouring German troops more than ever before. They were prominent in his mobile armies, and dominated the new élite 'palace' cavalry (the *scholae palatini*) he created as imperial lifeguards. For the first time, the very highest army commands, including the new Masters of Cavalry and Infantry, were opened to officers of German origin. What the Illyrians had been in the armies of the third century, the Germans became in the fourth.

Constantine's military policy – which was followed by his successors – departed from Diocletian's in an important way. He maintained and even raised the enlarged size of the armies, and continued the basic distinction between first-class, mobile troops (cavalry and infantry) and second-class, static border troops. But Diocletian's great defence system had been a provincially based one, in which the two worked in mutual support. The mobile forces had normally acted as a backstop to the *limitanei* in their chains of forts, ready to destroy an invasion whose impetus had been absorbed and broken by the latter. They also buttressed the morale and training of the *limitanei,* since both had the same function of defending provincial frontiers. But Constantine, doubtless owing to his experience in fighting civil wars, reverted in effect to the earlier policy of Aurelian, and again grouped all the first-class forces in a single offensive mobile army, attached to the Emperor, with no special connection with any frontier. The mobile army and the frontier army thus became permanently separated in their command structure, functions, and in the long run, political interests.

In the last analysis, Constantine's military doctrine meant that protection of the throne itself took precedence over protection of the provinces. The mobile army could help any province threatened with serious invasion, but in the crucial interval the *limitanei* in the forts had to hold out alone. Frontier defence was measurably weakened in favour of the central field army. Nonetheless, this did not reach dangerous levels in Constantine's time. He continued to build and garrison the frontier forts and kept up the strength of the frontier forces, and on both Rhine and Danube he followed the same active, aggressive policies the Tetrarchy had done. The frontiers were kept secure in his time.

Constantine did not repeat Diocletian's abortive attempt to curb inflation by price laws. More significantly, he abandoned as impossible Diocletian's goal of restoring a universal, stable silver currency. As inflation devalued the poor quality denarii still further during the first decades of the fourth century, the rich and powerful scrambled to amass gold, whose value had doubled, then trebled, against the denarius. Gold hoards, plate and jewellery that had been withdrawn from circulation in the long crisis years, now reappeared as coin. The State joined the scramble, and being the most powerful of all, secured the lion's share. Pagan temples were mercilessly ransacked by Constantine's fiscal officials using every possible pretext. Rents on imperial estates were levid in gold; two distinct new taxes, on business and on senatorial lands, were introduced with the express aim of raising gold. It became possible for Constantine to succeed where Diocletian had failed, and recreate a gold currency for widespread use. His new *solidus,* struck at 72 to the pound, became the stable means of transaction in the upper classes of bureaucracy, land-owners, soldiers and men of property, and was to retain its weight and purity for seven centuries. But this was achieved at the cost of severing gold permanently from the everyday copper (nominally 'silver') coinage of the poor, who consequently became the losers.

The marvellous engine of taxation which Diocletian had designed was keenly appreciated. Although on one conspicuous occasion Constantine reduced the *capita* of Autun when he ruled Gaul, it is near-certain that overall, he used the lever of the annual budget to raise the State's estimated needs, and hence the burden on each subject. Of his two new taxes, payable in gold, it was the *lustral* tax on manufacturers and traders that brought urban commercial resources firmly into the same net as landed wealth. (Even prostitution was eventually subject to this tax.) Constantine changed the five-year cycle of the census of resources to 15 years, but otherwise he had every reason to extend and use the new tax machinery, exploiting all the possibilities it opened. Payments in kind became translated into payments in gold where possible. But the convertibility of tax obligations into State services of every form was developed most thoroughly by his administration. Having registered what everyone owed, officials could be paid by simple exemption from municipal services, or granted titles in lieu of salaries.

As we have already seen, such a comprehensive plan of requisitions and obligations presupposes a fixed population, tied to its tasks in the economy. It was under Constantine that compulsory social organisation, the regimentation and virtual enserfment of whole sections of the population, came steadily into force. The binding of workers to hereditary corporations, of *coloni* to their lands, and *decuriones* to their municipalities, became clearly established in law. A *colonus* who left his landlord was to be forcibly restored to him; the *decurion* class was forbidden to leave the cities of their birth, and even required permission to travel; their sons automatically inherited their onerous municipal obligations. If they migrated, they forfeited all or part of their property. Everywhere, men's resources – in money, land, commercial capital or just labour power – were held as surety by the remorseless State. The command economy in which all had to serve in their respective stations, took on a firm and unrelenting shape.[7]

By Constantine's death in 337 the radical transformation of the Roman world was virtually complete. The most conspicuous signs of change to men of the time (depending on their viewpoints), were security of the frontiers; a mighty, bejewelled Emperor ruling the world from his new and splendid capital in the East; the new religion of Christ, visible everywhere in the building of churches and the influential figures of bishops, hurrying about their affairs like high officials; the thriving country estates and villas of the great landlords; the fat jobs in the civil service, the proliferating new titles, uniforms and dignities; the locust-like army of officials with their endless head-counts and tax reckonings; and the tightening of servitude on the poor man and the peasant. Behind it all was an intelligent plan of survival, first engendered in the ad hoc expedients of Aurelian and the military Emperors, then consciously worked out, expanded and put to use by Diocletian and his colleagues. The machinery had been used equally by Galerius, Maximinus Daza, Maxentius and Licinius: its logic and necessity transcended the interval of civil wars and the fortunes of individual rulers.

The great problem of stability and succession was painfully mastered, though not in the way Diocletian had envisaged. Dynastic loyalty again replaced the artificial ties of the Tetrarchy. But despite Constantine's personal example, rule by a single Emperor from a single capital was henceforth to be the exception, not the norm. Constantine's descendants rediscovered the old truth that the Empire was too vast, its enemies too many, to be ruled by one man. After his death, dual rule between imperial kinsmen (or occasionally adopted colleagues) became the general pattern: between Constantius and Constans, then Gallus, then Julian; then the brothers Valentinian and Valens; then Gratian and Theodosius. Its most successful prototype had been the dual rule of Diocletian and Maximian. Although there were still periodic intrigues, coups and civil wars for the purple, these were far fewer than in the third century. The armies still had to be placated, and still had a recognised ceremonial role in the election of Emperors (and usurpers), but there was no return to the earlier, self-perpetuating military anarchy in which any powerful general could compete.

There are several reasons for this all-important achievement. The new, elevated position of the Emperor now dominated the two strictly separate civil and military establishments. Army commanders were powerful, honoured, carefully handled functionaries in a larger imperial system that enclosed them. Under Constantine the infantry formations of the field army became more numerous but smaller: the 'legion' was permanently reduced to about 1,000 men, for greater flexibility but also (one strongly suspects) to make commands more impersonal. A military *dux* or *comes* under the Late Empire commanded a variegated assembly of units and had less control over their pay and supplies, and no civil jurisdiction at all over the territories he occupied. Moreover, the German officers increasingly favoured by Constantine had no social or administrative qualifications, and would not have been accepted in a Roman magistrate's chair. Rebellion was possible, but more difficult: and in several crises during the fourth century the civil ministers on the spot dissociated themselves from the revolt and remained obstinately loyal to the distant Emperor who had appointed them.

The 'barbarian' generals and soldiers had a high regard for the claims of blood kinship and personal loyalty (as distinct from a Roman law they barely understood) which naturally inclined them to defend a hereditary dynasty. Even more important, as they reached towards the highest commands, they knew they would never be acknowledged as Emperors in their own right. They might wield the power of the sword, but they were still socially overawed by the culture and manners of civilisation.

The new order of the fourth century solved many problems, but at the cost of creating new ones, which were managed or concealed for a time, but would later grow to serious proportions. So long as the Emperors remained strong monarchs, commanders-in-chief in fact as well as name, the German military element could be kept in control. Yet the same social barrier that excluded their leaders from the purple, prevented them ever being integrated into the State and civilisation they defended. For a long time the balance of advantage lay with Rome: these men were first-class warriors who loyally fought the 'barbarian' enemy that was ethnically akin to them. But as the armies became predominantly Germanised, leaders like Dagalaif, Arbogast, and Silvanus acquired a pivotal concentration of power like Chinese warlords, which could neither be institutionalised, nor held indefinitely in check by social deference.

The need for manpower was acute, because Roman rural populations, especially in the West, did not recover in numbers from the depopulations during the earlier crisis, despite the return of security. The tax burden on the Empire's finite agricultural resources grew to an enormous size, many times that of the Early Empire: it now had to support far larger armies, a swollen State bureaucracy, and alongside that a second, growing bureaucracy of the Church. The cities did not revive their old position. The rich did not return to them, but consolidated their power in great landed estates. The small farmers and peasants were bought up, driven into serfdom by taxation, and gradually wiped out as a group, particularly in the West. In both town and country the middle levels of wealth were vanishing. Emperors saw the symptoms and made honest attempts to stem the process, but since a major cause was the upkeep of the State machine, and since the upper officialdom and clergy were themselves great land-owners, the State was in practice bound to the landed nobility, whatever its sentiments and legal decisions might decree.[8]

The top-heavy apparatus still held the State together. For all its costly and cumbersome machinery, it performed the essential task of State bureaucracies, which is to limit the disruption caused by unavoidable power struggles at the top. But with the external pressures unabated, the Roman State now had fewer resources to draw on. And where Diocletian's design had envisaged a rough justice, an equitable sharing of sacrifice, the reality was to prove anything but equitable as the century wore on.

chapter seventeen

·IN THE LONG RUN·

It was in the late 370s that intelligence first began to suggest to the Roman frontier commanders that the tribes beyond the Danube were undergoing disturbances on a new scale, resulting from the arrival of a hitherto unknown people, the Huns: an event which, in retrospect, was to set off a new and worsening series of crises that permanently altered Rome's relations with its neighbours.

Emerging from Southern Russia, this terrible nomadic horde with its seemingly irresistible cavalry system had crushed and subjected the Alans, broke the Ostrogoths and then, on a great battle on the Dneister, defeated the Visigoths and driven them too from their lands in Dacia. Alarm was communicated through the different Gothic tribes. A great host united under the Visigothic chiefs Alavivus and Fritigern to seek a new and safer homeland. Arriving on the northern banks of the Danube, they respectfully petitioned the Eastern Roman Emperor Valens for lands in Thrace on which to settle under the usual terms of tribute and military service to the Empire. Their request was granted.[1]

The immigration, which might have been to the Empire's benefit if accomplished gradually, was badly mismanaged. The sheer numbers proved such that all computation and control were lost: 'the ill-omened officials who ferried the barbarian hordes across, often tried to reckon their number, but gave up the vain attempt'.[2] The imperial administration could not immediately cope with the organising and feeding of such a population. They still had most of their arms, they were hungry, and their plight was shamefully exploited by the rapacious officials Lupicinus and Maximus, who sold them food at enormous prices, which even entailed them enslaving some of their children. In desperation they revolted, defeated Lupicinus, and proceeded to plunder Thrace without serious resistance. In the confusion their Ostrogothic kinsmen likewise crossed the Danube en masse, unhindered by frontier controls.

The threat they posed was so great that Valens now had no option but to march against them. Encouraged by the partial success of his local commanders, he arrived to confront them with his main field army outside Adrianople. Here he made two more blunders. He allowed the artful Fritigern to spin out truce negotiations, while the Ostrogoths came to reinforce his already considerable host. Yet Valens himself was persuaded not to await the arrival of Gratian's army from the West, before giving battle. Negotiations broke down, and the issue was put to a decision on an open plan on 9 August 378. The left wing of the Roman cavalry scored an initial success, but was unable to break through to the enemy camp for lack of support. Then the shock of a combined cavalry attack by Goths, Alans and Grethungi routed the Roman horse, and surrounded their unprotected masses of infantry. They were in the fatal position of being locked in close order, unable to move or manoeuvre, menaced by a combination of missiles and heavy cavalry:

> Because of the clouds of dust the sky was obscured from sight, and echoed with fearful cries; the arrows, whirling death from every side always found their mark with fatal effect, since they could not be anticipated. When the barbarians poured down in great hordes, trampling horses and men, and in the tight press of ranks there was no room for retreat and no openings for flight, our soldiers, in extreme contempt of death, struck down their enemies while receiving their own fatal blows: on both sides the strokes of axes split helmet and breastplate ... the ground, slippery with blood, gave them hardly any foothold, so they could only strain every nerve to sell their lives dearly: they resisted the assaults of the enemy so fiercely that some were killed on the weapons of their own comrades.[3]

After several hours it was all over. The remnants escaped with nightfall. The Emperor Valens himself was lost under the heaps of dead, and two-thirds of his Eastern field army were destroyed, perhaps 40,000 of the best soldiers. The disaster ranked with Cannae, six centuries before: its effect on manpower and morale at this critical time was incalculable. The shock of Adrianople reverberated throughout the Empire. A whole nation of Visigoths was now established on Roman territory, no longer as suppliants or subjects but, as they saw it, by right of conquest.

Valens' successor Theodosius realised that expelling them was neither possible nor, in the present manpower situation, even desirable. Skilfully using the fortified cities and strongpoints which the Goths had proved unable to capture, he checked their marauding, restored the nerve of his troops, and scored several victories which were more important for prestige than strategic effect. But it enabled him to bring them to a treaty in 382, formally settling them as *foederati* in lower Moesia, with obligation to provide military help when required.

Theodosius had been adopted by Gratian as his most suitable colleague in the emergencies. He was an energetic and astute ruler who was able to accommodate the Goths and rebuild his army, learning from the Gothic heavy cavalry tactics and enlisting many of their warriors under his command. He was able to fight and win two costly civil wars against the Western usurpers Maximus (383) and Eugenius (394). But the very policies he was compelled to pursue indicate that he saw without illusion just how weak the Empire had now become in the face of the external threat. In theory, the settling of barbarians was just an extension of the long-established policies of the Illyrian Emperors. But this was illusion. Their settlements had been managed after Roman victories, the peoples carefully distributed, and subject to Roman law and administration. *Foederati* were whole Germanic nations in arms, retaining their own chieftains and political identities, bound only by flimsy 'treaties' to give military aid: advertised as a measure of friendship, the policy was palpably one of weakness and necessity.

On paper, the military strength and organisation of Rome at the end of the fourth century still looked extremely formidable – a total army of some 600,000 men in East and West. But this too was deceptive. Two-thirds of these were *limitanei,* immobile peasant militia whose quality had deteriorated with their isolation. Of the main field forces, many were in practice tied to a particular province; many were upgraded *limitanei* of varying effectiveness – the 'legions' which appear in such profusion in the *Notitia* were small, light infantry units bearing no resemblance to the highly trained divisions of the past. Of the best fighting units a great proportion were Germanic, under their own commanders – often not even nominally Roman subjects, but pure mercenaries on short term contract, whose homes and peoples were beyond the frontiers.

While the notion of a conscious Teutonic fifth column is exaggerated, the fact that so many German officers fully understood the military system they were operating and had natural links with various enemies they were opposing, inevitably meant a shift in outlook and real balance of forces. The mercenaries fought purely for gold and had no affinities whatever for the provincials they were defending; though they fought well enough, it became judicious for the Masters of Infantry and Cavalry to plan carefully which enemies they could and could not be used against. Intelligence of imperial weaknesses and troop movements could now be gathered by a skilled German war chief such as Fritigern in a way that would have been impossible a century earlier. Such leaders no longer held the Roman military machine in awe, but calculated its strengths and weaknesses just as Roman generals did their own. In place of a margin of superiority on the Roman side, the two were coming to resemble one another.

It is not surprising that the policy of Theodosius after Adrianople was to cultivate and manage the Germans as best he could, both inside and outside the Empire. He could not possibly dispense with this great reservoir of fighting men and skills, though fully alive to the political danger. For him, it was a choice between an Empire protected by strong but uncertain allies, and one barely protected at all. Diplomacy henceforth assumed a new importance in external and internal politics, since simple military opposition to the Germanic world as a whole, was no longer practical.[4]

How had the State come to this? The westward migration of the Huns was a new element in the world situation, but it occurred when the society and government of the Empire were already dangerously brittle, top-heavy and polarised, above all in the West. The economic plight of cities was worsened by the fiscal measures of Constantine's successors, who deprived them of most of the rents on their corporate lands. Meanwhile the great rural land-owners, self-sufficient and dominant in their territories, had grown into almost independent magnates, negotiating with the State from an increasingly strong position. Most of them collected the taxes themselves, which meant avoiding most of their own share at the expense of their *coloni.* In a time of low population they held tenaciously onto this peasant labour, preferring to meet the State's military conscription by money payments instead of men, which in turn led to the hiring of more barbarian mercenaries instead of internal recruitment. These great lords could offer the small man various kinds of protection from the agents of the State, whether in the courts, or by purchasing his debts, or sheltering him from the threats of officials. Some even organised small private militia. Since the State's total budget actually doubled in the 40 years between Constantine and Valentinian, since the poor always paid more than their share, and the protectorless paid extortion on top, the burden on the urban poor and the peasantry had become utterly oppressive. Despite their shackles, many still fled; town curials escaped into the clergy if they could; banditry increased again.

These trends were all more exaggerated in the less urbanised Western provinces, where the cities had been completely dependent on the countryside. The old senatorial nobility of Italy and Gaul had been deprived of its political influence by Diocletian, but not its great landed wealth; and as time went on they had consolidated and improved their relative economic position to an extraordinary degree. Concentration of wealth in fewer hands owing to low birth rates and intermarriage among noble families had led to a position where an average senatorial income was perhaps five times what it had been in the first century. Many had multiple estates in Italy, Spain, Gaul or Africa; a typical senatorial annual income was about 120,000 solidi, compared with 1,000 for a court official and five for a peasant.'

By 400, most of Gaul and Italy was owned by less than a dozen great senatorial clans, whose wealth once again allowed them to dominate the provincial governorships. These circles affected an aristocratic 'republican' style which despised the military Emperors, and whose general concern was to insulate their own family fortunes and position from the demands of the State. They gained financially both as land-owners and governors: fierce imperial laws against bribery, extortion and other malpractices were dutifully published by the very officials against whom they were directed. To the peasant, the price of 'security' which the State exacted from him, was serfdom or beggary. To the small town-dweller it was the choice between bankruptcy under the State or under the 'protection' of a great magnate. To the poor, Germanic settler-soldier of the *limitanei,* what he was ultimately expected to defend were the huge estates and villas of the rich – against 'enemies' whose way of life was perhaps closer to his own. The proverbial 'decay of civic spirit' in the West was made up of such elements

In the Greek East the same essential problems existed, but there were sturdier resources to meet them. Native population was far greater. Cities were much more numerous and managed to preserve greater economic viability, partly through their commercial and manufacturing life, on which they had depended since Hellenic times. Alexandria, Antioch and soon Constantinople were the great trading centres of the Mediterranean. A larger proportion of private wealth was therefore tied to the cities, and for this reason civic life was not extinguished: there was no wholesale relapse into a purely rural economy, as in the West. Nor was the peasantry dominated by great magnates to the same extent: they were tied to their land holdings, but often in independent village communities rather than great estates. The tendency towards economic polarisation certainly operated, but it was blunted by the more urban, commercial, and indeed governmental character of the civilisation, which went back to before Roman rule. Many of the cities received imperial subsidies, and Constantinople itself grew rapidly into a great imperial and commercial metropolis. The middle ranks of wealth, the urban gentry, small land-owners and artisans were squeezed but not wiped out by the organised demands of the fortress Empire. Certainly there were wealthy land-owners who occupied the upper State officialdom. But they still lived in the cities, their wealth was more modest and widely distributed, and they were overwhelmingly the new Constantinian aristocracy of State service, the mandarinate of parvenu senators, whose social position was tied to their public careers in a way that the older Italian nobles' certainly was not.

In consequence, the Emperor in the East kept a far better grip on the upper class through whom he ruled. Avoidance of tax and service obligations, corruption and abuse could be kept within limits, and a higher level of accountability and professionalism maintained in the civil service. The administrative machine, cumbersome and immensely costly though it was, operated closer to the model Diocletian had originally designed, and from a distinctly wealthier base. The grain from Egypt actually went, more or less, to the various destinations the Prefect assigned to it; the State-controlled factories and industrial corporations delivered their assigned quotas; the land-owners and villages produced their levy of recruits. No huge and powerful group was able to sidetrack the imperial government on a massive scale in the way the Western nobility did. After 363 the Persian frontier was again stable for a long time. There were no civil wars fought in the Eastern provinces, and very few usurpers arose there.

All this was due not only to its economic strength and State organisation, but to a strong, indigenous Hellenic tradition of loyalty to the State and its divine rulers, and a long acceptance of State bureaucracy and management. The slow shift Eastwards in the political centre of gravity, culminating in Constantine's new capital, had been no accident. Here were cities, strategic strongholds, population, industry, wealth, and a controllable centre of power. The Eastern senatorial mandarins did not look disdainfully down on the soldier-Emperors, but were proud of the New Rome, proud to be *Rhomaioi*. Although the new barbarian shock first fell on the East at Adrianople, the great and significant fact is that the East managed to weather the terrible storms of the fifth century, while the West eventually went under.

The fall of the Western Roman Empire has been a potent stimulus to the moralistic, legendary and romantic imaginations of nearly every succeeding age. As Bury points out, we must beware of seeing it as something fated and inevitable. It was not the 'natural effect of immoderate greatness', but of failure to adapt to a new scale of crisis. By the 380s it was unavoidable that parts of the Empire's territories would become Germanised by one method or another. The problem, as Theodosius saw, was to integrate these numerous and powerful peoples into its political framework somehow. They were still simple warrior aristocracies, without the skills to administer viable independent states of their own. What they wanted was their own lands, opportunities for war with rewards, and high honours for their chieftains. To utilise and contain these new, primitive forces within a continuing Roman polity was a task demanding a high order of statesmanship, but it was not impossible. Had Theodosius reigned longer or had capable successors, the fusion of Roman and German populations in the West might have taken a different form.[6]

In 395, however, Theodosius died, leaving two quite immature sons, Honorius and Arcadius, to occupy the thrones of East and West respectively. He had adopted as their guardian the Vandal general Stilicho, but this did not offset the grave weakness of having two child Emperors, whose courts became centres of intrigue by rival factions, and whose divisions could be exploited by the new barbarian 'allies'. Stilicho was highly popular with the armies and *de facto* ruler of the West, and attempted to extend his control to Illyricum, which was still the main non-German recruiting ground. Had he himself not been a 'barbarian' he might have made himself Emperor, and possibly kept the West united. As it was, he was thwarted and opposed by the aristocratic party at court, who eventually engineered his disgrace and downfall.

The Visigothic *foederati* under their new king Alaric took early advantage of the instability to break their treaty, plunder Greece and threaten Constantinople. They were deflected westward after considerable machinations by the Eastern court. Stilicho defeated Alaric several times, expelled him from Italy, crushed an Ostrogoth invasion and suppressed a revolt in Africa; but in doing so he was compelled to abandon Britain and strip the Rhine defences, which collapsed under a huge invasion of Vandals, Alans, Suevi and Burgundians that overran Gaul and entered Spain. In the emergencies the Western court moved from threatened Milan to its final secluded refuge at Ravenna. In 408 it brought about the downfall and execution of Stilicho – an act, as Gibbon points out, which could hardly have been more disastrous had the courtiers been the paid agents of Alaric. Large numbers of Germanic soldiers deserted at this treachery to their leader, and the government was quite impotent to prevent Alaric re-entering Italy and sacking Rome.

The imperial 'government' of the West was in fact directed from a cloistered, ineffective court at Ravenna which sheltered a succession of personally weak Emperors both from the invaders and from the realities outside their palace. It continued to issue its paper proclamations, and conduct its ceremonies and intrigues like some ghostly theatre. But Italy was split from Gaul, taxes failed to be gathered, the breakdown of security issued in repeated peasant uprisings, and regional Prefects and army commanders assumed delegated power to make war or treaty as circumstances allowed. The Visigoths were manoeuvred into crushing the Vandals in Spain and rewarded with their own territory in Aquitaine. But the Vandals were able to create their own brief kingdom in Africa which cut the grain supply to Rome and held Italy to ransom. A more durable Roman sub-province was maintained in Gaul by Aetius, which was able to organise a coalition of Romans, Goths, Franks and Burgundians to meet and repel the terrible westward sweep of Attila's hordes. But once the great emergency was past their unity crumbled, and Aetius himself fell victim to a palace plot and was executed shortly afterwards. The Western Provinces degenerated into a shifting assemblage of territorial fragments ruled by Romans, Visigoths, Ostrogoths, Vandals, Franks, Burgundians and Alemanni, many of them bound by nominal ties of allegiance to the Empire, their kings having titles such as Master of the Army, or Patrician. The Emperors at Ravenna, who had ceased to be trained in warfare or command their own armies, became the arbiters, collaborators and eventually the mere puppets of the Germanic warlords, who found it temporarily useful to manipulate the prestige of the imperial throne rather than occupy it themselves.[7]

The East was in a perilously weak state at the beginning of the fifth century, having to face both the Visigoths in Thrace and a torrent of Huns from the Caspian who were ravaging Syria and Palestine. The Huns were eventually defeated and the Visigoths moved westward, but Ostrogothic *foederati* in Phrygia revolted, and were only defeated after great damage, and treachery on the part of the Gothic general sent to deal with them. Despite many blunders and failures, the government and population acted vigorously to meet or avert the multiple dangers. Unlike the West, the people were generally defiant and patriotic, prepared to resist even when the means were lacking. Citizens formed themselves into crude militia to defend their city walls. After Gainas, Gothic Master of the Army, collaborated with the enemy and blackmailed his way to temporary control of the government, religious and cultural tensions at Constantinople were inflamed against Germans: the orator Synesius publicly attacked them as wolves within the fold. A popular riot led to a massacre of Goths and their expulsion from the city, after which they made little headway against the harassment of the peasantry. Although other Germanic sections of the army were still needed, the Emperors were henceforth very sparing in the policy of granting lands for settlement, preferring the lesser evil of temporarily losing a province or two, which might later be recovered.

The Praetorian Prefect Anthemius, regent after 408, constructed massive new land fortifications around Constantinople, secured a durable peace with Persia, and strengthened the Danube fleet against the Huns to the North. The East's military forces were still not strong enough to repel every invader, but its diplomacy was assisted by two further factors. Most of its great fortified cities, and pre-eminently Constaninople, could not be taken: they formed a network of strongpoints which prevented a half-organised invading horde from securing its hold on the central territories. At the same time its economic strength was still great enough both to hire soldiers, and offer considerable bribes of gold to different barbarians, adroitly playing off Germans against Germans; and (since by now many of them were Christian) using the added antagonisms of Arian versus Catholic as a dimension of its policies. Where it could not contain them, it tried to deflect their impetus westward, as it did with Alaric, Attila and Theoderic the Ostrogoth. The Emperors Leo and Zeno deliberately worked to reduce the power of the Germans in the army, counterbalancing them by recruitment from the Isaurian mountain peoples, who became a rival military élite: a goal that was largely achieved by the end of the fifth century.[8]

The passing of Roman Europe was seen and felt in quite different ways by those who lived through it. To the German tribal kings it was primarily a difficult struggle for their own personal supremacy, and for the life of their own peoples, later enshrined in the heroic legends of the *Volkerwanderung*, the mighty wars and migrations of peoples from which the Niebelugenlied was woven. To Augustine or Pope Leo, it was vivid confirmation that the power and might of worldly states are transitory clay, and that the only lasting City is Christ's eternal kingdom, whose earthly counterpart is the Church. The overall character of the change was neither a sudden collapse into savagery, nor – as some pro-German historians have suggested – a gentle shift from Roman to German overlords which went largely unnoticed by their subjects. Rather, it was both of these things and others too, depending on when and where one lived. Many of the German kings were already partly Romanised, and became more so through settlement, marriage alliance and Christianization, although this did not filter down to the mass of their followers. It became something of a mission among the less prejudiced, more realistic Romans to do all they could to civilise their new rulers. The words attributed to Athaulf, the Visigothic king who married Honorius' very able sister Placidia, may be idealised, but they reflect an attitude that was growing:

> At first I wanted to erase the Roman name and convert all Roman territory into a Gothic Empire: I longed for Romania to become Gothia, and Athaulf to be what Caesar Augustus had been. But long experience has taught me that the ungoverned wildness of the Goths will never submit to laws, and that without law, a state is not a state. Thereofore I have more prudently chosen the different glory of reviving the Roman name with Gothic vigour, and I hope to be acknowledged by posterity as the initiator of a Roman restoration, since it is impossible for me to alter the character of this Empire.[9]

At one extreme, after the Western puppet empire had finally been extinguished, the rich senators of Italy experienced the barbarian Ostrogothic kingdom of Theoderic as a minor alteration in their way of life. True, they lost one-third of their lands to Gothic settlers. But it was done in an orderly way, thinly disguised under the old Roman billeting law of *hospitalitas*. And their ownership of the remainder was protected from depredation in a way which had eluded the last Emperors. They continued to live under Roman law and administration, to enjoy their consulships and festivals, collect their enormous rents, entertain the populace with circus games and indulge in the ostentatiously cultured social life as before. Romans and Goths lived in Italy as separate societies, and Theoderic's government continued most of the old imperial styles and offices, managing the administration through a Praetorian Prefect in the old manner.

In Italy, Spain, and particularly Gaul, the elements of Roman culture and administration continued in an attenuated way, because the conquerors had nothing to put in their place. Conversion of the Goths and Franks to Christianity greatly enhanced the essentially Roman influence of the Church with its network of bishops and dioceses, superimposed on the old municipal administration. In both East and West during the century of crisis, strong bishops often assumed the earlier role of city magistrates. The unity of geography and administration that had once existed, slowly went under: but it left rich residues of the old civilisation which were never destroyed.

But at the other extreme, the Romano-British *civitates,* always a tiny minority in a peripheral province where Latin culture had never sunk deep roots, did face a virtual Dark Age. After the last troop withdrawals and the relinquishing of Britain's defence, the Angle, Saxon and Jutish invaders progressively took over the south-eastern part of the island, cutting the cities off from all communication with the Gallic mainland, while they were also threatened by new invaders from north and west. Valiant attempts were made to organise the native Celtic population to resist; the cities may have expected a Roman return if only they could hold out for a period. Local kings sprang up, and tried to hire Germanic mercenaries in exchange for land settlements, which soon proved disastrous. Here, there was hardly any civilising of the invaders, mingling of peoples, delicate diplomacy or prestigious marriage alliances: only relentless, shifting hostility and warfare between British and Germans which slowly drove the Celtic boundaries back, isolated communities, and one by one put out the last beleaguered remnants of a Romanised way of life. Britain descended into a welter of ephemeral little statelets whose struggles left hardly any literary or even archaeological records. Only a few names, and the terrible laconic reports of the much later Anglo Saxon Chronicle give us glimpses of the times:

Aelle and Cissa beset Andredes cester [the old Roman fort of Pevensey] and slew all who dwelt in it, nor was there one Briton left.[10]

But as the Volkerwanderung abated and the Hun 'Empire' collapsed, the Eastern Empire gathered strength. The synthesis of Greek culture, Roman law and government, the Absolute monarchy and Orthodox Christianity evolved into a distinct and powerful civilisation of great durability, which within a century began the *reconquista* of Italy, Illyricum and Africa. The essential State machinery and social organisation of Diocletian and Constantine maintained it as the richest, most powerful and most sophisticated state in Christendom until the Arab conquests. Its fiscal system, for example, was incomparably more effective than anything the Frankish kingdoms even contemplated. From Gibbons' distorted perspective, the whole of Byzantine history was one protracted degeneration from Roman virtue into oriental vice, despotism and monasticism. But it is a strange kind of degeneracy which resists multiple enemies using all available weapons, which again and again recovers lost provinces, and actively spreads its religion, literacy and manners throughout its huge Slav neighbours. Its culture and artistic heritage are abundant in the countless churches of the East: Greek, Serb, Bulgar, Russian. Its political will to survive is still eloquently proclaimed in the monumental double land walls of Constantinople, the greatest city fortifications ever built, on which Goths, Huns, Slavs and Arabs dashed themselves vainly for almost a thousand years.

·APPENDIX I·

·DIOCLETIAN'S· ·PROVINCIAL· ·REORGANISATION·

The most recent detailed review of the reorganisation is in Barnes, *The New Empire of Diocletian and Constantine*, Ch 7 and 8, on whose work this draws.

The Severan Provinces

Creta et Cyrene	Moesia Inferior	Belgica
Aegyptus	Dacia*	Gallia Lugdunensis
Arabia	Dalmatia	Gallia Narbonensis
Phoenice	Macedonia	Aquitania
Cyprus	Achaea	Britannia Sup.
Syria Coele	Epirus	Britannia Inf.
Mesopotamia	Pannonia Sup.	Baetica
Palaestina	Pannonia Inf.	Hispania
Cilicia	Noricum	Lusitania
Cappadocia	Raetia	Mauretania Tingitania
Galatia	Agri Decumates*	Mauretania Caesariensis
Bithynia et Pontus	Germania Sup.	Africa
Asia	Germania Inf.	Sardinia
Lycia et Pamphylia	Alpes Maritimae	Corsica
Thracia	Alpes Cottiae	Sicilia
Moesia Superior	Alpes Graiae et Poeninae	Numidia

*Both evacuated prior to Diocletian's reorganisation. Two new provinces of Dacia were created south of the Danube by Aurelian.

Diocletian's Dioceses and Provinces

(Based on the Verona List, as amended by Barnes, *op. cit.*)

DIOCESE OF ORIENS
Libya Superior
Libya Inferior
Thebais
Aegyptus Iovia   (created 314–15)

Aegyptus Herculia   (created 314–15)
Arabia Nova
Arabia
Augustia Libanensis
Palaestina

Phoenice

Syria Coele

Augusta Euphratensis

Cilicia

Isauria

Cyprus

Mesopotamia

Osrhoene

DIOCESE OF PONTICA

Bithynia

Cappadocia

Galatia

Paphlagonia (divided after 384?)

Diospontus

Pontus Polemoniacus

Armenia (divided after 381?)

DIOCESE OF ASIANA

Lycia et Pamphylia

Phrygia Prima

Phrygia Secunda

Asia

Lydia

Caria

Pisidia

Hellespontus

DIOCESE OF THRACIA

Europa

Rhodope

Thracia

Haemimontus

Scythia

Moesia Inferior

DIOCESE OF MOESIAE

Dacia

Dacia Ripensis

Moesia Superior

Dardania

Macedonia

Thessalia

Achaea

Praevalitana

Epirus Nova

Epiris Vetus

Creta

DIOCESE OF PANNONIAE

Pannonia Inferior

Savensis

Dalmatia

Valeria

Pannonia Superior

Noricum Ripense

Noricum Mediterraneum

DIOCESE OF ITALIA

Venetia et Histria

Aemilia et Liguria

Flaminia et Picenum

Tuscia et Umbria

Campania

Apulia et Calabria

Lucania et Bruttii

Sicilia

Sardinia

Corsica

Alpes Cottiae

Raetia

DIOCESE OF GALLIAE

Belgica Prima

Belgica Secunda

Germania Prima

Germania Secunda

Sequania

Lugdunensis Prima

Lugdunensis Secunda

Alpes Graiae at Poeninae

DIOCESE OF VIENNENSIS

Viennensis

Narbonensis Prima

Narbonensis Secunda

Novem Populi

Aquitanica Prima

Aquitanica Secunda

Alpes Maritimae

DIOCESE OF BRITANNIAE

Britannia Prima

Britannia Secunda

Maxima Caesariensis

Flavia Caesariensis

APPENDIX I

DIOCESE OF HISPANIAE

Baetica

Lusitania

Carthaginiensis

Gallaecia

Tarraconensis

Mauretania Tingitana

DIOCESE OF AFRICA

Africa Proconsularis

Byzacena

Tripolitana

Numidia Cirtensis ⎱
Numidia Militiana ⎰ reunited in 314

Mauretania Caesariensis

Mauretania Sitifensis

·APPENDIX II·
·DIOCLETIAN'S EDICT·
·ON MAXIMUM PRICES·

The following is a brief extract from the great lists of maximum prices and wages attached to the Edict of 301. The most convenient translation is probably the Appendix to Tenney Frank, *Economic Survey of Ancient Rome* (Baltimore, 1940).

The prices for individual items which no one may exceed are listed below

I wheat 1 army modius	100 denarii
barley	60
rye	60
millet, crushed	100
millet, whole	50
panic grass	50
spelt, hulled	100
. . . .	
spelt	30
vetch	. . . .
beans, crushed	100
beans	60
lentils	100
chickling	80
peas, crushed	100
peas	60
chickpea	100
bitter vetch	100
oats	30
fenugreek	100
lupines, raw	60
lupines, cooked	4
kidney beans, dried	100
flaxseed	150
rice, cleaned	200
barley, cleaned	100
spelt, cleaned	200
sesame	200

hayseed	30
alfalfa seed	150
hemp seed	80

II Likewise, for wines

Picene 1 Italian pint	30
Tiburtine	30
Sabine	30
Aminean	30
Setine	30
Surrentine	30
Falernian	30
one year old wine, first quality	24
one year old wine, second quality	16
ordinary wine	8
beer, Celtic or Pannonian	4
beer, Egyptian	2
Maeonian wine, boiled down one-third	30
chrysattic wine	24
must, boiled down	16
must, boiled down one-half	20
spiced wine	24
wine with wormwood	20
rose wine	20

IX, 5 For boots

boots for mule drivers, or farm workers, first quality, without hobnails, pair	120
boots for soldiers, without hobnails	100
shoes, patrician	150
shoes, senatorial	100
shoes, equestrian	70
boots, women's, pair	60
shoes, soldiers	75

IX, 12 For sandals and Gallic sandals, pair

Gallic sandals, for farm workers, double-soled, men's	80
Gallic sandals, single-soled, men's	50
Gallic sandals for runners	60
oxhide sandals, double-soled, women's	50
oxhide sandals, single-soled, women's	30

VII 1 For wages

farm labourer, with maintenance, daily	25
stone mason, with maintenance, daily	50
cabinet maker, with maintenance, daily	50

carpenter, with maintenance, daily	50
lime burner, with maintenance, daily	50
worker in marble paving and walls,	
with maintenance, daily	60
worker in wall mosaics, with maintenance, daily	60
worker in tessellated floors, with maintenance, daily	50
wall painter, with maintenance, daily	75
figure painter, with maintenance, daily	150
wagonwright, with maintenance, daily	50
wagon blacksmith, with maintenance, daily	50
baker, with maintenance, daily	50
shipwright, seagoing vessel, with maintenance, daily	60
shipwright, river vessel, with maintenance, daily	50
fired brick maker, for every 4 bricks of 2 ft,	
and for preparation of the clay	2
sun-dried brick maker, for every 8 bricks,	
and for preparation of the clay	2
camel driver or ass driver and hinny driver,	
with maintenance, daily	25
shepherd, with maintenance, daily	20
mule driver, with maintenance, daily	25
. . . .	
model maker, with maintenance, daily	75
other plaster worker, with maintenance, daily	50
water carrier, working a full day, with maintenance, daily	25
sewer cleaner, working a full day, with maintenance, daily	25
polisher, for a sword, used	25
for a helmet, used	25
for an axe	6
for a double axe	8
for a sword scabbard	100
parchment maker, for a quaternion, one foot,	
white or yellow parchment	40
scribe, for the best writing 100 lines	25
for second quality writing	20
notary, for writing a petition or legal document	10
. . . .	
elementary teacher, per boy, monthly	50
arithmetic teacher	75
shorthand teacher	75
teacher of manuscript writing or palaeography	40
teacher of Greek or Latin literature or Geometry	200
of rhetoric or public speaking	250
advocate, for opening a case	250
for pleading a case	1,000

XVII For transportation

fare per passenger, per mile	2
freight, 1,200 pound wagon load, per mile	20
freight, 600 pound camel load	8
freight, one ass load	4

·APPENDIX III ROMAN EMPERORS· ·FROM MARCUS AURELIUS TO· ·THEODOSIUS·

		MANNER OF ELEVATION	AND OF DEATH	
161–180	Marcus Aurelius	adoptive heir	d. naturally	Marcomannic wars
161–169	Lucius Verus	adoptive heir	d. naturally	
180–192	Commodus	dynastic heir	murdered by courtiers	
193	Pertinax	elected by Senate and Guards	murdered by Guards	
193	Didius Julianus	elected by Guards	murdered by Guards	
193–194	Pescennius Niger	elected by army	killed in civil war	
193–197	Clodius Albinus	elected by army	killed in civil war	
193–211	Septimius Severus	elected by army	d. naturally	
211–217	Caracalla	dynastic heir	murdered by army	
211	Geta	dynastic heir	murdered by Caracalla	
217–218	Macrinus	elected by Guards	murdered by army	Pressure on Rhine and Danube
218	Diadumenianus	dynastic heir	murdered by army	
218–222	Elagabalus	dynastic heir	murdered by Guards	
222–235	Severus Alexander	dynastic heir	murdered by army	
235–238	Maximin (The Thracian)	elected by army	murdered by army	Military anarchy becomes permanent
238	Gordian I	elected by Senate	killed in civil war	
	Gordian II			
238	Pupienus	elected by Senate	murdered by Guards	Rise of Sassanid Persia
	Balbinus	elected by Senate	murdered by Guards	
239–244	Gordian III	dynastic heir	murdered by Guards	
244–249	Philip (The Arab)	elected by Guards	killed in civil war	
249–251	Decius	elected by army	killed in battle against Goths	
251–253	Trebonianus Gallus	elected by army	killed in civil war	Collapse of Rhine and Danube fronts
253	Aemilianus	elected by army	murdered by army	
253–260	Valerian	elected by Senate and army	d. in Persian captivity	

Dates	Emperor	Accession	Death	Events
270–275	Aurelian	elected by army	murdered by bodyguard	Invasions of Italy
275–276	Tacitus	elected by Senate	murdered by army	Illyrian Emperors regain
276	Florianus	elected by army	murdered by army	military mastery
276–282	Probus	elected by army	murdered by army	
282–283	Carus	elected by army	d. naturally (?)	
282–284	Numerian (Aug from 283)	dynastic heir	murdered by Prefect	
282–285	Carinus (Aug from 283)	dynastic heir	murdered during civil war	
284–305	Diocletian { (both retired 305)	elected by army	d. in retirement	
286–305	Maximian	adopted	killed in civil war after renouncing retirement	
293–306	Constantius { (both Aug	adopted	d. naturally	Tetrarchy and New Order
293–311	Galerius { from 305)	adopted	d. naturally	
305–307	Severus (Aug from 306)	adopted	killed in civil war	End of Tetrarchic system
305–313	Maximin Daza (Aug from 308)	adopted	killed in civil war	
306–312	Maxentius {	dynastic heir, elected by army	killed in civil war	
306–337	Constantine I (Aug from 307) {	dynastic heir, elected by army	d. naturally	Restoration of stable dynasties on collegial principle
308–324	Licinius (Aug from 308)	adopted	killed after civil war	
337–340	Constantine II	dynastic heir	killed in civil war	
337–350	Constans	dynastic heir	murdered by army	
337–361	Constantius II {	dynastic heir	d. naturally	Establishment of State Christianity
351–354	Gallus (Caesar only) {	dynastic heir	executed	
355–363	Julian (Aug from 361)	dynastic heir	killed in battle	Germanisation of armies
363–364	Jovian	elected by army	d. naturally	
364–375	Valentinian I {	elected by army	d. naturally	New frontier pressures
364–378	Valens {	dynastic kin	killed in battle	
367–383	Gratian {	dynastic kin	assassinated	Westward migration of Huns
375–392	Valentinian II {	dynastic kin	assassinated	
378–395	Theodosius I	adopted	d. naturally	Foederati and erosion of Roman control in West
392–408	Arcadius { Partition	dynastic heir	d. naturally	
392–423	Honorius { (of East & West)	dynastic heir	d. naturally	

{ bracketing of Emperors indicates collegial rule

·APPENDIX IV·
·BIOGRAPHICAL NOTES·

Diocletian Augustus. Retired 305 ⎫
Galerius Caesar (Augustus after 305) ⎬ Dynasty of Jove
son-in-law of Diocletian ⎭

Maximian Augustus. Retired 305 ⎫
Constantius Caesar (Augustus after 305) ⎬ Dynasty of Hercules
son-in-law of Maximian ⎭

Prisca wife of Diocletian

Valeria daughter of Diocletian, wife of Galerius

Eutropia wife of Maximian

Theodora daughter of Maximian, wife of Constantius

Carausius rebel Emperor of Britain and coastal Gaul

Allectus minister and successor to Carausius. Crushed in 296

Domitianus rebel Emperor of Egypt

Achilleus minister of Domitianus and effective leader of the Egyptian revolt. Crushed 298

Vahram II Great King of Persia. Signed treaty of 287 with Diocletian

Narses successor to Vahram. Invaded Syria but defeated by Galerius 298

Tiridates III King of Armenia. Ally of Rome against Persia

Severus appointed Caesar in West 305. Abdicated and died 307

Maximinus Daza nephew of Galerius. Appointed Caesar in East 305

Maxentius son of Maximian. Seized power in Italy 306. Defeated by Constantine and killed 312

Constantine son of Constantius. Seized power in Britain and Gaul 306. Subsequently recognised as Caesar, then Augustus. Defeated Maxentius, then Licinius, to become sole Emperor after 324 with the foundation of a new capital of Constantinople

Fausta second daughter of Maximian. Married Constantine 307

Licinius appointed Augustus 308. Forms alliance with Constantine 313. Defeated Maximus Daza and rules in the East. Finally defeated by Constantine 324

Lactantius Christian rhetor at Nicomedia during the Tetrarchy. Witnessed persecutions after 303 and subsequently wrote a strong polemic against Diocletian and his colleagues, with the exception of Constantius, father of the new Christian Emperor Constantine

·BIBLIOGRAPHY·

Abbreviations used in Bibliography and References

CAH   *Cambridge Ancient History*
CIL   *Corpus Inscriptionem Latinarum*, Berlin, 1862–
CJ   *Codex Iustinianus*
Dessau H. Dessau, *Inscriptiones Latinae Selectae*, Berlin, 1892–1916
FIRA   *Fontes Iuris Romani Anteiustiniani*, 2nd ed., Florence, 1940–1943
IGRR   *Inscriptiones Graecae ad Res Romanas Pertinentes*, Paris, 1906–1927
JRS   *Journal of Roman Studies*
RE   Pauly Wissowa, *Real-Encyclopaedie*
SHA   *Scriptores Historiae Augustae*, London, 1932

Main Sources: Classical

Lactantius, *De Mortibus Persecutorum*, ed. S. Brandt, Vienna, 1897 (Trans. W. Fletcher, *The Works of Lactantius*, Vol II, 1871)

Sextus Aurelius Victor, *Liber de Caesaribus and Epitome*, R. Grundel, Teubner, Leipzig, 1961

Eutropius, *Breviarium*, ed. H. Droysen, Auctores Antiquissimi 2 Berlin, 1878

Eusebius, *Historia Ecclesia* and *De Martyribus Palestinae* (Trans. H. Lawlor and J. E. L. Oulton, London, 1927)

Panegyrici Latini, ed. R. A. B. Mynors, Oxford, 1964

Zosimus, *Historia Nova*, Teubner, Leipzig, 1887

Zonaras, *Epitome*, ed. Lindorf, Leipzig, 1868–75

Scriptores Historiae Augustae, (Trans. D. Magie, London, Loeb, 1932)

Codex Iustinianus, ed. P. Kruger, Berlin, 1967

Notitia Dignitatum, Bodleian Library, Oxford

Main Sources: Modern

T. D. Barnes, *The New Empire of Diocletian and Constantine*, Harvard University Press, 1982

J. B. Bury, *History of the Later Roman Empire*, Vol. I, London, 1923

Cambridge Ancient History, Vol XII

Cambridge Medieval History, Vol IV

Edward Gibbon, *The Decline and Fall of the Roman Empire*, Chs X-XVII

A. H. M. Jones, *The Later Roman Empire 284–602. A Social, Economic and Administrative Survey*, Oxford, 1964

A. H. M. Jones, J. R. Martindale and J. Morris, *Prosopography of the Later Roman Empire 1: 260–395*, Cambridge, 1971

R. MacMullen, *Roman Government's Response to Crisis*, Yale, 1976

Pauly Wissowa, *Real-Encyclopaedie der classischen Altertumswissenschaft,* ed. W. Kroll, Stuttgart, 1894–

O. Seeck, *Geschichte des Untergangs der antiken Welt,* Berlin and Stuttgart, 1910–1921

O. Seeck, *Regesten der Kaiser und Papst fur die Jahre 311 bis 476,* Stuttgart, 1919

W. Seston, *Dioclétien et la Tétrarchie, 1. Bibliothèque des Écoles françaises d'Athènes et de Rome,* Paris, 1946

E. Stein, *Histoire du Bas-Empire 284–476* (Trans. J. R. Palanque, Paris, 1959)

Select Bibliography

Alföldi, A., 'Des Usupator Aureolus und die Kavalliereform der Kaisers Gallienus', *Zeitschr. für Numismatik,* XXXVII and XXXVIII (1927–28)

Alföldi, A., 'La Grande Crise du monde romain au IIIe siècle', *L'Antique Classique,* 7, 1938

Alföldi, A., *The Conversion of Constantine and Pagan Rome,* Oxford, 1948

Alföldy, G., *Noricum; History of the Provinces of the Roman Empire,* London, 1974

Altheim, F., *Der Krise der alten Welt,* Berlin, 1943

Altheim, F., *History of Roman Religion,* (Trans. H. Mattingly), London, 1935

Anderson, J. G. C., 'The Genesis of Diocletian's Provincial Reorganisation', *JRS,* 1932

Anderson, P., *Passages from Antiquity to Feudalism,* NLB, London, 1974

Arnheim, M., *The Senatorial Aristocracy in the Late Roman Empire,* Oxford, 1972

Bailey, C., *Phases in the Religion of Ancient Rome,* OUP, 1932

Barnes, T. D., 'Lactantius and Constantine', *JRS,* 1973

Barnes, T. D., *Constantine and Eusebius,* Cambridge, Mass. & London, 1981

Baynes, N. H., 'Three Notes on the Reforms of Diocletian and Constantine', *JRS,* 1925

Baynes, N. H. and Moss, H., *Byzantium,* Clarendon, Oxford, 1948

Birley, A., *Marcus Aurelius,* Eyre & Spottiswoode, London, 1966

Boak, A. E. R., *Manpower Shortage and the Fall of the Empire in the West,* Oxford, 1955

Bowder, D., *The Age of Constantine and Julian,* London, 1978

Brown, P., 'The Diffusion of Manichaeanism in the Late Roman Empire', *JRS,* 1969

Brown, P., *The World of Late Antiquity,* London, 1971

Bulić, F., *L'imperatore Diocleziano,* Split, 1916

Bury, J. B., 'The Notitia Dignitatum', *JRS,* 1920

Bury, J. B., 'The Provincial List of Verona', *JRS,* 1923

Bury, J. B., *The Invasion of Europe by the Barbarians,* London, 1928 (repr., New York, 1963)

Bushe-Fox, J. P., 'The Saxon Shore Forts', *JRS,* 1932

Calza, R., *Iconografia Romana Imperiale III 287–363,* Rome, 1972

Christiansen, H., *L'Iran sous les Sassanides,* Copenhagen, 1944

Collingwood, R. G. and Myres, J. N. L., *Roman Britain and the English Settlements,* Oxford, 1936.

Costa, G., 'Diocletianus', E. de Ruggiero, *Dizionario epigrafico,* Vol 2, 1922

Cumont, F., *The Oriental Religions and Roman Paganism,* Chicago, 1911

De Blois, L., *The Policy of the Emperor Gallienus,* Nederlands Instituut te Rome, 1958

Demougeot, E., *La Formation d'Europe et des invasions barbares: des origines germaniques a l'avènement de Dioclétien,* Aubier, Paris, 1969

Dodds, E. R., *Pagan and Christian in an Age of Anxiety,* Cambridge, 1965

Domaszewski, A., *Religion des Römischen Heeres,* Trier, 1895

Duncan Jones, R., *Pay and Numbers in Diocletian's Army*, Chiron, 1978

Eichholz, D., 'Constantius Chlorus' invasion of Britain', *JRS*, 1953

Ensslin, W., *Zur Ostpolitik der Kaisers Diokletians*, Akad der Wissenschaft, 1942

Ensslin, W., 'Valerius Diocletianus', Pauly Wissowa, *RE*, Vol 14, 1948

Ensslin, W., 'Maximianus Herculius and Maximianus Galerius', Pauly Wissowa, *RE*, Vol 14, 1930

Erim, K. and Reynolds, J. 'The Aphrodisian Copy of the Diocletian Edict', see *JRS*, 1970, 1971, and 1973

Ferguson, J., *The Religions of the Roman Empire*, Thames & Hudson, London, 1970

Finley, M. I. (ed.), *Slavery in Classical Antiquity*, Heffer, Cambridge, Mass, 1960

Frank, T., *Economic Survey of Ancient Rome*, Baltimore, 1940

Frend, W. H. C., *Martyrdoms and Persecutions in the Early Church*, Blackwell, 1965

Frere, Sheppard, *Britannia*, London, 1967

Frye, R., *The Heritage of Persia*, Weidenfeld, London, 1962

Ghirshman, R., *Iran, Parther und Sassaniden*, Munich, 1962

Goyau, G., *La Tétrarchie: sommaire d'une étude d'ensemble*, Études d'histoire juridiques, Paris, 1912

Haussig, H. W., *History of Byzantine Civilisation*, (Trans.), Thames & Hudson, London, 1971

Hendy, M., 'Mint and Fiscal Administration under Diocletian', *JRS*, 1972

Holland Smith, J., *Constantine the Great*, Hamish Hamilton, London, 1965

Homo, L., 'L'empereur Gallien et la crise de l'empire', *Revue Historique*, CXIII, 1913

Honoré, T., *Emperors and Lawyers*, Duckworth, 1981

Howe, L., *The Praetorian Prefect from Commodus to Diocletian*, Chicago, 1942

Johnson, A. and West, L., *Survey of Byzantine Egypt*, Princeton, 1949

Johnson, S., *The Saxon Shore Forts*, Paul Elek, London, 1976

Jones, A. H. M., *The Roman Economy* (collection of papers), Oxford, 1974

Jones, A. H. M., 'The Roman Civil Service', *JRS*, 1949

Jones, A. H. M., *Constantine the Great and the Conversion of Europe*, Oxford, 1948

Jones, A. H. M., 'Date and value of the Verona List', *JRS*, 1952

Kagan, D., *Decline and Fall of the Roman Empire*, Boston, 1962

Keyes, C. W., *The Rise of the Equites in the Third Century*, Oxford, 1915

Kinch, K. F., *L'arc de triomphe de Salonique*, Paris, 1890

Lewis, M. and Reinhold, M., *Roman Civilisation: Sourcebook II The Empire*, Harper Torchbooks, 1955

Liebeschutz, J. H. W. G., *Continuity and Change in Roman Religion*, Oxford, 1979

L'Orange, H., *Das Spätantike Porträts*, Oslo, 1973

L'Orange, H., *Art Forms and Civic Life in the Late Roman Empire*, (Trans.) Princeton, 1965

Luttwak, E., *The Grand Strategy of the Roman Empire*, Johns Hopkins, 1976

MacMullen, R., *Soldier and Civilian in the Late Roman Empire*, Harvard, 1963

MacMullen, R., *Enemies of the Roman Order*, Harvard, 1967

MacMullen, R., *Constantine*, New York, 1969

Manley, I. J., *Effects of the Germanic Invasions on Gaul, 234–284*, Univ. Calif. History XVII

Mann, A. J., *The Persecution of Diocletian*, Cambridge, 1876

Marasović, T. and J., *Diocletian Palace*, Zara, Zagreb, 1968

Millar, F., *The Roman Empire and its Neighbours,* London, 1967

Millar, F., 'Dexippus: The Greek World and the Third Century Invasions', *JRS,* 1969

Millar, F., *The Emperor in the Roman World,* Duckworth, 1977

Miller, K., *Die Peutingersche Tafel,* Stuttgart, 1962

Mitteis, L. and Wilcken, U., *Grundzuge und Chrestomathie des Papyruskunde,* Leipzig and Berlin, 1912

Mócsy, A., *Pannonia and Upper Moesia: History of the Provinces of the Roman Empire,* London, 1974

Mommsen, T., *Romische Staatsrecht,* Leipzig, 1887–8

Nischer, E., 'The Army Reforms of Diocletian and Constantine and their modification up to the time of the Notitia Dignitatum', *JRS,* 1923

Nock, A. D., *Conversion: the old and the new in religion from Alexander the Great to Augustine of Hippo,* London, 1952

Noeldeke, T., *Geschichte der Perser und Araber,* Leiden, 1879

Oliva, P., *Pannonia and the onset of the crisis of the Roman Empire,* Akadamie Ved, Prague, 1962

Ostrogorsky, G., *History of the Byzantine State,* New Brunswick, 1957

Parker, H. M. D., 'The Legions of Diocletian and Constantine', *JRS,* 1933

Petrikovits, H., 'Fortifications in the North-Western Roman Empire from the Third to the Fifth Centuries AD', *JRS,* 1971

Piganiol, A., *L'empereur Constantin,* Paris, 1932

Preuss, T., *Kaiser Diokletian und seine Zeit,* Leipzig, 1869

Puech, H. C., *Le manichéism, son fondateur, sa doctrine,* Paris, 1949

Rostovsteff, M., *Social and Economic History of the Roman Empire,* Oxford, 1957

Salway, P., *Roman Britain,* Oxford, 1981

Seston, W., *Du Comitatus de Dioclétien aux comitatenses de Constantin,* Historia 4, 1955

Shiel, J., *Greek Thought and the Rise of Christianity,* Longmans, London, 1968

Skeat, T. C. (ed.), *Papyri from Panopolis 298–300,* Hodges Figgis, Dublin, 1964

Sperber, D., 'Denarii and Aurei in the time of Diocletian', *JRS,* 1964

Ste. Croix, G. E. M. de, 'Aspects of the "Great" Persecution', *Harvard Theological Review* 47, 1954

Stade, K., *Der Politiker Diokletian und die letzte Grosse Christenverfolgung,* Weisbaden, 1926

Sutherland, C. H. V., 'Diocletian's reform of the coinage', *JRS,* 1955

Sutherland, C. H. V., 'Denarius and Sestertius in Diocletian's coinage reform', *JRS,* 1961

Sydenham, E., 'The Vicissitudes of Maximian after his Abdication', *Numismatic Chronicle* 14, 1934

Syme, R., *Emperors and Biography,* Oxford, 1971

Thomas, J. D., 'Epigraphai and Indictions in the Reign of Diocletian', *Bulletin of the American Society of Papyrologists,* 1978

Thompson, E. A., *The Early Germans,* Oxford, 1965

Todd, M., *The Everyday Life of the Barbarians,* Batsford, London, 1972

Van Berchem, D., *L'Armée de Dioclétien et la réforme constantinienne,* Paris, 1952

Van Sickle, L. E., 'Conservatism and Philosophical Influence in the Reign of Diocletian', *Classical Philology,* XXVII, 1932

Vogt, J., *The Decline of Rome,* Weidenfeld, London, 1964

Vogt, J., *Konstantin der Grosse und sein Jahrhundert,* Munich, 1949 and 1960

Vryonis, S., *Byzantium and Europe,* London, 1967

Wade, W. V., 'Carausius, Restorer of Britain', *Numismatic Chronicle* 12, 1953

Walbank, F., *The Decline of the Roman Empire in the West,* London, 1946

Walser, G. and Pekary, T., *Die Krise der Römischen Reiches,* Berlin, 1962

Warde Fowler, *Roman Ideas of Deity,* Macmillan, London, 1914

Webb, P. H., 'The Reign and Coinage of Carausius', *Numismatic Chronicle* 7, 1907

Webb, Mattingly, and Sydenham, *The Roman Imperial Coinage,* London, 1938

White, L. (ed.), *The Transformation of the Roman World,* Berkeley, LA, 1966

Wilkes, J. J., *Dalmatia: History of the Provinces of the Roman Empire,* London, 1969

Other selected classical works

Ammianus Marcellinus, *Historia,* (Loeb Transl., Heinemann, 1939)

Anonymous Valesianus, (Loeb Transl., Heinemann, 1939)

Constantine, *Oratio,* (Transl. in Nicene & Post-Nicene Fathers, Oxford, 1890)

Dio Cassius, *Historia,* (Loeb Transl., Heinemann, 1927)

Eusebius, *Vita Constantini,* (Transl. in Nicene & Post-Nicene Fathers, Oxford, 1890)

Herodian, *Histories,* ed. L. Mendelssohn, Leipzig, 1883

Jerome, *Chronicle,* Eusebius Werke 7, ed. R. Helm, Berlin, 1956

Lactantius, *Divines Institutiones,* ed. P. Monat, Paris, 1973

Malalas, *Chronographia,* ed. L. Dindorf, Bonn, 1831

Orosius, *Adversum Paganos,* Teubner, Leipzig, 1889

Tacitus, *Germania,* (Loeb Transl., Heinemann, 1914)

·REFERENCES·

Prologue (pages 9–12)

1 Antony Birley, *Marcus Aurelius,* Ch. VI
2 The only serious military actions in the reign of Pius were the occupation of Southern Scotland beyond Hadrian's Wall in 142, and a revolt in the ungarrisoned province of Mauretania in 145 which required the despatch of legionary units from other provinces. Birley, *ibid*
3 Dio, LXXII, 36. Standard sources for the reigns of the Antonines are first, Cassius Dio's *History,* books LXIX–LXXIV, parts of which are lost, and the surviving texts being in epitome only. The *Historia Augusta (SHA)* is as usual of mixed reliability. Other useful but sparse information is found in the two Victors, Eutropius and Orosius. Other modern biographies of M. Aurelius include H. D. Sidgwick (Oxford, 1921) and A. S. L. Farquarson (Oxford, 1952)
4 *SHA, Vita Marci,* 22
5 Dio, LXXI, 33
6 Marcus Aurelius, *Meditations,* VI, 30
7 *SHA, Vita Marci,* 9
8 Birley Ch VI; *SHA, Vita Pii,* 12, *Vita Marci,* 8
9 Dio, LXXIII; Herodian I, ii
10 Dio, LXXV—LXXVII; also Antony Birley, *Septimius Severus,* 1971

1 The Third-Century Collapse (pages 15–23)

1 Principal modern sources on the character and migrations of the Germanic peoples in the third and fourth centuries include A. Alföldi in *CAH*; J. B. Bury, *The Later Roman Empire,* Ch IV; J. B. Bury, *The Invasion of Europe by the Barbarians*; E. Demougeot, *Le Formation d'Europe et les invasions barbares*
Gibbon in Ch IX bases his picture of the Germans too heavily on Tacitus, who was describing a much earlier state of affairs and who knew next to nothing of the eastern Germans. See also I. J. Marley, *Effects of the Germanic invasions on Gaul, 234–284*; M. Todd, *The Everyday Life of the Barbarians*; on the growth of the retinue, see E. A. Thompson, *The Early Germans*; on Germanic skills, E. A. Thompson, *A Roman Reformer and Inventor*; also P. Anderson, *Passages from Antiquity to Feudalism,* I, 4 and II, 1
2 Tacitus, *Germania,* 33, 37
3 Caesar, *Bell, Gall.,* Ch IV
4 This important point is well brought out in Luttwak, *The Grand Strategy of the Roman Empire*
5 Tacitus, *passim*
6 On the rise of Sassanid Iran, Christensen and Ensslin in *CAH*; Christensen, *L'Iran sous*

les Sassanides; T. Noeldeke, *Geschichte der Perser und Araber*; R. Ghirshman, *Iran, Parther und Sassaniden*; Richard Frye, *The Heritage of Persia*

7   Zosimus, I, 23

8   Sources for the brief and turbulent reigns from 235 to 284 are scattered and often unreliable. The essential facts narrated in the notorious *SHA* are supported by coin and other evidence, but much of the accompanying detail is either erroneous or fabricated, especially the 'documents' which the authors purport to reproduce. Cf. R. Syme, *Emperors and Biography*. Herodian, the two Victors, Zosimus and Zonaras provide scanty biographies, but much has been reconstructed from corroborating evidence such as coins, inscriptions, papyri, rescripts, *fasti*, etc. It is the general opinion that some of these writers drew on a single source, now lost, the *Kaisergeschichte* of Enmann. Cf. A. Enmann, *Philol.*, suppl. IV (1884)

9   Wilcken, *Grundzüge und Chrestomathie*, 402

10 The various facets of the crisis are dealt with by a number of modern authors, the foremost being A. Alföldi, *La grande crise du monde romain au IIIe siècle*; Ch VI of *CAH*; *Die Gotenbewengen und die Aufgabe der Provinz Dacien*. See also W. Ensslin in *CAH*; G. Pauly Wissowa, *Real-Encyclopadie*; A. H. M. Jones, 'The Anarchy', in *Later Roman Empire*; G. Walser and T. Pekary, *Der Krise der romischer Reich*; R. MacMullen, *Roman Government's Response to Crisis*. See also Rostovtseff, Frank, Seeck, *op. cit.*

11 Origen, *Matt. Comment.* series

12 MacMullen, *op. cit.*, Ch. 1. The plague is recounted by *SHA*, Eusebius, Zosimus, Zonaras, Orosius and others

13 After the great invasions of Gaul in 276–7. On depopulation, see esp. Boak, *Manpower Shortage*

14 *Oxyrhynchus Papyrus*, XII, 1477

15 *CIL*, Vol III, 14, 191

16 See particularly F. Millar, *P Herennius Dexippus: The Greek World and the Third-Century Invasions*

17 For Postumus' revolt, *SHA, Tyr Trig.*, III and *Div. Aurel.*

18 In the power vacuum created between the defeat of Valerian and the final overthrow of Palmyra. The revolt of Firmus is obscure, and Seston suggests the *SHA* confused many of the details with the later Egyptian revolt of Achilleus in 297. See Seston, *Dioclétian*, pp 145–8

19 On the defeat and capture of Valerian, Zosimus, I, 1; also Wickert in Pauly Wissowa, *RE*, 402

20 Diocletian's origins. Precise dates and details of Diocletian's origins have been the subject of extensive arguments, which are well rehearsed in A. H. M. Jones *et al.*, *Prosopography of the Late Roman Empire*, and more recently T. D. Barnes, *The New Empire of Diocletian and Constantine*, which is critical of Jones at several points. See also Seston, *Dioclétian*, pp 38ff; R. Syme, *Emperors and Biography* p 223 and *passim*; T. L. Skeat (ed.), *Papyri from Panopolis*
    All that is really indisputable is that he came from Dalmatia. That he was born or brought up at Salona is generally deduced from the fact that he retired there. Lactantius, *Mort. Pers.*, 9 tells us that his pre-imperial name was Diocles. Victor in *Epitome* (39.1) claims this was derived from his mother, who derived it in turn from

her town of origin, Dioclea (presumably Doclea). The two stories, that he was the son of a scribe and/or the freedman of the senator Anullinus, are in Eutropius, 9, 22. Beatty in Skeat, *op. cit.*, concludes that Diocletian's official birthday as Emperor was 22 December, and Barnes considers this was probably his actual birthday. The *Epitome* (39.7) suggests that he died early in 313 aged 68 (cf. also J. Moreau's commentary on Lactantius) which would put his birth in 244. But Barnes suggests his death may have been in late 311 or early 312, following Lactantius' account that he starved himself to death after the destruction of his and Maximian's statues by Constantine. If he was aged 68 this would put his birth in 243 or possibly 242. Jones, *op. cit.*, considers it possible the *Epitome* refers not to his death but his abdication at the age of 68, which would put his birth as early as 236

21 J. J. Wilkes, *Dalmatia*

22 *ibid*, p 385. The whole chapter on Salona is a useful background. See also the handbook of Split Archaeological Museum. The Museum is currently in the process of purchasing the Tetrarchic busts in Solin

23 The two broad social groupings within the citizen body, *honestiores* and *humiliores*, gradually emerged as citizenship spread to include more and more of the freeborn population in the second century. By the time of Septimius Severus the two categories were explicitly recognised in criminal jurisdiction. *Honestiores* included the Senatorial and equestrian orders, the municipal curial class, and soldiers of all ranks

2 Virtus Illyrici (pages 24–38)

1 Gallienus is portrayed in *SHA* as a frivolous tyrant, a portrait Gibbon reproduces in Chapter X. Modern research has rehabilitated him as an energetic Emperor and skilful military innovator during the worst period of the Empire's calamities. For a general assessment, see esp. Homo in *Revue Historique*, CXIII, and more recently De Blois, *Policy of the Emperor Gallienus*

2 *SHA, Vita Gallieni,* and *Tyr. Trig.*; Zosimus, I, 40; Zonaras, XII 25

3 Gallienus' military changes are discussed at length by De Blois, *op. cit.,* who draws on Alföldi, Ensslin, Pflaum and others who have reassessed this important reign. On the development of the cavalry arm, see especially Alföldi, *CAH,* Ch V and VI; *Des usupator Aureolus und die Kavalliereform des Kaisers Gallienus,* ZN, XXXVII. Also Wickert in Pauly Wissowa, *RE,* 364; W. Ensslin in *CAH,* II, IV and XI; Altheim, *Soldatenkaiser.* Many writers have seen in Gallienus' cavalry reforms the prototype of the later *comitatenses* of Constantine and (allegedly) Diocletian. I do not share this view, as explained in Chapter 7

4 On the abolition of senators in legionary commands, Victor, *Caes.,* 33ff and 37. Cf. also Keyes, *The Rise of the Equites in the Third Century*; Arnheim, *The Senatorial Aristocracy in the Late Roman Empire*; Seston, *Dioclétien,* p 309ff; W. Ensslin in Pauly Wissowa, *RE,*1326; and De Blois, *op. cit.*

5 On the *Protectores,* see Deisner in Pauly Wissowa, *RE,* 1113ff; Alföldi, *Hauptfaktoren*; Von Stauffenberg, *Das Imperium uber die Volkerwanderung*

6 Von Domaszewski, *Rangordnung,* p 189ff; Jones, *Prosop.,* p 609

7 Pflaum, *Carrières,* II p 901–5; Jones, *Prosop.,* p 980

8 For the greater social mobility among the soldiers, see R. MacMullen, *Soldier and*

Civilian in the Late Roman Empire; Keyes, *op. cit.*; Jones, *Prosop.*; Pflaum, *op. cit.*; De Blois, *op. cit.*

9 Zonaras, XII, 31. That Diocles served under Aurelian and Probus is claimed in *SHA, Vita Probi,* and, more importantly, implied in *Pan. Lat.,* 11(3)

10 Lactantius, *Mort. Pers.,* 9 and 10

11 Luttwak, *Grand Strategy of the Roman Empire,* p 3

12 *SHA, Vita Carini,* XIII

13 Gibbon, Ch XIII

14 Portraiture. Apart from the Nicomedia head and the statue at the Villa Doria Panfili, Rome, the majority of surviving statues are in the masklike 'expressionist' style, as in St. Mark's Square in Venice, which deliberately render each Tetrarch identical. But for an interesting intermediate portrait, see the porphyry head, probably of Diocletian, in Worcester Art Museum, Mass. (see plate 2).
Some books, including the *Encyclopaedia Britannica,* persist in reproducing the 'Capitoline' bust as one of Diocletian, despite the fact that students of the subject recognised this erroneous identification nearly a century ago, and that the style is obviously foreign to late third-century portrait sculpture.
The same divergence between naturalistic and expressionist heads is found on the coins, but even the naturalistic portraits rarely offer genuine likeness

15 For the rise and outlook of the *Illyrici,* see most of the modern writers quoted above, esp. Alföldi, *CAH,* and *Hauptfaktoren*; and Pflaum, in Pauly Wissowa, *RE,* 1278ff. Also R. Syme, 'Emperors from Illyricum' in *Emperors and Biography*

16 For abundant examples, Webb, Mattingly & Sydenham, *Roman Imperial Coinage*

17 For the rise of Odenath and Palmyra, *SHA, Tyr. Trig.,* XV; Peter the Patrician, *Excerpta.* In 261 Gallienus declared Odenath *Dux Romanorum, Imperator* and *Corrector Totius Orientis.* Jones, *Prosop,* p 638. See also Fergus Millar, *JRS,* 1971

18 *SHA, Vita Gal.,* XIV; Victor, *Caes.,* 33.21; Zosimus, I, 1; Zonaras, I, 10; Eutropius, IX, 8

19 *SHA, Div. Claud.*; Zosimus, I, 46; Zonaras, I, 9; Eutropius IX, 8. Much of the detail in *SHA,* and certainly the supposed letter of Claudius, is bogus

20 Zenobia's rise and fall are described in *SHA, Tyr. Trig.*; Zosimus, I; Victor, *Caes.* For the reign and wars of Aurelian, *SHA, Vita Aurel.* and *Tyr. Trig.*; Victor, *Caes.*; Victor, *Epitome*; Eutropius, Zosimus and Zonaras. Aurelian's truly great military achievements have not perhaps received their due historical acknowledgement, partly because of the dearth of trustworthy detail on his wars

21 *SHA, Vita Aurel.* and *Tyr. Trig.,* XXIV

22 It was begun by Aurelian and probably completed by Probus

23 *SHA, Vita Probi* and *Tacitus*; Victor, *Caes.*; Victor, *Epitome*; Eutropius; Zosimus

24 *SHA, Vita Probi* and Julian, *Caesares*

25 *SHA, Vita Probi*; Zosimus, I claims that Probus settled some of the German captives in Britain

26 R. MacMullen, *Soldier and Civilian* and *Roman Government's Response to Crisis*; A. H. M. Jones, *Later Roman Empire, passim*

27 A. H. M. Jones, *Inflation under the Roman Empire*; MacMullen, *Roman Government's Response,* Ch 5; Oertel, Ch V in *CAH*

28 *CJ*, 11.59

29 *SHA, Vita Probi*, XXI; Victor, *Caes.*, 37.4

30 *SHA* and Victor, as above; Eutropius, IX 17.2 give the latter reason. Zosimus and Zonaras merely retail the revolt of Carus and the murder of Probus by his troops

31 *SHA, Vita Cari* etc; Victor, *Caes.*, 39; Victor, *Epitome*, 38; Zosimus I, 72; Eutropius, IX, 19

32 *SHA, Vita Cari* etc; Victor, *Caes.*, 39.1 and Zonaras, XII, 31 say that he was 'domesticos regens'. His suffect consulship (as distinct from an ordinary consulship commencing on 1 January) is indicated in *Chronicon Paschale*, and by the fact that his first consulship as Emperor, for 285, was officially recorded as Consul II. See Seston, *Dioclétien*, p 46

33 For Carus' Eastern war and death, *SHA, Vita Cari* etc; Victor, *Caes.*, 38; Victor, *Epitome*, 38, Eutropius, IX, 18

34 For modern speculation about the intrigue around Numerian, O. Seeck, *Geschichte der Untergangs*, I; Seston, pp 48–9

35 *SHA, Vita Numer.*; Gibbon, Ch XII

36 On the death of Numerian, *SHA, ibid*; Victor, *Caes.*, 39; Victor, *Epitome*, 38; Eutropius, IX 18

37 On the elevation of Diocles, *SHA, Vita Cari* etc XIII; Lactantius, *Mort. Pers.*, 17; Victor, *Caes.*, 39; Victor, *Epitome*, 38; Eutropius, IX 20; Zosimus, I 73. The date and place of the event are now generally agreed as 20 November (not 17) at Nicomedia (not Chalcedon). See Seston, Ch I; Skeat, *Papyri from Panopolis,* and esp. Barnes, *NEDC*, Ch. 4

    His oath of innocence and the public killing of Aper are common to several sources. *SHA* adds the picturesque detail, almost certainly invented, that he quoted from Virgil as he stabbed Aper ('Gloriare, Aper, Aeneae magni dextra cadis!')–witnessed, we are told, by Vopiscus' grandfather once again, and doubtless added to give the flavour of authenticity (*Vita Cari* etc XIII)

38 On the ceremony of army elevation, Dio, *passim*; *SHA*; Ammianus Marcellinus. The inflation of the times precludes even a guess at the size of the money donative. On the military insignia and equipment, see studies of the Arch of Galerius, the Arch of Constantine, and the reliefs at Dura; the *Notitia Dignitatum*; and references throughout *SHA* and Ammianus. We know from *Oxyrhynchus Papyri* 47 (J. Baines, London, 1980) that he was still known as Diocles in Egypt by March 285. I have assumed that the change was made before the Battle of Margus, but at present that cannot be definitely proved

39 See biographical notes on Chapter 4

40 Mentioned in De Blois, *Gallienus*

41 *SHA, Vita Cari*, XVI

42 For the brief revolt of Julianus, Victor, *Caes.*, 39, 1; Victor, *Epitome*, 38; Zosimus, I 73

43 For the battle of Margus, *SHA, Vita Cari*, XVIII; Victor, *Caes.*, 39.1; Victor, *Epitome*, 38; Eutropius, IX, 20. The assassination of Carinus is contained in the two Victors and Zosimus, but Eutropius merely says he was betrayed by his army. There may in fact have been more than one engagement. See Seston, p 53

3 Jove and Hercules (pages 41–60)

1 Zonaras (XII, 31) is alone in claiming that Diocletian immediately proceeded to Rome to begin a persecution of Christians there. But this is nowhere mentioned by contemporary Christian chroniclers of the persecutions, who would surely have mentioned it. He did, however, briefly visit Ticinum in 285, as testified in an inscription. See Barnes, *NEDC,* p 50

2 Victor, *Caes.,* 39, Jones, *Prosop.,* and Barnes, *NEDC.* Seston, p 204 discusses these conciliatory gestures

3 Victor, *Caes.,* 39. He was indirectly attacking the cruel retribution of Constantius in his own time. It is likely Diocletian's clemency was less surprising: by 285 the upper administration was coming to expect 'business as usual' after the frequent changes of Emperor

4 A probable Sarmatian campaign of Diocletian in 285 is deduced, like many other Danube campaigns, from the imperial victory titles: see Barnes, *NEDC,* p 50. Warfare of varying intensity against Sarmatians, Goths, Carpi and others was near-continuous along the Danube during this whole period, making individual campaigns difficult to distinguish. For the invasions and internal rebellion in Gaul, *Pan. Lat.,* 10 (2), Victor, *Caes.,* 39, Eutrop., IX, 20. Coins exist of Amandus but not Aelianus

5 The precise dating of Maximian's elevation to Caesar has been notoriously problematic. See Seston, pp 57–81. *Pan. Lat.,* 10(2) and Eutrop., IX, 20 clearly suggest he was despatched to Gaul with the imperial title in mid-285. More recently Barnes, *NEDC,* pp 4 and 57 reconsiders the evidence, including an inscription attesting Diocletian's presence at Ticinum, and concludes that Maximian was probably elevated to Caesar at Milan on 21 July 285. It is most likely that Diocletian would personally perform such an important and premeditated enactment so early in the reign. However, I am persuaded by Seston's argument that Maximian's subsequent promotion to full Augustus so soon afterwards was probably forced on Diocletian by the crisis of Carausius. The hypothesis is still consistent with Maximian's promotion early in 286, not in November as Seston suggests

6 Maximian was probably born in 250, cf. Victor, *Epitome,* 40, 10–11 which also says his parents were shopkeepers near Sirmium. See also Victor, *Caes.,* 39, and *Pan. Lat.,* 10(2). Ensslin, *RE,* 14 2486 discusses his probable career before 285

7 Gibbon, Ch XIII

8 Lactantius, *Mort. Pers.,* 8

9 Victor, *Caes.,* 39. *Pan. Lat.,* 10(2). Seston, pp 57–81

10 For the revolt of Carausius and Maximian's abortive expedition, Victor, *Caes.,* 39, *Pan. Lat.,* 10(2) and 11(3). See esp. Seston, pp 57–81 and S. Johnson, *The Saxon Shore Forts,* London, 1976. Carausius' proclamation of himself as Augustus cannot be dated more precisely than 286. See Barnes, *NEDC,* p 10

11 *Pan. Lat.,* 10(2) 11–12. This was delivered in 289 before the failure of Maximian's naval expedition

12 Seston, pp 76ff. Against Seston, Ensslin, *RE,* 2490, and Barnes, *NEDC,* p 4, accept the evidence of *Chron. Min.,* 1.229 that Maximian's promotion to Augustus was on 1 April 286, when Diocletian was probably at Byzantium. Assuming it was prompted by Carausius' revolt, it therefore places that event early in 286

13 *Pan. Lat.,* 10(2) of Mamertinus stresses throughout the unity of the Augusti, their relation with Jove and Hercules, and with one another

14 Maximian's western affairs are best described in *Pan. Lat.,* 10(2) and corroborated by victory titles as well as ancient writers and other sources. These are: the campaign against the Heruli, late 285 or early 286; the expedition across the Rhine, 287; the meeting with Diocletian, 288; the treaty with Gennobaudes, late 288; described respectively in *Pan. Lat.,* 10(2) 5, 6, 7, 9 and 10. See also Seston, pp 57–81

15 The 285 Sarmatian campaign is deduced from the victory titles, and the 289 campaign likewise, plus *Pan. Lat.,* 11(3) and 8(5). See also Seston, p 129 ff, and Barnes, *NEDC,* pp 50–51 and 255

16 *Pan. Lat.,* 10(2) and 8(5). Cf. M-L Chaumont, *Récherches sur l'histoire d'Arménie de l'avénément des Sassanides à la conversion du royaume,* Paris, 1969

17 See Chapter 8. The distinction was being made by 291, although the separation of offices was only at an early stage

18 See Chapter 9

19 Dio, LIX, 6, 3; quoted in F. Millar, *Emperor in the Roman World,* p 3

20 Lactantius, *Mort. Pers.,* 7

21 *Pan. Lat.,* 11(3) and S. Johnson, *The Saxon Shore Forts,* Ch. 2

22 Webb, Mattingly, and Sydenham, *Roman Imperial Coinage.* Also R. A. G. Carson, 'The Mints and Coinage of Carausius and Allectus', *JBAA,* xxii (1959)

23 For the meeting and celebrations of 290–1, *Pan. Lat.,* 11(3) of Mamertinus. Seston, pp 210–230 discusses at length the unfolding theology of the Jovian and Herculian houses

24 *Pan. Lat.,* 11(3), 12

25 *Pan. Lat.,* 11(3), 10

26 *Pan. Lat.,* 11(3), 11

27 Webb *et al, Rom. Imp. Coinage*

28 See the shield designs in the *Notitia Dignitatum.* However the reliability of these has been seriously criticised by Robert Grigg, *JRS* 1983

29 *Pan. Lat.,* 10(2), 11

4 The Tetrarchy (pages 61–70)

1 R. A. G. Carson, *op. cit.,* also Webb *et al, Rom. Imp. Coinage.* See also Shepherd Frere, *Britannia,* Ch. 16

2 The suggestion that Carausius' success, with its threat of major fragmentation in Gaul once again, was a spur to the Tetrarchic system is strongly pressed by Seston, in my view convincingly. For what little it is worth, the *SHA* also states this in a general way

3 *Pan. Lat.,* 10(2), 14

4 On the origins and careers of Galerius and Constantius, see the usual ancient sources, plus in particular R. Syme, *Emperors and Biography,* Jones, *Prosop.,* and Barnes, *NEDC,* for summaries of the often conflicting and insufficient evidence. The linking of Constantius to the earlier Emperor Claudius II is wholly bogus, as probably is the nickname Chlorus. There is a persuasive tradition, supported by Barnes, *NEDC,* as well as others, that he was Maximian's Praetorian Prefect at least after 288, and that

during this tenure he married Theodora. This is based primarily on references in two Panegyrics 10(2) and 8(5).

Barnes, p 62, argues from *Pan. Lat.*, 8(5) and Diocletian's attested movements, that Galerius was invested as Caesar on 1 March, 293 (not 21 May, as Seston, p 88ff suggests, following an alternative tradition): and probably at Sirmium, not Nicomedia as Lactantius states. Lactantius is not to be discarded lightly on simple matters of fact, but the Justinian Code's clear evidence of Diocletian's movements in 293 makes it highly unlikely he could have been at Nicomedia on either of these dates; and investiture by proxy, which Seston suggests, seems improbable. (It had happened with Maximian's elevation to Augustus, but that had been in emergency)

5 *Pan. Lat.*, 8 (4), 4

6 Constantius was born not later than 250, and his son Constantine probably in 272 or 273. Barnes, *NEDC*, pp 39–43

7 Galerius was born some time before 260 at Romulianum, where he was buried. The slander against his mother Romula comes from Lactantius, *Mort. Pers.* 9, who also accuses her of infusing him with anti-Christian sentiments. Most of this can probably be discounted, as we know very little about Galerius' parentage. He originally bore the name Maximianus (unconnected with Maximian Augustus) and this appears on coins and in the official titulature; but to avoid confusion I have referred to him throughout by his more usual name. For his drinking habits, *Anon. Vales,* I, 4, 11. According to Lactantius, Galerius later had an illegitimate son Candidianus, whom Valeria his wife adopted. His daughter, Valeria Maximilla, may either have been the issue of an earlier marriage, or of his marriage with Valeria. (Lactantius is unclear about Valeria's childlessness, and may only mean that she was unable to have other children.) If Maximilla was the daughter of Valeria, this would place the marriage before 293. See especially Barnes, *NEDC* Ch 4, who places no reliance on the traditional accounts that the two Caesars divorced their wives and married into the imperial families in 293, since these all stem from Enmann's lost 'Kaisergeschichte', a source which we know confused the chronology of the Tetrarchic period. In the case of Constantius, the Panegyrics support the view that he was both Praetorian Prefect and son-in-law to Maximian before 293. But Galerius' earlier marriage is less certain, and his possible Prefecture (cf. Barnes Ch 8) merely conjectural

8 Lactantius, *Mort. Pers.*, 7. For the size of later Roman armies, see Luttwak (1976), part 3

9 Victor, *Caes.*, 39

10 As Lactantius himself virtually admits, in *Mort. Pers.* 7

11 *SHA, Vita Cari,* XVIII

12 Seston, p 185ff inclines to this view. If the territorial divisions were definite, then at least they were not exclusive. Barnes, *NEDC*, Ch 11 discusses the evidence and concludes that while there may have been a formal fourfold division, it was often overridden. In practice the more substantial division was into East and West, and even this was disregarded when necessary

13 Dessun, *Inscriptiones Latinae Selectae,* 629

14 Victor, *Caes.*, 39

15 For the shift in power in Persia, cf. Chaumont, *op. cit.,* and Seston, pp 165ff

5 Victory and Consolidation I–Britain, Africa, the Danube (pages 71–77)

1 Seston, p 102. The main ancient sources for the British reconquest are *Pan. Lat.*, 8(5), Victor, *Caes.*, 39, and Eutropius, 9. Among modern accounts, which vary in their interpretations, see Seston, pp 101–113; S. Frere, *Britannia*, Ch. 16; S. Johnson, *The Saxon Shore Forts*, Ch 2; D. Eichholz, 'Constantius Chlorus' Invasion of Britain', *JRS*, 1953; W. V. Wade, 'Carausius, Restorer of Britain', *Numis. Chron.*, XII, 1953; N. Shiel, *The Episode of Carausius and Allectus* (BAR 1977)

2 *Pan. Lat.*, 8(5), 6

3 Eutrop., 9, 22 and *Pan. Lat.*, 8(5), 12. The mercantile motives for the coup are suggested by Seston, pp 101–113

4 K Miller, *Die Peutingersche Tafel*, Stuttgart, 1962

5 *Pan. Lat.*, 8(5), 15

6 This seems improbable, and may well be a rhetorical flourish only

7 *Pan. Lat.*, 8(5), 16

8 For Maximian's Mauretanian campaign, *Pan. Lat.*, 8(5) and 9(4), Eutropius, IX, Zonaras, XII. Much of the evidence derives from inscriptions. For a thorough review of the sources, Seston, pp 114–128. Also B. Warmington, *The North African Provinces from Diocletian to the Vandal Conquests*, Cambridge, 1954; M. Rachet, *Rome et les Berbères: un problème militaire d'Auguste à Dioclétien*, Brussels, 1970

9 For the several Danube campaigns of Diocletian and Galerius the main sources are Panegyrics, victory titles and inscriptions. Again, see Seston, pp 128–135. On the Ripa Sarmatica, A. Mócsy, *Pannonia* and *Upper Moesia*; A. Alföldi, in *Third Congress of Roman Frontier Studies*, and *passim*. Also Luttwak, *Grand Strategy*, Part 3

10 See Chapter 7

6 Victory and Consolidation II – Egypt and Persia (pages 78–88)

1 The chronology for these very important events in the Orient has been the most difficult of all for students of the period, precisely because so much explanation hangs on it. For example, did the Tax Edict precede the Alexandrian revolt, or follow it? Was it one of its causes, or a subsequent measure of pacification, or neither? Was there any deeper connection between Achilleus' revolt and Narses' invasion than mere opportunism, and did Diocletian and Galerius believe there was? Is the hypothesis of Manichean involvement in the rebel movement plausible, and if so, did Narses assign the Manicheans – perhaps as unwitting tools – a role in his strategy?
A good summary of the problems is given in T. C. Skeat (ed.), *Papyri from Panopolis*. Essentially Boak and Youtie in *The Archive of Aurelius Isidorus*, and Seston, *Dioclétien*, pp 137–183, favour the view that the Alexandrian revolt began in 296. The Tax Edict of Optatius has been securely dated to 16 March 297, which suggests to Seston that it followed the revolt's suppression. However the Panegyric of 1 March 297 at Trier mentions victories on the Nile, which may well refer to the defeat of the Blemmyes, but it does not mention Alexandria – that is only referred to in a Panegyric delivered 18 months later. This would suggest at most that the end of the siege was not yet known by March 297, which makes it most implausible that a new tax policy, influenced by the grievances which had led to revolt, could have been worked out and put into law in such a short time. Cf. Barnes, *NEDC*, p 230–1.

An alternative version to this, adopted by A. C. Johnson in 'Lucius Domitius Domitianus', *Classical Philology*, 1950, rejects the dating above and argues that the March 297 Edict preceded, and quite possibly provoked, the Alexandrian revolt. This would entail that the Thebaid troubles, at least, had other causes than the Edict, since they preceded it. This general view is supported by Vandersleyen, *Chronologie des préfects,* and by Beatty in Skeat (ed.), who shows from recent Papyri that Diocletian was travelling northwards down the Nile in September 298. It is difficult to believe he spent a whole 18 months settling the affairs of Egypt if at the same time there was a major crisis on the Persian frontier following Galerius' initial defeat. T. D. Barnes presents the most recent chronological argument, and it is this I have generally accepted. According to this account, the probable sequence of events is as follows. Galerius suppresses the Blemmyes in 294. The Persian invasion, occurring in late 296, occupies the two Emperors' attention. Early in 297 Galerius is defeated at Callinicum, and the Tax Edict is promulgated. The revolt in Egypt erupts violently, first in the Thebaid and then in Lower Egypt, including Alexandria itself. Realising its seriousness, Diocletian returns to Egypt in mid-297 with an army which is employed both in quelling the cities and beseiging Alexandria, which holds out until the spring of 298. After this, Diocletian spends most of 298 pacifying Egypt, possibly releasing some troops for the Persian front. In the spring of 298 Galerius launches his new offensive, is victorious, and returns up the Euphrates late in the year. Having travelled down The Nile, Diocletian leaves Egypt for Antioch in the winter, and finally joins Galerius at Nisibis in the spring of 299 for the conclusion of the peace treaty.

I do not deny problems with this interpretation. If Coptos (and Busiris?) did revolt in 290–1 (cf. Seston, p 141) this must have been at best only remotely connected with the later full-scale national revolt of Achilleus and Domitianus. However, Coptos at any rate does seem to have taken part in the later and larger revolt, since Paniskos' letters from Coptos are dated according to the reign of the rebel Domitianus, suggesting a connection between the movement in the Thebaid and Alexandria. Against Seston, I think it unlikely that the Blemmye raiders were allied with the urban populations of the Thebaid. The revolt probably did have multiple causes, but I think it more plausible to view it as a single coalition, many of whose elements remain obscure to us, than to postulate an outright opposition between the Thebaid and the Delta. Whether Paniskos actually was a Manichean remains conjectural, as is the extent to which Persia made use of this religion. Clearly Diocletian saw them as an insidious enemy influence, but the fact that his famous constitution against Manicheanism was in 302, not 297 (cf. Barnes, pp 55 and 169) perhaps weakens Seston's arguments that they were an active fifth column in the Egyptian uprising

2 On Manicheanism, see P. Brown, 'Diffusion of Manicheanism in the Late Roman Empire', *JRS,* 1969; also P. Brown, *The World of Late Antiquity*; J. Ferguson, *The Religions of the Roman Empire*; Nock, Burkett and Leitzman in *CAH*, Vol XII; H. C. Puech, *Le manichéism, son fondateur, sa doctrine;* Seston, *L'Egypte manichéene,* Chronique d'Egypte, 1939

3 *Oxyrhychus Papyrus,* 2,142, quoted in Seston, p 140; and Seston more generally for a sketch of Egypt's economic troubles. Cf. Wickwitz, *Geld und Wirtschaft im röm. Reich*

des vierten Jahrht n. Chr., Helsingfors, 1932. Also A. H. M. Jones, *Inflation under the Roman Empire,* and *Taxation in Antiquity*

4 Galerius' expedition is deduced from *Pan. Lat.,* 8(5), 2; Eusebius, *Chron.,* 227 and Jerome, *Chronicle,* 226. *Oxyrh. Papyr.* also supports this. See Barnes, p 62

5 On Paniskos, see Winter, 'The Family Letters of Paniskos', *Journal of Egyptian Archaeology,* 1927, and Seston, pp 143 ff. The tax reform and edict of Optatius are described in Chapter 9

6 On the initial defeat of Galerius, Victor, *Caes.,* 39, Eutropius, IX, 24, Festus, *Breviarum,* 25. Seston, *op. cit.*

7 Ammianus, XXIV, 6, 8

8 Ammianus, I, 14, Eutropius, IX 24, Orosius, VII, 25. I am persuaded by Seston's suggestion and by the likely chronology that this was probably an invention of the next century

9 On the Egyptian revolt, Jerome, *Chron.,* 226, Eutropius, IX, 22. Seston, *op. cit.,* but see Barnes, *NEDC,* pp 12 and 230. On the motives of the revolt, Kubitschek, 1928, *Zur Geschichte des usurpators Achilleus*

10 Eutropius, IX, 24; Orosius, VII, 25; Malalas, *Chron. Antioch.*; Jerome, *Chron.,* 226. Seston, *op. cit.* On the Thebaid settlement, Procopius, *Bella Persica,* 1, 19, 27 and *IGRR,* 1.1291

11 Cf. Duncan Jones, *Chiron,* 1978

12 T. C. Skeat (ed.), *Papyri from Panopolis, 298–300,* for the quotation and description of the imperial progress. Also *Oxyrh. Papyr.,* 1416

13 *FIRA,* II 544–89. Barnes, *NEDC,* dates it to 302 from the tenure of Julianus, not 297 as is generally believed

14 Galerius' successful campaign is attested by his triumphal arch at Salonica; Lact, *Mort. Pers.,* 9; Victor, *Caes.,* 39; Eutropius, 9, 25; Festus, *Brev.,* 25; *SHA, Vita Cari.* Despite its being pressed into the artificial symmetry of the Tetrarchy's official celebrations, the scale of Galerius' military achievement by all traditional standards, cannot be disguised. It was the greatest single victory of the Tetrarchy, and the most decisive victory gained by Rome over Sassanid Persia until Heraclius in the seventh century. Although Lactantius no doubt exaggerates, it must have enhanced Galerius' prestige considerably, and with it his subsequent influence in Diocletian's counsels

15 Petrus Patricius, frag. 12 and 14; Ammianus I, 24–25; Procopius, *de Aedificus,* I, ii

16 Seston, pp 173–4; Stein, *Histoire du Bas Empire,* vol I

17 Cf. Johnson and West, *Survey of Byzantine Egypt*

18 Pliny, *Natural History,* V, x, 58

19 The great distinction between the liturgy state and the classical slave-owning system, with its fundamentally different political development, was first brought out, I believe, by Max Weber in his consideration of Egypt

7 Defence in Depth (pages 91–101)

1 *SHA, Vita Aurel.,* 44. This Chapter relies heavily on Luttwak's interpretation of both Gallienus' and Diocletian's military reforms, in *Grand Strategy of the Roman Empire,* to

which I am greatly indebted. The traditional view (Seeck, Grosse, Baynes, Parker) which is still found in the majority of general works, is that Diocletian expanded the armies to create at least essentials of the new, dual system: Empire-wide mobile field forces (*comitatenses*), perhaps evolved from Gallienus' innovations, which were geographically and strategically distinct from the static frontier troops (*limitanei*); and that Constantine perfected and formalised the division with a new command structure. The view was first challenged by Nischer (1925), and supported by Van Berchem's very influential *L'armée de Dioclétien et la réforme constantinienne,* (1942). Seston (1946 and 1955), Jones (1964) and Luttwak (1976) accept with increasing emphasis this alternative picture. Essentially, it is that while Diocletian certainly established static fortress troops on the frontiers, he actually broke up and redistributed the mobile forces, attaching them to the newly-organised frontier defence systems. They retained their tactical mobility, but within a regional strategy, not the Empire-wide one of Aurelian and Probus. References to Diocletian's *sacer comitatus* merely denote the Emperor's escort, and not a fighting field army in any sense. The *comitatenses* of the Late Roman Empire were a definite departure from Diocletian's strategy by Constantine, who reverted to single-Emperor rule after 324 and whose greatest wars were civil ones rather than on the frontiers. For a rehearsal of these arguments, see the above writers, and especially Luttwak, pp 187ff

2 Eusebius, *Vita Const.*

3 Malalas, *Chron.,* 12, 38

4 Luttwak, Part 3; Seston, *passim*

5 The actual size of Diocletian's armies is still arguable. Lactantius suggests he simply quadrupled it as he did Emperors and courts, which would have produced the miraculous figure of over a million men in a *standing* paid army, something no Ancient Empire could have supported for long. Estimates from the *Notitia Dignitatum* have put the Roman armies at approximately the end of the fourth century at between 496,000 (Szilági) and 737,000 (Nischer) but these would all include a large proportion of part-time, mainly self-supporting farmer militia, which came into existence after Diocletian's time. A figure between 500,000 and 600,000 soldiers of all types is to date the most reasonable estimate for the Tetrarchic period

6 The total of 53 legions comprises 33 Severan legions, six more by 284, and 14 more definitely identified under the Tetrarchy. Nischer (1925) believes the Tetrarchy raised no less than 34 new legions, and Jones in *LRE* endorses this.

A crucial question that is still argued is the size of the standard Tetrarchic legion. Luttwak seems certain that, while lower than the old 5,500 infantry plus supporting cavalry, they were definitely not the small, 1,000-man units misleadingly named 'legions' which appear under Constantine and are listed in such profusion in the *Notitia*. But just how large were they? Recently Duncan Jones (1978) has attempted to answer this from analysis of surviving pay receipts of army units in Egypt shortly after the end of the revolt. His calculations yield, for example, Legio III Diocletiana, 1,716 men; vexillation of Legio II Traiana, 1,109 men; vexillation of Legio III Diocletiana, 1,035 men. The conclusion is hardly avoidable that these were all parts of legions, not full legions. In the *Notitia*, well over a century later, Legio III Diocletiana is listed in five different locations. Thus, although there was already a discernible tendency towards smaller units among the mobile cavalry *alae* and the now static *cohortes,* the new legions raised by the Tetrarchy (and by implication, the restored Severan legions too), were not far short of the traditional 5,500 level

7 Boak, *Manpower Shortage*
8 For a discussion of the new forts, Petrikovits in *JRS,* 1971; Luttwak, Part 3
9 Vegetius, *De rebus bellicis*
10 This is the view of S. Johnson, *The Saxon Shore Forts*
11 Zosimus, II, 34. He contrasts this strongly and favourably with Constantine's policy, which involved weakening the frontier forces and basing the *comitatenses* in the cities, where they allegedly became softened by luxuries and oppressed the citizens

8 The Recasting of Government (pages 102–114)

1 Lactantius, *Mort. Pers.,* 7
2 Among the most useful modern works on the administrative reforms (concerning whose details and timing there are various disagreements) are: W. Ensslin, Ch XI of *CAH;* N. H. Baynes, *JRS,* 1925; J. G. C. Anderson, *JRS,* 1933; Seston, *Dioclétien, passim;* A. H. M. Jones, *LRE,* Vol I; R. Macmullen, *Roman Govts' Response;* and most recently Barnes, *NEDC,* esp. Chs 12 and 13. On more specific aspects, see J. B. Bury, *JRS,* 1923 and A. H. M. Jones, *JRS,* 1952 on the Verona List; Howe, *The Praetorian Prefect;* Arnheim, *Senatorial Aristocracy in the Late Roman Empire;* Keyes, *The Rise of the Equites in the Third Century.* For individual careers, the readiest sources are Jones, *Prosop.,* and Barnes, *NEDC*
3 MacMullen, *op. cit.,* and Honoré, *Emperors and Lawyers,* on the dwindling output of rescripts during the crisis years
4 Victor, *Caes.,* 29, 43. Among many examples of routine extortion by *frumentarii,* see the accounts in *Rev. de Philologie,* XVII (1943), 111–119, quoted in Sourcebook, p 402
5 See esp. Arnheim, *op. cit.*
6 While the total reform of the governmental machinery, including separation of civil and military authority, undoubtedly took decades, it has been argued by Seston, and more recently Barnes, *NEDC,* p 224ff, that subdivision of the provinces and creation of dioceses was probably done all at once, with only minor changes afterwards—the most probable date being 293. Several further alterations were made after Diocletian's reign, in 314–15
7 Valuable discussion on the reasons for the policy of provincial subdivision is found in Anderson, Seston and Jones. There is no need to postulate a single or even principal motive, and every reason to suppose that it served several complementary purposes
8 *CJ,* III, 3, 2
9 Shepherd Frere, *Britannia,* p 341ff. This conflicts with the assumptions in Collingwood and Myers, p 280. For the full list of Diocletianic provinces, see Appendix I. On the date and interpretation of the Verona List, see Bury, Jones and Barnes, *op. cit.*
10 That the line of authority was not simply a downward transmission belt, is assumed by Ensslin and Seston, and may perhaps be inferred from the system of appointment and removal, as well as the traditional avenues of legal appeal and petition. But its precise workings are still obscure and merit further study

11 Keyes, *Rise of the Equites*. There has been argument over whether the gradual exclusion of senators from governorships as well as military commands was simply a continuation of the policies begun by Gallienus. See L. Homo, *Revue Historique*, 1913, 1921; Keyes, *op. cit.*; Baynes, *JRS*, 1925, Anderson, *op. cit.* The steady encroachment on senatorial preserves by the Illyrian Emperors is well established, and of course, exclusion from military command often meant, *a fortiori*, exclusion from governerships as well. Diocletian carried this to its logical completion, with the exception of Italy and the few much reduced proconsular provinces. However, I agree with Baynes and Arnheim that the explicit policy of separation of military and civil estabishments was a distinctly new one initiated by Diocletian and later completed by Constantine

12 So the heading on the Verona List asserts, although only eight are named in the manuscript. Cf. Barnes, *NEDC*, p 218

13 See Arnheim's compilations in *Senatorial Aristocracy*, and that of Barnes in *NEDC*

14 *Pan. Lat.*, 10(2)

15 From the inscription recording his rebuilding at Birdoswald on Hadrian's Wall

16 *Pan. Lat.*, 9(5)

17 *Oxyrh. Papyr.*, 58 (Select Papyri no 226)

18 See Chapter 11

19 The structure of the Late Imperial Court is best attested in its completed form under Constantine; see Ch 16. How much of it was a continuation or development of practices already present under Diocletian, is still conjectural. The first mention of a Consistory is Tetrarchic; and it is possible that the later supreme legal minister, the Quaestor of the Sacred Palace, originated with Diocletian. See Jones, *LRE*; Ensslin in *CAH*; Bury, *Later Roman Empire*, Vol I; Millar, *Emperor in the Roman World*, *passim*

20 Our knowledge of the Praetorian Prefects of the Tetrarchy is still woefully meagre, a lack which is all the more acute since so much of the work of reorganisation must have hinged on them. It seems clear that the power and status of the Prefect reached its zenith under the Tetrarchy, with the exclusion of the senatorial element in provincial government and the great expansion of administrative machine. Yet Prefects still had military responsibilities as well, although these were probably declining overall, with the greatly reduced role of the Praetorian cohorts.

We cannot be certain how many held office simultaneously, how these offices were distributed, or – except in a few cases – who the occupants were. However, the secure identification of Asclepiodotus in 296, makes it near-certain that each of the four Emperors had a Prefect, though it is possible they were transferable in times of need. The most accessible modern lists are in Howe, *The Praetorian Prefect*, and Barnes, *NEDC*, Ch 8. Barnes' suggestion is that both Constantius and Galerius were Prefects to Maximian and Diocletian respectively before their elevations in 293. The latter is less secure, however. This leaves us with the following list of Praetorian Prefects:

285	Aurelius Aristobulus	PP to Carinus, then Diocletian
285–292?	Afranius Hannibalianus	to Diocletian?
285–292?	Julius Asclepiodotus	to Maximian?
288–293	Flavius Constantius	to Maximian

296	Julius Asclepiodotus	to Constantius
302	Asclepiades	to Diocletian
303	Flaccinus	to Galerius?

Other possible Prefects (in addition to Galerius before 293) are Januarius, Pompeianus, Tryphonianus. It is also possible Allectus was the Praetorian Prefect, not the rationalis, to Carausius (Seeck, *RE,* 1894)

21 *CJ,* VII, 62, 64

22 On the 'Orientalising' of the imperial style, Victor, *Caes.,* 39, 1–8, Ammianus 16, 10, Eutropius, 9, 26, *Pan. Lat.,* 2(3). See also Ensslin, Ch X in *CAH;* MacMullen, *Constantine,* and *Roman Govt's Response, passim;* Seston, pp 185–9, 245ff; Bury, *Later Roman Empire,* Vol I

23 *Pan. Lat.,* 11(3), 2

24 Victor, *Caes.,* 39, 2

25 Gibbon, Ch XIII

26 Lactantius, *Mort. Pers.,* 14

9 Finance, Taxation, Inflation (pages 115–125)

1 A great deal of scholarly work has gone into the reconstruction of Diocletian's fiscal policies, the most comprehensive and satisfying results of which are probably to be found in A. H. M. Jones, *LRE,* Vol I and especially his collection, *The Roman Economy;* and R. MacMullen, *Roman Government's Response to Crisis,* especially Chapters 5, 6 and 7. But see also Alföldi, Ensslin, Mattingly, Oertel in *CAH,* Vol XII; Seston, Part II; Rostovtsev, *Social and Economic History;* Bury, *Later Roman Empire,* Vol I; and numerous articles mentioned below

2 The famous *Constitutio Antoniniana* of 212, see Dio, LXXVIII, 9. It has been disputed whether the main motive for universal extension of the franchise was fiscal

3 MacMullen, *op. cit.,* Ch 5; Jones, *Inflation under the Roman Empire,* in *The Roman Economy,* above

4 Jones, *ibid,* and Jones, *LRE,* Vol. I. Both figures are conservative approximations for the period circa 150–260

5 Jones, *Inflation;* MacMullen, Ch 5

6 Jones, *op. cit.;* MacMullen, *op. cit.;* also C. H. V. Sutherland in *JRS,* 1955 and 1961 on Diocletian's currency reforms; D. Sperber, 'Denarii and Aurei in the time of Diocletian', *JRS,* 1966; M. Hendy, 'Mint and fiscal administration under Diocletian', *JRS,* 1972

7 Jones, *op. cit.,* and *Taxation in Antiquity,* in *RE;* MacMullen, *op. cit.,* chs. 5–6. Seston, pp 261–294

8 See the above, and especially MacMullen's excellent Ch 7 for the systematization of the economy in kind and its integration with Diocletian's tax system

9 On the new emphasis on *capitatio, CJ,* XI, 55, 1 and IV, 49, 9. MacMullen, Ch 6; Seston, p 262ff; Jones, *Capitatio and Iugatio,* in *RE*

10 A. E. R. Boak, *Études de Papyrologie,* II (1923), 1–8

11 On the new census of resources, see the works above, plus Jones, 'Census Records in the Late Roman Empire', *JRS,* 1953; Stein, *Histoire du Bas-Empire,* 1, 74. The Caranis

and Theadelphia declarations are quoted in Johnson and West, *Survey of Byzantine Egypt,* Ch II. See also Barnes, *NEDC,* Ch 14 on the dating and novelty of the census

12 Syro-Roman Law Book, cxxi. The combination of land and people into one overall tax assessment is first attested in the Table of Brigetio, *FIRA,* 1, 93. On the interpretation and possible interchangeability of *iuga* and *capita,* see Jones, *Capitatio and Iugatio;* MacMullen, Chs 6 and 7, for the most useful discussions. It is generally conceded that a uniform and exact system throughout the Empire never operated, and was probably not attempted. On the interchangeability of the term, see above, plus *Cod. Theod.,* XI, 1, 5 and XI, 20, 6

13 On the Thera Records, see Jones, *Census Records.* Other records of uncertain date survive from Lydia, Caria, Asiana, Chios and elsewhere

14 Jones, *LRE,* Vol I and *Inflation.* On *superindictio* see *Cod. Theod.,* VII, 4, 32 and Bury, *Later Roman Empire,* Vol I, Ch II

15 Bury, *op. cit.*

16 Quoted in Skeat (ed.), *Panopolis Papyri* 2

17 Cf. the Panegyric to Constantine delivered in Autun, probably in 312; *FIRA,* Vol 1, 93; Table of Brigetio; also, *Cod. Theod.,* VII, 20, 4 for a constitution of 325

18 Skeat (ed.), *Panopolis Papyri* 2

19 Lactantius, *Mort. Pers.,* 7; Victor, *Caes.,* 39, 32

20 Lactantius, *Mort. Pers.,* 7

21 *ibid*

10 A Command Economy (pages 126–139)

1 Again cf. Jones, MacMullen, above for inflation and the fiscal measures against it

2 Rylands Papyrus no 607

3 Preamble to the Price Edict. For a full translation of the Edict, see Appendix to Tenney Frank, *Economic Survey of Ancient Rome,* Baltimore, 1940. More recently see Erim, Reynolds and Cornford in *JRS,* 1970, 1971 and 1973 on a newly discovered copy of the Edict

4 MacMullen, Ch 5 points this out

5 Lactantius, *Mort. Pers.,* 7

6 Jones, *Inflation in Antiquity.* See also Ch 16 below

7 On the origins and development of State organisation of economic groups, there is widespread literature. Perhaps the strongest documentary evidence is in the pattern of laws appearing in the Theodosian Code from the early years of Constantine onward. However, evidence from the Justinian Code, as well as papyri and references in ancient sources, is generally accepted as establishing that much of the policy was initiated in the Tetrarchic period. Cf. J. B. Bury, 'Compulsory Social Organisation', in *Later Roman Empire,* Vol I; Oertel and Ensslin in *CAH;* Tenney Frank, *op. cit.;* Rostovtsev, *Social and Economic History;* Boak, *Manpower Shortage;* Jones, *LRE,* Vol I and *Roman Economy;* MacMullen, *Soldier and Civilian,* and esp., *Roman Government's Response,* Chs 6–7

8 On the burden of *decuriones, Cod. Theod.,* XII, 1 *passim.* On Diocletian's compulsory civic obligations, *CJ,* X, 32, 6 and X, 10, 59; MacMullen, *Roman Social Relations,* and *Roman Govt's Response,* Ch 7. On hereditary status, *CJ,* VIII, 47, 7 and X 39, 4; MacMullen, *op. cit.;* Seeck, *Gesch. der Untergangs,* 2

9 On navicularii, *Cod. Theod.,* XIII, 5, 1 and 2

10 See esp., Boak, *Manpower Shortage*

11 On fabricae, Beatty in *Panopolis Papyri*; Cod. Theod., XII, 1, 37; *Notitia Dignitatum*; and esp. MacMullen, *AJA,* 1960, *Roman Govt's Response,* Ch 7 and *Soldier and Civilian.* See also Haussig, *Byzantine Civilisation,* Ch 2

12 On the colonate, cf. the laws in *Cod. Theod.* and *CJ*; MacMullen, *op. cit.,* Ch 7; Jones, *LRE,* Vol I and esp., 'The Roman Colonate', in *RE.* Also Haussig, *op. cit.* Tenney Frank, *Econ. Survey*; Oertel in *CAH*

13 For a discussion of late Roman slavery, W. Westerman, *Slave Systems of Greek and Roman Antiquity*; also Rostovtsev, 'Problem of Serfdom in the Roman Empire', *Journal of Land and Public Utility Economics,* 1926. On *Inquilini,* cf. Jones, *Colonate,* and MacMullen *op. cit.,* Ch 7

14 *Cod. Theod.* V 17, 1

15 Oertel in *CAH* describes it most misleadingly as 'State Socialism'. See notes to Ch 11 below

11 The New Order (pages 140–150)

1 The surest evidence of Diocletian's movements is from the date and place of his rescripts from the Justinian Code. See Barnes, *NEDC,* pp 49–56

2 *SHA, Vita Cari,* 10

3 R. MacMullen, *Roman Government's Response to Crisis,* Ch 9

4 Cf. Karl Wittfogel's all-embracing category in *Oriental Despotism,* Yale, 1957. Though anti-communist, Wittfogel employs a distinctly Marxist approach which consistently tries to account for the political and cultural superstructure of a state from its underlying economic relations, and consequently underestimates the great differences due to legal and religious institutions

5 Mommsen, *Staatsrecht,* quoted by Bury in *LRE* Vol I. Bury contrasts sharply with Wittfogel in according great significance to the legal forms of the Late Roman monarchy, and even perhaps dignifying what were at most conflicting traditions of legitimacy into explicit parts of a constitution. The idea of a 'legal right of revolution' sounds almost contradictory until we distinguish this very clearly from more modern concepts of revolution, which connote not just a leadership coup but the overthrow of a constitutional order. The fact that the army (and later, the army in concert with the ceremonial Byzantine senate) could depose an Emperor, represented simply a violent method of succession within an unchanged monarchical establishment

6 For the operation of the imperial power, and the attitudes of rulers and ruled towards it, see especially F. Millar, *The Emperor in the Roman World.* On Diocletian's rescripts and his legal policy I rely heavily on T. Honoré, *Emperors and Lawyers*

7 *CJ,* IV, 44, 3

8 *CJ,* V, 5, 2

9 Honoré, *op. cit.,* pp 119 and 129

10 *CJ,* VII, 4, 3

11 *CJ,* III, 37, 5

12 *CJ,* I, 14, 4 quoted by Bury, Ch I

13 *Basilica,* II, 6, 9 quoted by Bury, Ch I

14 Gibbon, Ch XIII

15 See Vogt, *The Decline of Rome,* Ch. 1, and especially Oertel in *CAH,* who actually talks of the growing regimentation as 'State Socialism', perhaps with the Soviet Union in mind. Comparison with modern totalitarian states is apt to be badly misleading. In the Roman Empire technology, economic limitations and speed of communication greatly constrained the actual power and surveillance the Government could exert on the individual, or at any distance from the court. The 'secret police' (*agentes in rebus*) employed from the time of Constantine onward (and perhaps before him), spied erratically on higher officials; they did not and could not maintain the watch on the whole population which is possible to modern political police. There was no censorship or organisation of cultural life as we understand it. There was widespread evasion of the Government's edicts, and a correspondingly large measure of discretion to administrators in carrying them out. Tradition was tenacious in all classes, both rulers and ruled, and it was not possible for Emperors to sweep away old institutions in the manner of modern revolutions. The broad ruling strata on which they depended, whether noble or parvenu, received or aspired to a 'traditional' education, for there was no other, and this remained true even when most of them had become Christian. The age was quite foreign to the idea of continual change, let alone 'progress', and so there could be no radical revolution of official values to support new policies, of the kind that happened in Russia after 1917 and Germany after 1933. Even the adoption of Christianity was a gradual process of absorption of traditional religion, and involved very little political change on the part of the State. Although the change they brought about was profound enough to be recognised by us as a 'revolution' in State and society, both Diocletian and Constantine had to adapt existing institutions, and for the most part stress publicly the continuity, not the break, with Rome's sacred heritage. While both centralised direction and collectivist policies became pronounced, and resulted in greater institutionalised oppression, they were evolved for quite pragmatic reasons of survival, not inspired by any ideological motives. The only exception to this general rule was perhaps the exalted imperial cult and ceremonial; this was pure propaganda, designed to exaggerate rather than dissemble the imperial power, and it too sprang from the same imperative

16 Vogt, *Decline,* Ch 1

17 For the changes in architecture and art, see Vogt, *ibid,* and especially L'Orange, *Art Forms and Civic Life in the Late Roman Empire*

18 T. and J. Marasović, *Diocletian Palace*

12 The Gods are Alive (pages 153–162)

1 FIRA, II, 544–89

2 Dio LII, 36

3 Among the many works on Roman religion and the cults of the Empire, see for example Nock, Baynes, Alföldi *et al* in *CAH*; F. Altheim, *History of Roman Religion*; Cyril Bailey, *Phases in the Religion of Ancient Rome*; J. Ferguson, *The Religions of the Roman Empire*; P. Brown, *The World of Late Antiquity*; F. Cumont, *The Oriental Religions and Roman Paganism*; A. D. Nock, *Conversion: The old and the new in religion from*

Alexander the Great to Augustine of Hippo; J. H. W. G. Leibeschutz, *Continuity and Change in Roman Religion*; Warde Fowler, *Roman Ideas of Deity*

4 See for example the account of Augustus admonishing childless senators in Dio, LIV, 1–11. Also the numerous inscriptions alluding to the tomb as the final abode, see Ferguson, *op. cit.,* pp. 132–136

5 Emile Durkheim, *Elementary Forms of the Religious Life*

6 Lucan, *Pharsalia,* VII

7 Varro's fragment of religious antiquities, quoted in Augustine, *Civ Dei,* vi, 2; cf. Warde Fowler *op. cit.*

8 Hence, of course, the charge that the Christians were atheists

9 Horace, *Carmina,* 3, 6

10 Zosimus, II, 5–7

11 Hymn to Demeter (*Hom. Hymn,* 2, 480), quoted in Ferguson, *op. cit.,* p 101

12 Lucretius, *De Rerum Natura,* II

13 Ferguson, *op. cit.*; P. Brown, *op. cit.*; and esp. R. MacMullen, *Enemies of the Roman Order,* on the growth of magic and of the popular mystical strands in later philosophy

14 See esp. P. Brown, *op. cit.,* pp 49–57

15 *Pan. Lat.,* 11(3), 6

16 Cf. Ferguson, *op. cit.,* Ch XII; Vogt, *Decline of Rome,* Ch 1–2; MacMullen, *Roman Govt's Response,* Ch 2

17 *CJ,* V, 5, 2

18 Cf. Warde Fowler, *op. cit.*

19 *Pan. Lat.,* 11(3), 18

13 Politeia Christi (pages 163–172)

1 Sybilline Oracles, VIII 91–95 (Trans. M. Terry, New York, 1890)

2 Cf. P. Brown, *World of Late Antiquity,* and R. MacMullen, *Enemies of the Roman Order*

3 Tertullian, *Apologeticum,* 50

4 *Ibid*; also Vogt, *Decline of Rome,* Ch 2

5 Origen, *Contra Celsum*; more generally J. Shiel, *Greek Thought and the Rise of Christianity,* London, 1968

6 Cf. especially P. Brown, *op. cit.*

7 Arnobius, *Adversus Nationes,* 2

8 Pliny, Letters X, 96, and Trajan's reply; Tertullian, *Apologeticum*

9 On the Valerian persecution including the protest of Bishop Dionysius, Eusebius, *Hist. Eccl.,* 7; Lactantius, *Mort. Pers,* 5; Cyprian Letters, LXXX

10 Acta Maximiliana, R. Knopf and G. Kruger, *Ausgewählte Martyrerakten,* 1929, 19

11 Passio Marcelli, Knopf and Kruger, 20

12 Eusebius, *Hist. Eccl.,* 8, 4

13 Lactantius, *Mort. Pers.,* 10

14 Cf. Fliche et Martin, *Histoire de l'Église,* Vol 2, pp 458ff

14 The Great Persecution (pages 173–185)

1 Lactantius and Eusebius, our principal sources, both say that the army purge of Christians preceded the first Edict of general persecution by some years. I am assuming here that the purge of Veturius and that ordered by Diocletian are the same,

and probably occurred in 299. Between 299 and late 302 when they met at Nicomedia, Galerius and Diocletian were at different residences. Cf. Barnes, *NEDC*, Ch 5

2 Lactantius, *Mort. Pers.*, 11; Eusebius, *Vita Const.*

3 Victor, *Caes.*, 39, 33

4 For example, A. J. Mann, *The Persecution of Diocletian*, tries hard to mitigate Diocletian's personal responsibility. See also Stade, *Der Politiker Diokletian und die letzte Grosse Christenverfolgung*; and N. H. Baynes in *CAH*, Vol XII, Ch 19

5 If Prisca and Valeria were secret Christians (Lactantius 15) they seem to have kept the secret extremely well. There is no record of either of them declaring their faith openly, even after Galerius' Edict of toleration in 311; nor do Christian stories record either of them secretly helping their co-religionists in any way; nor were they honoured posthumously, even when Constantine's propaganda was straining its efforts to denounce Licinius – their murderer – as a persecutor of Christians. Though many modern writers accept the assertion without comment, I have always been sceptical. At my own Catholic primary school during the coronation of Elizabeth II some nuns were also half-convinced that the popular young princess was a 'secret Catholic' who was inwardly reluctant to take the oath of Defender of the (Anglican) Faith

6 Lactantius, *Mort. Pers.*, 11

7 *ibid*

8 Eusebius, *Vita Const.*, 50

9 Lactantius, *Mort. Pers.*, 11

10 Lactantius, *Mort. Pers.*, 12–13; Eusebius, *Hist. Eccl.*, 8

11 Lactantius, *Mort. Pers.*, 15. His own testimony seems sufficient evidence that, in the beginning at any rate, Diocletian's strategy was civil persecution rather than outright bloodletting

12 Quoted in A. H. M. Jones, *Constantine the Great and the Conversion of Europe*

13 H. Chadwick, *The Early Church*, Ch 7. Also A. Momigliano (ed.), *The Conflict of Paganism and Christianity in the Fourth Century*; Jones, *op. cit.*

14 Lactantius, *Mort. Pers.*, 14; Eusebius, *Hist. Eccl.*, 8; Constantine's *Oration to the Saints*

15 Lactantius, *Divines Institutiones*, 7

16 Lactantius, *Mort. Pers.*, 14; Eusebius, *Hist. Eccl.*, 8

17 Eusebius, *Hist. Eccl.*, 8

18 *ibid*

19 Ruinart, *Acta Sincera*; Knopf and Kruger, 22

20 Eusebius, *Vita Const.* By the time Eusebius was writing, official propaganda demanded that not only Constantine but even his father be represented as Christians during the persecutions. In Chapter 16 he offers the preposterous story that Constantius demanded pagan sacrifice from members of his court on pain of dismissal, and then deliberately rewarded those who had refused. The truth would surely be that he was prudently carrying out a bloodless purge, quite consistently with his other measures of demolishing churches but refraining from executions (Lactantius 15)

21 Lactantius, *Div. Inst*, 7

22 *ibid*

23 Eusebius, *Hist. Eccl.*, 8

24 Chadwick, *Early Church*, 7; A. J. Mann, *op. cit.*; J. Holland Smith, *Constantine the Great*

25 Eusebius, *Hist. Eccl.*, 8
26 *ibid*
27 *ibid*
28 *ibid*
29 *ibid*, and *Martyrs of Palestine*

15 Abortive Renewal (pages 186–200)

1 Professor Marasović has suggested to me that the palace must have been begun in the 290s at the latest, if it was to have been even near-complete in 305

2 Main sources for the triumph and retirement of the Augusti are Lactantius, the two Victors, Eutropius, Zonaras and Jerome, *Chronicle,* plus the *Latin Panegyric,* 6(7) to Constantine. There is no evidence of a long-standing plan to hand over power at a definite time, and every indication that the detailed decision was not made until late 303. The marriage of Maxentius to Valeria Maximilla is attested in *ILS* 667 and 671

3 Lactantius, *Mort. Pers.,* 17. Eutropius IX

4 See also the story in *SHA, Vita Cari,* XX

5 Lactantius, *Mort. Pers.,* 17

6 Lactantius, *Mort. Pers.,* 18

7 *ibid*; *ILS,* 667 and 671

8 Lactantius, *Mort. Pers.,* 18

9 Lactantius, *Mort. Pers.,* 19, 26; Eutropius X; Zosimus II

10 Cf. *Cambridge Medieval History,* Vol. 1, p 3

11 Lactantius, *Mort. Pers.,* 19

12 Victor, *Caes.,* 39, 8

13 Victor, *Caes.,* 39, 47. See Jones, *Constantine the Great and the Conversion of Europe,* who surprisingly attributes to Diocletian shame about the persecutions

14 T. and J. Marasovič, *Diocletian Palace*

15 *SHA, Vita Aurel,* XLIII

16 On Constantine's flight and elevation, *Pan. Lat.,* 6(7); Lactantius, *Mort. Pers.,* 24; Eutropius, X; Victor, *Caes.,* 40, 4 and *Epitome,* 41, 3; Zosimus, II, 9 *Anon. Vales.,* 3, 4; Jerome, *Chron.,* 228

17 On Maxentius' seizure of power and Severus' death, Lactantius *Mort. Pers.,* 24, 26; Victor, *Caes.,* 40, 7; Eutropius, IX, 10; and X, 2; *Anon. Vales,* 3, 4; Zosimus, II. On Galerius' invasion and Constantine's marriage to Fausta, Lactantius, *Mort. Pers.,* 27; *Pan. Lat.,* 7(6)

18 Lactantius, *Mort. Pers.,* 28–9; *Chronica Minora,* 1.66, 231; Victor, *Caes.,* 40, 17. Zosimus, II

19 On the Carnutum conference, Lactantius, *Mort. Pers.,* 29, Victor, *Caes.,* 40, *Chron. Min.,* 1.231. Victor, *Epitome,* 39, 5 mentions Diocletian's eulogy to his cabbages

20 *Pan. Lat.,* 6(7); Lactantius, *Mort. Pers.,* 29

21 On the Edict of toleration, and Galerius' death, Lactantius, *Mort. Pers.,* 33–5; Eusebius, *Hist. Eccl.* 8; *Anon. Vales,* 3, 8; Victor, *Epitome,* 40.16

22 Lactantius, *Mort. Pers.,* 39–50; Eusebius, *Hist. Eccl.,* 8. The *damnatio* of Maximian was not immediately after his death, but at the time of Constantine's break with Maxentius, i.e. 312 or late 311. But Constantine later rehabilitated him. Cf. the discussion in Barnes, *NEDC,* Ch 4

23 Ammianus, XIV, 8

16 Constantine's Completion (pages 203–210)

1 Eusebius, *Hist. Eccl.*, 10. See bibliography for the various biographies of Constantine
2 On the famous war with Maxentius, *Pan. Lat.*, 12(9), Lactantius, *Mort. Pers.*, 44; *CIL*, I, p 274
3 Eusebius, *Hist. Eccl.*, 20; Lactantius, *Mort. Pers.*, 48
4 *Pan. Lat.*, 6(7) for the bogus lineage; also R. Syme, *BHAC*, 1971 and various coin inscriptions in Webb *et al.*; Lactantius, *Mort. Pers.*, 52. See *Notitia Dignitatum* for the survival of the Jovian and Herculian legions
5 Zosimus, II, 22–28; Victor, *Epitome*, 41; Lactantius, *Mort. Pers.*, 47–50
6 Cf. R. MacMullen, *Constantine*, for a graphic description of his imperial cult
7 For the distinct reforms of Constantine, see in general *Codex Theodosianus, passim*; *Cambridge Medieval History*, Vol IV; A. H. M. Jones, *LRE*, Vol I, and *Constantine the Great and the Conversion of Europe*; MacMullen, *Rom. Govt.'s Response* is very useful. On the final shape of the Court and bureaucracy, J. B. Bury, *Later Roman Empire*, Vol I. On the military reforms, Van Berchem and Luttwak, Part 3. On fiscal policies, A. H. M. Jones, *op. cit.*, and *Roman Economy*. On relations with the Church, Jones and Bury, also Vogt, *Decline of Rome*, Ch 2
8 See esp. Boak, *Manpower Shortage*; A. H. M. Jones, *LRE*, Vol I. On the great increase in the tax burden and the gulf between rich and poor, Jones, 'Taxation', in *RE*; Bury, *Later Roman Empire*, Vol I; Anderson, *Passages from Antiquity to Feudalism*, I, 4

17 In the Long Run (pages 211–219)

1 Our best source for these events is undoubtedly Ammianus, XXXI
2 Ammianus, XXXI, 4
3 Ammianus, XXXI, 13
4 On the reign and policies of Theodosius, see Zosimus and Victor, *Epitome*. More usefully, A. H. M. Jones, *LRE*
5 Bury, *Later Roman Empire*, Vol I, Ch II; Peter Brown, *World of Late Antiquity*, p. 34. On the contrast between the economic strength and resilience of East and West, see the above, plus Jones, *LRE*, Anderson, I, 4; Boak, *Manpower Shortage*
6 See esp. Bury, *op. cit.*, Ch IX. He does not seem however to acknowledge the role of manpower shortage in the crisis of the West
7 On the final stages of the Western Empire, see Bury, *op. cit.*, Jones, *op. cit.*, Vogt, *Decline of Rome*, Ch 3; P. Levine and Hollister in White (ed.), *Transformation of the Roman World*
8 Useful works on the beginnings of Byzantium include *CMH*, Ostrogorsky, *History of the Byzantine State*; Baynes and Moss, *Byzantium*; Haussig, *Byzantine Civilisation*; Vryonis, *Byzantium and Europe*, and Vryonis in White (ed.), *Transformation of the Roman World*
9 Orosius, VI, 42
10 *Anglo Saxon Chronicle*, on the conquest of Sussex, AD 491

·INDEX·

·INDEX·